D1583842

A Taste of Power

The Politics of Local Economics

◆

Edited by
MAUREEN MACKINTOSH
and HILARY WAINWRIGHT

VERSO

London · New York

First published by Verso 1987
© Maureen Mackintosh and Hilary Wainwright
All rights reserved

Verso
UK: 6 Meard Street, London W1V 3HR
USA: 29 West 35th Street, New York, NY 10001 2291

Verso is the imprint of New Left Books

British Library Cataloguing in Publication Data

A Taste of Power.
    1. Local government——Great Britain
    2. Local government——Great Britain
    ——State supervision
    I. Mackintosh, Maureen   II. Wainwright
    Hilary
    352.041   JS3091

ISBN 0-86091-174-8
ISBN 0-86091-886-8 Pbk

Typeset in 10pt Parlament by Leaper & Gard Ltd, Bristol, England
Printed by Thetford Press Ltd, Thetford, Norfolk

To Frank Campbell and to Jeannette Mitchell, GLC colleagues and friends, who both died while this book was being written. They are much missed.

Jeannette, writer and campaigner for better health care, inspiration and critic of her friends, died of cancer in October 1986 at the age of 33.

Frank, a former construction worker and socialist agitator, renowned for his commitment and his wit, died in February 1985 at the age of 43.

Contents

Preface

'The Greater London Council is typical of [the] new modern divisive socialism. It must be defeated. So we shall abolish the Greater London Council,' said Norman Tebbit in March 1984 with that knack he has of spelling out the ideological motives behind Government action. But in fact, in March 1986, it was democracy which the GLC abolition attacked. The government not only abolished a right to vote: to vote for the people who run London's underground and bus systems, and its fire brigade, who plan the use of its land, who sustain its facilities for arts, entertainment and sport and, not to be forgotten, who arrange the disposal of its solid waste. It also tried to stop dead the 'Livingstone' GLC's attempts to widen the scope of democracy in London beyond the vote: by providing resources and a political platform for movements and organisations outside conventional party politics. To Norman Tebbit this was all part of 'modern socialism'. For the government that meant an alternative centre of power in the capital city, it meant living proof of an alternative way of governing it; it meant a focus for malcontents; above all it meant trouble, unpredictable and uncontrollable. And it was infectious. The authors of this book intend to spread the infection.

The work for the book began life as part of the consultation process on the GLC's Industrial Strategy. This involved public meetings in local communities, day long workshops with workers in different industries and services and interviews with individuals who either worked for enterprises funded by the Greater London Enterprise Board, or were associated with

ix

'voluntary sector' projects funded by the GLC. A group of us decided to complete the writing up of this work and see it through to publication. Some of us went to work at the London Strategic Policy Unit, the unit set up by eight London Boroughs to continue and develop, with much diminished resources, the new initiatives — in relation to women, ethnic minorities, planning, transport, industry, employment and the arts — begun by the GLC.

As a whole, the book is a cooperative rather than a collective effort, many people contributing to different chapters. It was edited by Maureen Mackintosh and Hilary Wainwright, who are therefore the only people who can be blamed for the shape of the book as a whole. They also wrote the introduction and conclusion. The authors of the different chapters are listed below. At the end there is a note on people who helped and contributed, and a list of further reading and sources.

'Setting an Example: the GLC as Employer' was written by Paul Soto. Maureen Mackintosh wrote 'Women's Work', with help from Liz Heron. Ray Collingham wrote the chapter on 'Labour's Plans for Construction', on the basis of discussions and interviewing with Frank Campbell. Eileen Davenport drafted the GLC's 'Property Strategy' and Lliane Phillips wrote the chapter on Docklands, with help from Betty Presho and Bob Colenutt. Maureen Mackintosh wrote 'Public Transport Engineering: the GLC and the Transport Unions', and also worked with Dave Welsh on the chapter on 'Jobs and People's Lives: one person operation on buses and tubes'. The chapter on 'Socially Useful Production' was the product of many minds: Geraldine Hackett, Steven Marks, Mike Hales, Maureen and Hilary all contributed to the draft. Teresa Hayter wrote the chapter on Enterprise Planning in the Greater London Enterprise Board, with some input on equal opportunities from Irene Breughel and Jay Thacker. The other chapter on GLEB, on different approaches to industrial strategy with furniture as a case study, was written by Hilary Wainwright. Sheila Rowbotham wrote about London Health Emergencies, Dave Spooner wrote the chapter on Transnationals, and the enthusiasm for the 'Jobs Festivals' is John Hoyland's.

There were many others, not elsewhere acknowledged, who helped. We are very grateful to them all. Slim Hallett made us feel it was worth doing when we had our doubts. Julia Phillips contributed to the discussions, especially on grants and women's work. Gordon Donald was always willing to do research and administration and did it with great competence. Trevor Richardson, one of that rare species, a socialist administrator, along with Christine Geesley, were essential to the early work for the book. Pam Gordon cleared many bureaucratic obstacles with apparent ease. Mike Ward and Robin Murray, our political and executive bosses, have been in their own distinctive ways a constant source of both argument and encouragement.

1
Introduction

> I was suspicious, and so were the majority of people around here. It wasn't long since we had been fighting the GLC, over the tower blocks. I said, we don't want them, we don't want them down here, no way.

Connie Hunt, a tenants' leader from London's Docklands, was talking from long experience of a constant, weary warfare that she and many like her find themselves waging against their local councils, Labour and Tory. And here was the new GLC threatening to come down to Docklands, and start poking its nose into their local organisations.

Like it or not, from 1981, many community organisations, trade unionists, women's groups and others found the GLC on their doorstep demanding time and involvement in GLC activities and — sometimes — offering resources in return. Many people found themselves giving up much unpaid time to work with well-paid GLC employees; some now feel it was worth it, others feel resentful. But most of those who were drawn into the GLC network — going to meetings, patiently (or not) answering demands for information, scooping up yet more GLC post off the mat — agree that it was different at least in scope and generally in kind from the demands made by local councils in the past.

Political Activity as Economic Policy

The 'Livingstone' GLC was different however, not only in the

1

level of demands it made on people, but also in *why* it made those demands. From early on, many people in the GLC came to see the working relationships which developed between the council and its constituents as a crucial element — even *the* crucial element — of economic and industrial policy. This book explains what this meant, how these relationships were established and why they were important. It explores the contradictions involved in a more democratic approach to economic policy supported from within the state. And it argues that the most important lessons to be learned from the GLC about future Labour economic policy making, at local and national level, are about these relationships between the state, and the majority of its citizens: or in other words about the political *process* by which a state authority develops and implements alternative economic policies. These are precisely the lessons which policymakers are presently ignoring.

The new GLC administration came in with an unusually detailed economic policy in its manifesto. The aim was to create jobs and improve employment conditions, through the coordinated use of all the different powers by which the GLC could influence the economy of London. The policies included the formation of the Greater London Enterprise Board (GLEB) to invest funds in the private sector, the improvement of employment and working conditions within the Council, and the use of Council powers such as purchasing and grant giving as tools of economic intervention.

In addition, the manifesto sketched a commitment to an innovatory *method* of making economic policy. It was to be developed with the participation of working people. It aimed to strengthen the control of working class Londoners over resources and policy. In the manifesto's words:

> Our vision of the future is a city in which the elected representatives take the lead in economic planning — with maximum community involvement — for a prosperous London.

And, somewhat more forcibly:

> We shall set out to increase the element of democratic control over industrial decisions: control by elected authorities and control by working people in their workplaces.

The manifesto gave few details of how these very general aims were to be achieved, beyond a commitment to developing structures of industrial democracy within the Council, to trade union involvement in planning agreements for firms in which GLEB invested, and to support for workers' resistance to closures and redundancies.

Right from the start, therefore, economic policy at the GLC contained an unresolvable tension: between on the one hand centralised, 'strategic' economic intervention, run by an arm of the state, and on the other hand the democratising of economic policy, which meant giving up some control over economic policies and resources to those people affected.

These tensions rapidly became acute in all areas of economic policy. As the manifesto had promised, the new councillors set up an Economic Policy Group to advise the new Industry and Employment Committee. These new recruits, or 'officers' as professional local government staff are called (appropriately given the almost military hierarchy of local government), came generally from outside local government. They had experience in trade union organising, research and support work, community organising, journalism, academic research and teaching. The new officers had the experience and contacts to work with outside groups. To put flesh on the bones of sketchy policies, they needed information, allies and ideas from outside the Council. And many argued from their own experience that the best way both of defending and generating jobs and of involving people in GLC policy making, was to provide support for non-GLC organisations: campaigning groups, trade union and community resource centres, women's groups, and co-operative development projects.

As the chapters of this book demonstrate, the most effective GLC economic policies were developed and implemented through these tension-ridden alliances. Where the GLC failed to develop a popular basis for its policies by working with organised groups of Londoners, then the policies tended to founder or to become captive to establishment wisdom. As a result, the history of the development of these working relations between the local government politicians and staff, and the GLC's constituents, with all the failures, problems and contradictions that they involved, provides many of the most important lessons to be learned from the GLC. But these are the kind of lessons which get lost behind the statements of policy and proposals for spending which were the main written products of GLC work.

This book then, is an attempt to retrieve and spell out these lessons. It is not an exhaustive history of GLC economic policies. It contains instead a series of case studies of how the work was done, and what was achieved, and why, in different areas of economic policy. Their central theme is that *how* policy was made determined what was achieved. And they show that therein lie important lessons for future socialist economic strategy at a national as well as a local level.

Policy and Practice

It quickly became clear to the new GLC employment officers that any commitment to going out of County Hall and opening up its resources and decision making to outsiders demanded a wholly new way of working for local government. Far more than most borough councils, the GLC had always been a rather Olympian institution, shut away behind the elaborate hierarchy and formality of County Hall. There were few precedents, and no rules, for a more open working relationship with Londoners. Formally, and within the established traditions of local government, the task of the new staff was to propose to Council committees policies based on the manifesto commitments and their own work. Once approved by the Council's own lawyers as something the Council could legally do (an increasingly serious hurdle as legal constraints were tightened by the government), the proposals would then become 'Council policy', backed by the financial resources agreed by the committee concerned. These policies would then be implemented by other Council officers and the newly established Greater London Enterprise Board (GLEB).

The manifesto description of the new officers' job had contained echoes of this formal division between policy and practice: the new officers' concern, it said, 'would be with overall planning, and not with detailed implementation'. But such a description of how things actually get done is naïve. Local government is notorious for generating Committee papers which don't get much beyond the Committee, the files and the dustbin. Although the new breed of officers knew this, they became known for producing bigger and more ambitious papers. The big policy documents — such as the London Industrial Strategy — often seemed an irrelevant self-indulgence to the small groups outside County Hall struggling to extract some resources from the GLC. But the proposals in the papers depended for their success on the input from groups in the community. This meant going beyond the traditional methods of research and consultation, and often brought conflict with long serving GLC officers — although it attracted some surprising allies amongst those officers. It also wiped out the neat distinction between policy making and policy implementation.

The manifesto commitment to economic democracy was extremely vague about who was to be involved in policy making and how. A lot of questions immediately emerged, and were answered in practice, unsystematically and in a hurry. For example, which parts of the community were to be involved in policy making, since one cannot involve seven million people individually? How, most seriously, were those people who were the least organised, with the least power, to be involved? How was people's control over their working lives to be increased, and did this imply the transfer of resources to groups in the community and the unions? If so, what happened if those groups used resources in ways which went against Council policy? Or against national trade union policy? What sort of commitments should be asked for in return for the resources? Should the GLC officers work with shop stewards and trade union activists, or only with trade union officials?

These were only a few of the major problems raised by an unspecific commitment to democratic economic planning. In turn, these issues raised questions for the people drawn into the GLC net. How much autonomy would and should they give up in return for GLC resources? How much energy should they devote to trying to influence the GLC, as opposed to an approach of 'take the money and run'? Different answers to these questions by different groups affected the outcome of much GLC policy. The following chapters explore these contradictions, showing how the new GLC staff answered the questions in practice, and arguing about whether the answers were right or wrong. They also reflect at least some of the views of those on the receiving end of the GLC's economic policies.

But first, it will help to understand those answers if we look briefly at the assumptions and ideas with which the new councillors and staff approached the problems. Many of these assumptions came from the experiences and movements of the 1960s and '70s.

Influences and Tensions: Trade Union Initiatives and Restructuring for Labour

The tension between planning state policy, and transferring power to others, was there from the start in GLC policy towards public investment in manufacturing industry. Ideas about this in the GLC were influenced by workers' initiatives during that brief, confident period of trade unionism in the 1960s and 1970s, before the recession had really set in. Faced with the threat of closure and redundancy many shop stewards' organisations, especially in the engineering industry, took militant action such as occupations and 'work-ins'. In a few instances they put forward their own alternative plans to the company's schemes for 'rationalisation'. In the early '70s, the prospect of national-isation in shipbuilding and aerospace, promoted in particular by Tony Benn, stimulated trade unionists in these industries to prepare detailed plans for industrial democracy: 'workers' control with management participation' as stewards from ship-yards on the Tyne put it.

In particular, hopes of government support encouraged the shop stewards' combine committee at Lucas Aerospace to develop a plan for converting their factories and skills to the production of different, more socially useful products. The Lucas workers' plan had become something of an international symbol of workers' control initiatives in the age of multinationals and defence-led, computer-controlled technology. In the GLC, the Lucas plan was an important model to both politicians and officers. It contributed to a strong initial focus on manufacturing industry and to rather over-optimistic assumptions about trade union strength and levels of organisation in London in the 1980s. It contributed too to a wider conception of economic policy — the early basis of 'popular planning' — which saw GLEB invest-ments and other GLC economic initiatives arising out of alter-native plans for jobs and services, based on social need, which the GLC would itself help people to prepare.

These workers' initiatives had also by the 1980s helped open up a small but important crack in the rigid division within the British labour movement, that keeps economic policy as the politicians' concern, and restricts trade unions to the defence of wages and conditions. The economic crisis, and the vast rise in unemployment, made some trade unionists more determined to make a substantive trade union input into local economic policy. Regional trade union officials had been involved in discussions of Labour's GLC manifesto. And in the manifesto there was at least a nod towards closer union and local authority co-operation on making economic policy.

When it came to the aims and organisation of GLEB the 1974-79 Labour government provided a further cautionary tale. For the period when Tony Benn was Minister of Industry there was a brief glimpse of an industrial strategy with some involvement of shop floor workers. But under pressure from the CBI (intending on its own admission to take action outside the law if Benn's policies came anywhere near implementation), the City and the Civil Service, the policies collapsed into the timid, secretive corporatism of Harold Wilson. The disillusion from this experience led a group of trades councils and shop stewards to investigate what had gone wrong. Their report, 'State Intervention in Industry, a Workers' Inquiry', influenced those in the GLC arguing for firm political control over the Greater London Enterprise Board, and the establishment of political objectives for its investments, including the strengthening of labour in the firms where it invested. The tensions in the management of GLEB between the commercial objectives, and the social and political objectives — the latter embodied in the concept of enterprise planning — persisted throughout GLEB's history under the GLC.

Alongside the trade union history, the 1970s had also seen the development of a network of 'committed' researchers: people with research skills, working in the academic world or in trade union resource centres, or research organisations like the Low Pay Unit, the Hazards Centres, Labour Research or local resource centres for community campaigns. Researchers in these networks had been trying to do work useful to the labour movement and the women's movement. This involved learning from people working in particular industries, and providing them with useful information. In addition, they had developed an approach based on a particular strand of Marxist theory, which required a detailed study of how work was organised and the technology used in particular industries. Its subject was labour, rather than the markets of conventional economic analysis.

From these influences came the idea of 'restructuring for labour', as the guiding aim of GLC economic intervention. Generally, this meant intervening in the London economy in a way which strengthened the position of labour. For a major economic restructuring *against* the interests of labour was already underway, pushed by the market and government policy.

One way of intervening in the interests of labour was to provide resources for the labour movement, and particularly shop floor workers, to help them influence policy. The Popular Planning and Industrial Development units both set out to channel resources to trade unionists in London, to help them research and develop alternative plans. The Project Development Unit gave grants to trade union resource centres in London. In other words, resourcing the self-organisation of labour was regarded in itself as a tool of economic intervention, as well as a way of generating inputs to the GLC's industrial policy and demands on GLEB for investment funds.

'Restructuring for labour' was also embedded in the structure and aims of GLEB itself. GLEB was set up with trade unionists on the board who would, it was intended, report back regularly to the South East Regional TUC. One of the aims with each GLEB investment was to involve each workforce in 'enterprise planning'. In theory this was closely related to the work of strengthening and resourcing labour. However there was a constant tension in GLEB between its relationship with private sector managers and owners and its social and strategic objectives. One chapter in this book examines how these tensions worked out in practice, with detailed case studies.

There were other tensions too. The concept of 'restructuring for labour' at its most ambitious meant industrial investment which sought to reorganise, and make viable, whole sectors of the London economy in a way which strengthened labour in that industry. In principle, it meant 'working from below' with workers where ad hoc demands in failing factories might well conflict with the overall approach 'from above' to investment in a sector. This implied learning from workers in particular industries and providing information in exchange which could be of immediate use to them. One chapter of this book discusses this issue in detail for one industry.

Other Influences: Community Struggles and Feminism

'Restructuring for labour' potentially included public sector intervention, and attempts to develop production and provision for social need. The work on technology, discussed in one chapter of this book, began from the idea of creating jobs from the provision for need. This stress on need was also a central theme in two other major influences on the GLC's work: community struggles and feminism.

In Wandsworth, Southwark, Coin Street in Waterloo, and parts of Docklands, strong campaigns had grown up in the 1970s against land and property speculators and for community control of land. Local groups fought public enquiries, drew up their own plans and lobbied councillors and would-be councillors for a commitment to use their planning powers to halt the specu-lators. The campaigns' demand was that councils should develop the land to meet the housing and employment needs of local people. These were an important influence on the new GLC, especially Michael Ward, chair of the Industry and Employment committee and George Nicholson, chair of planning. GLC staff were put under political pressure to respond to these local groups, and to provide resources for them to develop alternative plans for areas of land, including land held by the GLC and land subject to private development. Two chapters in the book — on property-based employment initiatives, and on the Docklands campaign — discuss this work, looking at the issue of choices over which campaigns to support, the problems involved in work with community groups, the difficulty in establishing effec-tive local employment projects and some of the inherent conflicts with sector-based industrial strategies and investment.

Another set of influences on the GLC came from feminism. The concerns of feminists to improve women's job opportunities and working conditions brought them into conflict with many of the initial assumptions about where the GLC would put its energy and resources. In addition to women who went to work for the women's committee, a number of feminists made an (uphill) effort from the start to bring the special interests of women into the wider economic policies, including research, grant giving and investment policy. A chapter of this book discusses some of these efforts and their very limited success. An attempt to shift the focus of work towards women meant arguing for the need to try to change the division of labour in rather drastic ways. It also meant trying to work and spend resources on areas of the economy outside the initial focus on better organised, better paid manufacturing industry. This led to a recognition of domestic labour, unwaged as well as waged, as an important sector of the economy and to research on and funding for childcare. It also led to some work on sectors of waged employment with abominable pay and conditions, such as hotels, catering, cleaning and much of the clothing industry. And it led to an increasing emphasis on change within the public sector itself.

On the other hand, feminism also influenced the methods of work, in ways which were rarely explicitly acknowledged. It had been the women's movement which had argued most forcibly in the 1970s that the *process* of political activity was integral to its content. It was feminists who had argued for a practice which started from people's experience, and involved working with them and promoting self-organisation. In a watered-down way, some of this had got into the principles of *some* of the wider Left by the 1980s.

Missing Influences: Anti-racism

Many of the weaknesses as well as the strengths of the GLC economic policy work stemmed from these initial influences and the gaps and assumptions which underlay them. By far the most important missing issue, in the assumptions behind the employment work, was in relation to race and anti-racism.

The 1981 manifesto had contained a commitment to an Ethnic Minorities Committee, and many of the Labour politicians were acutely aware of the issues of racism and black unemployment in the wake of the 1981 riots in Bristol and Brixton. But nevertheless, the needs and organisations of Black people in London were not integrated into the wider employment policies.

This was in large part because the other influences just discussed were all in different ways racially exclusive. Consider each in turn. The kind of trade unions which provided the models of industrial intervention were based in the better organised sections of British manufacturing industry. These were areas from which, even during the economic boom of the 1960s, black workers had been largely excluded by the action or lack of action of both management and trade unions. Similarly, many of the community campaigns over land and property were based in predominantly white working class organisations, even in areas with substantial black populations. The concept of the community these organisations were fighting to defend, in the wake of the departure of their traditional employer, tended to exclude local black residents. Feminism, too, had been a movement with a strong bias towards the needs and interests of white women, which was only beginning to be forced in the late 1970s to learn from the needs, circumstances, ideas and interests of black women.

As a result of this political history, the people hired at the beginning for the Economic Policy Group — later the Industry and Employment Branch — were not only almost all white, they were also largely ignorant of the struggles and organisations of black people in London, and they tended to ignore the issue of racism.

This was rightly a source of a great deal of criticism of the GLC's work. Under pressure from black organisations, the GLC first began to respond to the needs of black communities through the work of the Ethnic Minorities Unit and the Police Committee. The Industry and Employment Branch was much slower to start to integrate anti-racism into its practice. It was in practice left to the efforts of some of the black officers in the Branch, most of whom were not hired until 1984 or later, to start a serious debate on black employment policy. Some relevant work was done, but too late to make much impact on the use of resources.

It is largely as a result of this history that there is no chapter on anti-racism and black employment policy in this book. The chapters were generally written by those involved in the areas of work discussed, and often by people who felt at least in small part responsible for the outcome. Those most qualified to write about race and employment in the GLC felt unattracted to the task for a number of reasons. Some black staff in the Industry and Employment Branch had found the struggle to develop black employment policy, late on, without sufficient political support or commitment from colleagues, difficult and demoralising. The prospect of looking back was depressing, creating remembered resentment and anger at the lack of scope and resources for the work, and there were few achievements to write about. Some felt that they had learned what was involved in forcing a different and more productive starting point for work on black employment, but that they were better employed going on from there than looking back, at least at present. Others felt, more strongly, that to write a chapter on black employment or anti-racist work was not appropriate in this book, because it would serve to legitimise a policy making process which did not in fact have anti-racism as a central theme, and a book over whose editorial process black staff had had relatively little influence. There is therefore perhaps some justice in the absence of a chapter on this subject: the conclusion however contains a summary of some of the issues raised by black staff and other people interviewed for the book, written by the editors.

While the failure to make a priority of black employment work was a specific problem, it was also symptomatic of a wider problem in the GLC's approach to employment. Many of the influences on employment policy stemmed from a period of stronger trade union organisation and higher employment than existed in the London of the 1980s. The economic recession had undermined trade union organisation drastically in London, and further polarised the fate of the organised and the unorganised, the working and the unemployed. The GLC, with its commitment to working with outside groups, and the (chronic) haste in which it did everything, tended to end up working with those organised in ways with which it was familiar, particularly those in trade unions or long established pressure groups. Many people — working class women, the unskilled, as well as black people — got by-passed again, their forms of self organisation largely unrecognised and unsupported. There were many in the GLC who saw the contradiction, but several chapters, especially the chapter on women's work, show the extent to which it was never resolved.

Finally, there was another, quite different kind of gap: knowledge and experience of commercial practice. Throughout the Labour GLC's history there were never enough people working for it who were both sympathetic to its aims and had the accounting and commercial skills needed for successful investment and intervention in the private and public sectors. The GLC often lacked the skills effectively to challenge plain bad management, to make good investment and management decisions, or to rethink the management strategy and practices of large organisations such as London Transport, then under GLC control. This is bound in part to be a chronic problem of the Left, but it showed up as a particularly telling weakness for this kind of economic policy. The chapters on 'sector strategy' at GLEB and on London Transport engineering discuss some of these issues.

The Economic Problem and the GLC's Leverage

Looming above all these influences, though, was the fact that the problems were much greater than the resources available. The GLC was a big local authority. Its revenue budget of £800m a year had a substantial impact on the London economy. On the other hand, it was rather an odd local authority: having lost much of its housing stock and some of its other powers, its spending was concentrated by 1981 on transport, the fire brigade and waste disposal, and arts and recreation; its own in-house staff were working on land and planning issues and scientific and other services not visible to its constituents in the way that the housing and social services functions of borough councils are. On to this rather curious institution, the manifesto proposed to graft economic policy by two means: the use of the '2p rate', (the rate money available for general spending), largely for industrial investment, through GLEB; and the use of the other spending powers of the GLC, including the purchasing on behalf of other institutions and the pension fund, for the purpose of economic intervention.

The available resources however paled before the scale of the economic crisis in London. Even a brief description of the scale of the job loss and unemployment in London brings on a feeling of helplessness. A dramatic summary is that the Thatcher government has seen the destruction of more of London's factories than Hitler's blitz. The statistics show that between 1961 and 1981 nearly 800,000 jobs were lost in manufacturing industry in London: a decline of 60%. Predictions show another 100,000 jobs going in the 1980s. Most of the service industries have lost jobs too, and London now has around half a million unemployed.

Against this trend, a local authority, however large, has precious little leverage. Investment decisions in the private sector, which sustain or destroy employment, are made by large, often multinational, firms with an eye to their balance sheets. These firms can control budgets the size of nations, far larger than the GLC. In 1981, 75 of these firms had factories in London; by 1986, at least twenty had found it more profitable to sell their London site and invest elsewhere. These firms' decisions affect industrial organisation, technology, working conditions and commercial survival, not only for their own employees, but for competitors and for a mass of small and medium size suppliers and contractors who go under when they leave. The investment decisions are backed up by London's powerful financial institutions. Controlling assets estimated at £1000bn, these big institutional investors operate too often on a short time horizon for industrial investment and profitability, and have substantially contributed to the London-based property boom which has made the London industrial closures so profitable. This is a vicious circle for London employment, very hard for a local authority to break into.

The other force shaping the London economy — and increasingly linked to the forces of the private market described above — is the government and the vast, unco-ordinated public sector. Nearly one third of London's waged employment in 1981 was in the public sector. The Thatcher government, pursuing private profitability, the destruction of union strength and reduction in the size of the public sector, has cut public sector employment, sold state enterprises to private owners, and opened up state services to bidding by private firms. This has meant a major attack on the jobs, wages and conditions of one million London public sector workers. In 1983/4 alone, London health authorities cut the equivalent of 4000 full time jobs, a far higher rate of decline than elsewhere in the country. British Airways shed nearly 13,000 jobs at Heathrow in preparation for privatisation. Just because London has for so long been a centre of service employment, it is suffering badly from the attack on the public sector.

In this situation, the way people in the GLC thought about the best use of the GLC's (small) leverage changed over time. Initially, a lot of attention was concentrated on the £30m a year which could be used for industrial investment, through the establishment of the enterprise board. The aim of the Greater London Enterprise Board (GLEB) was to save and create jobs, but to do so in an 'exemplary' way: to concentrate on the quality as well as quantity of employment, and to take a longer term view.

Over time, the focus of the economic policy work shifted from industrial policy to use of the GLC's other spending powers. The GLC was a major public purchaser and contractor. It purchased on behalf of itself, the Inner London Education Authority (ILEA) and many London Boroughs. It also spent heavily on building contracts in addition to employing its own direct labour force in London Community Builders. In principle these purchasing activities gave the GLC considerable leverage over working conditions in the firms to which GLC contracts went. In 1983, the Council set up two Contracts Compliance units to try to make the most of this leverage. The aim of the Equal Opportunities Contracts Compliance Unit was, as its name implies, to use GLC contracts to improve job access and working conditions for ethnic minorities and women in the supplying companies. The Construction Contracts Compliance unit sought to use the threat to remove firms from the list of those approved to tender for contracts as a lever to enforce direct employment (rather than the 'lump'), better working conditions on site especially in health and safety, and trade union access to sites.

The manifesto had also contained a commitment to establish municipal enterprises producing goods otherwise bought from private suppliers. The intention was to create more and better jobs than those in private suppliers. This project never got underway, nor did the scope of direct labour in construction expand. One chapter in this book reports the views of workers in London Community Builders on the reason for this missed opportunity and assesses the work of the Construction Contracts Compliance unit.

Later on more attention was also paid to the working conditions of the GLC's own workforce. The GLC employed 22,000 people, including the fire brigade, which made it one of the biggest employers in London. In principle, here was an opportunity to improve conditions and involve the workforce. In practice legal and financial blocks, resistance within the unions and by senior officers and problems in thinking through and implementing changes, greatly limited what was done. One chapter of this book documents the changes that were made, notably the expansion of opportunities for women and for members of ethnic minorities, but then goes on to discuss with GLC workers and councillors why so many hierarchies and relationships remained the same.

The GLC was also until 1984 the responsible political authority for the 60,000 transport workers employed by London Transport. Here the dominant issue became the defence of jobs and conditions against a management intending further to run down the industry, against the GLC's aim of expanding it. Two chapters look at aspects of this history: the attempt to keep open London Transport's engineering works, and the research into the problems created by the management's attempts to introduce more one person operation of buses and trains. A central theme in these chapters and several others is the need to turn a formal relationship between GLC politicians and full time trade union officials into a more open working relationship between GLC officers and different levels of the trade union movement. Different points of view are expressed on what was learned from these experiences.

The GLC's last financial lever was the power to give grants, and this became an increasingly important part of the work of the Industry and Employment staff. This is not conventionally seen as a source of economic power. But given the rhetoric of increasing people's control over economic activity and policy, the transfer of resources to trade unionists, women's groups, the unemployed and Black organisations was clearly a way of furthering this aim. If 'sharing power' meant anything, it began from getting resources — funds primarily, but also research and information — out of County Hall to those groups who could use them. Grant giving work grew rapidly, and several chapters — on health campaigning, on local initiatives in Docklands, and on organising against multinational management — show the extent to which these resources allowed a sharp rise in the confidence, scope and strength of independent action by these groups.

Naturally, there were problems. Despite the rhetoric, the Branch had not been prepared for the rapid flow of applications for cash, and had no clear policy for dealing with them. It tended to be the best organised and most vociferous who had best access to resources. Those who worked on giving grants — often people with community or trade union experience — were cut off from the rest of the Industry and Employment Branch and not given time to work with and develop organisations to be funded, or to create links between those organisations and other Branch work. Further, there were problems for those funded, in a loss of autonomy, and the danger of overexpanding and then being unable to sustain the organisation without GLC support. The chapters on women, and on anti-racism, and on some of the campaigning work, discuss these issues.

Finally, it was not just financial and research resources that the GLC could offer. It was also publicity, a platform, political clout, which boosted confidence in a period of low morale. The chapters on Docklands, on health, on multinationals all provide instances of this process. Increasingly, the GLC came to realise that it got most done, had most impact, where the work it did was enhancing an existing movement. Where there was no groundswell, nothing much happened. The section on arms conversion illustrates some of the difficulties of pushing a 'good idea' from County Hall without a base in the relevant industries.

The State and its Citizens

Progressively, especially as the likelihood of abolition increased, the GLC came to see its role as much in resourcing and supporting the struggles of others as in doing anything directly through its own spending and investment and powers to command. It also became increasingly aware of the importance of such alliances to the effective use of all its other powers. Most of the attacks from the Right were over this resourcing. But many on the left worried about the dangers of incorporating organisations into the state, and by making them clients, weakening them.

Many if not most of the people who worked on GLC economic policy had started from a political position of opposition to the state, including the local state's lousy record on public services. But many had also come to conclude that movements and trade union initiatives also needed state support, and had a right to demand it of Labour authorities. For many people, the GLC was an opportunity to explore the possibilities and dangers of trying to use the state's resources both to support working class organisation, and to implement some of their aims.

In this the GLC was not alone. The new role of some Labour local authorities in trying to form alliances with some of their constitutents against central government has been a feature of the 1980s, but the ground had been prepared for decades, with the growing centralisation of power in central government. The inflation and the spending cuts of the mid-1970s, implemented largely by a Labour government, had fallen heavily on the services provided by local authorities, so the basis for confrontation was already there. The cuts in resources forced on local government, especially in the cities, by the present government were only the final straw.

In this situation there was clearly a material basis for local authorities and citizens to get together to look for alternative economic policies for their local areas. The councillors and officers trying to change local government came from similar backgrounds and political influences. While they would mainly describe themselves as socialists of one stripe or another, they had no serious illusions of being able to 'plan' their local economies, whatever the titles of some of their fancier publications. The best that could be done was to try to understand what was happening and look for points where intervention was possible to halt decay, to redirect some kinds of development and to support the regeneration of self-organisation among their constituents. The 'socialist' content of their work, where people felt it existed, was probably chiefly in the last point.

The proper 'constituency' for the economic and industrial policy was a much fought-over terrain. In principle it included all the working people of London, including the lower paid, out of work, non-unionised and unorganised. In practice it was more often the better paid and better organised who gained most, however fragile their strength.

It is true however that the number of people who came into contact with the GLC, or supported some of its ideas, was much wider than those who worked directly with County Hall or got a grant from it. The diverse community had no shared political expression, no lasting focus, certainly not the Labour Party. Few members of the public would have made any clear distinctions between the employment work and the wider activities of the GLC: the women's committee work, the ethnic minorities committee, the festivals. The high profile of the GLC, the way it tried to mix politics and entertainment, its effect in drawing younger people into some connection with politics, was exemplified in the big 'Jobs Festivals', the subject of a chapter of this book. The last one attracted a quarter of a million people, and they functioned as publicity for the GLC, as concerts, as political platforms and vast markets for ideas and information between hundreds of active groups.

The final test of the extent to which the GLC's activities did or did not give more power to working class people in London, is the question, what is left now? The GLC was under tremendous pressures, early on, from the probability of abolition, and those pressures affected the way resources were used. Did the GLC resources strengthen organisations or, as some feared, undermine them? No one in the GLC thought we were creating socialism now, but most of those who have written the chapters of this book believe that using state resources to strengthen the organisations of working class people, and developing the capacity of those organisations to put pressure on the state, is an essential element of working towards more economic democracy. It is not a very large ambition, when stated like that, but it is very difficult to do.

This then is a book about the GLC's economic policy, but about *how* as much as *what*; about political process as much as economic policy ideas. It does not cover all of the GLC's economic policies, and indeed omits several major areas of work of the Industry and Employment Branch. Though most of the chapters are written by people who worked for the GLC, we have tried throughout to put forward and discuss not only our own views but also the views of those who were on the receiving end, those who were 'GLC'd'.

All the experiences, diverse as they are, show very clearly that *how* policy was developed determined what was achieved. In this, we think lie the most important lessons for future national or local policy makers. The most general ambition of the book is to try to inject into current discussions of Left economic policy a stronger sense of the way such policy must be shaped by a democratic political process. Any future political authority which thinks it can construct a progressive and successful economic policy without developing a *method* of constructing and implementing it in association with (and also sometimes in active contradiction with) those in whose interests it is intended to operate will be wrong. And thinking about the contradictions and the new ways of working this involves — especially at the national level — has to go forward now.

2
Public Transport Engineering: The GLC and the Transport Unions

... as far as our relationship with the GLC was concerned, whenever we asked they tried to help us ...

Tom Holland

The GLC gave us limited help ... allies we could turn to to get us professional advice ... and the opportunity to speak to the Transport Committee was of value.

Dan Stringer

... after all the GLC were the bosses, and the man who pays the piper calls the tune ... at that time we believed they were going to be able to ... we didn't know about Bromley and Fares Fair and all those things that came later.

Julia Tinsley (London Transport trade unionists, 1985)

The most popular policy of the new Labour GLC administration in 1981 was its promise to improve London's rotting public transport system: to lower fares, to increase services, and to invest in better stations and new buses (to be built, said the manifesto, in London), and in general to give priority to public transport. It is not surprising that the proposals were popular, in a city highly dependent on good public transport (only a small minority of London's one million commuters drive in), and where services had been declining, and fares rising, almost continuously for three decades.

The policy making process seemed, initially, rather straight-forward. Since 1969, the GLC had controlled and financed London Transport. It paid the subsidy, borrowed and provided the capital, approved the budget, and decided policy for the organisation. It therefore seemed to most people, politicians included, that the Council could freely decide how the organisation should operate.

The legal defeat of the Fares Fair policy ended that illusion and made clear the struggle that would be involved in developing more progressive transport policies for London. The GLC had rapidly implemented its pledge to lower fares, cutting them by on average thirty per cent and proposing a supplementary rate to pay for the expected increase in subsidy needed. The subsidy was however challenged by Bromley Council in the courts. At this point it became clear that the policy was popular: local groups were formed all over London, involving public transport users, local residents and some trade unionists, to defend the lower fares and improved services, and the Council's right to implement its manifesto commitments. Use of the public transport system rose quite rapidly.

The court case went all the way to the Lords, where the GLC lost. The Lords' judgement took the view that the GLC's decision was based on insufficient preparation, analysis and consultation, and also cast doubt — to the horror of transport planners — on the powers of the Council to subsidise public transport at all. Fares doubled in 1982, and passenger use of public transport fell off sharply. The Council's transport policies were in a mess and its supporters angry and demoralised.

That was the low point. After that it was, with considerable effort, uphill most of the way until July 1984, when the government finally took control of London Transport away from the council. The GLC got itself better legal advice and constructed, after consultations with London Transport, a 'Medium Term Plan': a moderate proposal, with much more detailed argument, for a drop in fares of twenty five per cent associated with the introduction for the first time in London of a common transport pass which could be used on bus or tube, the Travelcard. The proposal was tested in the courts, and was introduced in May 1983.

It was regarded at that time as a poor second best to the original Fares Fair proposals, but in fact it was a phenomenal success, far greater than even the optimists in the Council had expected. In the first year underground use rose forty four per cent, and bus use went up ten percent despite many people switching to the tubes. The additional subsidy needed to pay for the Travelcard was far less than predicted even in the first year. Success seemed finally to have set in.

Job Losses: Engineers, Conductors and Others

Just after the Travelcard was introduced, however, in July 1983, the Conservative government was re-elected on a pledge greatly to increase privatisation and cuts in the public sector, and a new collection of problems set in. These centred on employment. In addition to its transport policies, the Livingstone administration had come in pledged to try to defend and create employment in London. Public transport was a major employer: 60,000 jobs, largely manual, employing many Black workers and women workers who would find it particularly hard to find alternative jobs with half a million unemployed in London. Although there were problems with wages and conditions, the transport jobs were usually secure and were unionised: not a common feature of manual jobs available to inner city residents.

London Transport management decided in the new political climate that they could make further major 'savings' in employment. Already in 1982, when the GLC had effectively lost control of London Transport policy, employment in the organisation had been falling. In 1983, with the new expansion of services, this should have ceased to be a problem. On the contrary, London Transport management now began to propose thousands more job losses.

This chapter is about the attempts to prevent these job losses and the privatisation and dismemberment of London Transport that lay behind them. It looks at the sometimes tense working relations that developed during this time between GLC politicians and officers, GLC appointees to the London Transport Board, trade union officials and active trade unionists — like those quoted at the beginning of the chapter — in London Transport's bus and rail engineering works.

It is a curious story. Here you had the spectacle of the management of a major transport undertaking actively resisting the attempts of a Council which appointed it to give it more money to employ more people and run a better service. You had a Council in control of a public transport service employing 60,000 people, with an administration committed in its manifesto to creating employment in London, yet struggling to find legal powers to prevent thousands of job losses from its own public transport services. In the GLC, there was a group of new employment officers trying to develop links with the London Transport trades unions in order to try to defend the jobs — and in the process upsetting some long serving Council officers who

Credit: Carlos Guarita/Reflex

The most popular policy of the new GLC administration in 1981 was its promise to improve London's rotting public transport system. This included the maintenance and development of its engineering works.

thought this quite incorrect. And finally, you had a trade union movement split over whether it should deal directly with the Labour GLC in defence of jobs, or whether it should continue only to negotiate with London Transport management in the manner of the traditional bargaining relations.

The struggle to defend London's public transport therefore raised problems the manifesto writers had not anticipated: the limits of GLC powers for a start; and then the need to develop with the trade unions better arguments about how the public sector should be managed. The GLC needed alternative industrial policies for the public transport industry, to defend jobs, develop skills, and to develop the services and back-up work, like engineering, in ways that would create new jobs — and in the process to develop a critique of the management's privatisation proposals which would if necessary stand up in court. At the same time, the GLC also needed to work with the trade unions to make those policies effective: by providing information and assistance it could help support and give the trade unionists confidence, but on the other hand it depended on the trade union fight to give the GLC nominees to the London Transport Board, and the Transport Committee, a basis of strength from which to argue. As a result, the GLC, the transport workers' ultimate employer, found itself supporting trade union organisation against the decisions of the management it also employed.

This chapter explains this story, and draws out of it some lessons for the future about the relations between unions and public authorities in developing policies for the public sector. Those lessons centre as much on the *process* of policy making as on its results.

The background to the London Transport management's proposals to cut jobs was the 1983 Transport Act. This put a new obligation on public transport operators to put 'appropriate' activities out to tender from the private sector. The London Transport management argued that this legal obligation required and justified contracting out much of the engineering work, and that this would imply the closure of one big bus engineering works (Aldenham works, in West London), and major job losses elsewhere in engineering. They also began actively looking for other opportunities for privatisation: building, cleaning, catering were all under threat, though not then the bus driving itself (that came later).

When the first major proposal to contract out engineering work came to the GLC in October 1983, it became clear that the

London Transport management did not intend to ask the Council's consent to these redundancies and the 2000 job losses which might be involved. The management argued that they did not need the Council's agreement since they were simply obeying the new law, and merely extending an existing practice of putting some work out to tender. Always before the London Transport Executive, as the management board of London Transport was called, had required the Council's consent for all major policy changes, and it was on this power to give or withhold consent that the Council had relied to exercise control. So here was a new challenge to the Council's powers to control transport policy.

It was followed by more proposals to cut jobs. At the end of 1983, London Transport submitted its proposed budget and future service plans to the GLC. Although transport use was expanding rapidly with the Travelcard London Transport was proposing not to expand services. Furthermore, it was proposing to reduce jobs by another thousand, not counting the engineering job losses, mainly by going over to more 'one person operation' (OPO) on the buses and to driver-only trains and by reducing station staff. For all this part of the job losses, however, they were at least proposing to consult the GLC.

So, the GLC was faced with a major enterprise under its own — shaky — control which was proposing to shed jobs at a rate which would swamp other efforts at job creation. This went against the GLC's commitment to job creation — and against all economic logic in the middle of a recession. But the legal constraints on the GLC were such that it could not just say no. To prevent the job losses, it had to prove that it had the legal right to make the decision, and then that it would be reasonable, given the Council's legal duty to run an efficient transport service, to retain the staff and keep the engineering services in-house.

At this point we should stop saying 'it' about the Council. For though the administration was clear on its aims on this issue, the Council officers were deeply divided on the facts and the logic of transport policy. Many professional transport officers felt employment issues had no place in transport policy; they also believed that further decline in public transport was inevitable. Against this employment officers and a few transport officers were constructing an argument that the service could be revived, that demand could be expanded, and that the transport spending — about a quarter of the whole current budget of the GLC —

was a tool of intervention in the economy to promote employment, both directly, through transport jobs, and indirectly through improving the functioning of the London economy by giving people access to jobs and services.

In effect, the Livingstone administration began with a transport policy, but no industrial or employment policy for the transport industry. The initial employment policies had concentrated on the private sector and on the direct GLC labour force; transport and employment policies had been compartmentalised into separate areas; and the scale of the pressures to come from the government on the public sector had been underestimated. So there was no detailed policy on how the public transport sector should be managed. This had to be painfully developed, under pressure from events, from 1983 on. This chapter looks at the issues faced in the engineering works. The next discusses the equally important issue of the staffing of operating services, and particularly the issue of one person operation of buses and tubes.

The London Transport Board and the Trade Unions

When Labour was voted into power in 1981, the London Transport Board, or Executive, had four executive members — the Chairman Peter Masefield, soon replaced by Keith Bright, the managers of the bus and rail operations, and the finance director — and at that time only one non-executive member. The Board had some autonomy from the GLC, and was responsible for the day to day running of the operation, while the GLC had overall policy direction. The precise limits of the powers of the two bodies had really never been tested in practice, but in the past, industrial relations had been the concern of management.

The new GLC administration wanted to increase industrial democracy in London transport, and to give trade unions a greater say in policy, but they also subscribed to the view that industrial relations were primarily an internal matter between LT unions and management.

Dave Wetzel, the Chair of the GLC Transport Committee (and an ex-bus conductor), described the discussions with the unions in the early days. From the start, he held quarterly tripartite meetings with the London Transport unions (stewards and officials) and management, where issues of policy — budget and fares, Fares Fair and the Law Lords — were discussed. This was a substantial departure from the past for Chairman Peter

Masefield. Dave Wetzel and the trade unionists agree that the meetings were useful, but did not significantly increase the involvement of the unions in policy. The unions did not meet before hand, treating the meetings chiefly as information gathering sessions. The GLC did not meet the unions separately at all. As Wetzel described it: 'London Transport invited the unions ... it was very rare that we met [the unions] individually.'

Why not? 'That's a good question ... Looking back on it, it was a mistake that we didn't. Certainly they never asked for it: that's always the politician's easy way out of doing anything. At the time it didn't seem necessary ...'

At these meetings, the question of internal industrial democracy in LT, and workers' representation on the Board was raised. As Wetzel describes it:

> I particularly wanted ... that the London Transport Executive and the workers should get together and tell us the procedures that *they* wanted for worker participation in management decisions. I actually set that as an objective, I said, I don't think it is for the GLC to tell you as workers ... how you should structure yourselves. I want both sides ... to come up with a structure ... that we can ... take through the Council's machinery.

Neither the unions nor management rushed to implement this objective. Many people in the trade union movement of course have great doubts about the value of worker participation in management. Wetzel again: 'You know, there's a whole dichotomy within the union movement about worker participation ... I imagine the management probably played on that ... They created a working party — I shall never ever allow a working party again — nothing ever ever came of it.'

Wetzel's first proposal, he says, was for LT workers elected to the Board. As a second best, he proposed union representatives of some kind to sit on the second decision-making tier, for the rail, bus, building works, and other separate internal businesses the management were then creating. He hoped that 'experience and confidence at that level of participation' could then lead to workers on the Board itself. Nothing happened, other crises took over; 'it was always something in the back of my mind'.

The issue reappeared, however, when the GLC finally decided in 1983 that it would have to put its own appointees on the Board, in order to get its policies implemented. Initially, there had been no intention to 'pack' the Board in this way. But there had been a number of disputes over GLC policy proposals, including the Council's wish to implement an equal opportunities hiring policy in LT.

Wetzel remembered that 'the final crunch' came when, after the May 1983 fares increase, the London Transport Chairman he had appointed (Keith Bright) submitted a three year plan which was far too cautious in the GLC's eyes. The Transport Committee was looking for an ambitious plan to build on the Travelcard's success, including more services and more capital spending on station improvements; the London Transport management was looking over its shoulder at the government's exhortations for redundancies and reduced services ... and at their future employment prospects. As Wetzel describes the argument:

> Before ... the bank holiday, I was saying, 'Can I have a draft? I want to see that what you're asking for are things that we want to deliver ... and I want you to ask for more than we can deliver ...' He [Bright] was saying to me, 'It's still up here in my head'. Then we came back from the bloody bank holiday ... and they published this glossy brochure of the LT Three Year Plan. What he was asking for was a *cut* in bus services ... Already at this stage ... his gallery was Ten Downing Street and he was playing to the gallery. Then we wasted a hell of a lot of time lifting that Three Year Plan to something almost recognisable as a GLC wish. It was a struggle.

After that, Wetzel began to look for new Board members who would implement GLC policy for London Transport. The question immediately arose of the number and position of trade union representatives who should be put on, and in particular, whether these should be regional or national officials, or representatives from the London Transport workforce. At this point 'Bright made the request that we shouldn't have workers employed by London Transport on the Board.'

The GLC, not anxious to provoke a serious crisis at that point, agreed. Looking back, says Wetzel: '... we should never have made that concession. We should have said "no" to Bright. However ... we agreed that the union representatives should not be workers in London Transport. We talked to the unions, they wanted one representative.'

Wetzel recalls that his first choice was Bill Morris, a national official of the Transport and General Workers' Union, partly because of his knowledge of the bus industry, partly because he wanted, for the first time, a black person on the Board. But the main problem, he now feels, was finding trade union represent-

atives with enough commitment. Busy members of union executives tend not to give tasks like this priority, or to take risks.
Wetzel said of the national official (not Morris)who was eventually appointed to represent all the main unions: 'I was disappointed. There's no way he made it his first priority, he was
very busy, not able to give the time expected from a Board
member.' Now, he says 'I am against union executives deciding
who should be union representatives on Boards.'

In 1983 and 1984, the Transport Committee put onto the
Board an increasing number of its own appointees in an effort to
gain control of London Transport policy. These appointments
were controversial, and the new members were attacked in the
press, notably for their lack of transport expertise. (This attack
looks rather ironic now, since they appear to have had between
them more knowledge of transport than the new appointees put
on by the government after July 1984, when LRT was formed.)

The new Board members formed by early 1984 a majority of
the Board, and could therefore in principle overrule the executive
members, although the position of a non-executive group
composed largely of part-timers is complex. However, despite all
the discussions about workers' participation, no clear discussion
was undertaken at that time about the relations between the
unions and the new Board members. When asked whether the
issue was discussed with the new Board members, Wetzel
reflected: 'I can't remember that it was ever consciously ... no
decisions were ever taken. There was more discussion of the
relations with us.'

Others have suggested that some politicians too might have
found such a direct Board/union link undesirable, taking control
away from County Hall. As a result of this lack of preparation,
once the future of the engineering works became a serious issue,
relations between the Council and the shop floor trade unions
had to be constructed ad hoc.

Bus and Rail Engineering in London

After years of speculation and rumour, the Chairman of London
Transport has advised the Trade Unions that it is the declared inten-
tion to close Aldenham Works and transfer its functions to Chiswick
Works.

Trade Union Joint Committee document, London
Transport 1972

> Aldenham Works should close at a time to be subsequently agreed but not later than December 1984. ... At this stage the staff reductions would be between 1300 and 2000.
>
> London Transport management, Bus Workshop Strategy Review 1983

> These proposals [from the London Transport management Acton Works Study Team] imply the effective closure of Acton Works, with the loss of the maintenance capacity it contains and of 850 jobs.
>
> GLC Committee Report 1984

Aldenham, Chiswick and Acton Works were in 1981 the main bus and rail engineering works in London Transport. Between them, they employed more than 3500 workers. Their function was then to undertake major, regular overhauls of buses and underground trains. It was this preventative maintenance that kept them in service over the long periods for which many of London Transport's vehicles had lasted: twenty five years, for the well known Routemaster buses with the open-back platforms, thirty six years at least for the Underground trains. In between major overhauls, the Underground depots and the bus garages did routine maintenance and repair. Along with the Works and Buildings department workers, the skilled and semi-skilled engineering workers did all the maintenance work (apart from road maintenance) which kept London's buses and tubes running.

Closure of Aldenham bus works had been proposed before by London Transport. In the 1970s the bus service had been seriously flawed by the frequent break-down of buses, especially the new generation of Leyland-built buses for driver-only operation. The trade unions had been writing papers in the 1970s complaining about the problems of poorly designed buses, lack of spares and poor management of maintenance; and about a management process which saw constantly cutting the bus fleet, buying untested buses and lengthening maintenance cycles as the right response to poor reliability. They had also been complaining about the trade unions being blamed for these failings.

Reliability had been improved in the late 1970s by changing the type of buses bought, and reorganising maintenance. However, in 1983, the London Transport management announced a new decision: privatisation of much of the bus engineering work. This followed a management study called the 'Bus Works Strategy Review', stimulated by the management's interpretation of the new Transport Act, and also by the recent investigation of the bus works by the Monopolies and Mergers Commission. The Bus Works Review concluded that money could be saved by closing much of the in-house engineering capacity and contracting the work out to a large number of private suppliers, mainly working out of London. Given the simultaneous collapse of much of the rest of West London's vehicle engineering firms, there would be few jobs in London to replace those lost.

Management announced the closure of Aldenham works to the trade union officials and delegates, and then the next day to a mass meeting of workers. After the mass meeting, the stewards from all the unions on the two sites met. They set up a committee which included three members of the TSSA, the union representing white collar staff. Elected as individuals by the meeting as a whole, these representatives played quite a key role in what followed. As Tom Holland and Julia Tinsley, two of the stewards on the committee, explained:

> We decided that the best way to defend outselves was to involve everybody ... some of the expertise that was on the [committee] we hadn't traditionally been able to use in our set-up, and that was of great value.
> We then started to meet regularly, but we had no official standing. So through a set-up negotiated with management there was a committee drawn up, of full-time officials and the different organisations we belong to. We officially got recognition for that committee.

The committee was given a room, and the LT management agreed to give them a few weeks to respond. Given the historic lack of co-operation between unions in LT, the establishment of this joint committee, especially involving the staff unions, was a considerable achievement.

Choices for Trade Union Strategy: Argue or Fight?

The trade union joint committee at this stage was facing a difficult choice of strategy, one which people continue to argue about to this day.

'The alternative really [that] all the politicians were giving us at that time,' says Tom Holland, was 'either you can fight and say no, forget the information whatever it is, we're going to fight for our jobs. Or you can go up the avenue which you're choosing, to seek to destroy the argument for closure.' In other words, should they fight the closure by threatening industrial action, and at least at the beginning refuse to discuss the detail? Or should they take on the management's arguments and try to prove them wrong: try to prove in other words that it was not cheaper or better for London Transport to close the works and sub-contract the maintenance to the private sector?

The unions chose the latter course, while not at all unaware of its dangers. And they chose it for two reasons: they knew that there was not the support at that stage for an all-out strike, and they believed that they could prove that private contracting would be disastrous. If they could prove that in-house labour was as efficient as the private sector on a fair comparison, then a negotiated reorganisation could save the works, or a new one on the same site.

The trade unionists knew people in the works were demoralised, they had been hearing for years that they might lose their jobs.

> Since the sixties there's always been the threat of closing Aldenham ... you know, closing, then we're saved, closing ... the change to the GLC I think stopped it in the early seventies ...
>
> You'd have had a job to have a *lunchtime* strike at Aldenham. Each time we had a mass meeting ... the first question was always about voluntary severance and why didn't they increase it?
>
> I think we knew from the very beginning that a total out and out stoppage, a strike, to prevent the closure of Aldenham wouldn't have stood a chance.

Later, the work done by the committee provided the basis for two highly successful days of action, and a mass lobby of London Transport headquarters, which in turn put pressure on management to rethink, but most of the stewards still believe that they were right to work up to this action by first proving that they had a case.

Involving the GLC

At this point, the works committee came to the GLC — among many other organisations — for help. By this time, there were fewer illusions about GLC powers. As Tom Holland remembered, the Chair of the GLC Transport Committee, Dave Wetzel, warned the unions about the consequences of the GLC getting involved in the argument.

> We wanted help ... professional people who could advise us on the way [London Transport] had done their books, money, accounts, people who could advise us on the structure of buildings ... the GLC helped us tremendously. But ... they did tell us right at the initial stage ... if you go down the avenue of seeking to prove [the London Transport management] wrong, if you don't succeed in proving them wrong, then you're left with [the fact that] they're right. And if you put the GLC into helping you do that, then it is tied to the outcome.

Whatever the doubts about which strategy to choose, the unions found in GLC a serious concern about the scale of job loss, and the loss of the skilled engineering resource for London represented by Aldenham and Chiswick works. The Council officers also knew that this was only the beginning. The politicians listened and told the officers to do something. But the officers, many new to local government and snowed under with the problem of job losses all over London, were not organised to work with the unions in this way, as Julia Tinsley remembered:

> It became the standing joke that whenever we went to the GLC ... there wouldn't be one person from the GLC that would be at the whole meeting. Some of them would be there when we started and leave halfway ... and somebody would come in and ask a question that had already been explained ... the moving population of the GLC ... lovely people, well meaning, but God were they in a muddle.

Issues of Public Engineering Policy

The first task of the GLC officers was to work out whether the GLC had the right to be consulted on the tendering proposals, and to give or withhold consent for the decisions on the future of the works. Legal advice said that, on an issue of this importance, it did have those powers, but that it had to establish that it was 'reasonable' to withhold consent: that is, that the cost savings from tendering were not what they appeared, or that the effects on the bus service would be serious. Loss of employment in London, in itself, was not sufficient reason in law. As a result, the GLC needed to evaluate the proposals for itself. To do this, they needed to work with the unions, both to draw on their knowledge and to support them in developing their own case and convincing their members.

The GLC therefore began by getting professional advice, from GLEB and from consultants: people to work with the unions on evaluating the management proposals. This process exposed, as so often in the GLC's experience, the scarcity of sympathetic people able to think creatively about industrial policy. The unions discovered this too: some people were good, some — larger consultancy firms in particular — took the money and did the minimum, and patronised the trade unionists into the bargain.

The arguments on strategy centred on three points. The first was the question of the comparison of in-house and outside costs. Since the management argued that they were legally bound only to keep in-house work that was 'viable', by which they meant cheaper than contracting out to the private sector, the question of proper costings and a proper basis for comparison became crucial.

The second argument was over the question of the organisational structure of the work which remained. The management wanted a structure of small industrial units to replace the big integrated bus works: easily closed down should times change or management be unable to manage them successfully. The unions were aiming for a single new works to house all the in-house activities, which they felt would be easier to defend later, and which they were convinced would be cheaper in the long run.

And the third dispute was over the issue of the longer-term strategy for engineering maintenance and the proper approach to raising productivity in a works which had become too large for LT's reducing scale of operations. Management wanted to contract the scale of engineering, to cut the level of regular overhaul or even move away from regular overhauling altogether. The trade unionists on the other hand saw possibilities of raising productivity by returning to an older practice of taking in outside work on contract, while the GLC wanted to retain the works as a basis for future expansion of public transport.

The second argument was decisively won, with the help of an architect consultant who threw himself into designing a new and appropriate building, in collaboration with long-standing trade unionists who knew the work it had to house. Julia Tinsley described the collaboration.

The architect ... and his quantity surveyor, they were really invaluable. Reg, who had all the engineering knowledge, he did a plan of the factory ... and arranged it [in ways] that made it more efficient. ... the architect went away and drew a scale drawing and came up with all sorts of statistics for us on how much more economic it was to have it as one unit, rather than all the little ones.

The collaboration worked well, and the argument was won.

The difficult argument however was the first one. The trade unions and the GLC were both convinced that the management view that contracting out was cheaper was based on poor information about the costs of in-house work; a judgement backed up by the Monopolies and Mergers Commission report which had criticised costing methods. They also believed that the outside contractors' estimated prices were artificially low, and that contracting would at best bring a few short-term savings at the expense of higher costs and worse service in the long run.

The arguments were gradually formulated into a series of issues which the trade unionists summed up in the question of 'fair competition'. These included the following.

How should the private sector's prices be estimated? What would prevent private contractors from offering a low initial price, which they would raise once they got the contract, and how could you prevent them delivering lower quality work than existing in-house maintenance?

How should in-house costs be assessed? What was the justification for adding 'notional' rents for buildings owned by London Transport? How should higher quality of in-house work be allowed for?

How should 'activities' to be put out to tender be divided up? At present, virtually all work was done by direct labour. Breaking down the work into tasks, and privatising some, loaded overheads on the others and made them 'unviable' too. How could this 'cascading' privatisation be prevented?

How were the additional costs of supervision, quality testing, co-ordination and organisation of tendering and private work, to be allowed for in costing the privatisation option? If they were not, the real costs of privatisation were underestimated, and in-house costs appeared too high.

How should the additional risk inherent in private contracting be allowed for, including the loss of passengers should the buses again become highly unreliable? At the time, the management were arguing that there would be no effect on the service at all of dispersing the maintenance to numbers of private suppliers, which would all have to be co-ordinated.

How should wages and conditions in private firms be treated? Should private firms be allowed to gain work simply by under-cutting negotiated rates and conditions in the public sector? How could this be prevented?

Some of these issues were about methods of cost calculation, and some were about the principles of how direct and private labour should be compared. All of them were of concern to both the GLC and the trade unionists. The trade unionists wanted to demonstrate that they could, on a 'fair comparison', do the work efficiently in-house. The GLC was concerned with that too — all the contracted-out work was likely to leave London, given the rundown state of the London engineering industry — but they were also concerned very centrally about the impact of privatis-ation on public transport as a whole. The research done among other operators which had tried privatised maintenance fully justified this concern. As London Transport's *own* report pointed out:

> Executives of public transport undertakings we have spoken to recount horror stories of their experiences with subcontracting over-haul and maintenance, including tales of long deliveries and broken promises, lack of priority, additional expense not quoted for, poor quality work requiring extensive rectification etc. etc. None would recommend subcontracting.
>
> London Transport Bus Works Strategy Review Report 9B

Most of the detailed cost arguments were put together by the white collar trade unionists, several of whom worked on sta-tistics and costings. It turned out to be very hard to find account-ants who understood the issues, could handle industrial accounts and who could also work with trades unionists.

> The accountancy people came in and they took away a whole load of stuff, and we never got any results from them at all. On the costings ... we mainly put our own stuff together in the end.

As a result of organisation, pressure and argument about shoddy costing (as well as GLC threats to go to court), the works committee won an agreement from the Aldenham management to test the 'fair comparison prices' through trial tenders. The trade unionists examined in detail the quality of the work coming back from trial orders from private contractors. Their worst fears were confirmed: '... we haven't had a single job come back to the standard they would have had at Chiswick [the other main bus works, also under review].' The prices of private firms were often unreasonably low, as the trade union side also succeeded in demonstrating: '... sometimes the materials costs were more than the prices they were quoting.' Internal costings were also dodgy: '... there were twenty seven sets of figures, of which we proved fairly conclusively that twenty three were in error.'

While this was going on, the management were also reorganising Aldenham works to cut costs. The unions accepted this process, despite the implied job losses, believing that they could compete, surely, with overhauls done in the Midlands or further north — by Midland Red, or Leylands — and believing this was the best way to save a bus works in London. Not all the trade unionists were sure this was the right approach, but the committee maintained its view.

At the same time, the GLC, GLEB and the unions were trying to find alternative outside (private or public subcontracted) work, to increase throughput at the works, and so save jobs and maintain transport engineering work. The GLC was aware that the works represented one of last big engineering shops in London, and that loss of them would mean a loss of skills (by 1983 the London Transport apprenticeships represented half the engineering apprenticeships left in outer North West London), and of capacity to expand transport in London in the future. The GLEB technology division became involved in investigating possibilities of establishing new transport manufacturing activity in the works — for example, for a vehicle chassis — and in looking for work which could be contracted in. The GLEB-based London Transport Technology Network grew in part out of these links.

A debate also began on public transport maintenance, with the GLC becoming increasingly concerned that, if larger scale maintenance facilities were scrapped, vehicles would be less reliable and last for a shorter time. It also became clear that there was a serious bus design problem for London's transport. Whereas LT had previously had a hand in designing its own buses — it had helped to design and build the Routemaster — later, when Leylands closed down bus building in London in the late 1970s, LT had shifted to buying available buses, with front and centre doors, which lasted fewer years and were less suitable for dense London traffic and passengers. The Council therefore also began looking at whether LT should not be using its engineering capacity to develop better London buses. The Transport Technology Network began investigating the design and cost issues, and it became clear that it would be viable in cost terms to design a better bus specifically for London.

This type of debate on the fundamentals of engineering policy also arose in the debate over the future of Acton rail works. Its scope, and the importance of the issues being debated, along with the fact that decisions taken then could preempt the possibility of a more effective public transport system later, showed up the weakness of the public transport industrial policy debate up to that time.

But by early 1984, it seemed clear that the government was indeed likely to succeed in removing control of London Transport from the GLC. The trade unionists' main concern therefore was to get an agreement with management on the future of the works which would stick beyond the GLC, and which would save a substantial proportion of the jobs.

Acton Rail Works

While the trade unionists at both Aldenham and Chiswick works were engaging in the endless task of inspecting the results of trial orders from the private sector and arguing with management about the basis of a fair comparison of work, Acton rail works was facing similar pressures. The big Acton works at that time regularly overhauled the underground trains and their equipment as well as doing crash repairs and modifications of new trains (such as putting in ventilation when the passengers started to pass out in summer on the new District Line trains). LT management had done a similar study to that at Aldenham and Chiswick, and in 1984 it came up with similar results concerning closure and job losses, though this involved more internal reorganisation and less contracting out.

At Acton, management proposed to close most of the works in 1985, dispersing the periodic overhauling of the bodywork of the trains to the various depots around the underground system. These depots had done only minor and emergency maintenance, not major overhaul, and so faced a big jump in workload. The management review claimed that this change would provide huge cost savings. In addition they were intending to contract out much of the skilled overhauling of the trains' mechanical and electrical equipment to the private sector. A total of about 850 jobs would go, plus the engineering capacity represented by the works.

At Acton, a works committee was again formed including the NUR and the craft unions on the site. The committee again responded by criticising the proposals in detail, but they refused to co-operate with the process of preparing for tendering and the transfer of train overhaul work. At the same time, they too contacted the GLC.

The GLC was again in a complicated position. It could not, given the constraints of the 1983 Transport Act, direct the London Transport management not to save money solely in order to maintain employment. On the other hand, it was clear from discussions with the trade unionists that there were serious implications for rail services of the closure of London's sole rail workshop. Given the size of the underground system, the length of life of the trains, and the experience of other railways which were trying to operate without proper overhaul facilities, the loss of central overhaul facilities seemed likely to threaten the rail service in the future. London Transport International was actually at this time engaged as consultants in advising New York to put in an overhaul works to improve its standards of subway maintenance!

As before, therefore, the Council found a consultant to advise themselves and the union. This consultant — an engineering management specialist — agreed with the works committee that there were serious problems with the basis of the management decision. The basis of the costings again appeared to be incorrect: the cost of refurbishing Acton to continue the work there appeared very high, and was based on no discoverable detailed study, while the costs of doing what management claimed was the same work at the depots appeared far too low.

After looking at the proposals in some detail, and visiting the works (including discussions with local management), the consultant came to the conclusion that the proposals were in fact designed to achieve two other aims: to reduce the amount of maintenance on trains and to break up union organisation and regain management control over the rail maintenance work in the face of a historically well organised workforce. These views were reinforced by management's claim that the decision was urgent, for which urgency he could find no evidence, and by the failure to include in the cost calculations the additional capital costs of scrapping trains earlier. This is the way the consultant put his conclusions in his report to the Council:

> Acton works is an invaluable asset to LT, it represents LT's ability to 'refurbish and run' rolling stock, rather than to 'scrap and replace'. To lose this facility would severely constrain LT's ability to run a satisfactory service in the future if limitations in the supply of capital make a 'scrap and replace' policy unviable.
>
> Chris Lakin. Consultancy Report to GLC, May 1984

In other words, for doubtful financial savings, London Transport was willing to run down its maintenance programme and so risk its long term operating capacity.

The unions also pointed out that the change involved a sharp deterioration in working conditions, as well as in efficiency of work. For example, at Acton workers washed the trains and raised them on bogies before overhaul, but the proposal at the depots was to do the work from pits, on unwashed trains still on their wheels.

The Acton Works committee saw the GLC consultancy work as an 'enormous help'. They compared it with help they might have got from their own officials, had those officials had the time, expertise and resources to provide it. In fact, trade unions cannot find those kind of research resources, and local government, looking for knowledge, involvement and support for its own policies, and so needing union help, can therefore appropriately fill a gap.

But the balancing act involved is complicated. The GLC officers involved were conscious of trying to balance several aims: to inform themselves, understand and contribute to the union case, yet not in any way to become mediators between union and management, nor to undermine the independence of the unions in fighting their own case.

The Acton Works Committee produced their own 'Counter Report' to the management proposals. In this, they made retention of overhaul of trains at Acton a precondition for negotiations on other reorganisation proposals for the works for the purpose of cost cutting, or for discussions of tendering. In other words, they decided, unlike the Aldenham unions, not to co-operate with trial tenders on equipment, or cost reductions at Acton, until the dispute over the removal of train overhaul was resolved.

At this point, the management proposals for virtual closure of Acton works came to the London Transport Board, causing serious divisions between the London Transport management and recent GLC appointees to that Board.

The Board and the Engineering Works Committees

By the time both Aldenham and Acton works came to the London Transport Board, the GLC appointees were in a majority. But on the other hand, a government take-over from the GLC and the formation of LRT was imminent, and the trade unions were very aware that what they wanted was an agreement which would stick beyond July 1984.

At this point, the lack of policy on the relations between new Board members and the unions became a problem. The members of the works committees sought from the start to influence the Board. But neither the management nor indeed the national union officials were happy about direct relations between the works committees and either the Board or the GLC officers. Some trade union officials went to the point of complaining to the GLC politicians about officers talking to their members.

The works committee members agree the issue was unresolved. 'In the early days it was very very difficult to get hold of some of the Board members.' Some Board members thought it was their job to talk to the local trade unionists; others not. The TGWU national official, who was the only union representative on the board, did not involve himself directly in any of the debates between trade unionists and the Board members on the defence of the engineering jobs. And in the case of one Board member (John Palmer, also a GLEB director), a sharp conflict developed with the union committees over tactics. 'He thought, and he made no bones about it, that the workforce should resist at all costs,' the stewards recalled.

The unions, shop floor and officials, had an eye to the longer term and to agreements that might stick when the GLC was gone, and they knew their own members. They tried to stick out, with the new Board members' support, for a clause stating that there should be no compulsory redundancies as a result of the Aldenham reorganisation, but management refused to sign this. The Aldenham works committees otherwise stuck to their agreement with management that the works should be cut and re-organised in return for a promise of a new works once the cuts were achieved. The GLC-appointed Board members, faced with the imminent creation of LRT, accepted this.

The problems between the works committees and their own officials on the issue of union-GLC and union-Board relations were generally quite rapidly resolved. The officials agreed quite quickly to allow the works committees to present their arguments directly to the Board, recognising that it was the in-house trade unionists who had the knowledge to argue their case. On Acton, the NUR put an official from Acton works itself in to work with the committee, and this resolved liaison problems. Tom Holland, previously works committee chair, and now an official himself, reflected ruefully that 'the role that I now play will be seeking to protect what ... my union has.' Nonetheless 'I hope I don't change in as much as I feel people at the grass roots should have direct contact.' When the question of Acton works came to the Board, it divided sharply between the management members and the majority of non-executive GLC appointees, who met the Acton trade unionists and agreed that management had not made the case for closure. The management agreed to stop preparations for partial closure of the works but only because of the coming transfer of London Transport out of GLC control. The dispute would have been very different, had the LRT Bill not been close to the statute book.

Lessons?

There are, within this story, issues of procedure and issues of policy. The GLC officers and politicians came rapidly to believe that they could develop alternative policies for London Transport, which would retain jobs, while improving efficiency, expanding services, and staying within the law. But to do that they needed detailed information and advice. And the only source of this knowledge was the union works committees, not the officials who also had neither time nor inclination to be intermediaries. Hence direct contact was essential: but it went against all the established procedures of trade unions and local government.

The policy proposals which the GLC evolved for London Transport engineering reflected this joint work between GLC officers and works committees. They argued for integrated management, instead of fragmentation into numerous small management units, or 'profit centres'. They argued for the efficient in-house management of repair and maintenance, as against privatisation and putting out to numermous different private suppliers. They argued for criteria of fair competition which take good wages and conditions of work as a proper aim of the public sector. And they argued for an expanding public transport industry — an argument which has been justified by the continuous increase in passengers since the introduction of the Travelcard: seventy per cent on the Underground and fifteen per cent on the buses between May 1983 and early 1987.

The intellectual argument about the costs and risks of private contracting was substantially won. But as a result of renewed financial and political pressure from government, and a management and Board much more dedicated to short-term cost cutting, LRT has returned to cutting the overhaul and engineering maintenance work done. In effect, major preventative maintenance is no longer being done as before, but the effects are not yet visible, and the costs will be paid later. Acton has now been largely closed with the loss of 650 jobs, losing all the train overhaul work to the depots; in those depots people are working harder in worse conditions. Aldenham lost the major overhaul work which was its mainstay, with the LRT bus business shifting away from preventative maintenance towards repair when buses break down. Despite demoralisation, the Aldenham workers fought hard for the management to go out and look for work which could be brought in; despite the success in finding a lot of contract work, Aldenham has now been closed, and the previous agreements with the trade unionists abandoned. The long term costs of this destruction of London's public transport system remain to be counted, though the short-term costs in job losses and worsened working conditions have already been felt.

Reflecting on the experience of GLC appointees on the Board, the trade unionists we talked to were divided on the solutions. Some maintained their opposition to members of the workforce on the Board, feeling that it was better to have sympathetic outside Board members. Others thought a mixture was right: 'I think you should have ... a cross section, some representing the public, public interests, some representing the workforce's interests, some representing public business interests ...' They saw of course the problem of worker representatives being outvoted, and faced with conflicts of interest. One trade unionist argued for half the Board to be elected from the in-house work-force, despite recognising the problems. Others were prepared for a minority. But what united them all was that, were there to be worker representatives, they should be from the shop floor, not only officials. This was on the grounds, above all, of expertise, and secondly of contact with members. Dan Stringer expressed the feeling of many trade unionists. In a similar future situation: 'They ought to try to get participation on the Board more at worker level. If you don't have worker participation from the industry, you lack something.'

The trade unionists' chief criticism of the GLC Board members was their lack of expertise in the details of London Transport operation. 'We spent so much time explaining what we meant. It was so hard getting things over.' The Chairman appointed by the GLC — Keith Bright — came in for exactly the same criticism. The Board members however largely got points for commitment to the organisation, whereas the Chairman, since knighted by Mrs Thatcher, did not. All felt the Chairman's appointment had been a serious mistake. 'If they couldn't find someone suitable they should have left it empty.' This is a view, in retrospect, with which Dave Wetzel would probably agree. In line with the general lack of relations with shop floor unions, no-one had asked the unions at Bright's previous job about his record before he was offered the LT job.

The tensions in running public service organisations will continue to be there. The experience of London Transport engineering suggests however how important it is that the issues should be discussed explicitly between the politicians and the trade unions concerned. It also points up how important it is to achieve the difficult task of finding public sector management willing to work in a more collaborative relation with in-house unions. It is clear that the unions at all levels need to contribute more to policy formation for public sector services, including the question of management strategy and methods. The trade union officials need to accept direct shop floor participation — and so do politicians and management. But the national union officials also have an important role to play in representing the wider interests of labour outside the organisation in question.

Furthermore, a working method needs to be developed linking Board members, whoever they are, to the 'constituencies' to which they are supposed to be accountable: this is as true for shop floor workers as any others. Otherwise any Board members become cut off from the development and operation of the enterprise, and lack the base for making judgements. Several of the GLC-appointed Board members felt they needed clearer links to the GLC, and clearer information about the GLC's aims, as well as better relations with the unions. This in turn involves finding local government officers or other public officials who can develop the working relations between all these groups.

Only a working process of this kind, linking different levels of the unions to the political process of decision making, and the decisions on the Board, will allow a clear alternative industrial policy to be developed and put into practice for the public services, to counterpose the present tendencies for privatisation, fragmentation and decline, which are now putting the capacity of London's crucial public transport system under threat.

3
Jobs and People's Lives: One Person Operation on Buses and Tubes

I'm now two people ... and I can't mix it.

When I was a crew driver ... I never used to worry about the people on the back ... But now ... I worry about the doors ... I worry that I'm going to catch a kid by his clothing and by his arm, and miss him in the mirror, and drag him along ...

As a conductor I used to pride myself that I wouldn't let anyone override ... I did the job properly, and you should feel proud of that ... As a one man driver, you know there's about six or seven people upstairs that have gone further than a 20p fare; and you know you can't do anything about it, and that's going through your mind as you're driving.

How seriously should a local authority, employing a large number of people, take the effects of their policies on the working conditions of their staff? Should they try to find out if their policies are worsening the health and safety of staff? If intensification of work saves money, how should they balance that against possible effects on health and safety? What are the effects on the economics of an industry or public service, of policies which undermine health and safety of staff?

Put like that, these questions are clearly important. But big public sector employers, like other large employers, do not have a very good track record on health and safety issues. Financial issues can easily appear more urgent. It could be said of the last GLC's employment policy too that it was more concerned with numbers of jobs created, saved or existing, than with the kind of jobs; more concerned with quantity than quality of employment. Health and safety issues did not form a central part of the GLC's

46

employment policies, nor did the GLC have a clear employment policy for its own transport services. However, it became clear later that an important way of intervening in the London economy was to improve the employment levels, management and working conditions of their own employees. Furthermore, once the Industry and Employment Branch began to look at the question of health in London as a serious concern, it was clear that working conditions and conditions of life were a far more important determinant of people's poor health than even the decay of the London health service.

This chapter looks at this issue of working conditions in a major London service industry: public transport. It discusses research done by GLC officers working closely with bus and underground workers, on the effects of job intensification on those workers' lives. In the process it discusses the politics and problems of political research. It also argues that investigations into occupational health and working conditions should not continue to be seen as a secondary issue after numbers of jobs and pay, but as a central concern, focussing on how the public sector can increase its employees' control over the conditions of their whole working lives.

The quotations that start this chapter are from a discussion with London bus workers in 1983. They are talking about the strain of moving from doing one job, be it driving or conducting, to doing in effect two jobs at once, both driving the bus and dealing with the passengers. The policy which had brought this about was the change to one person operation of the buses — OPO for short — as the London bus fleet changed over from the familiar open platform buses with a conductor, to the bigger buses with doors and just a driver up front taking the money.

OPO became an issue on both buses and tubes in the early 1980s. In 1981, when the Livingstone administration came in, just under half of London's buses were OPO, mainly on the less busy (though often still quite bustling) outer London routes. Most of the bus routes through central London were still 'crew', that is, run by driver and conductor. Most British cities had, by 1980, lost most of their conductors, but London Transport had found that central London was too busy for OPO buses. As a result, London Transport still employed 7,000 conductors.

On the underground, in 1981, all the trains still had guards except for the Victoria Line trains which had been built for nearly-automatic operation. Although London Transport had long been looking for ways of saving money by cutting their jobs, the unions had resisted OPO, and there had been doubts about the safety of driver-only underground trains. However, in the late 1960s the NUR had relaxed its opposition in principle although technical preparations and negotiations took until the late 1970s.

By 1983, London Transport had decided to go ahead with more OPO on both buses and trains. As the quotations suggest, this meant a major intensification of work for both bus and train staff. On the buses, OPO drivers have to take the money, check passes, open and close the doors, watch for problems, deal with any trouble *and* drive; on underground trains, the OPO drivers have to open and close the doors, watch for problems leaving the platform, drive, and deal with any problems (like stopping in a tunnel) as best they can without leaving the cab and without help. Previously, the guards and conductors had done all the jobs except the actual driving. While the worries about OPO in the GLC in 1983 centred on the unemployment it would create, it also quickly became clear that there might be other implications for working conditions and for the service provided.

OPO: Who Decides and How?

> OPO on trains and buses is sheer madness. It's terribly unsafe to have passengers on a train or bus with only one staff member. People have said that we are trying to halt progress, and that there have been no forced redundancies. The problem is — there'll be fewer jobs — people's children will not be getting those jobs.
>
> Underground guard on the Metropolitan Line

> One Person Operation helps reduce costs.
> London Regional Transport Annual report July 1985

OPO meant a sharp cut in jobs in London Transport — a major London employer — at a time of high manual unemployment in London, and just when the GLC was trying to create more employment. In its Three Year Plan written in 1983 (the plan Dave Wetzel complained about in the last chapter), LT proposed to cut 1000 jobs on the buses by introducing OPO on more bus routes; and it also proposed to take guards off the Hammersmith and City line trains as an experiment. If this was successful, they planned to go on to OPO on the District and Circle line in 1984. Including cuts in staff at stations, this meant a

PAY HERE

Exact fare, please.
ke your ticket. You
ay need to show it.

Welcome a

Tham

BATTERY ISOLATOR
BEHIND DRIVER'S SEAT

Credit: Judy Harris/Format

The introduction of one person operation on the buses dramatically affected the working conditions of all bus drivers.

loss of about 1000 jobs on the underground over three years, with more cuts in the longer term.

In the face of criticism, London Transport persisted in congratulating itself on the creation of further manual unemployment in the London economy. Job cuts were referred to as 'savings' achieved: 'For the move from 53% to 65% o.p.o. which is contained in the ... Three Year Plan, the financial benefit is £5-6 million per annum ... Net job savings are about 1,000.' said the London Transport Executive in a Memorandum to the GLC in September 1983.

'Financial benefits' in this means a reduction in London Transport's financial loss. In other words, the GLC were being informed that LT wished to cut a thousand jobs, in order to save up to £6 million per year.

As with engineering, the question then became, who should decide, and how? One view was that LT should be left to decide: the 'management should manage' view. The GLC could not accept that — they had the overall policy responsibility for London Transport. Some trade unionists took the same view as LT however, feeling that the GLC should not meddle in negotiated union-management agreements on staffing. This was one reason why debate on OPO focussed initially on the buses. The rail union, the NUR, was in favour of the OPO experiment on the Underground, while an official from the transport union, the TGWU, came to the GLC Transport Committee to oppose further OPO on the buses. The London Bus Section of the TGWU firmly opposed the job cuts in the Three Year Plan.

Another view, prevalent among Conservative London borough politicians, was that LT was right to consider chiefly its financial position. London ratepayers, went the argument, paid for LT's subsidy, and it was the GLC's duty to keep it down. Furthermore, the government had already begun to set financial targets for LT's subsidy well below those the GLC thought appropriate. With government takeover of LT already being proposed, the management were under conflicting pressures if they wanted to keep their jobs.

A third view was the official policy of London Transport, and was accepted by many GLC officers. This was that finance was not the only consideration; it was also important to measure how OPO affected all transport in London. It was agreed that for those who use London's roads, car drivers, van drivers, pedestrians, cyclists, OPO means more congestion. The OPO buses hold up traffic; a worse service on public transport pushes more people into private cars. Traffic slows down. LT therefore tried to put a monetary value on this loss of time and congestion, and set this off against the money saved by OPO. It was, they said, still worth increasing OPO. The GLC had doubts, disputing their figures on congestion caused and bus passengers lost.

A fourth view was wider than that. It said, you do not only take into account the effects on transport. You also look at the effects on employment. The GLC was responsible for the London economy, not just for its transport. How could it be sensible to wreck with one hand what you were doing with the other? LT only measured the cost to the economy of OPO-created unemployment by the redundancy pay it had to give the conductors. But the costs to the conductors and to those who might have got work as conductors are far greater. Furthermore, OPO affected people doing other jobs in London's economy, such as working in shops, because the increase in unemployment would mean less money to spend, and worsening public transport undermined town centre shopping.

Many in the GLC felt strongly that these costs should be taken into account in the decision. But the GLC's limited legal powers made this very difficult. If unemployment costs had been taken into account, the balance of the arguments about OPO would have been very different. As an economist who studied the problem for the GLC put it: 'If all unemployment costs are included, it would not at present be worthwhile to proceed with further OPO conversion.' (P.B. Goodwin, 'One Person Operation of Buses in London' Report to the GLC, March 1985, p. 7) Passengers were just as well aware of the point. When asked, in discussion group surveys of opinion, whether they would prefer conductors or lower fares (a rather tendentious choice), most pointed out that there was more to the choice than that. Fewer conductors meant more unemployment: 'that's *more* people on the dole, if you put it that way.' 'You're saying x number of people have got to lose their jobs so we can have lower fares — that's a terrible responsibility.'

Worst of all, London Transport was proposing *both* to create more unemployment *and* to raise overall public spending, while giving passengers a worse service. The money London Transport saved by reducing conductors' jobs was *less* than the cost to the Exchequer of the extra unemployment pay. But the GLC was not allowed by law to take those calculations fully into account in its decisions, and government's recommended methods of making such decisions left them out too.

Furthermore discussions with bus workers quickly made it clear that the costs to them of OPO were not limited to the costs of unemployment. For those who remain in work, OPO is a way of getting far more work out of fewer staff for only seven to twelve per cent more basic pay. And in parallel with the OPO conversions, London Transport has also been changing the shifts around in order to increase the number of hours worked in any one day. The effects of all this on the staff were not assessed, and therefore could not be taken into account. As the London Bus Section of the TGWU put it: '... the industry has shown scant interest in the health of its employees ... by not undertaking medical studies on the whole question of stress and related problems which can include various heart disorders arising from OPO work.'

In other words, as in other parts of the public sector such as the health service, money savings were being proposed at the cost of working conditions of the staff. London Transport argued on the basis of sickness absence statistics that there were no adverse health effects to be taken into account, but there was no independent evidence on the effects of the increased workload.

Finally, for passengers, OPO on buses and trains means a worse service, less speed, less safety. Buses get slower, spending far more time at each stop, as people queue to get on. The buses are hard to get on to, especially for less able passengers, passengers get less help with pushchairs or directions, and relations between passengers and staff become strained as drivers struggle to do several things at once. On the Underground, hard pressed drivers have sometimes opened the doors on the wrong side by mistake, an error which puts passengers' lives at risk. The loss of staff around in uniform compounded by taking staff off stations makes passengers, especially women, feel less secure. None of this was taken into account in London Transport's decision process, as the GLC Women's Committee in particular was quick to point out.

What was the GLC to do about all this? Committed as it was to the attempt to turn round the public transport system in London from its chronic decline, the Council knew that the process would take time and money. But it was under great pressure from the government and Tory borough councils to cut short-term costs whatever the long-term consequences. In these circumstances the Council decided that the first thing it needed was more information. It commissioned an outside consultant to look at all the issues in more detail, and postponed a decision on further OPO on the buses until the study had been done.

No study however can remove the issue of political choice. How much weight should be put on the different issues? One issue, in particular, showed up as very poorly understood: the effects on health of the speed-up in work on the buses through OPO. This was potentially an important issue, and one with which the GLC ought to be concerned both as ultimate employer and as local authority. And it was one on which staff and management disagreed sharply, while evidence was almost entirely lacking.

OPO and Health on the Buses: What Kind of Research?

There has been for many years growing concern amongst busmen ... regarding the health problems associated with the dual role of driving and conducting.

TGWU London Bus Section 1984

I've started getting migraine again, and it's the first time since I was thirteen ... pains in your shoulder and down your back ... I'm smoking twice as many as I used to.

London bus drivers in a garage which has recently gone OPO, 1983

Analysis of sickness data ... shows that when adjusted for age and experience the sickness rate is about 3% lower [for OPO] than for crew drivers.

London Transport Executive, 1983

Does bus work make you ill? Does OPO driving make you worse? If so, why? These were not questions with which the GLC had previously been concerned, although it had been the local authority responsible for London Transport since 1970. London Transport stated that sickness was on average no higher for OPO than for 'crew' drivers, and that as conductors had the worst health and were more subject to assaults, the removal of conductors would improve the average health and security of bus staff. The OPO drivers argued that OPO was undermining their mental and physical health judging from their own experience and observation of their garages. London Transport dismissed this as unscientific.

The GLC decided to investigate. This meant undertaking primary research, a decision which fitted in with other work going on in the GLC at the same time on health. One of its researchers, Jeannette Mitchell, argued that research clearly showed that 'our conditions of life are a far more important influence [than medicine] on how long we live and how well we are. Governments and local authorities wishing to improve health must pay attention to the quality of our work and home lives.' As a result, the GLC committed itself to 'conduct an audit of Council policies for their potential impact on health' (London Industrial Strategy, Health chapter). Health became an issue in the development particularly of the GLC's food policies, and health and safety considerations began to be introduced into work on construction and office work among others. In transport, where the GLC was an employer, this commitment could only be fulfilled if research was done first.

But what kind of research, and with what aims?

There were political issues here too. The GLC employment researchers were committed to the idea that working people being 'researched' should be involved in what was happening, for straightforwardly democratic reasons, and because this meant the research would be more reliable. People should rapidly get access to the information they had helped generate, and the research should serve the interests of those researched as well as those of the Council. In other words, research came to be seen as a means of developing working relations between the GLC's constitutents and the Council, and not simply a way of collecting information the Council thought it would be nice to have.

The research into the health effects of OPO on the buses developed into an attempt to put these principles into practice. This was as much a result of pressure from bus workers as of the principles of the researchers. The research was being designed at a time when a campaign against more OPO was getting under-way among busworkers. For the drivers and conductors, investigating the effects of OPO was also a way to get their colleagues on the buses to think and talk about the issues and about the effects of the job on themselves, part of a campaign against speed-up.

These effects had been quickly visible, and had led bus staff at several garages into starting to investigate the problem for themselves. Brian Collins, then an OPO driver, and union branch secretary at Romford garage, described this process: 'Well after our garage had gone 100 per cent OPO, as the months were going on, we were seeing big changes in the staff, their attitude to work, to each other ... they changed in personality ... they went quiet ... and some of these men were the comedians of the garage ...'

Brian and others became convinced that there was far more stress and increasing ill health in the garage since OPO had come in, including serious illness, and also showing up in the increasing isolation of people and increasing tension. They had decided to try to do a survey of the effects of OPO in one or two garages when someone from the GLC rang up, having heard that they were interested and wanting to come down and discuss the issue.

The result was the taped discussion from which some of the quotations above are taken. The drivers said that they could see among their colleagues that the strain of doing two jobs — driving and dealing with the public — was putting additional strain on people already under stress from a difficult job and shiftwork, and that this was undermining their health and their home lives. It was clear from this anecdotal, but deeply felt, evidence, that there was something to be investigated. But given that some drivers were intending to do their own investigation, should the GLC keep out? There was a precedent for a 'workers' investigation' of bus work and health: a study in 1980 by a TGWU Branch in Leeds. This had been designed and undertaken by the union members, with support and advice on method and questionnaire design from a local WEA centre. London drivers had seen and discussed the Leeds study in detail already, and had thought of areas which had not really been covered and which they would want to investigate.

The Leeds study, though carefully done, and producing reliable results within its fairly small scope, did not allow a satisfactory comparison of crew and OPO driving, because at that time there were relatively few crew routes left in Leeds. The London drivers also felt that it missed some elements of the job. But the London bus workers did not have time or finance for a larger-scale reliable study.

Resources were what the GLC had to offer. As Steve Johnson, another driver, commented: '... we were very pleased that [the GLC] involved themselves, because we didn't have any idea how we were going to finance it and we had originally intended to do just our patch of outer East London.' On the other hand, the resources brought GLC interference and changed the nature of the study, reducing trade unionists' sense of being in control. Brian Collins described the mixed feelings: 'Well looking back to

the beginning of the survey, when we were telling the membership that the GLC were involved in what started off to be our
own survey in our garage ... there was some bad feeling: this is
our survey, it is about us: they did not want state bureaucracy
poking its nose in.'

The tension expressed in these two points was present
throughout the project. For the bus workers — and in principle
for the GLC officers — the maximum involvement and control by
trade unionists was desirable for its own sake, and for the sake
of the quality of the research. But on the other hand, the GLC
had its own interests. It wanted to ensure that the research was
done in such a way that the results would not be assailable on
the grounds of poor research method; pursuing that, the Council
put up the resources, paid a consultant (a doctor with research
experience in 'epidemiology', the study of the disease rates in the
population) and a full time worker, and therefore ended up with
the control inherent in doing a lot of the work. The study was
formally based at the London Hospital Medical College, where
the consultant worked, but had a lot of GLC involvement.

It quickly became clear that research would have to be done
involving several thousand bus workers, if statistically useful
results were to be obtained. This meant working throughout the
bus fleet. While the GLC was talking to trade unionists about the
research, the regional and local officials of the London Bus
Section of the Transport and General Workers Union, responding to repeated expressions of concern by delegates to the
London Bus Conference about assaults and health problems on
the buses, had been pressing London Transport to look at these
issues. So when the GLC approached the TGWU formally for
their views on the proposed study, there was a very positive
response. But when the GLC approached LT proposing that it
should co-operate in facilitating the research, London Transport
formally refused saying that it was proposing to undertake its
own (much more expensive) research on the same subject.

This put the GLC — and the TGWU — in a difficult position.
On the one hand, two studies on the same subject would confuse
people, some of whom would be answering the same questions
twice. If one study was done properly, one was enough. On the
other hand, there were a number of objections to the study
London Transport was proposing to do, as the union was well
aware. The TGWU had, in one official's words, many 'reservations' about the LT proposals from the start.

The first problem was the involvement of the London Transport medical service. Any driver who develops particular medical conditions, such as high blood pressure, cannot continue to drive. Bus drivers over forty-five (recently changed from fifty) are given regular medical checks for this purpose. Not surprisingly, then, while the LT medical service was seen by the staff as generally competent it was also regarded partly as a mechanism for weeding people out of their jobs. As one of the drivers involved in the health survey put it: 'You have medical officers seeing all these people come up with very serious illnesses and they ... pass the ones they think are fit and let the other ones go, and they don't see it as any sort of responsibility to stop what is going on.'

In addition, LT had recently announced a change in the rules on sickness absence. In an attempt to reduce time off sick, which they believed to be unreasonably high, disciplinary action against those taking sick leave had been increased, and the TGWU commented that the employers had begun enforcing the existing procedures 'more vigorously' than in the past.

As a result, there was a fair amount of suspicion around the garages when the London Transport management announced that, instead of co-operating with the GLC survey, they would prefer to do their own. Despite protestations by the medical officer, no doubt sincere, of unbiased research and confidentiality, many busworkers lacked faith that the findings could not be used against them in their job, or find its way onto their files.

There were also problems with the method proposed for the LT study. The LT research was based on individual confidential interviews with a sample of bus workers from the entire fleet. The questionnaire was to be drawn up independently of the union, indeed it was argued that the questionnaire could not be discussed with the union as this would bias the study! As a result the union could have no input into the content of the study. And the individual interview format would not give bus workers confidence in the anonymity and confidentiality of their replies.

For these reasons, the TGWU Regional Officer for London's Buses, Terry Allen, decided to support the proposed GLC study, despite the evident confusion of two studies running at once, provided that the GLC study was designed as trade union-based study over which the union had substantial control. Such a study would give the TGWU independent evidence on a subject of major concern to their members.

Buses and Health Research Method: A Trade Union Based Study

The GLC and the TGWU therefore decided to go ahead with their own study. As the study had to be done with no formal co-operation from LT, by then transformed into London Regional Transport under government control, all the work was done through the union, based on the union branches in the garages. The regional office of the union gave the study official backing, assisted and ensured that the branches were informed and asked to support the research. The GLC provided the funding, including payment for a medical consultant, a full time researcher and research expenses: the Council also provided its own input of research and statistical expertise, processed the data, and administered the organisation of project.

One of the first activities of the TGWU was to publicise the study among its membership. The union's London Bus Section of the TGWU has a rather unusual structure, based on a regular delegate conference of representatives from all the garages in the fleet, and this structure helped get the study underway. As one of these reps remembered: 'Well the first time the survey was mentioned was naturally at the T&G conference of all the reps, and we were told by the union to give as much assistance as possible.'

In general, the official backing of the Regional Office of the union was crucial in getting the study done.

In order to ensure a substantial and continuing trade union input a project steering committee was set up. It included a TGWU official responsible for one of the London Bus districts (Ollie Jackson), two lay delegates to the union's London Bus Conference, the GLC researchers involved, the medical consultant, and the full time project worker. As the project developed two ex-drivers, George Collins and Brian Collins, took a very active part in the research, and joined the steering committee. George had been driver, conductor and active trade unionist since he had started work on the buses in 1946. Recently retired, his experience, and the confidence in the project which his involvement inspired in the union members, was, in his fellow trade unionists' words, 'invaluable'. Brian, who had been an OPO driver and branch secretary when the project began, had by the end of the project been medically retired with spinal spondylosis, a disease to which heavy vehicle drivers are particularly subject. (Whether OPO increases the probability of contracting that particular very serious illness, because of the continual twisting sidewise in addition to the stress of driving, was something the research was not able to resolve because the sample was too small and the timescale too short.)

The research was designed to produce statistically satisfactory results together with considerable participation of drivers and conductors. Far from being incompatible (as London Transport argued), these two elements are highly complementary. The detailed involvement of the bus staff in the questionnaire design, including the lists of issues and illnesses, and the organisation of the questionnaire, was the best way of ensuring that the questions asked were the relevant ones. It was also the only way to ensure that the questionnaires were widely distributed and returned: many people would only take the trouble to fill out a long difficult questionnaire if they felt there was some useful purpose to doing so. Finally, the research also aimed at starting a wider discussion within the bus fleet about the relation between bus work and health, of the kind the Leeds study had also sought to stimulate. This, the steering committee hoped, would be assisted by the simultaneous production of a video discussing the issues.

The study was done in thirteen garages, meaning that questionnaires would be distributed to about 4000 drivers and conductors. In addition, a fourteenth garage would be used as a pilot, to test the questionnaire. The branch committees in each garage chosen were closely involved in the study, and particularly in distributing and persuading people to fill in the questionnaires.

There was still the tension however between the fact that the day to day work was done by the paid workers, particularly the project worker, Tina MacKay, and the wish to give the bus staff as much control as possible. So did the GLC take over, or did it genuinely involve people? The balance of opinion varies. As the trade unionists pointed out, there is always a problem when the local government people have paid time to do the work, and the bus staff are fitting it in in their spare time, around shift work, when they are tired. The TGWU official on the steering committee, Ollie Jackson, who worked hard on the study, nevertheless commented that 'to my regret I was not able to devote as much time to it as I would have liked to because of the pressure of business.' As one driver involved described it: 'originally when we were drawing up the questionnaires, and giving them out in the garages, and George Collins and Brian Collins went round the thirteen garages and involved the local trade union branches ... it was very much felt we were in control. But of course once the results went off to County Hall, and we waited quite a long time for the results to come out, the meetings were less frequent and we weren't so much involved at the final production end.'

The greatest involvement of union members was definitely early on. The steering committee, and trade union activists from several branches, helped draw up the questionnaire, and criticised successive drafts. As the process went forward, some conflicts emerged between the bus workers' interests and those of the GLC. The bus workers were particularly interested in the design of the buses and its effect on the drivers, and drew up detailed questions about drivers' views on the cab design and other aspects of the bus.

They also wanted a number of questions on shift work, feeling that shift work damaged workers' health. The GLC people, anxious for the survey to get full results on the *differences* between OPO and crew operation, wanted to cut down on issues common to both types of work. A compromise was struck (involving a long questionnaire!), but there was clearly a tension between undertaking a survey which would get bus workers thinking and talking about the whole range of ways in which their jobs affected their health, including many areas common to both crew and OPO work, and doing a study focussed on the differences between the two. Both were aims, and probably the second was better achieved than the first.

The bus workers involved were very clear about these distinctions: 'the health project was very much a trade union oriented idea. You know, from our point of view the reason why we did it was that people were being seriously affected health-wise. But also we felt that it could be different ... it is quite a nice job if you don't have to work such long hours, if you get a reasonable amount of pay, if you don't have the isolation of one person operation. And it would create jobs rather than, you know, disable people, which is what it is doing at the moment.'

Bus Work and Health: The Issues

A number of decisions were made about the issues the study could and could not address. It could not look in any detail at major longer term illness such as heart disease and high blood pressure which cause people to leave bus work, to retire or even to die. To do so would have required access to those who had left either because of serious ill health or because they could no longer tolerate bus work and so might be susceptible to serious illness. What the study could do was threefold: look at the prevalence of illness concentrating on everyday ill health; look at stress using various indicators including people's feelings about their lives; and look at other causes of ill health, especially smoking, drinking or housing conditions.

The questionnaire took at least half an hour to fill in and there were questions people might resent. As Ollie Jackson put it, 'at the end of the day, a person's medical standard is very private', so there was a lot of reluctance to overcome. The questionnaire began with some personal information — the kind of jobs and routes worked. It went on through shiftwork and the design of the buses: the most familiar areas for people, and the most straightforward. The next sections were on road conditions and their effects, on problems with dealing with passengers, and with concentration while driving. The last three sections asked about feelings about the job, about experience of accidents and assaults, and finally about people's health: recent poor health, poor health over the last year, hospital treatments, drinking and smoking.

For the people from the GLC and the London Hospital, the detailed discussions on the questionnaire with bus staff led them in a number of unexpected directions. The bus workers were concerned from the start with stress, not only for its effects on their physical, but also on their mental well being and home and social life. These were issues which had also been strongly emphasised by the Leeds study. The OPO drivers made the point that the source of stress was not only the speeding up of work, but also the resultant loss of control over work and lower job satisfaction. And it was people at home who got the worst of it: 'Stress is not funny; it's invisible ... you don't realise its creeping up on you until you actually start giving it away.' Discussing the move to OPO, one of the drivers said: 'I asked my wife last night, I said (we'll be possibly talking about it tomorrow), "well what's the one thing you've found how it's come out?" "You bring it home to me and the kids" she said, "and I'll never forgive you for that."' And another: 'I used to come home and the kids used to climb straight over me; but now mum says "leave dad alone, let him unwind" ... it's as if I've come in with the plague.'

Doing their job badly because of too much pressure changes people, and the lack of any break in the day wears them down. 'When I started driving, I used to really enjoy it ... At the end of the day I could feel like I had painted a picture. I've made a pot. It's something to be proud of. But now ... I can't concentrate on driving ... it's just a bind ... there's no satisfaction any more.' 'It's killed me as a person.' The isolation changed people, and changed relations in the garage: 'I think the whole garage has suffered ... the darts and the snooker matches, it all seems to be fading away now, because people are becoming so insular; they just sit at their table with their cup of tea and their own little flask ... they've just become recluses really.'

In addition, the discussions produced a long list of types of ill health and other related problems, some of them quite specific to bus work.

In getting people to complete the questionnaire, the crucial issue was confidentiality. This problem was reduced for this study by the non-involvement and partial hostility of management (a bonus that made up in part for the lack of LRT statistics). Even so, as Ollie Jackson remembered, 'in the early stages ... people genuinely believed that the employer might be getting a feed back', and the trade unionists involved, especially George, had to do a lot of explaining, persuasion and reassurance. The potential confusion with the management study, however, never emerged. In Ollie Jackson's words, 'LT's proposals died a natural death ... We saw it as a façade because they were aware that we were participating in your study.' This loss of interest was, in Ollie Jackson's view, part of a general retreat by LRT management from co-operation with the union after the GLC lost control.

Interestingly, neither staff nor union wanted the union involved in processing the results, on the grounds of confidentiality. But most were prepared to believe that the GLC would keep the results confidential, and after much discussion, the questionnaires were handed out with envelopes to be sent direct to the GLC's data processing centre. No names, numbers, or precise ages were on the questionnaires. In addition some of the busworkers involved visited the data processing centre where GLC part-time employees were coding the questionnaires for processing. The women explained what they were doing, and demonstrated that the forms themselves were not touched by the GLC officers involved in the survey or by the union.

About half the people who received questionnaires returned

them. For a survey of this kind, this is a very high rate of return, and was undoubtedly the result of all the time spent in the thirteen garages explaining, helping and encouraging people to fill them in, and all the efforts made by the branch committees.

Unasked Questions

But there were, undoubtedly, unresolved problems. While the questionnaire was designed to look at the health of conductors as well as drivers, the bus staff involved in drawing up the questionnaire were mainly drivers, and the questions were not as well designed for conductors. Issues of stress particular to them got missed off.

Worse, the questionnaire missed off some of the issues important to women staff. There were a couple of questions that were for women only, concerning health and discrimination in applying for drivers' jobs. But there were no questions on harrassment specific to women, and the questionnaire was much less carefully discussed with women than with male staff before being used. This was partly due to the smaller number of women staff — there are in particular too few women drivers to get any reliable results from the questionnaire about their health. But it was also bad research planning: not making enough effort to talk to women, and to get clear what issues most concerned them. Ollie Jackson commented: 'I got the impression that our women were very reluctant, especially the women drivers; the prejudice is still there about women drivers, and they needed ... a lot of persuasion even to speak to you.'

This impression was confirmed when an attempt was made later to fill in some gaps by interviewing women staff in more detail about their working lives and health problems. These discussions raised a series of issues about stress on women missed in the study.

One problem of course was child care: 'I don't think it's fair to have children while you're on this job ... it's the shifts you have to do, you need someone permanently to look after that child.' Women's need to change shifts for this reason was not recognised: 'The main point [is] being able to work your shifts around childcare arrangements ... I had an arrangement with another clippie for three months until someone cottoned on ... she liked doing lates ... I love doing earlies because I could be home for the kids and for three months we worked out a swopping system

... then someone raised an objection, and we were told we could not do it any more. The garage manager said, "we are not here to arrange our service round your needs". But if my driver wanted to play in the football team it was OK.'

Another problem specific to women was the non-recognition of serious menstrual pain as a reason for absence: and working in that kind of pain is likely to be even more difficult if you are doing two jobs at once. The highly irregular shift pattern — more damaging, many staff felt, than it needed to be — made menstrual problems much worse. Other issues included the lack of decent toilets for women staff, and food which suited them: salads, lighter food. And there was some serious sexual harrassment reported; the worst was reserved for women who decided to try to go driving, subjected sometimes to a stream of innuendo and deliberate discouragement. It's all considerable additional stress: 'looking at pornographic magazines mainly in order to wind you up.' 'Places like the canteen and the games room are really a male environment, and the women who are accepted are accepted by turning a blind eye to the way the men behave or becoming one of the lads.'

And then there's the usual innuendo about sexuality faced by women in male jobs, designed to harrass the lesbians, undermine other women, and divide the women from each other: 'The garage manager ... I went in about my probation or something ... he got the conversation round to where did I live ... who did I share with? Is it a man or a woman and do you share the same bedroom? He wouldn't be asking this of any man.'

Women conductors of course, faced with OPO, can choose driving or the dole: but going driving is a far harder option than for men. As OPO increases, the number and proportion of women workers on the buses drops sharply. Black staff are also more likely to lose their jobs, which makes black women doubly vulnerable. 'When I first started ... it was roughly 50/50 black/ white ... when I left the number of Black staff was starting to go down. The vast majority of new staff were white, male and young, and that's got worse since OPOs have come in.'

The black women staff interviewed were on the whole reluctant to talk about racial harrassment, although they admitted it existed, and many of the incidents they described with passengers included racist abuse. There were several descriptions of racism at the training centre for drivers, especially directed against Asian staff. But this evident source of serious stress was the other important issue not explored by the questionnaire.

There were several reasons for this. There are substantial numbers of black staff on the buses, many of whom were recruited direct from the Caribbean, especially Barbados, during the period of acute labour shortage in the 1950s. The GLC's original intention had been to include a question on the questionnaire concerning the race of the person filling it in, plus questions on racial harrassment. However, when we discussed this with black officials, lay delegates and black staff on the buses, they were all unanimously opposed to this. They felt strongly that it would be unacceptable, and undermine the project. Given this unanimity — itself a commentary on the situation on the buses — we left the questions off. As a result, we have no way of discovering whether the health and general stress experienced by black staff is worse than that experienced by white.

We do however think from the discussions in the garages that the response rate from black staff has been lower than that for white. Most of the people working on the project were white — though not all — and the black staff were simply not as prepared as the white staff to trust the researchers. They were also more cynical, and more likely to regard the whole thing as a waste of time. We wondered if literacy was also a problem, but an Asian branch official who was involved in the study saw this as a racist stereotype, arguing that as many white staff have literacy problems. There is no doubt that the questionnaire was not easy to fill in, required a lot of effort from many people who completed it, and discouraged some. But if we had done the whole study through interviews instead, we could have only talked to a tiny fraction of the 2000 staff who filled in questionnaires.

Bus Work, OPO and Health: The Results

We all held our breath when the results came off the computer. Up to that time, we had had no evidence but the anecdotal, and LRT was sure that we were wrong.

We were right. The evidence is extraordinarily strong and consistent for a study of this type. OPO drivers have worse health than crew drivers, and worse health overall than conductors as well. For the comparison between crew and OPO drivers this result holds across virtually the whole range of illnesses investigated. OPO drivers have worse problems of overtiredness and related problems, stomach problems, chest problems, aching joints and limbs, and problems of depression and anxiety. The gap gets bigger between the two jobs when we look at troubles over the past year as opposed to the past week, and more severe as opposed to less severe symptoms. (Hospital treatment shows the biggest difference of all). Various ways of averaging or adding up the results produced a consistent result: OPO drivers have worse health.

The results for conductors were rather different. The averages showed that conductors were healthier overall than OPO drivers, but less so than crew drivers; they also had a different pattern of illness. The conductors suffered particularly from arthritis, loss of appetite, flu and nervous problems, and markedly of course from swollen feet. They had less back trouble than drivers, and fewer problems with haemorroids. It should be remembered when looking at the amount of anxiety and depression (worst of all for conductors) that it is the conductors whose jobs are particularly at risk from the increase in OPO. Faced with the choice of retraining as a driver, which they may neither want nor be suited for, or redundancy, their anxiety is likely to be related to the future as much as their present situation. The fact that conductors are healthier than OPO drivers is striking since there are less stringent health requirements for conductors.

The results were analysed to see whether the ill health of the drivers and conductors could be explained by other factors than the job: for example, by smoking or drinking, age or bad housing. Perhaps, for example, OPO drivers smoked more or drank more, or perhaps they were simply older?

The results on this point are interesting. OPO drivers are certainly older: OPO pays better, and OPO drivers used to be taken on on the basis of seniority, although this is now breaking down as conversion to OPO increases. However, the age difference does not explain the health difference: within each age group, OPO drivers had worse health than the other drivers or conductors. Further more, and even more striking, the older OPO drivers, over 45, had *better* health than those between 35 and 44: for the other jobs, there was no strong relation between age and health. This may be because only healthier people have gone OPO driving in the past, it may be because the older OPO drivers are a 'survivor' population: those whose health has been undermined have left. Either way, age does not explain the greater ill health of OPO drivers.

Neither does smoking, or drinking, or the homes people live in. The study shows, exactly as expected, that people who smoke and drink more are less healthy. However, there is no difference in smoking and drinking between the three different occupations. As to housing, the better-paid OPO drivers, rather as expected, are more likely than the other categories to be owner occupiers in the suburbs. This on the whole ought to mean that they have better than average health, which makes their worse health more surprising.

What does appear to explain some of the worse health of OPO drivers, however, is pressure of work, and the stress involved in OPO driving. The study asked a lot of questions about people's feelings about their jobs, designed to show up how much under pressure people felt, how good their concentration was, how tired they were, how wound up or distressed, and conversely how much pleasure they felt in their job and how much satisfaction they got from it. Questions were also asked about sleep and tiredness.

Sleeping problems and tiredness were common to all the bus workers, and were closely associated with shifts. The sleeping problems were also closely associated with the measures of ill health: shift work undermines to some extent the health of all categories of bus workers, and improvements in the shift patterns would be likely to help everyone. For all the other measures, however, OPO drivers were clearly under worse stress than the others: especially more wound-up and distressed. They felt a greater lack of control over the job and a lower sense of competence, as well as difficulty in relaxing. These factors appear to explain a good part of the difference in ill health between the different jobs.

We also constructed what we called an 'aggravation index' for each type of bus, a measure of how annoying and irritating each was to drive. Startlingly, the new buses are all regarded as worse to drive than the old Routemasters (the twenty-five year old, open-platform buses), and this is only partly because the Routemasters are crew buses. It says little for modern bus design that the buses seem to be getting worse not better for the driver.

It is important to note that all the results reported above were for *men* only: ninety per cent of those who filled in questionnaires. The reason for this is that women's health patterns are different from those of men, and there were not enough questionnaires to do the analysis properly for women, especially women drivers. We did however compare the women conductors' questionnaires with those of the men. The women conductors over 45 had more ill health than men; before that women seemed to be in much the same or even better health. The most striking difference though was in experience of the job: women appeared both to be happier with the conducting job than the men — to get more positive satisfaction from it — but also to be more tired. This may well reflect the working day of the women outside the job, a view reinforced by some of the discussions with women reported earlier.

But is all this accurate? The study is entirely based on asking people how they feel and how their health is. Well, people say, why believe them, maybe they are just saying what they want you to hear? There are several answers to that. First, all medical studies are based centrally on 'self report', meaning asking people how they are, and that includes medical diagnosis. Second, while there is no doubt that people may both exaggerate or conceal their symptoms, there is no reason to suppose that this differs between the different jobs. People who chose OPO and intend to go on working at it are not likely to want to show that it is damaging them, and are as likely to under-report symptoms as are conductors. Under-reporting, not the opposite, is the chronic problem of this type of study. Finally, the group most likely not to have filled in the forms, or to have understated their ill health, are long-serving and older drivers worried about their medical test and afraid, despite all reassurances, that the questionnaire might get back to management. These older and longer serving people tend to be OPO drivers, so this would cause the results to show too small, not too large a gap, between OPO and other workers.

Worst of all, this study is only showing the tip of the iceberg. We have not looked at heart disease, angina, high blood pressure, the long term serious illnesses which cause people to be removed from driving. We have not talked to the people who were medically retired, or left before their health was further undermined: this is a health 'snapshot' of a rather tough survivor population who have adapted to or learned to cope with the job. The job is doing worse things to people than appears here.

OPO on the Underground, and the Politics of Videos

I saw the survey as far more important than the video, when the video was first thought of. But in this day of high technology, and people getting square eyes sitting down watching television every day, they do relate to moving pictures, and when you go to a garage and show the film, it generates debate.

During the time when we were doing the bus work and health study, two videos on OPO were made. One was made as part of the bus project, with a number of the trade unionists who also worked on the bus study. The other, about the effects of OPO on the tubes, was made by GLC staff, video makers and LRT Underground workers. Both were intended to stimulate discussion on OPO and health and safety generally.

Video making was probably one of the most effective methods the GLC used of reaching people and promoting discussion. Few people working for the Council had much experience of video making, and there was quite a lot of experiment with the politics of video making and participation.

OPO on the Underground began under the GLC with an experiment on the Hammersmith and City line: this was later extended to the Circle and District lines: these are all double track lines running just below street level, not the deep tube lines running in single-track tunnels. The NUR had agreed to this OPO extension, in return for increased pay for the new driver-operators. The GLC had not opposed this, in part because of the union agreement, although they had worried about the safety issues.

But doubts in the union were growing, as unemployment increased, and as LT began associating the push for more OPO with reductions in station and platform staff, thereby sharply reducing total staff on the underground. As Geoff Revel, a member of the NUR executive involved in the negotiations, pointed out: 'We can legitimately say that we entered into the agreement (on OPO) in that kind of atmosphere ... when we used to go on marches because there was a quarter of a million workers unemployed.'

In response to growing fears of unemployment, and growing anxiety about stress on one person operators on trains, the union tried to renegotiate the OPO agreement, before any further extension of OPO. The NUR's aim was to shorten the maximum OPO work without a break, hence reducing stress and job loss. LRT resisted, introduced OPO on the East London line in May 1985 without a new agreement, and took court action when the union called a strike without a ballot. The strike was patchy, and rapidly called off.

In mid 1985, then, there was considerable doubt and discontent at all levels in the union about further extension of OPO, especially to the deep level tubes where it would be more dangerous. Although by then it had lost control of LT, the GLC still had a legitimate interest in OPO on the Underground, because of its employment effects, and because of health and safety in a major London service industry. Some of these effects were much the same as on the buses: job losses — 2000 guards' jobs — and intensification of work: 'one person to do two people's jobs for sod all pay,' in one driver's words. For a number of trade unionists on the tubes, the introduction of OPO under the GLC was an example of what they had thought all along — the GLC was going to have good policies for passengers, but just be a standard, bad, employer when it came to the basic industrial relations issues of jobs, pay and conditions.

The GLC Industry and Employment branch really only began to talk to the trade unionists about OPO in late 1984. Again, the involvement consisted in research, trying to find out what the issues really were and what tube workers thought about OPO — and then making the results available through a process of interviewing and video making, working with trade unionists and offering support, advice and facilities.

The impetus for the video came in 1985. In June, the GLC ran a Transport and Employment conference, bringing together some trade union officials, lay officials and members, local government people working on transport policy, academics and people working on passenger campaigns. At this conference there was a workshop discussing the situation of workers in the public transport sector, by this time under very serious attack from the government. A number of trade unionists wanted to know where the GLC had been over the introduction of OPO on the tubes, and demanded that the GLC 'do something' to help.

This conference was the starting point for a series of meetings with guards and drivers to discuss the issues. The bus video was being shown by then, and a video was proposed to put on record the views of guards and drivers about OPO on the Underground. The audience would be other public transport workers and their passengers.

The video was filmed in the Underground, with the soundtrack made in County Hall. It had to be made without official backing, and was made by a small video company and the GLC, working with a large number of tube workers. Few tube workers were willing actually to appear in the film for fear of reprisals, an indicator of the changing situation within London Transport and the different nature of the debate on OPO on the underground. Few bus workers had expressed these fears. There was an accompanying booklet, containing more detail of the interviews, discussions, and background about OPO on the tubes.

What emerges most strongly from the interviews and this research, as well as from discussions around the video, is the importance of the health and safety issues, again, for OPO under ground. The debate was quickly widened by the trade unionists from the old lines — employment, or rather, actual redundancies — to health and safety issues for passengers as well as staff.

And on the underground too, these were serious, although the pattern was rather different. As on the buses, single drivers can never relax their attention, switching from concentration on driving to operating doors as well as watching the platform. There are the same worries about passenger safety: 'A guard looks out for people who either slip or fall against the train, who attempt to obstruct the train or who accidently slip between the platform and the train, and at some stations there are very big gaps. We are also looking for any problems: it is possible to shut a child in the car and leave a parent on the platform.'

With OPO, it is the drivers who are supposed to watch in this way, but they often cannot see. On the curved platforms, there are mirrors and TV monitors, but, as an OPO driver explained: 'The equipment was cheap, the TVs cameras, mirrors were positioned wrongly. You could hardly see down the platform. A lot of the cameras didn't work. You thought, this is ridiculous. It was soul destroying.'

As with OPO on the buses, the trains are slowed down and made more irregular. And there is the same feeling of isolation, especially because of fear of assaults, exacerbated as always by the feeling of isolation at being underground. Since OPO has been allied with reducing the staff on stations, the general feeling of isolation is increasing, and some black staff feel it particularly, faced with increasing racial assaults: 'I've had terrible fights going on on my train ... I've got to talk as a man with a black skin, you're in real trouble with OPO.'

Ironically, at the same time that LRT was taking staff off stations and trains, it was hiring extra police to deal with assaults. This, many tube workers firmly believe, is the wrong approach. Dave Wetzel echoed the views of many trade unionists: 'The maintenance of a civilised Underground is not a policing matter, it is a *staffing* matter. The government is very misguided if it thinks it is making a saving by creating a virtually deserted system with police rushing from trouble spot to trouble spot. Passengers will prefer to travel in other ways and revenue will be lost.'

But the worst thing about the Underground, which contrasts with the buses, is the *scale* of things which can go wrong. The worst worry for the drivers is that, under pressure of time, often unable to see the platform in places where the train cab stops in the tunnel, he or she (but there are few women) will open the doors on the wrong side, away from the platform. It has happened, several times already. So far no one has been killed, but with crowded trains, live rails and people trapped possibly against the tunnel wall, it is very dangerous. 'Many' District Line drivers had done it, said one operator.

Having two people can be crucial for other reasons. One of the guard's most important roles is to be there, on the train, if a driver collapses, if there is a fire or a serious problem, to deal with passengers, move the train, keep calm, keep people off the live rails, provide information and instructions. This is most important in case of a fire: there have been thirteen fires damaging trains and stations in the last five years, several of them serious. Fewer staff on trains makes fires more likely; fewer properly trained staff around in a fire makes the chances of passengers a lot poorer. Privatisation, meaning contractors unused to the Underground, increase the risks: a serious fire at Oxford Circus appears to have been started by inflammable materials in a contractor's store.

Making the videos turned out be half the problem. Distribution proved to be a major difficulty, especially after the end of the GLC. But for a small number of workers, involvement in making the videos was a valuable and demanding experience. The bus video in particular took an open approach to the debate, and included discussion of the good side of OPO — more money, contact with the public and working on your own for those who liked it. Bus workers were involved in research, script-writing and interviewing on camera.

Brian Collins described the process: 'I never thought anything could exist like that ... Instead of just the GLC deciding to make a film and deciding what workers would like or what policy dictated ... every single day of filming was done with bus workers present, helping to form questions and clarify things. The involvement was tremendous. And I must say, the film-makers bent over backwards to make sure that the views were valid bus workers' views. ... When the film was first edited it was shown, and anybody that was involved could have any parts clarified or removed.'

Not everyone was so happy with the process, arguing that too few people were drawn in, certainly fewer than were involved in the Underground video. But there is no doubt that the video raised and got discussed many of the wider issues the survey inevitably missed. One of these was the issue of racism, raised by black bus workers interviewed. Another was the stress of approaching redundancy. Another, only touched on in the survey, was the social effects on people's home lives, relations with wives, partners and friends. The video was shown (though still not widely enough) in garages, women's groups, Labour Party wards, and to many other interested people. It started wide discussion.

Some of the best discussion has been with passengers. Passengers and staff have often been in conflict: as a TGWU official summarised the strains on his OPO drivers: '... the public screaming at you and threatening you, treating you as dirt at times.'

The public have a strong tendency to blame public transport staff for all the failures of the service. And staff conversely have been known to treat the public as the enemy, and more public as worse. However, as the passenger interviews showed, there is genuine public sympathy, especially over unemployment.

The videos can help a bit of mutual understanding. As one bus worker who had been showing the video to groups of the public said: '... for the general public it was an eye opener ... they were saying things like, oh well we won't string the bus driver up when he's twenty minutes late tomorrow morning.'

They also help overcome the divisions among different parts of LRT's workforce. Not only did the bus video stimulate the Underground video, it brought different bus workers together: 'When you walk into a garage that knows nothing about the project, nothing about how it was made, the first thoughts are, that this is a propaganda film ... from either London Transport or the GLC, a body people know little about if they are not political. But once the film was shown in a garage and discussion took place afterwards, it united everybody, it united the conductor, the driver and the OPO driver because it was talking about the same thing, jobs and conditions in employment.'

As Ron Young from Wandsworth garage put it, 'Guys don't talk to each other in the canteen about their medical problem. ...

When they saw the video, they knew that they weren't individuals, they knew that what they had, the other guy had, and they started talking more openly about the health problems within the industry. Especially the marital side ... everyone turned it into a joke about the divorce rate on this firm ... and it's not just because of the shift work. That's the thing that struck us most, they were saying, Christ, the times my wife has said that, or the times I've said that.'

Local Authorities, Health and Safety and the Trade Unions

Is all this still relevant?
    I think it's even more relevant ... because all the propositions that management are putting to us mean that the membership will have to work longer hours with less buses on the roads. It's job intensification ... There is no doubt that the more pressure is put on people the more their health deteriorates.

Ollie Jackson, the TGWU official who worked on the bus study, was talking about the new pressures that bus workers have come under in 1985 and 1986. The chief pressures have come from increased privatisation, especially through putting out to tender bus services and many related services like catering. This tendering process has been used as a lever by management to try to enforce deteriorating conditions on bus workers, from fewer jobs, via lower wages, to worse working conditions.

The worse working conditions, the poor health that results, the lower levels of service, deteriorating relations with the public: these effects form a vicious circle. The stress on the bus and tube workers which comes from job intensification is a central part of that process. In some areas, like catering, the link is very direct. As Ollie Jackson put it, because of financial pressures, 'the catering facility is not what it used to be ... we're very conscious that unless we keep a tight grip on it, the junk food syndrome will take over, digestive related illnesses will be on the increase.'

As the public transport service is broken up into bits for easy privatisation, there is less and less future for people whose health is undermined. As Ron Young explained: 'What used to happen was, when they became unfit to drive a bus, there was a lot of what they called "light duty" jobs of which cleaning was one. . . . if we start losing out any of these jobs to privatisation, you're losing your own workforce that have given a large amount of time.' Though there are no clear figures, the union believes that numbers of medical retirements are rising.

Damage to staff and the safety of passengers are interrelated, as Ollie Jackson pointed out, discussing privatisation: 'Some of the so-called competitors are actually prepared to employ people whose medical standards are such that London Transport would retire them on medical grounds.'

All this, and OPO too. OPO is going rapidly ahead: nearly seventy per cent of bus services are now OPO, and the pressure for further OPO on the tubes continues. The GLC only delayed it on the buses, and did not affect the pace of introduction on the tubes. Many people feel that the work that has been described was too little and too late. Are there, then, any longer term effects or lessons?

There are several aspects of the story. One is an experience of doing research, and of trying to change the relations between local government and a part of the public sector workforce and trade unions through the research. Second, the work reinforced the importance of health as a trade union issue, and was a way to get people to think and talk about their jobs, and the effects of the jobs on their lives, a way to get the effects of job intensification on individuals more clearly on the agenda of local authorities as well as trade unions. Third, there was a strengthening of contacts between trade unionists in the already fragmented and further dispersing public transport service, through these discussions.

It is clear from the interviews that the work on the health research and the videos changed the view some transport staff had of the GLC — though not always for the better of course. It must be remembered that the GLC was the employer, and that the trade unionists were experienced cynics. Worse, when the Livingstone administration came in, with its early plans for cheap fares and more services, the bus and tube workers were intitially highly suspicious. They had had the Cutler administration as employer, and before that the previous Labour administration, which had been little different in its record on jobs and conditions. Employment in London Transport had been dropping steadily. The cheap fares policy had not been discussed in enough detail with the unions, certainly not widely discussed with the garages and depots in terms of its impact on staff, and many bus and tube workers suspected that they might be going to pay for these cheaper fares in terms of more work, and particularly more OPO. Steve Johnson, a bus driver, remembered this period: 'From the receiving end of the GLC as an employer, for the first couple of years there was no noticeable difference between them and Cutler ... I think to some extent the Law Lords decision worked in our favour — it is perhaps a contradiction ... because in 1982 they were talking about further one person operation as a way of, sort of balancing the books when it comes to cheaper fares'.

Steve argued that, once the Law Lords decision had been taken, reversing the cheap fares policy, then the relation between the GLC and the unions began to improve, of necessity: 'The politicians were then looking to us to ... fight their battles against the judges, ... and that connection then came into being between the GLC and the unions to resist central government.' A number of trade unionists saw this as the crucial background to a sudden greater interest in their welfare!

The interviews also demonstrate just how big is the gap, in class-divided Britain, between people who worked for the GLC in County Hall, and people who drove their buses. The bus workers were many of them both puzzled and amused when 'the GLC' started ringing them up: 'some of the early meetings were quite interesting in that, you know, someone from County Hall was coming down, and I suppose we had these stereotyped images of who would appear — you know, pin strip and bowler hat — and we were pleasantly surprised that they were human beings.' The curiosity was on both sides in the early stages: 'I think the people who came down from County Hall were pleasantly surprised to meet bus workers. ... They were very enthusiastic about some of the anecdotes we were telling them and some of the details, ... they were enjoying themselves finding out about bus work ... to the extent that we thought they were going to start applying for the job!'

In itself, these kinds of contacts, and the working relations that resulted, do not change much. At best, they give people a bit more confidence in dealing with and pressuring that distant beast called local government. But without these kinds of working relations, nothing will be learned. In the context of the 1980s, with trade unions under pressure and morale low, it was a common comment that the GLC expressing serious interest in the working conditions of bus workers, and the effects of policy on their lives, had an effect in boosting morale and giving people new energy.

The project itself, the video and the study, appears to have had some genuine organising effect in bringing garages together. People saw the video, discussed it, met others involved in the survey. In that sense, said one activist, 'the GLC were responsible for new links that were being forged between garages. We had an industrial dispute one day and it was only because of the involvement of the garages with each other over the project that immediate support was gained.'

The videos were undoubtedly more effective than the questionnaire study in getting discussion going on health and working conditions among the bus workers, although both helped. As Ron Young, one of the branch reps closely involved in the study in his garage in Wandsworth, pointed out, the discovery that the problem wasn't just your own, but was common, was important in itself: 'what they (the management) try and get across to you is that it's a problem that's only at Wandsworth — the sickness, the high blood pressure, the heart related diseases etc. is only a Wandsworth thing and we're all shirkers. And it's not until you actually got involved in surveys like the survey that was done that you realise that it is a problem that is widespread throughout the fleet, that every garage has got a high percentage of guys off with a similar type of complaint.'

In addition to helping to get discussions going in the London fleet, the GLC also brought Leeds and London bus workers together and held a conference where the work was discussed while it was still underway with other interested trade unionists. These discussions made clear just how unusual it still was for workers in a particular industry to get together to research the health and safety of their industry in a systematic way. The Kings Fund Centre — who hosted the Leeds/London workshop and were very sympathetic to the whole project — were nevertheless initially surprised that the proposed participants in a conference on occupational health on the buses were bus workers, not academic researchers.

The discussions also raised a serious question for some trade union officials about the proper role for local authorities in this kind of investigation. While the London study had full trade union backing, some union officials were unhappy about the GLC bringing together transport union members, including invitations to interested union members from outside London to discuss the research. They felt the hosting of such discussions by a local authority, even with officials invited to participate, constitued improper interference in the internal affairs of a union.

This is of course a legitimate point of view, and raises an issue which recurred in much of the work the GLC did with trade unionists. The GLC took a contrary view: in this case that health and safety in a major public sector industry — and one further-more under serious attack — was a legitimate activity for a local authority. And furthermore — and this is perhaps the point really at issue — given that the GLC was firmly in favour of research being done with the participation of ordinary trade unionists and branch delegates and officials, the Council also felt that discussion between interested trade unionists from else-where in the country could only benefit the London work. The difference of opinion neatly sums up some of the problems of a local authority taking an interest in the organisation, including, inevitably, bargaining issues in industries in their area. These issues of union-public authority relations need to be debated, on a case by case basis, if a better working relation between local authorities and the different levels of the trade union movement is to be established.

To come back to where we began: the GLC in 1981 had no history of involving themselves in any way with the working conditions on bus and tube, with the kind of jobs transport provided to its 60,000 employees. No one in the GLC in 1981 (with the exception of the chair of the Transport Committee) could have told you what it was like to work on a bus, or whether the management were running the public transport service as far as possible in the interests of the working conditions of the staff. Some officers argued that this was management's affair.

Looking back, this now seems an extraordinary commentary on the management of our public services by public authorities. It took us eighteen months to demonstrate conclusively what seemed perfectly obvious to the transport workers involved: that job intensification harms your health. In the process we learned something else: that the issue of occupational health, so often hived off by everyone — unions, workers, management and public authorities — as a side issue after numbers of jobs and wages, is in fact a central political issue. It raises the issue of people's need for greater control over the conditions of their working lives, the central concern of industrial democracy. And researching and discussing it is a very good way of helping people reflect collectively on their own needs, on what their aims might be in establishing more control over their work, and on the connection between their work and the rest of their lives. Such collective reflection is potentially a very radical political process, posing a considerable threat to established methods of managing the public sector. In the present situation, given the rapidly worsening working conditions in public transport, the most immediate issue however is whether the *way* the research was done helped strengthen trades unionists' capacity to resist.

4
Setting an Example?
The GLC as an Employer

First Impressions

When we walked into the room full of cleaners, messengers, building workers and electricians we weren't sure what to expect. It was July 1983, two years after Labour had taken power in County Hall, but only six months since we had started work in the GLC's Popular Planning Unit. Mrs Thatcher had just 'won' the Falklands War and we were in the middle of a general election campaign, the outcome of which many GLC officers and councillors hoped would mean that their policies developed at County Hall would be implemented in Whitehall. The stakes were high: the Conservative Party manifesto included the pledge to abolish the GLC.

A few weeks before some GLC blue collar trade union representatives had asked us to put on a workshop about abolition and privatisation for their members. We were eager to know what ordinary GLC workers felt about their two years under a radical Labour administration.

A GLC messenger in NUPE summed up the mood of GLC manual workers at that time:

> The GLC's Low-Pay Campaign was well publicised on the TV. They had lovely speeches but nothing came out of it; we were still working twice the amount of hours for a decent wage. Our wages are £69 a week — basic — and we tend to work about 72 hours a week. Another thing is that I feel I am subsidising the higher paid worker when I use the canteen. They earn three times more wages than me, and I pay the same price.

They discriminate against us. It is a class issue from a white-collar Staff Association [the GLC's main white-collar union]. Until recently, they would not allow us to participate in inter-departmental sports activities; we have just changed that. The caste system in India is quite superior to what operates here at the GLC.

The manifesto included a number of things to bring us in line with white-collar workers; but Carr [John Carr, the chair of the GLC's Staff Committee] and the rest of the councillors over there have just let it slide; I think that was because of opposition from the Staff Association, or rather the officers.

We have about four layers of management here. Then we have got the Labour councillors. We have found that the management here is Tory, and you cannot do anything about it. Ken Livingstone can preach like Christ coming out to proclaim salvation — we are not going to change management — we are manual staff — we are just a general dog's body — we are non-essentials here. If we have got any problem to solve and we take it to management, we get little or no satisfaction out of them. It takes years; the Union here have been virtually non-existent for so many years, but it is only in the last two or three years that they have had any guts to stand up to management now and again.

You never seem to get a situation where there is somebody in authority to say yes or no to a problem; it is always passing the buck and saying 'I've got to put it to this committeee, that committee', and you do not know who you are dealing with; and therefore you are always in the wrong, no matter what you do.

This is just one voice out of 22,000 at the GLC. Obviously the NUPE messenger was not representative of the architects, valuers, firefighters, secretaries and thousands of other different jobs in the GLC. But we soon found out that he was speaking for most GLC manual workers, who did not think that the new Labour administration had made much difference to their predicament in the last two years.

In this chapter we are going to compare the Labour manifesto's promises to GLC staff with the reality as these staff experience it. We will look at why Labour was more successful in implementing part of its equal opportunities policies than what became known as the 'socialist wages policy'. We will identify the obstacles faced by the Labour administration and how they affected the campaign to defend the GLC. Finally, we will highlight lessons and experiences which will provide other councils and other council workers with ideas for taking some of the policies tried at the GLC still further.

Promises, Promises

When the Labour administration took power in May 1981 it probably had the most detailed and radical manifesto seen in local government for many years. There was a clear commitment to sweep away most of the inequalities and low pay in the GLC itself. Amongst other things the manifesto promised a minimum wage, an integrated career structure to include blue collar workers, a series of measures to promote equal opportunities and a new system of industrial democracy. Ironically those commitments that the GLC came closest to carrying out were those which could be most easily imposed with the back-up of the law. Those which it did least to implement needed forms of worker involvement which only began to take off when, and perhaps because, it was too late and abolition was on the cards.

Like all authorities, the GLC was divided into departments along professional lines such as architecture and valuation. Below the professionals there was a grotesque and alienating hierarchy of workers. Administrative and support staff occupied the next rung, followed by manual craft workers and finally so-called 'unskilled' manual workers. Within these broad categories there were hundreds of different job categories.

The job hierarchy was reinforced by differentials in pay and conditions. The GLC Director General earned about ten times as much as his cleaning lady. Apart from getting much lower pay, manual workers also had to work forty hours instead of thirty five, got half the London weighting allowance and less paid holiday. A high proportion were on bonus schemes which meant that they lost income if they became sick or went on holiday. Although there are no accurate figures for the period before the Labour Administration, a substantial number of GLC staff were earning less than the poverty level of two thirds of average male manual earnings as defined by the Low Pay Unit.

The recruitment and promotion scheme in operation when Labour took power in 1981 guaranteed that most people for senior and middle grade professional and administrative jobs were recruited internally. Manual and junior clerical posts were filled from outside. Once in, employees were not allowed to apply for jobs that were more than a few pay bands above their present grade, and moving from a blue collar to a white collar job was virtually impossible. This system, often referred to as the 'class system' of recruitment, effectively kept most people without university degrees in the blue collar or junior

Credit: John Sturrock/Network

Suddenly in the fight to save the GLC the views and the potential power of the GLC workers became important.

clerical jobs in which they started.

The 'class system' created huge income differences. It gave senior officers a very cosy life indeed, while manual workers, and to a lesser extent junior clerical workers, could barely make ends meet. The system also kept women and black people at the bottom of the pile. Only 16 per cent of GLC workers were women in 1981 and only 7 per cent came from ethnic minorities even though 40 per cent of London's workers are women and 19 per cent of its population come from ethnic minorities. When the GLC carried out its first survey of equal opportunities in 1983 it found that there were only thirty five women and fifteen black people out of 550 senior officers. White men did most of the senior professional, craft and firefighting jobs. Women and black people worked as cooks, cleaners, messengers and junior clerical and administrative staff.

Class Divisions

These problems are not just a question of inequality. The way in which work was divided up and organised at the GLC was a fundamental barrier to providing a more effective and responsive service to users. In the trade union workshops on abolition organised by the Popular Planning Unit between 1983 and 1986, GLC workers constantly referred to the ways in which rigid hierarchies, unnecessary bureaucracy and prejudices about lower paid workers prevented them from getting more satisfaction out of their work and doing a better job.

To start with, the distrust and lack of respect for blue collar workers meant that they were subjected to two methods of work monitoring and motivation that do not apply to white collar workers. The first was the use of bonus systems and workstudy methods, and the second involved complicated systems of prioritising and checking work through job tickets. Both approaches centralised power in the hands of the administrative officers who often had far less understanding of the needs of users than the workers who directly provide the service.

A painter from London Community Builders said: 'We provide a unique service to tenants and schools. We have responsibility for repairing particular schools and estates so we get to know the problems. This means that the quality of our work is better than contractors'. If we do something wrong then we are called back to put it right. Most contractors won't do this unless they are taken to court. Any profits we make go back to improve the service.

'Our main problem is the government's Land and Planning Act: but we have plenty of other problems which *could* be put right *without* a change in the law. The way we are paid causes problems. In most cases a work study officer will set a particular time for certain kinds of jobs like painting doors. We then get a bonus for the number of doors we paint. The trouble is that most work study officers have never done the jobs they are supposed to measure and they set ludicrous times. For example, we may have to paint a door with a lot of panelling in the same time as a plain door. The only way to keep up is to do shoddy work. We don't enjoy this but most people are not prepared to make *less* for doing the job well.'

This kind of criticism was made over and over again by all manual workers on bonus. They also criticised the other major way in which they were motivated to work, the use of job tickets to monitor and set priorities for work. In some cases the monitoring and control became an end in itself. Here's how a worker at the Woolwich Ferry Boat Workshop described the problem: 'Not many people even know the GLC runs the Woolwich Ferry — they only put a sign up a little while ago. Yet we are one of the main links between the North and South Circular Roads. We carry fifty six lorries and cars across the river six times every hour every day except bank holidays. We provide a life-line for many of the people of North Woolwich. A lot of them do their shopping across the river in Woolwich Town Centre. If it were not for the ferry the only way across would be under the ¾-mile long tunnel. This is quite dangerous at night and very heavy going for anyone who's not young and fit at the best times. It's free to go on our boats.

'Fifty people work running the ferry and there are another fifty-four people on maintenance. Our workshop is now the biggest ship repairer's on the Thames. I love my work. I love to produce things and see things grow. But they put all sorts of ridiculous obstacles in our way. When the Tories ran down the construction branch and a lot of other GLC services they transferred a lot of technical and supervisory staff to other parts of the GLC. Before this, we used to have six administrative workers in our workshop, now we have twenty-six. Before, if something went wrong with one of the boats they would just report it directly to one of us and we would fix it. Now they have to fill in a requisition form which goes through about six people before we can finally get on with the job.

'It always used to be a thing among us that we would never let the ferry stop. We used to do the repairs while it was going across. You could get a whole team of men out on Christmas Eve if something went seriously wrong. But now the management don't care. The man in charge of the workshop before had been a ship repairer all his life. He really knew the job and we worked well with him because he respected us. Then they decided to upgrade the job and told him that he wasn't qualified to apply. The people we've got now don't know one end of a ship from another. They spend all this money on ridiculous projects and machines that we tell them won't work but they never listen.

'We have to put most of the major repairs we do out to tender. But we're not allowed to tender for other jobs ourselves. It's mad. Most of our men have a good twenty years' skill and we're the largest workshop of this sort on the Thames. Why can't we make more use of it?'

Building workers described the same problem: 'We have to put up with a lot of complaints from tenants which have nothing to do with us. For example, if a school caretaker finds out that a toilet is broken he can't just phone us up and ask us to mend it. He has to fill in a requisition slip which goes to about four different people for approval. About three months later we get the order to go down and fix the toilets. If we find out that the toilet next to it is broken we can't even mend that. The caretaker has to fill out another requisition slip which goes through the same procedure. It's not surprising that a lot of caretakers are now using contractors for small jobs.'

Blue-collar workers and junior white-collar workers also complained bitterly about disciplinary procedures. They said they were subjected to many humiliating rules and penalties which again had nothing to do with doing a good job.

Most GLC workers felt that instead of trying to get them to do things by unwieldy bonus systems or bureaucratic control, far more time could be spent on explaining why they were meant to do something and training them on how to do it. Lack of training and clear task-setting was worse in 'low status' jobs. But these jobs are often vital for the smooth working of an organisation. For example, GLC messengers complained that they were given virtually no training on where things were but were criticised for bringing letters back undelivered. The obvious solution was to dump letters in any old room if they couldn't find the right place.

Women in the word processing room also described how they

were looked down on and given unnecessary work by the more senior, male white-collar workers: 'A lot of people don't realise what word processing entails. I think it creates more work. Before a person would dictate exactly what he wanted to say, now he thinks, ah ... it's on the word processor so I can do it roughly, so it means a double job. A girl spends five hours key-boarding and it comes back so altered that she's got to spend three hours correcting it. They continue doing it because they can't be bothered to think. They don't bother to do things properly in the first place — so they're doing less work, thinking-wise and we do more.'

GLC workers also complained that managers took a very narrow view of costs and productivity. By using private business methods of splitting up the service into cost centres, and focussing on cutting costs and jobs in order to look viable and productive, management often defeated the very aims they were set up to achieve. A security guard provided a graphic example: 'We have to deal with really major burglaries and watch out for fires. And yet our job is made impossible for us and for staff. For example two of the entrances to the GLC have no security staff on them at all and yet we have instructions from management that we have to stop all staff without passes even if we know them. That means the real crooks are allowed in the back door while we are forced to harass staff.'

Building workers faced a similar problem: 'Contractors have another advantage over us. We are only given an allowance for public transport. That means that a carpenter will have to lug his tool box on the tube halfway across London. If he finds he's forgotten his hammer when he arrives he has to go all the way back by tube. Most contractors would just nip round in a van. In fact a lot of us use our own cars, although we are not paid for it.'

Workers argued that the service could be improved by proper planning rather than mindlessly cutting costs and jobs. For instance, building workers said that there was no proper system for planning the supply of goods and tools so they often ran out. 'A lot of these things could be solved by involving the workforce more in decision making and by making small changes like having a system of planned maintenance and a quick procedure for dealing with emergencies. Why isn't this being done?'

Finally, most people at the Popular Planning workshops said that the division of the GLC into baronial departments dominated by a particular profession resulted in empire building, over and under spending, and over and understaffing. An

extreme but small-scale example of this was described by a fire
station commander: 'I remember being phoned up on Monday
evening and told to get rid of £20,000 unspent money the next
day. We badly needed respirators and some other protective
clothing, but that was the wrong budget head. I finished up
carpeting half the fire station and getting every firefighter a
calculator.'

Most white-collar workers could provide examples of wasteful
expenditure at the end of the budgetary year. But there were also
lots of examples of underused resources. As we have seen, the
Woolwich Ferry workshop could have done a lot more work for
other parts of the public sector. But it wasn't even getting work
from many GLC departments. Instead they sent it out to contractors. Similarly, workers in GLC parks and sports facilities
often had ideas of increasing the use of the facilities they worked
for.

Clearly these workers were committed to the content of their
work, or they would have like to have been. But the extent to
which this commitment meant anything was inseparable from
their value and dignity as workers, in other words how much
they were paid and conditions in which they had to work. All the
manual workers at the workshops felt that they were looked
down on, and treated as if they were inherently lazy and dishonest. Why should manual workers have to clock-in when
white-collar workers can work flexi-time and are trusted to work
their hours without nearly as much policing? Why were white-
collar workers paid far better basic wages and trusted to carry
out their work without further financial incentives, when manual
workers get poverty wages and a bonus to make them carry out
specific bits of work?

Achievements

Before describing some of the bloody battles, sweet victories and
dashed hopes of five years of Labour administration, let's look at
the achievements.

By the end of its five years, the Livingstone administration
had undoubtedly made more improvements to the conditions of
GLC workers than any other administration at the GLC. It had
trail blazed many policies which other local authorities around
the country have now taken up. (They have been described in
detail in the publications of the Equal Opportunities Unit.)

Perhaps the most significant reform was the abolition of the 'class system' of rigid internal recruitment. All GLC jobs were externally advertised and anyone in the GLC could apply for any job. On the white-collar side, where the GLC was free from national negotiations to make local agreements, pay increases were made at a flat rate or bottom-loaded (more for lower paid). Differentials among white-collar main grades were reduced. Blue collar workers had a flat rate £6 increase in their London weighting allowance which reduced the £10 difference between blue and white-collar workers. Meal allowances were also equalised with white-collar workers.

The most marked achievements in job opportunities were a result of the work of the new administration's Equal Opportunities Unit. This was established within the Personnel Department and given considerable clout. The Unit organised many positive action courses designed to compensate for the discrimination women, black people, and people with disabilities face in education and job experience. Many of these courses were targetted at blue collar workers who traditionally lose out in in-house training.

The Unit improved the conditions for women with children. They introduced a new income-related allowance for all staff with dependants (up to £20 per week for a household with an income under £6,000). Two work-place nurseries were set up and all jobs made open to job-sharing.

Recruitment, promotion and disciplinary procedures were all revised with the intention of screening out direct and indirect discrimination against women, ethnic minorities, people with disabilities, gay men and lesbians. A disabilities team was set up to provide training and improve the employment opportunities of disabled staff.

Together, these equal opportunities policies resulted in a small but visible improvement in the number of women, black and disabled people employed by the GLC. The last GLC monitoring report showed that the proportion of women in the GLC had increased from 16 per cent in 1981 to 21 per cent in 1985, and the proportion of black people had increased from 7 per cent to 11 per cent.

Finally, the previous Conservative administration had cut five thousand GLC jobs, mostly through natural wastage and voluntary redundancy; the Labour administration stopped this process and kept the number of GLC jobs roughly stable throughout its term of office.

What Got Dropped?

A number of important manifesto commitments were not achieved. Labour did not establish a minimum wage — a central commitment. In 1985, 1,184 GLC workers were still getting less than the poverty level of £108 a week as defined by the Low Pay Unit.

Table 1

Low Paid Employment within the GLC in 1985:
staff earning gross weekly wages of a) under £108 and b) under £162
(numbers and %)

	a) *under £108*		b) *under £162*	
	Male	*Female*	*Male*	*Female*
White Collar				
Full-time	32 (4%)	49 (1.2%)	1189 (16%)	1640 (40%)
Part-time	0	2 (0.3%)	7 (1.8%)	144 (24%)
Blue Collar				
Full-time	305 (2.7%)	147 (11.1%)	487 (4.4%)	171 (12%)
Part-time	154 (38%)	495 (60%)	243 (60%)	610 (74%)
Overall				
GLC totals	491	693	1826	2565

Notes

1. Figures for part-time workers are expressed as equivalent full-time wages.
2. For white-collar staff, figures include basic pay plus allowances but not overtime.
3. For blue-collar staff, figures are based on earnings in one particular week and many include not just overtime but arrears of overtime, holiday pay, bonus pay and season ticket loans. Figures in the table, therefore, slightly underestimate numbers of low-paid staff.

Manual workers still received £4 less London weighting allowance and worked five more hours than white-collar workers, and those who made up their basic wages with bonus payments still lost them if they were sick or on holiday. Many others only escaped extreme financial hardship by working extremely long hours (i.e. over 60 hours) — an impossible option for women with children.

On the white-collar side differentials remained very wide. A head of department still earned five to six times the salary of his or her secretary, and about ten times the salary of his or her cleaner. The division of labour was also still extremely hier-archical, discriminatory and inefficient. Firefighting and manual craft jobs and senior professional and administrative jobs were still almost exclusively a white male preserve. And in any of the GLC's canteens you were almost certain to be served by a black woman.

Black workers at the GLC also had serious criticisms of the equal opportunities policies. Degraft Nunoo, Chair of the NALGO Black Members Committee, says: 'the only improve-ment is in the numbers of black people, but that hides a very disturbing picture'. In fact, the increase in numbers took place mainly at lower grades. According to Degraft Nunoo, the general excuse in the past for not hiring more black people at senior level was there weren't enough black people with qualifications. 'But the moment more and more graduates from the black community came over the tune changed to "qualifications do not matter, you've got to have experience".'

Degraft Nunoo also criticised the fact that most departmental equal opportunity advisors and many of the advisors on race issues were white. So interview panels and council committees were still taking decisions on behalf of black people with no black representation. This, he argued, meant that black people still faced discrimination in promotion and recruitment and came up against racial harrassment by supervisors, managers and workers. The NALGO Black Members Committee took up a constant stream of cases of this kind.

Finally although there were certain changes in the committee structure and management of the GLC there was very little decentralisation of power to the majority of ordinary GLC workers. After two years of negotiation, the system of industrial democracy that was finally agreed with the unions mirrored the worst aspects of the council and the trade union bureaucracy combined. It did nothing to build on grass roots trade union initiative; nor did it change the way that work was organised to give workers control over what they did.

Fred Farrer, a NUPE shop steward in parks, describes the end result: 'In my view industrial democracy has been just a good excuse to waste a lot of time. Management didn't take it seriously in the slightest. I'm talking now about my own neck of the wood. The plant managers had the right to veto anything you said. There was no majority decision actually taken. It just amounted to a pep talk from the manager where he asked for suggestions from the workforce.'

Why did these policies fail while others succeeded? The story of attempts to implement certain manifesto commitments provides some clues.

The Problem of Being Reasonable: 1. On Wages

In 1983 the GLC set aside £26.5 million to meet its 'socialist wages policy'; money was definitely not the main problem. The GLC had fewer manual workers and fewer on very low wages than other local authorities, and it was richer. But even in the London boroughs, where around 30 per cent of manual workers came below the poverty level, low pay policies have not proved to be as expensive as originally thought. In Camden the Minimum Earnings Guarantee only cost half a percent of the wages bill.

The reason the GLC did not go ahead with all of the 'socialist wages policy' lies in the relationship between trade union organisation, legal 'reasonableness', and the GLC's own approach to industrial relations.

Blue-collar wages are negotiated nationally by representatives of all local authority employers and all local authority trade unions. Trade union officials and Labour politicians argue that if a Labour authority pays more than the national agreement it gives Conservative authorities the green light for paying less! According to John Newe, the TGWU representative on the GLC's Joint Trade Union Negotiating Committee: 'The national agreement just lays down the minimum basic wages and conditions. It's nonsense to say that you can't pay above this.' In fact, most manual workers in London have negotiated local improvements to the national agreement. Some local authorities, like Camden, Hackney, Islington, Greenwich, Haringey and Sheffield, have given their lowest paid workers a weekly lump sum called a minimum earnings guarantee or low pay supplement. This is usually calculated as a proportion of the difference between actual pay and the poverty level. The aim is to get everyone above the poverty level in stages.

Although local authorities are free to decide their own wage levels, councillors must behave 'reasonably' according to the courts. In the past, the judges have interpreted 'reasonableness' in very unreasonable ways. In 1922 they sent the entire Poplar council to prison for giving their workers a minimum wage of £4 a week because they thought this was too far above wages elsewhere. Passing judgement, Lord Atkinson said that by paying the same wage to women and men 'the council would fail in their duty if they ... allowed themselves to be guided by a feminist ambition to secure the equality of the sexes in the matter of wages and the world of labour'.

The Poplar judgement made it clear that councils could pay above the nationally negotiated rates of pay and benefits, but that there had to be a good reason for doing so. It was not good enough to do it out of 'socialist philanthropy'. In other words the council had to behave like a normal employer; it had to look at the market rate for the job (not necessarily the nationally agreed rate) and could only pay more if it got something in return.

During the first year of the administration Ken Livingstone, as a Camden Councillor, was under the threat of surcharge and prison for paying Camden council workers more than the final national agreement. But Camden won the case. So why didn't Ken do the same thing again in the GLC?

GLC councillors say that the GLC faced more legal pressure than the boroughs. Westminster Council employed a number of lawyers to work on finding ways of taking the GLC to court. But John Newe has a simple explanation: 'The GLC could do everything that Camden has done and more ... Even if they did lose in the courts our members would understand ... The trouble with people like Livingstone and Carr is that they don't understand trade unions, they've got no tradition of industrial militancy. They talk about equal opportunity, but what about equal opportunity between manual and white-collar workers?'

The reality was more complicated than this. In his note on the GLC Socialist Wages Policy, the GLC solicitor argued that one of the main reasons Camden councillors were let off while Poplar councillors were sent to prison, is that Camden councillors acted under trade union pressure: 'They were faced with an unusually single-minded and effective union leadership ... The council was faced with a position where vital services had been so disrupted and real hardship was being caused to the elderly and handicapped, and to commercial concerns, and where the whole administrative machine of the council was in imminent danger of having to close down.' Taking this disruption of services into account, the judge found that Camden had acted reasonably in paying above the nationally agreed rates.

Turning to the GLC, the lawyer goes on: 'There seems to be little scope for presenting it (the socialist wages policy) as buying off pressure as in Camden. To a limited extent one could argue an enhancement of good industrial relations, but again, in the absence of any real union pressure for the package, this is limited in scope.'

In other words, the workers should have been irresistibly disruptive! So the 'socialist wages policy' hit a deadlock with the politicians arguing that they couldn't find a legal justification for the claim unless the unions took industrial action, and the trade unions saying that they were not in a position to do so, but that the politicians should stick to their manifesto commitments anyway. Could the council have got any further in this situation? We shall see that they could — but they were limited, first by their definition of industrial relations, and secondly, by their approach to forming alliances with their own trade unions.

The Problem of Being Reasonable: 2. On Grading

On another issue the impasse between GLC trade unions and the administration was broken. This was over white-collar grading systems in the summer of 1983. After months of negotiations the council suddenly announced that it had obtained a legal opinion showing that the existing white-collar grading system was discriminatory and illegal. They unilaterally revoked the old system and imposed their own 'classless grading system'. The Staff Association took immediate industrial action.

Both unions and management admit that the system was archaic and discriminatory. But it did provide a stable career structure for some. So there was a material conflict of interest between the council and its equal opportunities policies on the one hand and an influential section of the Staff Association membership. The Staff Association had its own proposals for reforming the grading structure which would have awarded many grades, including the lowest, a pay increase. But it was opposed to completely open recruitment and free internal mobility. After several weeks of industrial action the Staff Association reluctantly accepted the new system at the next pay negotiation.

Although the socialist wages policy was, as John Carr says, 'a manifesto commitment underlined in big letters' when they realised how difficult it was going to be, 'to be perfectly honest we went for something that was a bit easier to get moving quickly. We went for equal opportunities.'

But why should a policy on equal opportunities be so much easier to implement than one on pay? The answers are found both in the way the original policies were conceived and in the council and union machinery.

The contrast between the large amount of thought and preparation on equal opportunities policy by the women's movement and the minimal preparation by the left as a whole on industrial relations under a left-wing administration is striking. Judith Hunt describes the former:

'The GLC's Equal Opportunities Policy represented all of the best ideas of people who'd been working in the trade union movement, in the community, and women's groups. Unlike a lot of other units and new areas of work for the council, there was a clear policy statement right from the start that myself and others were coming to work around.

'One of the important developments, certainly as far as women were concerned, was the work that the NCCL had done on positive action which drew heavily on the experience of the States. But, there are significant differences. The trade unions are not a particularly key factor in the States. So one of our key commitments was to have negotiated arrangements with the trade unions. A joint union management monitoring group was established early on. So we drew on extensive research that's proven institutional discrimination, institutional racism and sexism, in every organisation you can name. When we first met with chief and senior officers, we said the GLC can be no different from anywhere else, there have to be patterns and procedures that have to be changed, because you do have a predominantly white workforce, predominantly male workforce. We weren't in the business of wasting two years to prove that.'

In contrast to all this past experience on equal opportunities there were few models to draw on for transforming the conditions of work throughout the council. This was not anyway seen as a priority by the Livingstone administration. Better industrial relations tended to be seen solely in terms of more equality — doing something *for* disadvantaged groups, rather than negotiating a clear set of objectives for the service, and building on the energy and knowledge of all workers in order to achieve them. And there were no adequate mechanisms for taking on board lessons learnt in the course of what was to many of them their first experience of local government power.

John McDonnell, Chair of the Finance Committee, says that there were no Labour group discussions about the GLC's overall strategy towards industrial relations before or after the elections. Part of the problem was that the Labour group had no real forum for policy discussions. The left-wing councillors were worried about having too many discussions at full group meetings because they had a very slim majority. So the key discussions tended to happen in the new policy group of committee chairs set up by Ken Livingstone. But this committee lurched from dealing with one government-created crisis after another. The rule among committee chairs became to live and let live.

The Equal Opportunities policies themselves suffered from not being integrated into a socialist approach to industrial relations. Ursula Huws, who worked at the Equal Opportunities Unit, argues that the American origins of the GLC's equal opportunities policy focussed on individual advancement within existing hierarchies. The emphasis was on getting more women and black people into management and non-traditional skills; she argues that more time should have been put into supporting collective attempts to reduce differentials, revalue skills and change the way work is organised. This also means making equal opportunities more central to mainstream industrial relations.

The problem with this approach is that it can cost more and it challenges the whole way in which work is allocated. So there are bound to be conflicts with officers and with trade unions who do not want the status quo disturbed.

On its own, individual advancement also isolates women and black people from the collective campaigns and demands of other workers. If the definition of equal opportunities had been broadened to include the elimination of low pay, reducing differentials and changing the way work is organised, it would have been far easier to build support for it among blue-collar workers. As it was many white male GLC blue-collar workers only saw equal opportunities as a threat to the gains that they had won through collective bargaining. The conflict would certainly not have disappeared with the collective approach, but it would have been easier to build bridges.

The GLC Machinery

When they walked through the doors of County Hall for the first time, the twelve Labour councillors who went to chair GLC Committees found themselves in control of a budget of over a billion pounds and a staff of 22,000 people. Most of them had never held office at the GLC. They had to learn on their feet.

At the time there were very few left-wing models of how to deal with such a large administration. According to Mike Ward many of the Labour councillors were affected by Tony Benn's descriptions of the 'bureaucracy' as the enemy. Ken Livingstone was one of the few leading councillors with previous experience of GLC officers and unions. In the early days of the Labour council he tended to make statements which lumped all GLC white-collar workers and unions together as a hostile force. Both Christianne Ohsan, NALGO Branch Secretary, and Arthur Capelin, the Staff Association General Secretary, complained that many active white-collar trade unionists who were sympathetic to the new Labour administration became alienated by having the actions and views of certain senior officers attributed to them.

But many senior and even middle grade officers *were* hostile to the new Labour administration. In the absence of any mass pressure or campaign, Labour councillors had a pretty formidable task in trying to deal with them. They tried two main approaches: one solution many councillors adopted was to create new committees, units and organisations in order to get round blocks in mainstream structures. The Greater London Enterprise Board, the Industry and Employment Branch, the Women's Committee Support Unit, the Ethnic Minorities Unit and many others, are examples of this approach. The advantage of these new organisations was that they were staffed by people who had been involved in trade union and community campaigns, the women's movement, anti-racist organisations, and many other struggles outside the town hall. They were able to draw on their own experience and develop innovating policies very quickly.

But implementing the policies was much harder. Few of the new officers had previous experience of town hall wheeler-dealing (although they learnt fast). The key problem was that their own new organisation separated them from some of the traditional centres of council power like the legal, finance and valuation departments. Dealing with these departments often required the committed support of more than one councillor responsible for a committee, and given the fragmented nature of the Labour group this was difficult to achieve. So to the end, many excellent policies remained good intentions.

The second approach, which seems to have been far more successful in terms of changing the GLC itself, was to set up teams of people within the mainstream departments. John Carr argues that the key to success is that 'if you want to make an equal opportunities policy work for you as an employer, you've got to get the personnel department involved and committed behind it. If you look at those councils where they made very little progress, or made progress very slowly, it's because the equal opportunities initiatives have been marginalised and put outside onto a women's unit or an ethnic minorities unit or an equal opportunities unit, separate from the personnel department.'

He did create a new equal opportunities unit staffed with experienced people from outside local government. But he placed this within the personnel department. The new unit was well placed for implementing the equal opportunities policies within its brief. However there were no equivalent units or posts for other aspects of industrial relations such as the wages policy. In these areas, John Carr relied on the advice of mainstream personnel officers. This was nearly always given in terms of the status quo.

But even if the Equal Opportunities Unit had been given a wider remit, or if another unit had been set up within the personnel department to deal with the socialist wages policy, this would not have been enough to mount a really serious challenge to the status quo. Degraft Nunoo, chair of the NALGO Black Members committee, did not believe change could be simply instituted by management: 'Most people who came in from the outside and were put in managerial positions were also presumed to be able to tackle racism. But that was a wrong calculation because once you put someone into a managerial position, whether they are old or new in that area, they will form alliances with the managerial structure. No matter how active politically they might be, they will find themselves unable to operate. In other words you put them in a straightjacket.'

Change is partly a question of strategic alliances at the top, he thinks, but more importantly, it needs to come from pressure from below, in this case from the self-organisation of black workers.

This brings us to the question of how the GLC Councillors related to the workers and their organisations.

The Union Machinery

When the new Labour committee chairs first met rank after rank of grey-suited, high-paid officers, they must have felt a little lonely. One would have thought they would turn to their natural allies — the trade unions — for support. In fact, many GLC politicians started off by being quite dismissive of their in-house unions.

The only link prior to the election between the Labour group and trade unions was with regional trade union officers on the London Region of the Labour Party. There were no joint GLC union-Labour group discussions either about the manifesto, or about the first steps after the election. A joint discussion about strategy would obviously have been particularly appropriate in the area of industrial relations. There was in fact no serious analysis of who the unions were and how to form alliances with them.

Trade union organisation in the GLC was as difficult to understand and come to terms with as the council bureaucracy (on which it was often modelled). Although trade union membership and organisation was quite weak in many areas, there were seventeen recognised unions each with a completely different organisation, set of procedures and policies. But the essence of the official GLC trade union negotiating structure was that it reflected and often reinforced all the main divisions between occupations, white and blue-collar workers, men and women, and black and white people.

Until the period before abolition, the unions had no joint forum for dealing with common problems or divisive conflicts. As usual in local government blue and white-collar workers had separate negotiating committees (the Trade Union Joint Negotiating Committee for manual and craft workers in GLC and ILEA, and the Whitley Council for GLC white-collar workers). Only one woman and one black person sat on each committee.

As the Trade Union Joint Negotiating Committee covered workers in both the GLC and ILEA, it was dominated by the big ILEA unions. The TGWU with only a hundred GLC members had four seats and chaired the committee, while the GMBATU, with no GLC members at all, also had four seats. The Fire Brigades Union, which actually negotiated separately, had two seats. The remaining craft unions had one seat each. That meant that NUPE, which was the main union representing the low paid in the GLC, could easily be outvoted.

With their smaller and more scattered memberships most craft unions have area branches rather than workplace branches. Unless convenors called regular members' and stewards' meetings there was no forum for GLC workers to feed their views into the negotiating structures. Their delegates to the TUJNC were sometimes full-time or lay officials chosen by the trade unions at a regional level. Delegates were not *necessarily* stewards and did not necessarily have any link to departmental or shopfloor trade union organisations.

For historical reasons NALGO had only one place on the Whitley Council and no places at all on the sub-committee that decided wages. The NALGO office usually heard about pay settlements through the Staff Association bulletin. So 2,500 GLC NALGO members were effectively disenfranchised. The Staff Association was the single most powerful union in the GLC. It is often caricatured as being completely reactionary. In fact it is an extremely competent trade union that has negotiated considerable benefits for many of its members. But although it had large numbers of lower paid workers, women and black people, it was middle and higher paid officers who were dominant in the organisation. These were usually white men. There was a convergence of interest between the personnel department and the Staff Association about the definition of normal industrial relations which certainly did not involve radical changes in the way work was organised and divided up.

So those who had the most to gain from challenging the pay and work structure had the weakest voice in the organisations that had the power to challenge them.

The two negotiating committees agreed everything among themselves before talking to management. But the unions representing higher paid craft and white-collar workers were threatened by claims about low pay. Many of their more powerful members could not accept cleaners, caterers and secretaries catching them up on the pay scales. There was also a conflict of interest over strategies for improving pay. While most men in manual jobs make up for low basic rates of pay by working overtime, and by negotiating bonus payments, women don't usually have this option because of their domestic work on top of their jobs. Women benefit more from a reduction in hours and increase in basic hourly rates. But with the composition of the trade union negotiating committee it is not surprising that the claims of the low paid, especially for the more radical change women wanted, were rarely pushed hard.

How, in hindsight, could councillors have built a positive relationship with the unions to help overcome the obstacles they faced from some senior GLC officials and the government? GLC councillors and many of the new officers felt understandably impatient with the structure of the unions. They tended to respond either with dismissive talk of 'smashing' the Staff Association, as if this would automatically improve the situation, or to opt for a new brand of paternalism. This consisted of paying lip service to formal trade union procedures (i.e. secret deals with a few key bureaucrats), but really zapping through reforms on behalf of the low paid, women or black people without their involvement. For example, we have seen that Degraft Nunoo says that black people were not asked to be involved in certain aspects of the council's policies against racism.

The trouble with both approaches is that they assume the council should make up its mind about priorities with only casual input from the people most affected. Sometimes the policies are right, but sometimes they are desperately inappropriate. Many of the staff at PPU workshops complained of well-intentioned policies that they knew couldn't work or which inadvertently ran roughshod over a hard-won collective agreement. This approach can produce some quick successes but it does little to build up the self-confidence, understanding and involvement of the workforce.

The third approach is for the councillors to support and build on the activities of workers who are already taking up progressive policies through their organisations. For instance, take the area of equal opportunities. All GLC unions had active union members who were also campaigning for equal opportunities and other progressive policies. They should have been the natural allies of the Labour administration; such allies existed on many issues on which the councillors were facing obstruction. But in fact almost invariably they went unheeded.

The unions themselves jealously guarded against councillors who tried to do what they called a 'Michael Edwardes' by getting round the official structures and talking directly to their members. One way of overcoming this fear is to provide, through the union, better information, education and other facilities for all union members. If the policies really are in their interest they will start to do things for themselves. But politicians are often reluctant to follow this course: with better education, information and time off to organise workers are more able to think for themselves and put their thoughts into action. When people do start doing things for themselves they often move faster and in different directions than the politicians intended.

Abolition

Ironically, it was abolition and the requirements of the campaign against it which led councillors to make a positive move towards an alliance with the GLC workforce and to break loose from the conventional, managerial roles they had taken on. Faced with the threat of abolition, councillors found that they needed more than duty from their workforce; they were fighting a common cause that needed support, commitment, imagination and enthusiasm. In 1984 and 1985 Ken Livingstone held a series of mass meetings with the staff. Some committee chairs held meetings with different branches of their departments. Each department was asked to say what special contribution they could play in the campaign. After many problems, the unions were given time-off for campaigning; staff were seconded to work with the unions; shop stewards and trade union members were given an opportunity — through day-long workshops and a newspaper — to talk about their work, its importance, how it could be defended and how it and the conditions under which it was done could be improved, how they could establish more direct contact with the users of their service. Suddenly the views and the potential power of the GLC workers became important.

All these resources and energy were seen solely in terms of the campaign against abolition. They were not integrated into a radical approach to industrial relations. This made it much easier for the government to take out legal injunctions against this kind of activity.

On the union side, the threat of abolition resulted in the creation of new inter-union structures that could eventually have provided a forum for breaking down some of the worst divisions between different groups of workers. GLC blue and white collar unions joined together for the first time to form a single campaigning body and joint trade union committees sprang up in many departments.

But there was neither the time nor the people to solve all the problems. Many GLC workers found it very difficult to take the sudden concern for their views seriously when they saw little progress in many of the day to day ways in which they were treated. They became seriously disillusioned with the public recriminations between councillors over rate-capping. The trade unions themselves were divided over the kind of action that was most appropriate for defending the jobs of their members. Eventually certain key officials and trade unions pulled out and the new joint structure and committees disintegrated.

Lessons

The first and foremost conclusion is a central tenet of most socialists, and is a theme of this book as a whole, but somehow it is rarely acted upon: non-managerial workers very often have a clear understanding of the things that are wrong with the service they provide, and how their own work could be made more effective for users and more satisfying for themselves. But the way in which work is divided up and rewarded is a fundamental barrier to putting this understanding into effect. Changing the division of labour in order to build on this commitment and knowledge is far more important in improving the service than creating formal procedures for industrial democracy or user consultation.

This requires a comprehensive industrial relations policy which considers workers not simply as wage earners but as producers and providers of services. In other words the focus of this policy should go beyond inequality and low pay to how bureaucratic and hierarchical payment and job structures reduce the commitment and effectiveness of the work that people are able to do. The conventional definition of equal opportunities also needs to be expanded to include supporting collective attempts to reduce differentials, revalue skills and change the way work is organised. The policies have to go beyond rhetorical statements of intent and be costed and turned into a clear set of objectives with a strategy for overcoming likely problems. Taking the initiative in this way would make it far harder to mount a legal challenge.

The ideal council machinery needed to implement these policies will depend on circumstances but it would be a mistake to rely too heavily on parallel units and departments which can easily be marginalised. Mechanisms are needed for controlling and coordinating the traditional centres of power both within and between departments.

The most effective council machinery and the most carefully devised plans will make very slow progress unless they are supported by the majority of people who are going to carry them out. That means negotiating a set of alliances with workers' representatives. Ideally, this should happen at the manifesto stage or before. However, given that trade union structures are usually based around the existing division of labour it is no easy task to develop the alliances necessary to challenge the status quo. Nevertheless, there are several steps that can make it easier.

The first is that the council must be seen to deliver on certain mundane issues such as eliminating bad management and supervision. The council must also be seen to have a clear strategy and time-table for dealing with more expensive and legally complicated problems such as low pay and the bonus system. Any more fundamental changes in the division of labour require very delicate negotiations about terms and conditions and a major council training programme linked directly into policy objectives and operational targets. Secondly, steps can be taken that strengthen the hand of those trade unionists who are themselves taking forward progressive policies within their own organisations. This can be done without undermining trade union autonomy by providing certain trade union rights starting with full access to council information on finance and staffing plus the resources to publish this information along with trade union comments through to their members. Then trade union representatives need time off to discuss policy, including policy for council services, they need the resources to carry out their own feasibility studies on proposals, and organise educational activities for their members. In addition to these resources for unions councils could organise high status discussions with trade unions across departments about the improvement of jobs and services.

In the past these kinds of commitments have generally been made under the immediate threat of a new piece of government legislation like abolition, or rate-capping. Under such emergency conditions there is rarely the time to implement any of the more significant policies and the calls for greater worker involvement can sound rather hollow. Labour parties need to develop the policies described in this chapter and carry them out from the day they achieve office. That way socialism would be seen to start at home and might be very much more convincing for doing so.

5
Women's Work

Think economics and you conjure a male world. Male economists, trade unionists, politicians still wilfully ignore just how different the world of work and the priorities of economic policy look from a woman's perspective. 'Economic policy' raises an image of manufacturing industry, trade union organisation, high finance; meanwhile the women who make up 40% of London's workforce work predominantly in lower paid, less organised, part time, service and office work — and in the home. When progressive state authorities intervene in employment, they still concentrate on men's job opportunities and conditions as the measure of their success. Women's different, even greater and sometimes conflicting needs can remain invisible and largely unaddressed.

The Labour GLC from 1981-86 is a good example of how hard it is to shift economic thinking and economic policies towards the interests of women. The 1981 Labour GLC manifesto proposed *no* specific policies to promote women's employment, beyond equal opportunities within the GLC itself. From that inauspicious beginning women within the Industry and Employment Branch had a series of difficult battles to get women's employment on the policy agenda; only to arrive at the conclusion that in the end only a small proportion of resources for economic policy had been effectively spent on promoting women's employment. This history demonstrates the difficulty of making women's employment a priority for local authority economic policy, and this chapter offers a cautionary tale on the lessons from what was done and what was not.

There were only nine women out of fifty councillors on the new GLC in 1981, and only a very slight commitment to women's particular interests. One of the women councillors, Valerie Wise, began as vice-chair of the Industry and Employment Committee; as a feminist she set up a women's advisory group to discuss what should be done. It was this group, which included women trade unionists, which developed the idea of a Women's Committee and began to look at women's work as a separate area of employment policy.

This group recognised that their problem was, as Irene Breughel, one of the new employment officers, put it, nothing less than to 'rewrite the agenda' of the GLC's employment policy, to deal with the way work — both paid and unpaid — should be organised. This meant recognising the enormous economic importance of women's unpaid work in the home, and the double burden it imposes. It also meant recognising the (related) concentration of women in low paid, part time work. And it meant rethinking the GLC's whole approach to both childcare provision and employment policy in order to try to improve those conditions.

Hilary Wainwright, the only woman among the five people who set up the Economic Policy Group, described how this commitment became Council policy: 'The way we found out that you make something policy without doing masses of research and going through all sorts of hoops, was by writing out a Leader's report, which the Leader (of the Council) then gives at the beginning of the Council meeting. He makes a statement, and that becomes Council policy, and then it goes through the Committees. So I drafted out a policy commitment based on all the work that this informal group had done, which included the commitment to domestic labour, and also other aspects of women's needs relating to employment. But that was the first time it became official policy, around April 1982.' However that Leader's report contained no argument about the specific needs of black women.

Once the Women's Committee was set up, in June 1982, it rapidly increased its spending. In 1982/3 its budget for grants to voluntary groups was £200,000, but by 1984/5 spending on grants for childcare alone was £5.2 million. As the Women's Committee was putting substantial resources into childcare, the women working in the Industry and Employment branch concentrated on employment projects, women's training, domestic work, and a few workplace creches. This chapter looks at all these areas, but its chief focus is the extent to which employment policy was reorientated towards women's needs.

Internal Blockages: The View from County Hall

Looking back, women who were involved in this work in the GLC feel that, while there were many successful childcare projects, and some good training projects, and while the employment position of women within the Council itself improved, relatively little was done to change women's employment and work conditions in the wider London economy.

The GLC Industry and Employment Branch hired a number of women who were feminists to work on employment policy, and as one of them put it, appeared to feel that as a result women's needs would get incorporated in all the work 'as a matter of course'. The women in question rapidly came to see it would not be so straightforward, and in September 1983 they set up the Women's Employment Project Team (WEPT) to coordinate initiatives on women's employment. WEPT was not a separate unit in the branch, but only a regular meeting of women in the Council whose work was in some way related to women's employment. It lasted, though often struggling, until abolition.

In assessing the results, consider the scale of the problem facing these women. They were fighting, in one woman's words, a 'rearguard action' from the very start. The GLC manifesto committed the Council to put the bulk of the economic spending — £30 million a year — into the Greater London Enterprise Board in pursuit of manufacturing employment. The trade union officials who had discussed it with the politicians came largely from the more organised bits of London's fast dwindling manufacturing sector. The Manifesto proposed a 'Manpower' plan, and was tacitly hostile to office or service employment.

In the face of this, the women in WEPT wanted to shift the whole emphasis of the employment policy to combat the forces which kept women doing more than half of the work in London for a very low return: in the lowest paid jobs with the worst conditions, as unpaid domestic workers in the home, and in a weak position in trade unions which took little account of their needs.

This would have meant major changes in employment policy: shifting spending (and GLC staff time) from men's to women's needs; changing the priorities from skilled manufacturing to other sorts of jobs; making equal opportunities central to the work on manufacturing; pushing for a shorter working week; and trying to combine all the ways in which the GLC could influence employment (through control of London Transport, by imposing conditions on contractors and suppliers, grant aid, campaigning and organising, as well as investing in firms) to further the interests of women. While there were achievements, this major shift in approach to employment policy simply never happened.

The most effective concentration of resources on women's employment needs was on the GLC's own employees. An Equal Opportunities unit was set up, under Judith Hunt, inside the GLC personnel department. Two GLC workplace nurseries were set up, and lower paid workers could get financial help with childcare costs. Positive action training schemes gave women a second chance at qualifications, basic literacy skills courses were introduced, job sharing and part time work increased, and the grading system was opened up (see Chapter 4). These reforms improved women's access to better jobs but low pay in the Council was not greatly improved, and there were no major changes in work organisation.

The GLC's Training board, too, devoted substantial resources to women's training courses, childcare, and funding for equalities issues on training projects, as well as lobbying against the bias against women in government training schemes. But the Industry and Employment Branch devoted few staff resources in total to women's employment needs. Several women worked within the Contracts Compliance unit on employment policies towards women in firms supplying the GLC. Otherwise there were never more than three or four women staff, working in research, project development or popular planning, concentrating on women's employment and domestic work — and often doing so in addition to other demanding work. In the industrial policy work, very few staff, male or female, spent time on the low paid, largely female sectors such as cleaning, catering, shopwork and clothing. Most serious, the Women's Employment Project Team never had resources of its own to spend on developing a programme of work.

Several of the women involved now argue that they should have pushed much harder for resources specifically for women's employment 'but politically we thought it important that work on women did not get ghettoised into particular posts. This was very naive.' WEPT, early on, argued that giving priority to

Credit: Maggie Murray/Format

Women form forty per cent of the labour force in London; they tend to be low paid and have a low level of trade union organization and involvement. The women at the GLC wanted to shift the emphasis of the employment policy towards these women's needs.

women's employment should be central to work on transport (while the GLC ran London Transport) and on GLEB, the 'flagship' of the employment work. But in fact, no one was taken on to push London Transport management into action on women's employment. GLEB's spending decisions were very hard for WEPT to influence from County Hall, and one woman, taken on by GLEB late in the day to work on equal opportunities for women, found herself isolated and given an almost impossible task.

The women in WEPT put a huge amount of time into getting women's work and interests written into the main GLC economic and planning strategy documents: as a result, the Greater London Development Plan acknowledges the importance of office work, and the Labour Plan (*not* the Manpower Plan) discusses women's work. And, unique among major public economic policy documents, the London Industrial Strategy argued that 'it is vital that the organisation of paid work make space for the work of looking after ourselves, each other and children', implying funding for childcare and other caring work, and *also* major changes in the organisation of paid work. All this was an achievement, and *perhaps* it will be harder for later manifestos to be quite so male chauvinist. But the way in which work was organised in the GLC still left a big gap between policies and how the money was spent.

Resources for Women's Work

The GLC had a variety of legal powers it could use to improve women's working conditions. These included giving grants and other support to groups investigating and organising on the problems of womens' secondary position in the economy; investing in firms which employed women or promoting the interests of women in companies where investments were made; improving women's working conditions in the GLC and in services run by the GLC such as the Fire Brigade and public transport; using the purchasing power of the Council to pressure private (and public) enterprises into ending discrimination against women; doing research and gathering information of use to women; supporting the independent self-organisation of women, and refusing to fund organisations whose activities ran against the interests of women.

The limits on what was achieved were imposed by the way the policy making process actually works in local authorities. GLC spending responded in practice both to politicians' priorities and to outside pressure. The investments tended to be dominated by firms which were in trouble *and* had an organised workforce to shout loudly; the work with unions tended to be dominated by those with the best line into County Hall; the funding of organisations tended to be dominated by those who were confident and ready to move in rapidly with a grant application, and then to make a noise if they did not get funded. Every element of this process tended to put women at the back of the queue and black women at the back twice over.

The work on low pay is a good example. Hotels and catering are one of the most important areas of manual women's work in London. The GLC funded a project, the Service Workers' Advice and Action project, aimed at support help with unionisation in the industry. GLEB supported several catering coops. But when it came to bringing cleaning and catering in-house or enforcing higher wages for cleaners on GLC contracts, other pressures took precedence. GLEB, for example, refused to employ in-house cleaners and catering staff, saying that this reduced funds for their investments. Within the GLC, much of the cleaning of fire stations and courts was done by outside contractors paying sometimes as little as £1.60 per hour. Councillors initially accepted legal advice that bringing the work in house would be 'unreasonable expenditure'. The contract cleaners were supposed to be covered by a 'fair wages' clause in the contract, preventing payment far below direct labour rates, but in all its years the GLC had never tried to enforce it. The clause was finally strengthened to make it enforceable but this took over a year. Five hundred women cleaners finally got an extra 40p an hour, some work began to come in-house, but there were never the resources to monitor the contracts and work with the cleaners to make sure the rules were applied. And by then, abolition had arrived.

Grant giving provides another example of the pressures. The Project Development Unit, set up in 1982 as the grant-giving arm of Industry and Employment, had made both women's and black employment priorities in principle. But, as one of the workers there remembered, 'very few applications relating to women and employment came in'. In 1983, without doing any advertising, the Unit already was 'flooded' with applications from groups who had heard that money was available. But most applications came from established and trade union-based groups: for trade union resource centres, cooperative development units and unemployed centres, all of which marginalised women's needs.

The Women's Committee had approached its grant giving differently. It had advertised very widely for applications, and as a result had been disastrously overwhelmed. 'We got two hundred applications ... a lot of them childcare, and in the early days a lot of them were from established groups.' Very few were for projects on women and employment, 'in part because that wasn't specified in the advert': women's employment had fallen down the gap between the Women's Committee and Industry and Employment.

It was partly this fragmentation of work in the Council which pushed women to the back of the queue. Women in contract compliance, grants work, campaigns, research, never got *together* to corner private sector employers. Grants funding was never properly seen as a tool of economic policy, on a par with investment in firms. In each area of employment work, women lost out separately.

As a result the best organised continued to get the resources. And, ironically, even the commitment to work with trade unions and community groups, through 'popular planning', tended to reinforce that. Sheila Rowbotham recalled the argument of one of the Economic Policy Group's founding members: 'He made the assertion that you had to organise with the people who were well organised already; they were the people who could best use resources. I contested this, because it is a very old argument, with men on the Left, on the grounds that it is wrong to assume that the people who appear to be well organised are the *only* people to be organised. There were times when people thought it impossible to organise workers who are now considered to be well organised — like car workers. What you need to do is to think of *different* ways of organising.'

And, added Mandy Cook who worked in the Project Development Unit, you need to recognise the scale of resources, in people and money, that needs to be put into the process, if you are to help the unorganised, or those organised in forms other than trade unions, to get together and put their own pressure for resources on a local authority.

Childcare

Childcare was the most successful area of GLC funding relevant to women's work. This was in part because feminists had argued for the reorganisation and support of domestic and caring work as a priority for the GLC. But it was chiefly because there was already an established network of groups campaigning on childcare. The existence of such a network gave the groups confidence, an identity, and also the capacity to respond actively to ideas for funding coming from the Council and to argue back.

The GLC both funded childcare projects, and also tried to strengthen the network of support for childcare work. In principle, this was the approach of 'popular planning': to help women gain the confidence, understanding and contacts to play an active part in policy making: to turn policy making into a flexible and creative process, rather than a collection of ideas from County Hall. This involved, amongst other things, developing contact between people inside and outside the funding authority so they could explore difficulties and divergent ideas. All this takes enormous amounts of time and resources — which were often not available.

The need for funding was beyond doubt. Childcare provision in London is hopelessly inadequate: in 1982/3 there were 93 nursery places per 1000 children under five. It is the lack of childcare which forces women into low paid, part-time or shift-work jobs. In Britain, unlike France, the state takes no general responsibility for the care and education of children under five, and the Women's Committee funding, oriented particularly to providing full-time high quality childcare with decent employment conditions, showed what could be done, as well as the high cost of doing it properly.

The sheer extent and variety of funding was a major achievement in itself. The Women's Committee by 1985/6 had put £14 million into childcare in 1985/6, and had supported over 200 childcare projects. They include workplace nurseries, drop-in creches, mobile creches, community nurseries, toy libraries, play-groups, and latchkey projects. Money was made available to help childminders improve standards and increase their resources; the Under Fives Working Group with support from the Popular Planning Unit set up a course for childminders in the Autumn of 1983. An Industry and Employment Branch grant paid for extra workers for the National Childcare Campaign. The Greater London Training Board funded short courses on 'Nurseries Now' and 'Running a Nursery' at the Polytechnic of the South Bank, to encourage nursery workers to develop new approaches to combatting racism and sexism in childcare practice. The Women's Committee paid for a 'special needs' worker at Market Nursery in Hackney to attend to the needs of children with disabilities, and it funded a 'home-care' worker at the Kingsway workplace nursery to look after sick children in their own homes. Conferences have been organised, workshops set up, newsletters and information packs produced, with the help of small grants that have given people a fresh impetus to act over childcare, and have, in the process, enhanced their expectations and their confidence.

At its best, the GLC funding drew on and extended existing initiatives. Pip O'Byrne describes how this happened in Greenwich. The Greenwich Childcare Campaign, set up in 1979, applied, successfully, to the Women's Committee for money for staff. Pip O'Byrne was the first of two development workers. She later went on to work for the newly funded Latchkey Development Group, an umbrella organisation co-ordinating twelve different projects all making out-of-school provision. She argued that the strength of the GLC was its support of voluntary organisations and its ability to act as 'a resource agency for a lot of the ideas and the things that you've wanted to put into practice. A lot of the workshops that the Popular Planning Unit have set up have proved to be a great base for initiating ideas.'

In Southwark the Women's Committee funded two new nurseries. The Rockingham Community Nursery began building work in July 1985 with room for twenty-five to thirty children; the Gumboots nursery opened in temporary premises at the end of 1985. Both owe their existence to the determined efforts of parents and community groups, as well as to the GLC's financial contribution. The GLC also funded a drop-off creche on the vast Aylesbury Estate. It has 200 children on its books, with parents rationed to two two-hour sessions a week — an index to how much more is needed. In Spring 1985 Southwark's *priority* waiting list for childcare stood at 850.

GLC grants also made it possible for some nurseries to meet the needs of disabled children. 'The implications of losing funding are dreadful', said Sue Greenwood, special needs worker at Market Nursery in Hackney. Although the Warnock Report recommended that children with disabilities should no longer be isolated in special schools, such recommendations are meaningless without the money to implement them. Market Nursery was keen to take on the disabled child of a parent with one child already in the nursery but had no money for extra staff. So the parent successfully applied to the Women's Committee for a helper. Sue Greenwood was appointed and not only were two children with 'special needs' subsequently offered nursery

places, but she has helped many other children faced with problems to do with illness.

The GLC also paid for seven extra full and part-time staff for
the National Childcare Campaign. Jenny Gudgeon, the
Campaign's London development worker, helped set up the
London Childcare Network which at the beginning of 1985 also
had substantial GLC support. She describes it as 'invisible
support': help and advice with the large scale typing jobs, photo-
copying and mail-outs that have to be done efficiently in the
early stages of a campaign. 'If it were just an informal campaign
plodding along I think it might have sunk by now under all that.'
Instead, it managed to draw in around thirty organisations and
over 200 individuals, keeping them in touch through a regular
newsletter.

These networks have encouraged rethinking among activists.
Laurie Mackensie of the National Childcare Campaign argues
that the Campaign had 'promoted a policy for the under-fives
which, if you look at it closely, represents a policy for three
upwards.' Strategies for children under two, she believes, are
'where change has to happen to childcare.' The Popular Planning
Unit funded the under-2s strategy group which led her to negotiate with Southwark Adult Education to teach a course for
nursery workers on the under-2s. She sees the London Childcare
Network as a forum that may influence social policy.

Sue Emerson, Southwark Childcare Campaign worker, is
convinced that the GLC has influened borough projects,
although she thinks there ought to have been more partnership
when setting up GLC-backed projects. According to Jenny
Gudgeon 'GLC funding has just raised the issues a lot more, and
a lot of borough councils are more aware that childcare's reasonably important ... it feels like the GLC's really raised London's
consciousness.'

The GLC also focussed on the status and training of childcare
workers. In Tower Hamlets GLC funding meant that Pre-school
Playgroup Association workers were paid a real wage for the
first time, instead of the £12 a day they had earned previously. In
fact, one of the most important lessons from these projects is just
how expensive good childcare is, as well as how important.
Many of the people involved hope that the conferences, workshops and support for campaigns will help defend the concrete
achievements. 'The networks that didn't exist before this GLC
support now have their own momentum', said Kath Falcon of
the Popular Planning Unit. Funding, even if discontinued, will

have given a basis for cohesive action — 'We'll still publish the newsletter, only on cheaper paper', insisted one determined member of the London Childcare Network.

Childcare and Employment

If the employment opportunities of women with children are dependent on good childcare, how did this affect the GLC's employment policy? The GLC's Greater London Training Board, which aimed to make its projects accessible to women, did begin, as one woman put it, to put childcare into its projects in a 'fairly routine way'. On the other hand, investments in projects providing employment for women were rarely backed up by childcare provision. An exception was Lambeth Toys. It was a small cooperative of Asian and Afro-Caribbean women, set up to make jigsaws with pictures of local black children, and dressing-up clothes from several countries, after an exhibition at Brixton Library provoked an unexpected demand for multi-ethnic toys. Initially Lambeth Mobile Creche helped out with childcare and later a creche worker was funded.

However, once GLEB was set up, and took over funding both coops and private firms, any attempt to integrate investment and childcare was lost. No one had the job of creating the links between GLEB and the GLC grant aid process which would have allowed proper funding of childcare — or indeed of women's training projects — to support women's employment in GLEB firms. Kath Falcon, who was taken on by the Popular Planning Unit in 1983 to give support to projects and campaigns in the areas of childcare and domestic labour, commented 'I certainly don't feel that what I did was at all integrated into Industry and Employment or even in the Women's Employment Project Team work.'

Industry and Employment did however fund workplace nursery projects. According to Mandy Cook, they hoped to establish projects which could survive without the GLC, and to 'assert to employers the issue of childcare costs and needs.' It was also a chance to involve the trade unions in childcare battles. The Project Development Unit funded three nurseries: the Kingsway nursery, the Fleet Street creche, and the Wandsworth shift workers' day nursery who were given a capital sum to extend their premises. They also funded the Norwood Children's Centres' Association.

The Kingsway nursery had long been regarded as a model of high quality, workplace childcare. It was set up in 1977 after a group of trade unionists convinced their employers of the need for a nursery in central London, but in 1983 the building it had occupied was put up for sale. The Women's Committee came to the rescue and bought the whole building with the aim of converting it into a centre for women's groups and childcare groups. The Industry and Employment Committee provided equipment for the new extended building, and it also funded Kingsway's homecare worker for sick children, as well as a researcher to monitor the homecare project.

The hard-won success of Kingsway depended on a group of well organised trade unionists, mainly professional workers. Among the employers who participated from the start were London Weekend Television, *Time Out* magazine and the Transport and General Workers Union. Clearly, non-professional workers have benefitted, but without the professional workers to make the case that the employer gains by retaining highly trained women workers, Kingsway would not have come into being. Even so, in 1983 it was threatened by the Inland Revenue's decision to treat employers' subsidies to workplace nurseries as a taxable perk for parents.

Kingsway was launched in a more generous economic climate than the Fleet Street campaign. It took the Fleet Street Campaign nearly six years to get their project set up, and needed substantial grant-aid from the GLC, and premises in the Kingsway building. Those employers who were sympathetic still would not give support on the scale Kingsway got to begin with, even though in one woman's words, Fleet Street was 'awash with money from the sale of Reuters' shares.' Yet the Fleet Street campaign had the official backing of both the NUJ and SOGAT, and was later formally supported by the film and TV union ACTT and the print union, the NGA. 'It's been a very hard battle to make it viable,' said Kate Holman of the campaign steering group. It took two to three years to win support from the unions (the campaign had its beginnings in a childcare workshop at a union conference). It raised £12,000 and a £50,000 GLC grant covered the first year's costs. Employers' donations would take the form of a covenant which enabled the nursery to hold charitable status and skirt the taxation trap. With places for twenty-five children the actual cost of each place came to £414 a month. After GLC funding and employers' contributions, parents were left to pay £30 a week. Clearly, the economics of setting up and running a workplace nursery are daunting. They need a combination of better-off employers, subsidy especially for start-up costs, and especially a strong organisational base among trade unionists.

For most women these conditions do not exist. An alternative is an area-based, employer-assisted creche. Such a nursery was one of the aims of the Norwood Children's Centres Association, an ambitious project which also wanted to open community cafes and laundries. A borough development worker had thought of the idea, and the GLC funded three workers for the project in 1983.

The project workers found clear local demand for full-time day-care and after-school care, but it quickly became clear that the aim of a local workplace creche funded by employers was unrealistic. Most of the local female workforce was unskilled or semi-skilled and un-unionised. They were in no position to bargain with employers for money to set up a central nursery, far less subsidise other facilities: 'The conditions are so awful that it's even difficult for people to get sick pay, never mind things like childcare,' said a project worker. Recognising this, the project shifted its goals to providing community focus, and an organising base for women's activities. By Autumn 1985 it had created a much-used drop-in creche, a boon to women students at the local FE collge and a vital regular support to others, a base for women's groups, a regular women and health course and a number of other women's activities, including advice on employment and childcare. In the process it had transformed itself into a project much closer to the successful women's employment projects the GLC funded in three boroughs.

Women's Employment Projects

'Women's employment is still a marginal issue raised by interested individuals,' commented a worker at the Lewisham Women's Employment Project. Marginal, she meant, to the economic policies of even supposedly sympathetic local authorities. The GLC funding pattern bears this out. The GLC funded several different types of projects on women's employment: borough- or area-based projects (in Lewisham, Haringey and Lambeth); sector- or industry-based projects (one concerned with office work, and another with women in construction); and issue-based projects, like the campaign to get women to sign on for benefits, and Women against Sexual Harrassment. This area of funding is notable for including some projects which can really be called 'exemplary', in that they show what can be done, with time, effort, resources and experience. The problem here was not lack of money, but lack of GLC staff time to get the money spent. As one of the workers in the Lewisham women's employment project said, 'more money's been available for women's employment projects than has been taken up from the GLC.'

The three borough based projects already existed before the GLC offered funding; they were already experienced, and rooted in their own areas. This allowed them to use the funding the GLC offered very effectively. Their growing range of activities was innovative, and shows what can be done with organisation, funding and imagination. The Lewisham Centre began work from a Women's Centre, and later opened a drop-in advice centre in Deptford. Haringey, too, started doing individual advice work. As one worker from Lewisham put it, the most important resource they have to offer is 'us', that is, friendly accessible help with employment problems, not least support in dealing with job centres and Lewisham Council's business advice centre up the road, where 'there's hardly room for a push chair' and women with crying kids are discouraged.

The Lewisham Centre has done a very wide range of work, starting from research and individual advice: identifying the needs and developing contacts. They produce a local magazine, they do a lot of knocking on doors talking to women, they also provide a place where women can come to read a book from the library or sew. They run courses, such as on DIY, pattern cutting, or signing for the deaf, and also employment-orientated courses like rights at work, and health and safety courses. For their first few years they did a lot of research: 'surveys all over the estates ... surveys of women who had done TOPS courses to see what happened to them ... looking at what childcare resources were available.' In its early stages the Haringey centre also concentrated on research.

Both the Haringey and the Lewisham projects identified child-care and training as crucial issues for women's employment. Both helped to establish women's training centres, working with the GLC's Training Board, which showed itself very open to initiatives from these projects. In Haringey, the Women's Employment Project did the feasibility study for the Training

Centre, 'and suddenly we were negotiating for a quarter of a million pounds — it was nerve wracking.' Both women's employment projects identified where women most needed training. This ranged from good quality training in manual skills, to electronics and computing. Women were also asking for advice on training in nursery work, community and social work, and business studies. The Haringey Women's Training and Educational Centre has technician, construction trades and computing courses as well as a big adult education programme.

Both these projects also do a lot of work on childcare. As a matter of course, 'childcare is provided for any event we run'. The Lewisham Centre helped to set up a mobile creche, which services trade union branches, council committees, and training courses, and sets up on estates.

The projects have also argued that good childcare is an important part of job creation. This has led to arguments with local councils who wanted to know, said an employment project worker, 'how many jobs we had created, and we talked about projects we'd been involved with, like the Women's Training centre and the mobile creche ... oh no, no, not them, they're not the real jobs, the real jobs are the ones in factories where they're getting £1.20 an hour ... we haven't created any of them, so we're not very high up in their estimation.'

This view of job creation was a common theme from the women interviewed. As the women in Haringey put it, the local authority view still is, 'proper jobs are in the private sector.' But the women's employment projects have seen the public sector as a crucial area for improving women's working conditions and access to jobs. As a result, they have developed working relations with local authority unions on women's employment. The Haringey project for example did research on the low proportion of the local council training budget that goes to women manual workers. This was used by a NALGO positive action group in 1983, to pressure the council to change their training policies.

The Haringey project's work on School Meals since 1985 has been particularly innovative. As one of the project workers described it, 'the project was set up jointly with NUPE, the public service union, initially to promote the school meals service, to give it a higher political profile,' and to combat the media image of unskilled work and poor quality food. From this came 'a conference with an emphasis on users, because the users were never taken into consideration: parents, community groups, with the school meals workers, trade unions and the voluntary sector all together.'

At the conference, says a project worker, 'it came out very strongly that everyone was prepared to fight for the service but wanted a say in it.' This brought out a need for an anti-privatisation strategy which concentrated on 'revaluing women's skills', and which also involved a training scheme, an anti-racist strategy, and education in nutrition.

The campaign developed through a formal link with NUPE. 'I think that kind of link brings skills to trade union organising and campaign work that aren't present,' reflected one of the women. 'The trade unions are very good at training people in negotiation and organisation, but not in how to campaign in relation to allies outside the trade union movement. It's a process of initiating ideas, and getting a not terribly positive response ... and then over the months you find that you get it quoted back, and things have moved ... it's about trust as well, it's not easy to get a joint project going with a trade union.'

Once launched, the campaign was sponsored by the London Food Commission and the GLC; this allowed the secondment of a school meals worker to the campaign. The project workers have tried to shift the campaign away from 'nutrition experts confronting one another', towards an attempt to 'tie progressive food policies to job creation', and towards accountability to users. As one woman commented, 'without this help you would never get a debate in a Parent Teachers' Association about food policy'.

The women's employment projects worked on other campaigns with the unions, including unionisation drives — 'hard work' — for example in shop work. The workers in Haringey pointed out that their area was 'moving very sharply into part time based employment, a growing proportion of home working and sweat shops.' They found that effective working relations with unions depend in part on the particular officials; some recognised 'that we have more contact with the women than they do', and welcomed help, while with others, 'it's like, go away'. What the women are clear about, however, is that when advising people about employment rights and whether they should join a union, they always discuss the problems, for instance, 'the negative experiences of racism and sexism that we know locally have been experienced. We couldn't advise somebody to go in there believing that the union was going to stick up for them.'

The projects have tried increasingly to concentrate on anti-racism and the interests of black women, and in both Haringey and Lewisham about half the project workers are black. The Lewisham workers said that the majority of the people who use the Resource Centre are black women. Haringey saw their work as 'focussed around black and working class women.' They have organised a conference for black women on education and employment, and carried out a survey of unemployed women, looking at the differences between the experience of black and white women, and the pattern of discrimination against black women in the area.

The results of this led them to campaign for shorter working hours, and against job sharing and part time work. 'We put a paper to the (Haringey) Women's Committee arguing against job sharing as a desirable position for the council to adopt,' said one of the project workers. 'We've put a lot into the argument for a 30 hour week. Job sharing can be seen as institutionally racist, in that it's accessible only to women on certain grades, which tends to privilege white middle class women's interests.' Employers, they say, are arguing with growing confidence that the shift to part time work is 'what women want', and they don't want to hear the opposite argument.

Their research on women's needs, especially those of black women, led the Haringey project workers to identify training as an area where they could work with unions to pressure private employers — and at the same time change unions' attitudes. One approach they developed was 'training audits' of local firms: an assessment of what the firms provided against what was needed. They sought joint sponsorship for these from unions (such as USDAW or the TGWU), from the local Council, and from 'community groups like ourselves, black groups and women's groups'. They proposed to link the audits to unionisation drives, and saw this as a constructive way to challenge racism and sexism in trade union structures. They also wanted to use them to push the local Council into a wider view of their powers and jurisdiction on employment policy.

Some unions were enthusiastic. 'From a union like BIFU [the Banking, Insurance and Finance Union], there has been a very positive response to running training audits and public enquiries spotlighting companies.' Bargaining over training, however, is complex for trade unions, because it raises issues of racism and sexism, and 'is very much about control at the workplace, who controls the labour process'. Or, as one woman put it, 'How do you get a trade union to say that the training needs of black women are equally important as collective bargaining for next year's wage rise? That confronts every traditional reflex.'

Sector-wide Women's Employment Projects

Borough-based or local area work is not the only way to develop women's employment projects. The City Centre project is a unique example of a different approach: a resource centre for office workers, based in the City of London itself. The Centre is unique because it has trade union support across rival union lines. Its success was due to an existing network of experienced women trade unionists, especially in BIFU, backed up by good development work by experienced 'research-oriented activists' based in County Hall. Enormously problematic to establish, it is now successfully pursuing a mixture of educational work, individual case work, research and campaigning in the interests of women office workers in the City. The project demonstrates both the difficulties and the enormous possibilities of resource centres for women workers in different areas of the economy, working with the unions but campaigning for women's employment needs within and across them.

WICAG — the Women In Construction Advisory Group — is an example of a different sort of campaign to break down entrenched attitudes. It was set up to work on increasing women's employment in the construction industry — a hard industry to work in, as chapter 9 makes clear. Again, the group involved women with experience in the industry. Their work in education took off very quickly: 'A day doesn't go by without us being asked to attend or support a conference, ... come and speak to a group, or visit a school or provide them with videos, exhibitions, leaflets.'

They work in both the public and the private sector. With private employers, it was going much slower, but after eighteen months, they had found employers who responded to pressure on recruitment and apprenticeships and were providing resources for them on *how* to change their practices. They developed a division of labour with the well-established group Women in Manual Trades: 'There's a lot of leg work to do ... talking to employers, about employment practice, hiring practice, interview and grievance procedures, advertising ... This has to go alongside women getting jobs and if possible precede it, because otherwise women find themselves in really hostile, horrible environments.'

They have worked with women in local authorities to get more women on to Direct Labour Organisations and with black employment projects on contesting discriminatory aptitude tests. All this detailed, repetitive, often discouraging legwork is an essential part of opening up job possibilities to women, side by side with other sorts of campaigning.

Learning from the Projects?

The women's employment projects all spent a considerable amount of their time trying to influence borough councils and the GLC. The GLC, they said, had been much more open, which was very productive, if chaotic at times: 'what they've done is throw the money up in the air and see what happens. All sorts of exciting things happen, and you get the odd disaster as well, but you get spontaneity or initiative'.

The GLC was less good, however, at drawing on the ideas it stimulated. Heather Macrae of the Lewisham project commented, 'we feel we've got more to contribute than there's space for, in terms of policy making'. There had been a much greater level of involvement in the early days of the Labour administration. While the project development officers who worked with them, she said, had always been supportive and 'interested', they too, within County Hall, lacked influence on policy. As a result, 'we came to be seen as one of the organisations the GLC funds, and not particularly an organisation with knowledge and information that was that important to what went on in County Hall. I think there were a few times when we felt quite annoyed about that'.

Moderate words, when you consider the ideals and ambitions of popular planning. Here were projects, in their own words, 'head down, doing the actual job', who had seen their influence in County Hall dwindle. The GLC was even less and less doing the job it was best suited to do of bringing together projects doing this kind of work to learn from each other. One project worker argued that, after several years, it was still true that 'the GLC's geared a lot of its work towards the unions, and hasn't really taken on board unorganised workers ... And that does exclude a large proportion of the London labour force.'

The WICAG workers also complained that their expertise was

often not used where it might have been useful, and their efforts to feed into policy received no reply. As they said, 'I think it would have been good that somebody from the Popular Planning Unit came down and explained the Industrial Strategy to us. And explained how the services of voluntary groups are used to further those aims.' Such consultation with funded groups rarely happened, and voluntary sector funding was not seen in that light by the GLC. WICAG argued that 'if the GLC was going on, they should be reviewing how much they are actually making use, in local government terms, of the experiences and the information about those experiences which is being gathered from ordinary people.'

The issue this raises is the GLC's accountability. The 'popular planning' ideas argued that democracy should be extended beyond the electoral framework. This meant new structures of accountability, and potentially projects like women's employment projects should have been part of that. But the groups the GLC funded were rarely drawn into that kind of dialogue. The employment project workers argued that, while they were responsible to the funding authority for proper audited accounts, and keeping to their funding agreements, they themselves were accountable chiefly to local women. As one worker put it: 'I think [accountability] is having the respect of the community'.

The potentially productive two-way relationship is fraught with difficulty, as the women admitted: small voluntary organisations may want to influence large statutory ones, but finding the time to do so is almost impossible. Requests from the GLC for help were sporadic and with too short a timescale; too often there was no feedback from meetings. On occasions their work was not only used by local authorities without attribution, but also reinterpreted. The GLC never thought through how to relate to organisations they funded; the result was the GLC's loss.

Funding, Accounting and Enterprises

The GLC's Industrial Strategy argued that it was possible to create paid jobs from the 'socialisation' of domestic work, at the same time helping lighten the burden for women of isolated work in the home. In practice, this came to mean support for community enterprises, particularly laundry projects, and some women's coops. The experience of these projects has some important lessons — particularly on the needs and problems of small voluntary organisations which expand into major projects employing numbers of people.

The Industry and Employment Branch funded one community laundry project and tried to get another under way. The background to the first, Westway Laundries, is explained in the London Industrial Strategy: 'These laundries were won in the teeth of opposition from private laundry owners between the wars, but gradually closed down in the 1950s and 1960s. Westway laundry in Notting Hill survived through the 1970s, with a devoted campaigning group arguing fiercely for its usefulness. With a GLC grant it was finally able to buy new machines for washing, drying and ironing, which were energy-saving. The laundry is vital for people without any washing or drying space on the nearby estate and it also does the washing for a nursery next door.'

Westway got its £63,950 grant by dint of solid campaigning in a part of London that had long experience of community activism and lobbying, and where there was, as a consequence, no shortage of know-how in the art of dealing with the bureaucracies of the local state. It helped that the struggle was to maintain an existing community service, and the premises were already there. When a group of tenants on the Coventry Cross estate in Tower Hamlets decided to set up a laundry, they had a good many more obstacles in their way, so it's not surprising that they failed where Westway succeeded.

There was an evident need for a laundry on the estate. The nearest commercial launderette was ten to fifteen minutes walk away and many households on the estate were without cars. The tenants' association also hoped that a laundry (and creche) would give the estate some positive community focus, an important goal given its thirty per cent Bengali population and the increasing manifestations of racism in east London. The idea for a laundry on the estate was first proposed to the GLC Housing Committee, but was turned down. 'It was the general belief that laundries are superfluous since everyone must have a washing machine. It wasn't the case on Coventry Cross. The kitchens in the flats don't even have room for them,' recalled tenant Bob Brett.

He took on responsibility for pursuing an application to the Industry and Employment Committee. The grant application demanded a cash-flow analysis for the first year's trading; it took ten to twenty hours with a calculator. 'That was a major hurdle to begin with, then there were bureaucratic hassles from then on.'

The next stop was registering as a co-op, something that would have been made easier with the help of a local co-operative development agency, but there was none in Tower Hamlets at that time. It took much longer and proved more complicated than anyone had anticipated. Premises was the next problem and planning permission was required from Tower Hamlets Planning Departments: 'The application form was in gobbledygook. There were things like how we would dispose of "trade effluent". Eventually we were advised to get on to the Environmental Health Department. We had to do all the costings on machine use, and deal with separate visits by gas, water and electricity about installation'. Progress was so slow that the grant money to buy machines and other equipment still hadn't been spent by the end of the financial year, and the project was faced with the prospect of making a new application or losing the money. Despite continued efforts, the project foundered in the end.

This story is not unusual in the sheer lack of assistance available to people trying to put together such a project, and a lack of clarity from the GLC on the scale of what they were taking on, in trying to provide the service as well as the jobs: 'basically you're being asked to set up a business, with no previous experience to guide you.' In this co-op of seven tenants no one had the necessary expertise or time to devote to setting up a business and they approached it as a process of trial and error. Disheartened in the end, they gave up, but another local estate learned sufficiently from that experience to get their own laundry project successfully under way.

The issue of co-ops and small businesses run by women also betrays a similar lack of clarity and commitment by the GLC. The Lewisham women's employment project got a lot of enquiries from women about setting up co-ops. They have run courses on accounting and on working collectively. A lot of women were looking for ways to earn money from the skills they already had: cleaning, dress making, hairdressing, cooking, decorating. For women to give these under-valued assets money-making potential through co-operative work is to question the arbitrary values placed on women's work. This is no easy process. Working-class women's lack of business experience and of 'being business-minded', along with the conflicting demands of their homes, stand in the way of turning dreams and schemes into realities.

The Lewisham project workers found that very substantial support was needed to make women's co-ops possible — but GLEB was unhelpful and unwilling to provide it. The local council had in the end been more helpful, and they felt GLEB's co-op funding criteria were harsher than banks sometimes required. 'I'm sure there would have been a lot more co-ops around if that had been made easier.' There are however problems with the economic viability of jobs from domestic labour; offering low returns because of the low incomes of people buying the service, they may need continuing subsidy. With GLEB requiring prospects of profitability after two years, those projects often fell down the gap between GLEB investment and GLC grant funding.

It was not only those setting up businesses who had problems. All those who struggled with complicated application forms for financial assistance and unfamiliar financial calculations, confusing procedures and administrative catastrophes, also suggested ways in which these could have been avoided, leaving more time for the projects' real work.

Pip O'Byrne pointed out the need for some training in book-keeping and accountancy. Jenny Gudgeon thought that a small amount of financial advice would have been enormously helpful for projects unused to preparing detailed budgets and handling large sums of money. Sue Emerson noted that substantial grants had overnight turned some Southwark campaigning groups into managerial groups with new responsibilities for paying wages and other bills.

Dealing with these was made less daunting through the adult education institute hours allocated to the Southwark Childcare Forum for courses in management. This kind of provision would have averted many problems had it been available on a wider scale. A peripatetic financial adviser would have been a benefit far outweighing its cost to the GLC. Even one day seminars on financial matters would have equipped groups with the basics and budget planning might have been more judicious. Ironically they often failed to provide for childcare or maternity leave, as well as training time or sickness and holiday cover — contrary to the political spirit and intentions of the funding.

Mandy Snell, employment officer in the Women's Committee Support Unit, added that there should have been model employment contracts for voluntary groups. Those doing the funding were snowed-under and inexperienced at the start, and learning too: 'we must often have seemed inconsistent and uncaring'. By the end, she said, 'we were beginning to realise what we should do'. They began to hold workshops for new groups, which greatly increased take-up of funds; they did more advising on finance, and a conference on networking in January 1986 showed the scope for helping groups to support and learn from each other.

Funding, Bureaucracy and Equal Opportunities

The problems of the relation between the voluntary sector organisations and the Council are not only practical: they raise important political issues. Those interviewed in funded projects have repeatedly described their relationship to the GLC as being like dealing with a faceless bureaucracy. Jenny Gudgeon's comment about the early days of that relationship is widely echoed: '... the great socialist idea of putting out money to voluntary organisations is great, but they didn't seem to know how voluntary organisations worked'. As project funding expanded contacts became impersonalised. Jenny Gudgeon again described a common experience: 'It's very analogous to phoning up about your broken down washing machine, and then you wait in and nobody comes and you get so angry because there's nobody who you actually know to have a go at about it. It's all so faceless on the whole.' There was no clear point of contact: '... we seemed to be shunted around, and they'd phone up and say, oh it's not me anymore, and it was somebody new every time, and you'd have to explain all over again who you were and what you were doing', recalled Sue Greenwood. Long delays were commonplace, and project workers were sometimes a week or two away from prospective redundancy before eleventh hour rescue arrived in the form of a reassuring letter or cheque.

It's undeniable that some of these difficulties were due to a tortuous bureaucracy and the time it took for newcomers inside County Hall to learn some of the skills of manipulating it (to say nothing of overcoming deliberate obstruction). But some were the result of inherent conflicts between state funding and democratic control of resources.

The GLC could never be simply a 'resource centre' because it was also a political and statutory institution with its own built-in interests, and constrained by legal provisions. Inevitably it had criteria for funding which involved choosing between applications for funding, and also imposing conditions on those funded. Undeniably, the GLC should have been clearer and more consistent in specifying those conditions and should have provided far more support to groups trying to comply with them.

But beyond that there is a dispute. Some groups feel interfering in the internal operations of the groups was actually wrong; others simply argue that it was done badly. This is a very important debate, and it centred particularly on the 'equal opportunities' issues: the demand that all projects funded should have an active anti-sexist and anti-racist practice, and that they should promote the interests and serve the needs of lesbians and women with disabilities.

There was a lot of confusion, and some bitter complaints from funded groups, about the pressures exerted over equal opportunities. A monitoring process was introduced after a number of groups — mainly the more established ones — had been funded, which required the groups to show progress on anti-racism, for example, in hiring staff and in what they did. Some groups welcomed the pressure and some were taking the lead. The Lewisham Women's Employment Project had already set out to shift the project's staffing to at least half black staff, and had set up an advisory group of black women to help them change the content of their work and also to support black staff when they were hired. Other groups found it more difficult, had monitoring reports rejected, and got into debates with the GLC which were, as Tina Dubois of the Westway National Childcare Campaign described, 'pretty difficult, pretty acrimonious; there's been a lot of conflict and a lot of emotion'. She went on to say that while the Campaign could still not 'be said to be a strong anti-racist organisation', nevertheless, 'the monitoring has forced regular reviews and discussions'. 'It's been useful, but I think there was quite a strong feeling, particularly from the workers, and particularly at the beginning, of resentment against it, and seeing it as a sort of policing role and unwarranted intrusion.'

Mandy Snell of the Women's Committee argues strongly against the view that these policies were an intrusion: 'One of the most significant things we ever did was to put our commitment to more disadvantaged groups of women into practice, through the equal opportunities conditions on grants,' she said.

What is not in dispute is that learning how to do the monitoring properly took time. If it was done badly it became purely formalistic. There was often not enough genuine consultation with groups. Shelley Adams of the Brent Trade Union Resource Centre saw the conflict as inevitable, because the pressure over race was real, but felt there was too much focus on 'the composition of the management committee ... rather than on the work.' She thought the speed of real change would have been faster if 'there had been a discussion, saying, this is what we're thinking of doing, what do you think are the issues we should raise? They didn't have to agree with us completely … but then people wouldn't have felt so threatened.'

Many groups said, and meant, that they were willing to meet the equal opportunities conditions. But this did not mean that they knew how to, or could afford to meet them, and the GLC offered too little help. Many groups pointed out that they were expected to improve their access for children with disabilities, without having suitable accommodation or enough staff. Nor was it recognised that widening the recruitment net could be expensive. Liz Southcombe described the dilemma of Hackney Community Nurseries Association: 'If you've only got a couple of hundred quid a year for your recruitment budget and you decide that every single time there's a job you put the advert in five or six of the ethnic papers, with one vacancy you've used it all up. The next time where does the money come from?' Who would disagree with her observation that carrying out an equal opportunities policy 'takes money, it takes resources, it takes training'?

After race, some of the deepest conflicts emerged over the rights and needs of lesbians. Some groups have argued that in their case this issue should never have been raised: for example in case of the Birner Women's Centre set up on what community activist Myra Garett described as 'a very, very deprived ex-GLC estate' in Tower Hamlets and used mainly by Asian women and pensioners. 'This issue about "was the centre discriminating against lesbians" just created enormous problems', recalled Myra Garett, who sat on the management committee. 'There was no way we could actually discuss it because of all the cultural and language things. And the GLC just insisted that the management committee make a policy statement about working with lesbians, and it seemed to us if they'd actually known what the centre was doing and how successful its impact was in terms of getting Asian women into the place to use it and be together and have some kind of collective support, that wouldn't have been an issue, and it just did seem an example of being out of touch with what was happening.'

Mandy Snell, of the Women's Committee Support Unit, disagreed strongly this view: while there was a lot of learning to do about how to respond to the needs of lesbians, and mistakes were made, she argued that the demands made were reasonable: to make literature available, to have a speaker, so that individual women in contact with the projects had access to information which would be very important to some of them. More was expected, she said, of long-established than of newly-formed groups. But groups should not, she argued, have been allowed to avoid this issue.

The GLC staff were themselves divided over linking race and lesbianism to funding. There was a view — argued, for example, by a woman working in the Popular Planning Unit — that it is one thing to compel employers (through Contract Compliance procedures) to change their recruitment policy in the interests of black workers: their opinions may not match their actions, but in the first instance these matter less than the removal of their power to discriminate against others. But, she argued, it was another to 'use the same kind of pressure' against groups of women in the community. 'Their perceptions do matter, and giving them room to develop and expand calls for far more sensitivity, generosity and permissive support.' She went on to argue therefore that, having funded a group, the GLC should not have imposed 'rigid political conditions', but 'was surely obliged to respect the differences in histories and circumstances that made uniform change impossible, and to recognise the richness and complexity of the processes through which people do come to see the world and one another in new ways.'

But others, while recognising the need to listen and support, argued that the GLC was right to insist on the equal opportunities criteria. While greater clarity and assistance were needed, when some long-established groups actively resisted developing anti-racist work (and some did), or even refused to discuss discriminatory activity, then the GLC, women grants officers say, was right to take a hard line. Because, as Shelley Adams put it, reflecting on the battle over anti-racist work by her project which she saw as in the end very productive, 'the pressure makes you think, you can't run away from it when it's coming from a funding body, and that's good.'

This debate is an important one, because it raises the contradictions inherent in a part of the state trying to promote the self-organisation of people who can, and perhaps should, then oppose it.

What might have been . . .

There was no real pressure from women outside on women's

employment, except for training where there was plenty, and it shows in the output.

Why, given the level of commitment of many people, was not more achieved? It is a question a lot of people talked about in the interviews for this chapter. One theme has clearly been that things were achieved most rapidly where there were already organised groups pushing from outside. Hence childcare and training were the most successful areas of funding for women; hence a number of other campaigns could be pushed forward because there was a nucleus of a campaign already: home-working for example, where the GLC strengthened an existing campaign. But where there was no pressure, there was, by default, no funding; regardless of need. 'The GLC could have done a lot more to generate projects around women's employment and training, but really what was being said was, the money's here and people aren't coming forward,' said one of the employment project officers. 'There should have been a lot more drive.'

Why did people not come forward, and why was little done to make up for that? It is not that women were not organising, but they were, it seems, putting their energies into areas other than employment, such as women's centres. And women were less experienced, less established in terms of Labour Party links than for example trade unions, and therefore less able to pressure the GLC effectively for resources.

What could have been done to change this? Well, some things were done, but not on the whole by the Industry and Employment branch. The Women's Committee, argues Mandy Cook, did far more than Industry and Employment ever tried to do, to 'open up power' to those outside. They did this in a variety of ways: by advertising very widely for grant applications, by holding meetings in every borough and funding a follow-up meeting run by local women, including doing the practicalities, like booking rooms and doing mailings and paying for the creche. As Mandy Snell recalled, 'In almost every outer London borough they took advantage of that ... That's where many women's centres came from.' Some of the effects of all this were negative: 'raising expectations is horrible', and the Women's Unit was swamped with demands. The results were inconsistency, far too slow decision-making at the beginning, and thus a great deal of anger from the groups who applied for money. But many more groups were drawn in than those who had initial access. Mandy

Snell argues that, in the last two years, this was changing the nature of the applications: the proposals were better, more realistic, and there were an increasing number from black women's groups.

Industry and Employment did not go out and create a constituency in the same way for women's employment work. It did not advertise for grant applications; it did not have co-opted members on the committee; and it did not discuss very effectively who its constituency was and how to work with it. As a result it did not successfully change the pattern of those who had access to its resources. Mandy Cook argues that 'women did not have the networks and the infrastructure' to develop and put forward projects on women's employment.

Changing that would have involved going out and helping to create the networks, the infrastructure, the organisational basis for the projects: doing the development work for the women's employment projects and campaigns substantially from scratch. This is what a number of people who came from the voluntary sector to work in the GLC expected to do. But in practice, they rarely had time, either in popular planning or project development, and those who made the funding decisions were separated from those who worked on policy.

One effect of this separation was that the funded groups, whose only point of contact was with the overworked grants officers, had little influence on employment policy. And in particular, Industry and Employment Branch policy makers (unlike the Women's Committee Support Unit) were insulated from the pressures on grants officers from outside groups over equal opportunities, especially race.

How could more resources have been spent on the employment needs of women, including black women and lesbians? Only, experience suggests, by spending far more staff time on developing the organisational basis for women's employment projects and campaigns of all kinds. This would have meant far less time doing other things.

This would have allowed, for example, far more work with women trade unionists, on developing resources and support for their needs. It is clear that there is a need for this. But the women activists within the unions, in the words of one grants officer, were 'overworked and fairly worn down'; the projects required experience, time and effort that were lacking. The City Centre project only serves to show what might have been.

It would also have allowed more project development work

with black women, and more time helping to develop lesbian employment projects. Industry and Employment funded only one lesbian employment project, in Lesbian and Gay Employment Rights. Changing this would have required finding staff early on who could work with existing organisations, and with people involved in wider projects like the London Lesbian and Gay Centre, to develop employment-related work.

If an effective source of pressure could have been created from outside groups for more funding for women's employment, this might also have helped change the pattern of internal use of funds. This would have involved major changes in other parts of the Industry and Employment Branch's work. It would have meant work on women's employment in London Transport, for example. It would have meant changes in the work on 'early warning' (that is, work with trade unions to detect where redundancies were likely to be announced before it happened) towards more work in the public sector, and more work with lower skilled, less organised groups of workers including women. And it would have meant a change in the use of resources put into GLEB.

While GLEB had a verbal commitment to equal opportunities, including women, it only created two jobs, late on, to work on it. While GLEB funded a few women's co-ops, it did not develop links with the grant funding which would have allowed it to provide childcare necessary for access by women to jobs in GLEB companies. It did not do a great deal to change the position of women in GLEB companies and their unions: it did not, for example, fund women to go on TUC courses for women trade unionists. And it did not establish an effective link up with the Training Board on training for women in the firms.

GLEB's equal opportunities policy within companies was made contingent on the (fragile) enterprise planning process described in chapter 6. One woman involved in GLEB came to argue that 'enterprise planning is inimical to equal opportunities': because it was an approach based on consensus, the enterprise planning discusions could only too easily end up ignoring employment opportunities for black people or women by tacit mutual consent between all the parties. This raises similar problems of political process and priorities to those found in the grant giving. While there are many obstacles to effective equal opportunities work in an enterprise board, GLEB was effectively protected by its relative independence from the GLC from serious challenge on this for much of its history.

As one woman argued, if one was serious about equal opportunities, a low 'cost per job created', which GLEB often claimed, would not be a matter for self congratulation. Early on, one of the women's employment project workers had been involved in arguing that childcare provision should be part of any GLEB job creation programme. She remembered that GLEB had replied that this would be too expensive. As she put it, GLEB was 'concerned to put forward a view of how to be more effective ... than capitalism itself ... if only it would do it this way we will retain jobs and we will retain control of our own economy ... I don't want to dismiss that, but somewhere, you know, the price was paid, and it was women'. She contrasted this with the Training Board, which in her view had 'made quite important inroads on training practice and ideas' as regards women's training.

More outside pressure from women might have changed the urgency with which women's employment was treated in other ways too. Interestingly, a number of people in the groups funded by the GLC which were not specifically women's projects perceived the pressure from the GLC on equal opportunities for women to have been rather slight. Shelley Adams argued that in terms of such pressure 'you never really got anything on women, you know, not in the same way as racism came over'. The result showed, she felt, in the work of the trade union resource centre, with more work on black employment issues than on women.

The women within the GLC, to come back to them at the end, feel rather the same. They feel that they were, in the end, probably too loyal, too conscientious, too taken in by (genuine) expressions of good will, too unwilling to demand resources, shout loudly, make trouble. And in the end it was resources that counted. A better policy would involve a higher proportion of staff working on women, more links between funding, development work, popular planning and research, and equal opportunities work in all the different areas of the Council's work. And more honesty maybe: as one of the women put it, 'If you are concerned with equal opportunities, and you are concerned with the *process* of work, which is working with people rather than on behalf or in the name of, then you have to accept that it takes enormous amounts of time and resources. And if you are not prepared to do that, if you do not have the resources to put back into it, then you just have to be clear about what you are not doing.'

Working out what the GLC was not doing on women is an important part of changing that next time round.

6
Industrial Democracy: the GLEB Experience*

Introduction

The Labour Party's manifesto for the 1981 GLC elections undertook to set up the Greater London Enterprise Board. One of its intentions was that GLEB should help to extend trade union control over company decision-making. 'Any intervention by GLEB', the manifesto asserted, 'in respect of its investment functions would be conditional on three-way talks, leading to agreement, between GLEB, the enterprise and the unions concerned covering in particular future patterns of employment and investment in the enterprise. Such local Planning Agreements would form part of the London Industrial Strategy ...' The term used by GLEB for this form of industrial democracy is 'enterprise planning'.

The manifesto reflected the tri-partism supported at a national level by the Labour Party with varying degrees of commitment. But its authors favoured the strong version of this theory, under which the state would not be neutral; the unions and public authorities were to act as allies. One of the most important elements in the original conception was the idea that enterprise planning would grow out of strong trade union organisation, as an extension of collective bargaining. It was hoped that trade unionists confronted by threats of closures and redundancies would, as the Lucas Aerospace workers had done, move from

---

*Note: The company names in this chapter are fictitious. The case studies describe the situation as it was at the end of the GLC (31 March 1986).

defensive trade union positions on to proposing alternative production plans for saving jobs, meeting social needs and introducing new technologies under trade union control. These plans could then be supported by GLEB.

Except in a few cases, and then only in a limited way, the original idea did not bear fruit. The idea of democratically determined enterprise plans rapidly lost its central position in GLEB's practice and theory. Few enterprise plans, in the sense of fully worked out business plans based on the involvement of the workforce, exist; those that do tend to bear little relation to reality. Instead, GLEB came to emphasise the idea that enterprise planning is a process, which involves the progressive extension of trade unionists' control over economic decisions. Moreover the process is a slow one, involving much hard work, extra costs for the enterprise and GLEB and the gradual building up of commitment and skills; no overnight miracles are to be expected.

The gap between the intentions and reality arises partly from an over-optimistic assumption that GLEB investments could be based on strong trade unionism in medium and large firms, partly also from an underestimation of the crisis of London's manufacturing industry. Attempts to fulfil the original intention came up against a number of problems. First, strongly unionised sectors of industry in London have virtually disappeared and those that remain are much weakened. Some of GLEB's investments have therefore of necessity been in sectors with no strong tradition of union organisation, such as the clothing or food sectors. Moreover, in the last decade monetarist economic policies have dramatically undermined trade union bargaining power throughout British industry.

Second, even though the GLC decided in principle that GLEB would not have a strategy of investing in small firms, the limited size of GLEB's resources has meant that in practice the bulk of its investments are in very small firms. Little more than a dozen projects, out of a total of around 200, have had more than twenty employees, and the largest has around 200. It makes little sense to talk of enterprise planning, or indeed any form of structured democracy, let alone effective collective bargaining, in a firm with six employees. Many of these small GLEB-funded firms are co-operatives. But they do not provide any real test of the relevance of co-operatives to the crisis facing major sections of British industry. The evidence in this chapter is therefore based on GLEB's experience in the small number of larger firms with twenty workers and over.

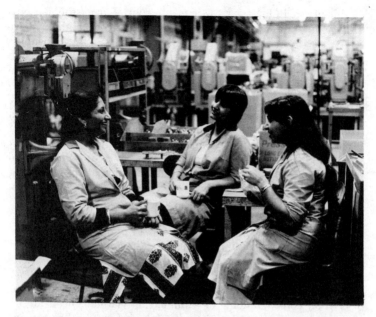

There was an over-optimistic assumption that GLEB investments could strengthen equal opportunities for women through strong trade unionism in medium and large firms. In reality, most of the firms were not unionised and almost without exception the women were in low paid jobs with few skills.

The third problem is that most of these slightly larger firms are in a state of crisis. Many of them were initially rescued from the receiver. GLEB, which has no powers of compulsory acquisition, has difficulty in engaging the interest of managers of successful companies in its proposals for investment, and would have little leverage over them if it could. Because its resources have been limited, they have usually been intended to achieve a minimum level of viability over a short period of time, shorter than that expected by some private sources of funds, even though this contradicts GLEB's own analysis that what is needed is long-term restructuring. There has been little moey available for development, new investment and training. There are considerable constraints on taking time off production for discussions on enterprise planning. And there is the additional pressure of having to retain existing management at least in the short term, simply for lack of alternatives.

Finally, GLEB of course has no control over the national environment. Many of the ideas about what it might achieve were based on the view that it could provide, in a microcosm, an image of what could become national reality. This perhaps led to excessive optimism about what could be achieved by a local institution with limited resources. Moreover when the manifesto was drawn up in 1980 and GLEB was established in 1982, there was a strong expectation that a sympathetic government would come into power in 1983 or 1984.

The sharpest dilemma which results from the economic pressure on GLEB has been between the need to ensure the survival of relatively small companies and the objective of strengthening the position of workers within those companies. The latter objective is likely to involve some costs, for example in improved wages and conditions. It also involves costs in terms of people's time: not only the time of GLEB staff in promoting and monitoring enterprise planning, but also the time of management and workers within companies, in negotiations, consultation, self-education, formal training and the provision of information. Because GLEB is an investment agency, there is no avoiding the fact that considerations of commercial viability need to be dominant, in the interest of saving jobs if for no other reason. Some would say that they were not dominant enough in GLEB's practice. Yet when short term commercial considerations overrode the other objectives set for GLEB by the GLC, this raised questions within the GLC and a minority of the board of GLEB as to whether the GLC had sufficient political control of GLEB.

However enterprise planning can also be seen as a benefit to management. One element of the GLC/GLEB view of enterprise planning is that the workers' greater involvement in planning will release their creative energies and ideas. More crudely, their greater understanding of the financial constraints and prospects of their enterprise may lead them to work harder, perhaps even to moderate their demands. Even though the GLC's guidelines for GLEB were insistent that enterprise planning should be based on trade union organisation and should strengthen rather than undermine it, it can, arguably, constitute a threat to the collective and independent organisation of the workforce. The fear of incorporation in management accounts for the reticence of many trade unionists towards any schemes for worker or indeed public participation in the private sector. But this fear is to some extent reduced when the enterprise is owned by GLEB or by the workers themselves, who are then the beneficiaries of increases in productivity and efficiency. These related questions will recur throughout the case studies which follow.

GLEB was set up with different divisions which roughly corresponded to the different objectives set for it. Since the abolition of the GLC it has been run by a group of London boroughs and its internal organisation is currently being changed, mainly as a result of the reduction in its resources. The original structures included property and finance divisions, a technology division, an investment division, a sector strategy division, an information division and a structural investment division (SID). The structural investment division had a unit of four people responsible for co-ops and two people with specific responsibility for equal opportunities. A further three/four people were responsible for enterprise planning and trade union matters.

Each of GLEB's projects was assigned to one division and had a 'project executive' in charge of it. The project executive had responsibility for commercial decisions about the companies they supervised. They were also expected to promote GLEB's other objectives. They did so with varying degrees of commitment and enthusiasm. The fact that some were unsympathetic, or even antogonistic, towards some or all of GLEB's social and political objectives demonstrates the difficulty of reconciling the various skills required and the need, as some would say, for more 'red experts'. This problem, again, is a recurring theme in the case studies which follow. Members of the structural investment division were sometimes asked to provide extra assistance in particular projects on enterprise planning matters; their effectiveness was limited by their small numbers and the consequent dispersion of their activities. They were assisted by 'support workers' on temporary contracts, who usually came from institutions responsible for trade union education.

Two years after GLEB was set up, it was decided that all investment proposals going to GLEB's Board should have an assessment from the structural investment division attached to them. This was mainly a result of SID members and others in GLEB and on the Board feeling that GLEB's social and democratic objectives were not being given enough priority. On the Board, however, little time was devoted to discussing these assessments; questions about enterprise planning were raised by only one or two members, who felt that they amounted to little more than a ritual. Thus one GLEB executive explained that: 'I've got to produce a progress report which is part of the proposal that's going to the Board ... but I think there are other factors which the Board are going to regard, frankly, as more important, more decisive.' Other executives — and a minority on the Board — felt there was a failure by the majority of the Board to take specific account of the progress of enterprise planning in determining priorities for investment, that this ought to be remedied, and that any costs associated with enterprise planning ought to be systematically quantified and allowed for in funding decisions. One way of doing this, which is now likely to be adopted by GLEB, is to account separately for commercial and 'social' requirements in funding agreements, so that the element of subsidy is clearly quantified and its effects can be more effectively monitored.

Further questions arise on the extent of GLEB's financial leverage. Its powers to promote any of its objectives vary with the nature of its financial stake in companies. GLEB may have total ownership (especially in companies which have been bought from the receiver), an equity stake (of varying sizes, but usually above 25 per cent), and/or loans. Loans clearly give GLEB least power to affect the policies of their recipients. In cases in which the loans can be disbursed in stages, or in which it is clear that further funding will be needed, GLEB can make such further funding conditional on compliance with its demands, which may include, for example, proper establishment of a trade union. In other cases, a quick injection of funding may be needed; it may be based on an enterprise plan, but if the plan is not adhered to, there is little that GLEB can do, short of calling in its loan, a procedure which has not yet been resorted to. Even when GLEB has substantial equity or total ownership, much depends both on the nature of local management and on the availability and commitment of GLEB executives themselves to monitor the situation, as the following case studies illustrate.

So there were failings and difficulties. But in spite of these, the activities of GLEB do provide a rich source of experience and lessons on the central question of democratic control of industry. GLEB's practice has not been uniform. It is basically a process of experimentation. In some cases GLEB's intervention has concentrated on achieving unionisation and on minimum gains such as the drawing up of procedural agreements, the issuing of contracts of employment, the establishment of health and safety procedures. As a supplement to trade union organisation, and at times as a substitute, GLEB has promoted the idea of worker-directors. In a number of cases there have been changes in legal ownership: some enterprises have become wholly owned subsidiaries of GLEB; some are owned partly by GLEB and partly, at least in theory, collectively by the workforce in workers' trusts; one company is owned partly by the print union SOGAT; some are or are becoming co-operatives. In some cases GLEB's interventions have conformed quite closely to the original intention of basing democratic structures on strong trade union organization. In this chapter, we attempt to provide illustrations of these various means of extending workers' power through a series of case studies. In addition, we include a section on equal opportunities which, in the proposals for GLEB, were intended to be part of enterprise planning.

Building Union Membership

GLEB has made considerable, though uneven, attempts to unionise the companies it funds. Some time after it was set up, an attempt was made to monitor union membership in GLEB-funded firms. This did not in all cases yield results, but GLEB publications state that 80 per cent of the workforce in GLEB's larger projects is unionised. The percentage in smaller projects is likely to be lower. This certainly represents an improvement on the situation before GLEB became involved. Financial agreements with GLEB specify that union organisers must be allowed access to the workforce, and this condition has generally been adhered to, although access has not always resulted in recruitment.

Not many more than half of the larger firms which GLEB came to fund were unionised before GLEB became involved, and in some of these union organisation was not well developed. In the new start-ups funded by GLEB, often with white collar workers, GLEB has usually succeeded in introducing a trade union. In perhaps a quarter of GLEB's investments in larger, existing firms, GLEB's support for union access has resulted in union membership for the first time. In at least one case, GLEB decided not to make an investment because the prospects for union recruitment appeared to be non-existent.

There are however cases in which GLEB staff have shown little interest in matters of unionisation. This may be because commercial considerations are paramount; if there is no company, there will be no workers. At times it is simply because

GLEB staff are overworked and nobody is available from SID to work on a particular project. The following situation is probably not untypical. A project executive, working on a new technology project employing some twenty people, 'believed' they had been recruited into a white-collar union, which he admitted was 'a bit odd' since they are manual workers. He did not know how many had been recruited. There was a shop steward but he had never spoken to him, even though he visited the company at least once a month. He did not know whether the regional official of the union had been involved.

In other cases a great deal of effort has been put into introducing and establishing the unions. For example in Free Wheeler, a record-making company employing fifty or so people, there was no union membership before GLEB became involved. GLEB had to approach five different trade union officials before one would go into the firm to recruit. There are now around twenty members. They have elected shop stewards, a secretary and a chair and are in the process of setting up bargaining procedures with the assistance of GLEB.

Another company, employing Asian workers, was not unionised at the time its owners approached GLEB. But before GLEB's loan was disbursed the company met the condition of union access and workers joined the union. Since then the union official has spent a considerable amount of time with the company and management has accepted the usual procedures and agreements. As a GLEB executive said: 'Before GLEB's involvement they had never seen the face of a union official. It only happened because of GLEB. We had a lot of trouble trying to convince people; there was a close relationship between management and the workers; we said you're going to grow big, when you have 100 workers you'll need structures.'

In another Asian-owned firm, Sumara, a huge amount of effort by both GLEB and the union at first produced only meagre results. It is only after two years, and after the close and continuous involvement of the union official and a recent intensification of monitoring by a member of SID, that the owner-managers appear to have accepted that the union is there to stay and to have dropped some of their anti-union attitudes. The company was typical of its sector. It was ununionised before GLEB became involved. The workers were paid very low wages, in cash, and conditions were bad. GLEB's intervention took the form of a loan to the owner-managers. Union access was not secured until some time after the initial loan was made. The first official met with a blank response. The owners had done nothing to explain to the Asian workforce what was going on and provided only minimal facilities. He was followed by a second official, who spoke the language of the workers; this official recruited most of the workers employed at the time and they 'managed to appoint a shop steward'.

Without the pressures from GLEB, it is unlikely that the union would be there at all. The biggest achievement, in the first two years after GLEB became involved in Sumara, was that the workers began to be paid nationally agreed union rates; tax and national insurance are regularly paid, and some progress has been made in health and safety measures. But in other respects progress was, until recently, minimal. As the official said: 'I have been twelve years in the union, I have never seen an employer like this; I have been over two years with this company, we have no contracts of employment, no company handbook, no discipline and grievance procedures, no grading structure. We're not one step up the ladder.' He has companies with a workforce of over a thousand; his union executive has told him to give up the work on this small company; the dues do not cover his expenses let alone his time. However, against all the obstacles, he continues out of loyalty to those who have paid their dues.

Again, without GLEB's involvement, it is possible that if any workers at Sumara had attempted to join the union, they would have been sacked , as has happened in other similar companies. As it is, some have been threatend with the sack if they join. One shop steward left because 'every time she took up a grievance she got no satisfactory response; she got fed up'; and her successor 'has been put under a lot of pressure; he has said that if this continues, he will be the next to leave'. A consultant sent in by GLEB to establish the true situation of the workforce received the co-operation of the management only after she made it clear that she represented GLEB and not the union. She was shocked by what she found: 'There were women crying; it was very depressing. One woman was injured; she got no treatment, she was just told to carry on.' The workers at Sumara appeared to have little knowledge about GLEB.

In the case of Sumara, the central thrust of GLEB's enterprise planning work has been the establishment of the union. As GLEB's executive put it: 'Our first job is to establish the union. After that, over a three or four year period, we can work on enterprise planning. There's no point in having a worker-director if we don't have stewards who can deal with grievances. They would just get sucked into management.' Yet the record shows with bitter clarity the difficulty of building trade union strength in a sector with competitive, small-scale, sweat shop industries and anti-union management, at a time of high unemployment. This is the case even with the backing of GLEB. GLEB does not have equity in the company and therefore has no direct control; no changes in ownership or control are currently proposed by GLEB. GLEB's financial leverage is therefore limited to 'drip-feeding': the owners were told they would receive a further loan providing they complied with GLEB's requirements, which included the issuing of proper contracts of employment and compliance with the union's other minimum demands.

For the time being, the combined pressures of GLEB and the union have borne fruit. Contracts of employment have finally, more than two years after GLEB first became involved, been issued to the workers. A company handbook has been prepared by ACAS and will shortly be issued. And the company has agreed to implement new wage rates. But there is no evidence that, if GLEB monitoring becomes less intense, this progress can be sustained.

GLEB staff, unlike the union, continued to express faith in the competence and goodwill of the current owners, who gave assurances that their compliance with union requirements was just a matter of time. The union official, asked before the latest achievement whether he believed there was any prospect for improvement under the current owner-managers, said he thought not. He would like the union to act as trustees for the funding, so that it could monitor its uses. Better still, he said, the union could run the company together with the workers as a co-operative, 'so that everybody has a say, and has the responsibility for producing'. The union would be able to supply the necessary professional management and marketing skills. He has indications that the workforce would be happier if the company was run as a co-operative. This is, then, a case in which union members themselves would like to take the initiative in going beyond their normal collective bargaining role, primarily because they feel powerless in relation to existing management.

There have been several other such cases: cases in which GLEB has felt it necessary to go along with existing management, largely because of the difficulty of finding competent replacements for them, and in which the workforce and unions, with their knowledge of the management, have felt strongly, and usually correctly, that management is not to be trusted. The next chapter provides an example in the furniture industry. In a sign-making company, Signwriters, GLEB was responsible for introducing the union for the first time. The company has a skilled, mainly male and white workforce. In this case, the owner-manager backed out before GLEB funding was agreed, and the company was re-started under GLEB ownership, with the prospect of it becoming a co-operative. One worker subsequently commented that he and other workers had been opposed to GLEB funding with the previous owner in charge, even though GLEB 'would have gone along with him'.

GLEB's first contacts with the workers in Signwriters centred on the introduction of trade unionism. GLEB staff made contact with the workforce well before any GLEB funding took place. The owner was told that union access was a condition of GLEB funding and agreed that, as first step, somebody from GLEB could come and talk to the workforce. At this meeting the GLEB representative explained the objectives of GLEB, mentioned the possibility of a workers' trust, a worker-director, and the necessity of having some sort of organisation on which enterprise planning could be based. There was little response. The owner put forward a proposal for a staff association. The proposal was accepted by the workforce; a staff committee was set up, with shop floor workers including the foremen. Later, when negotiations with the owner were not making progress, GLEB invited this committee to come to the GLEB office and suggested that part of the problem might be the lack of outside support of the sort that could be provided by a trade union. Eventually the workers agreed to invite a union official to come and talk to them and most of them joined. A trade union committee was formed. It had a number of discussions on the business plan which had been submitted to GLEB by the owner.

As it happens, the owner was unwilling to give the personal financial guarantees GLEB was asking for and the company went into receivership. The trade union committee carried on negotiations with GLEB and eventually the business was restarted under GLEB ownership. GLEB sent out forms to the workforce in order to determine who would be available for work and to ask whether they would be willing to work in a co-operative and would join a union. All but one of those asked agreed. However, since Signwriters has become a co-op, it has been less clear what the role of the union is (see below).

Even with the backing of GLEB, it is extremely difficult to establish strong trade union organisation in small firms without also making changes in management and perhaps ownership. But, as the following cases show, such changes may also at times make union organisation appear less necessary, or at least change its role. This has been the case both in some co-operatives and in some firms in which GLEB has relied on worker-directors as a means of promoting democratic control by the workforce.

Worker-Directors

The GLC did not originally intend that worker-directorships should be a central feature of enterprise planning. The intention was much more that democracy should be based on an extension of collective bargaining. The institution of worker-directors has been discredited in much of the labour movement, as a result of experiences in the steel industry and elsewhere. Even the Bullock Committee's proposal for 50 per cent worker representation on the boards of companies met with a mixed response from trade unions, some of whom feared that this would mean incorporation into management.

The GLC's position was that any worker representation should be based on trade union voting procedures and should be genuinely independent of management. Moreover the GLC, in its guidelines for GLEB, stated, for example, that: 'Negotiations should be modelled on traditional methods of collective bargaining'. But GLEB, as has been said, was confronted by a different reality from the trade union power of the 1970s. Strong trade union organisation, where it existed, was on the retreat. On its own it had proved incapable of stopping closures and redundancies, let alone making inroads into management power. In many cases it was simply absent. In such cases the institution of worker-directors seems to have provided an alternative means of worker involvement for GLEB to fall back on. It has not always been backed up by strong union organisation; in one case, the worker directors are not even members of a trade union. Where union organisation *is* strong, GLEB has also offered worker-directorships to the workforce, as one means of improving their access to day-to-day information on management decisions.

There have been worker-directors in roughly a third of GLEB's larger investments. GLEB has not implemented the Bullock Committee proposals for 50 per cent worker participation: it has either supported one or two worker-directors, or full co-operatives (see below). Its experience has shown, as was to be expected, that worker-directors in a small minority on boards are dependent on the goodwill of managers and owners and/or on the back-up of a strong union. On their own, they have little or no power.

For example, GLEB has set up a small company, Engco, based on several engineering divisions of a large corporation. These divisions were on a site which the corporation intended to close in order to consolidate its operations outside London. The work-force of twenty five is mainly white, male and skilled. Engco pro-vides an example of a harmonious relationship between management and workforce which appears to make the existence of a union unnecessary. There are perhaps three or four union members. Neither of the two current worker-directors is a union member, although both have been in the past. There is even doubt over whether any attempt has been made to recruit the workforce into a union. One comment from a GLEB executive was that: 'They know they would be absolutely, positively sup-ported if they wanted to join the union ... I think it's wrong to say, there's somebody coming down and you've got to listen and make a decision ... they do generally feel that they own a bit of the company they work for, and who needs a union when you do that.'

The workforce own collectively twenty per cent of the company through a worker's trust. But by far the most important reason why, in this case, the arrangement has worked well from the point of view of the workers, is the character of the manage-ment that they happen to have. (This will become clear from the second contrasting example, in which the ownership pattern is the same.) The managing directors at Engco have spent many years on the shop floor or close to it. In addition, because of the inexperience in financial and marketing matters of the existing workforce and management, they have had the full-time atten-tion of a consultant who was appointed by GLEB.

This consultant was originally recruited for his marketing expertise. He had no knowledge of the wider objectives of GLEB before he started work, and the subject of enterprise planning was not raised at his interview. But it turned out to be, as he put it, 'a happy match'. Before he came to his job, he had already taken an active interest in methods of involving the workforce in management decisions: he was convinced that that was the only way to 'make things work'. Asked for his definition of enterprise planning, he said that it meant: 'Explaining to the workforce in fairly simple terms what changes are required, and obtaining their ideas and commitment to the new path'. It is clear that he does in fact have an exceptional ability and willingness to make complicated financial and accounting matters clear, and that both he and the other managers have the respect and confidence of the workforce.

The experience of Engco shows also that much depends on the personalities of the particular individuals who become worker-directors. One of the original worker-directors thought he had been picked by his fellow workers because 'I think they got mixed up, they thought it was something to do with the union and they knew I was a union member and thought I would be the representative of the union.' But both he and the other worker-director had recently been replaced by workers who were considered by themselves and others to be more out-spoken. No doubt coincidentally, both new worker-directors had resigned from union membership. One was 'fed up' with the union, considered it had 'sold them down the river' over redundancies and had been of no assistance even in providing information; he resigned at the time GLEB took over. The other worker-director had also resigned from his union, after many years of membership, over a dispute about dues.

Neither was formally elected; as one of them said: 'They just went round, had a little chinwag among themselves. They thought I'd be the obvious person to represent them and I was prepared to accept it.' He did not think formal elections were necessary: 'I just think if they wasn't satisfied with what I was doing, then we'd have a little chat around and they'd nominate someone else.' In one case, the initiative for making a change appears to have come from management, who were pleased that more outspoken people had come forward and felt that this was an indication that the institution of worker-directors was felt by the workforce to be of some value.

One of the worker-directors certainly saw it this way: 'I like to know what's going on in the company. That's one of the reasons I've taken the job on. Also I like to see that the workforce is well represented. Anything that I get to hear about, I translate back to my workmates. Also if they've got any suggestions or anything which they'd like to put before the board, they tell me, I take notes of it and when there is a board meeting I can put those suggestions forward, and then come back to them on the differ-ent replies that I get.' Asked whether he felt he had some control over what went on at board meeting, he said, 'Let's put it this way: all of them up there on the board of directors, obviously, are quite familiar with all the paper work and that sort of thing. I did get some paper work in advance which I was able to go through. The Chairman pointed out different things to me ... and sort of kept me on the right track.' No formal training has been provided in management techniques: this worker-director felt that he had learnt a lot through asking questions but that if training was provided, it would be better to send someone younger than himself.

He also feels that his job is in fact a bit like being a union shop steward: 'If anything comes up that people think would be a good idea then obviously I can go straight into [the managing director] and see him. The same as what a shop steward would.' He did not think from his point of view that having a union in would give him any extra negotiating power; he felt that his position as a worker-director gave him 'about the same' negotiating powers as he would have as a shop steward. 'Unions are quite good in a lot of respects, but not in others ... no-one's approached me to join the union so I haven't ... if they'd stated I had to join the union, then obviously I'd join because I like it here.'

In addition to the monthly board meetings, there have been a number of general meetings, at which the whole workforce is present. These meetings have been led by the marketing consultant, who saw his task as getting it across to the workforce that the simple situation that they had had in the past, of merely carrying out orders from the parent company, no longer existed; that they had to compete in the open market, change their attitudes, and begin to make their own planning decisions. This, he said, made it harder for them, not better. Therefore: 'All the staff, including all the workers, were involved' in drawing up a business plan and subsequently in assessing progress in its implementation. As he puts it: 'they are at liberty to say we don't agree; but at the end they are a party to it. There are bound to be disagreements; there is no perfect way to run a business; one option is to close it down.' They don't have votes, but so far apparently there have been no serious dissensions: 'We talked everybody through it'. Information is displayed on large sheets on a board.

As one of the worker-directors explained, 'They just call a meeting and invite the directors and the workforce and we can attend or not ... then you're allowed to ask anything you want to ask, on any subject, whether it be on the workforce or the planning or whatever they want. It's not just confined to one person. They don't have to ask me to bring it up at the board, but you always get some people who are not prepared to talk.'

The minutes of the board meetings are generally available. One former worker-director said he did not put them up on notice boards, 'he had not been told to'; his successor said that he took them home to read, read them in tea breaks, and showed them to anybody who wanted to see them. One former worker-director said he didn't really report back; people who were interested asked. His successor confirmed this and said that after his first board meeting, 'this morning, when I came in, they said, what went on, and I told them exactly what went on, and they know as much as I do, to be quite honest.' He felt that a more formal system was unnecessary: 'Well, we all sit together sometimes. I don't have to say we're going to hold a meeting or anything.' This informal system does, however, leave out some people; for example an administrative assistant said that she 'would like to know more about what is going on'. She could not go to the general meeting because she was looking after the telephone and 'we're not issued with reports'.

The change in the workers' situation at Engco has made it necessary for them to work harder than they did under their previous ownership. A former worker-director said: 'I go home at night tired. We got lazy perhaps. The foreman comes round behind us (the same foreman as before); not with a whip.' A foreman said he had the feeling they were being 'used'; they did work for the same company which paid the same prices but often sent jobs back for them to be redone — thus deriving the benefits commonly associated with sub-contracting. Most people of course recognise that a change is necessary if they are to save their jobs. Management point out that on one occasion they volunteered to work at night in order to carry on producing while major refurbishment took place.

There is clearly also a considerable increase in flexibility; as one of the worker-directors put it: 'I haven't got sufficient work in to keep me going all day, so obviously I do something else'. And he added: 'It's not like a union firm where it's one man, one job. We all muck in and if someone knows a bit more than somebody else we help them and in return they can help us.'

Another change has been on the question of wages. One shop floor worker, agreeing that they now had more opportunity than before to have their say, added: 'But we haven't had much joy out of it'. He was referring to a big struggle they had had to get any wage rise at all; in the end they had achieved only one five per cent rise in the year-and-three-quarters since the new company was set up. Some of the workers expressed anger over this. Management said that the question of wage improvement would soon be considered; without accepting that all wages should be the same, there was nevertheless open discussion about what would be a more 'equitable' salary structure.

In general, it appears that workers in Engco not only have much greater access to information and to the process of making decisions, but also feel that they have a greater stake in it than they would in an ordinary company. Agreeing that this was so, one worker-director was clear that, for example, there was never any pressure for overtime to be worked: 'I don't think that comes into it. No, everybody, as I say, is quite willing to help out wherever they can'. Asked whether this was because they feel they have a stake in the company, he replied: 'Of course. If you're not going to get anything out of it obviously you work in a different environment altogether ... [In his former firm] we never had no say. But here it is different. I mean, nobody pressures you to do anything or anything like that ... As I say, I like it here.'

At the same time GLEB set up another company, Elco, based on another division on the same engineering site, with roughly the same ownership structure. There are two worker-directors on the board. The company is larger: when GLEB set it up, it took over a workforce of sixty people. The workers are mostly women and they do assembly work. Nearly all of them are union members, with separate unions for the shop floor and for staff and supervisory work. But there is no strong tradition of union organisation and militancy. The decisive difference between Engco and Elco seems to have been that, in Elco, there were considerable management problems. Unlike in Engco, a new managing director was recruited from outside the original work-force. In addition Elco failed to meet its financial targets. GLEB therefore decided that, if the company was to survive, the managing director would have to be replaced and, moreover, that redundancies had to be made. The story of redundancies, in particular, shows that in a situation of crisis, worker-directors have no effective power.

When the managing director was appointed, the unions were represented on the interviewing committee. It was felt in GLEB that this was 'quite a good test: future managers when they arrived with no warning were told that stewards were part of the interviewing committee'. The workers themselves, however, did not feel that they had had much say in the appointment. The appointment, as is frequently the case, had to be made in a hurry; it was made through an agency, and was not advertised. Not a great deal of effort was made at the interview to find out whether the person appointed was genuinely willing to make enterprise planning work. It was felt that it was hard enough to find managers who have the necessary experience and specific knowledge of the industry without imposing additional hurdles.

As it happened, the workers had no problems with the managing-director 'personality-wise'. He was willing to consult with the workforce, although 'sometimes he needed a little bit of pushing'. In GLEB it was said that 'to a degree he understood the things we were expecting him to say and he said them, and I think it's fair to say that actually in his first two or three months he tried to follow them through'. In order to improve the workers' access to information, new structures were set up. In addition to the worker-directors on the board, there was a negotiating committee, consisting of the two stewards from each union. This handled traditional union bargaining matters and initially was meant to meet the managing director once a week. The same committee, but in a different forum, was to discuss the wider issues of the business.

This system worked reasonably well although, as one GLEB executive put it, 'In the absence of somebody [from GLEB] kicking and saying look you've got to take them seriously, as soon as another priority emerged [the managing director] didn't see the maintenance of that kind of system as a real priority'. The stewards apparently failed to put effective pressure on the managing director to hold meetings. The matter was raised at the board by the worker-directors, with some effect at first. They also went in to see the managing director and complained about lack of information and the absence of a chance to talk about the business. In particular they wanted to talk about what type of equipment was being ordered. The managing director in turn complained that the worker-directors were not giving him enough support. He argued that since the workforce owned a share of the company, their representatives had a responsibility to police absenteeism and to exercise some sort of control; which in fact the worker-directors attempted to do.

But matters became much worse when commercial pressures started to bite. In this crisis, the major decisions were made in GLEB. They were then presented in a sanitised version to the board of directors. GLEB decided that before further funds could go into the company, the managing director would have to be sacked (and temporarily replaced by a GLEB executive). They further decided that 'costs must be reduced', which meant redundancies.

GLEB executives decided, after overruling some internal dissension, that the workforce, including the worker-directors, must not be told that redundancies were imminent although they found out by accident. The trade union officials were told one week before the official announcement of the redundancies. The view of the GLEB executives was that, if news of the redundancies got out, there was the risk that the workers would go on strike, and in that case GLEB's board would refuse to make an investment and the jobs would be lost. But, as the workers argued, they had worked on the site for many years, had decided not to move and were committed to 'making a go of it'; as one of them put it: 'I think some people, maybe some of the managerial side, don't realise how much loyalty there is on the shop floor. It's a shame really but they don't.'

There is of course, as the workers recognised, 'no nice way' of making redundancies. When the decision to make redundancies was finally presented to Elco's board of directors there was general agreement that something desperate had to be done to salvage the company. GLEB obtained the reluctant agreement of the union officials on a procedure for making redundancies. Redundancies were to be based on the areas of production that were and were not needed and profitable. The support of the worker-directors was enlisted in finding volunteers for redundancy. Their list did not match up to the needs. Therefore the new managing-director from GLEB asked individual department managers, on the basis of 'their knowledge of the people who worked underneath them' and of the survival strategy that was being pursued and the type of work needed, to draw up a list of the people in their department whom they thought should be made redundant. The list was scrutinised by the managing director and some people were taken off it, after further discussions with the managers.

But there appears to have been no procedure to ask the work-force what they thought about the chosen list. As one of the workers commented about the process of choosing: 'A lot of people wanted to know what gave them the right to make these decisions anyway, because we're all supposed to be one, we're all supposed to be working for ourselves.' Their view was that the choices should have been made, not solely by the unions, 'you can't put it on the workforce really, but I think the unions, the shop stewards, and the worker-directors should sit in on it ... then you can have the argument ... to see why they should go and why they shouldn't, and then you get a clear view of why they're going, why they're being made redundant.'

There was apparently also a failure to communicate the reasons even to the individuals concerned when the redundancies were formally announced: 'We was all outside and little slips of paper were given to the charge hand and he was told to send those people out here, so you was waiting for someone to come and say to you, can you go outside, and they was all told together. Now I think they deserved the right to be spoken to on their own, and be given a reason, not like a cattle market, you all go outside and you're told I'm sorry but you're being made redundant, you can go now if you wish, which is what they were told ... they should have been given letters or something like that ... or taken into the office and given a letter, so that they could ask for a reason why they were being made redundant ... because they came straight back out and put their coats on and left — this is the truth ... people were crying ...'

Both the worker-directors were made redundant. GLEB executives discussed, and rejected, the possibility of 'discrimination' in their favour. The new worker-directors felt, however, that there had been victimisation. In most cases they accepted that the decision was based on the commercial viability of particular areas of work They also accept that this was the case for one of the worker directors; his work was in an area that was clearly unviable. But the other worker-director, they felt, had been victimised: 'She was somebody who was very outspoken ... if somebody had a grievance she would go straight in and say I think you're being unfair ... once she got her teeth in it, she would not let it drop until she got an answer. And really I suppose she was a thorn in their side.' GLEB executives also said that the case for the loss of her job was less clear cut than in the case of the other worker-director. But they said that they did not have the view that she was excessively outspoken and that, on the contrary, they felt her contributions at board meetings were very useful. However, the workers were left with the firm impression that, in some cases, it was a case of 'the face not fitting'.

The redundancies have left a serious legacy from the point of view of the goals of enterprise planning. The new worker-directors (both of whom are women) feel that they have learnt a lesson: 'This is why we would never be as outspoken as (the previous worker-director) ... we've learned from her in that way'. Moreover, others hesitate to speak out at meetings. This is not because they are not interested in becoming involved, or just want to clock in and clock out, nor even because of simple nervousness about speaking in front of others; it is because they are afraid of being victimised: 'They'll moan, but when it comes to saying it outside, at the meetings, they'll let somebody else do it ... we've all felt it ... you would feel that if you did say what you'd like to say, you're then classed as a rebel — as much as you're not, as much as you're really doing things to help the company ...'

This points to a more general problem of control. The workers say that 'when we came into here, they had a big meeting upstairs, we all took the understanding that management and workforce were all one, we all worked together'. The workforce owns twenty per cent of Elco, and GLEB effectively has majority ownership. Both the new GLEB-appointed managing director and the staff at GLEB are adamant that they would not contemplate victimisation of workers for trade union activities, race or any other reason. And yet the workers feel insecure. This lack of control applies both to the question of redundancies and to the question of management appointment. Hiring and firing remains the prerogative of management: the workers have neither the power to decide who shall retain their jobs, nor the power to appoint or to sack management (as they would, legally, supposing they were a co-operative).

The workers feel confident in the goodwill of the current managing director from GLEB, and free to go and talk to him about problems. But they are aware that other managers 'do not like us going into him; we've opened our mouths you see and he's been up in arms about it ... not that he sides with anybody, he just likes the truth and he likes to be fair'. But his appointment is temporary; they do not know what their situation will be when he goes: 'This is what we are worrying about.' They would like him to stay; if not, they hope that they will have some say over who is appointed to replace him. They are doubtful about the prospects of gradually gaining more control: 'It would be nice, but I doubt it.'

There is clearly, perhaps stimulated in part by GLEB involvement, a strong desire on the part of the workforce to be kept informed. The present worker-directors accept the need not to report some things that are said at the board meetings in order not to damage the survival prospects of the company: 'it's mainly that if, in a particular month that we're not doing so well, or maybe we've not got orders we should have, that it can get out to other companies ... and it don't do us any good. Once you've explained that to people, then they're fairly understanding about it.' They do not have formal general meetings to report back to the workforce about what has happened at board meetings, although they have had them in the past, and they are again considering the idea; the problem is partly pressure of work and shortage of time; meetings outside working time would not be practical because most of the workers are women and have to get back to their families.

On the other hand a major failing so far under GLEB ownership is that the worker-directors feel that most of the information they get comes from 'upstairs', from the board meetings; they are not kept well enough informed about day-to-day decisions that are made 'downstairs' by management. The new managing director has instituted weekly meetings with the management team in order to obtain better information about what is going on on the shop floor. But the workers are not represented on them, either by their stewards or by the worker-directors. It did seem as though the new managing-director would be 'very happy to oblige' if they asked to attend the weekly management meetings, and had also said they could go in any time they wanted to, if there was any problem. But meanwhile they had not been invited to attend and 'you're not even aware that (the meetings) are taking place at the time ... if you're busy working you don't even notice these things ... unless you're right on top of the office ... Anything that goes on from down here, we're not told anything down here, although we're worker-directors ...'

Even from a management point of view, this clearly makes little sense. As the workers say: 'There have been a few things lately that have come out of the weekly meetings, which some people don't feel very happy about and it's the best thing really that, with the girls on the floor, if you explain to them before you do what you're going to do — it makes them happier, but if you do it and don't inform them, it makes them angry.' Such failure to inform appears not to be typical of GLEB-funded enterprises. It is also clearly an opportunity missed: it gives the lie to those who claim that workers are not interested in running their own workplace.

The present worker-directors at Elco do not feel that their role on the board presents them with a conflict of loyalties between the workers they represent and management. Both are union members, as are all except two or three of the workforce; one is a shop steward, the other is not. Initially the senior shop stewards were also worker-directors. But the current worker-directors felt that it was useful having different people performing different functions. The formal union negotiating structure continues to exist, although the union committee does not meet regularly. The two worker-directors were elected without opposition, at a general meeting of the workforce. They feel that it's important to go into the board of directors with an open mind, rather than with the idea of, for example, defending one person: 'Otherwise you're not really going to get anywhere if you go in there and regardless of what they tell you, you've got it in your head that downstairs aren't going to agree with that'. On the other hand the worker directors had some feeling that they were just there to make up the numbers; much of the discussion they did not understand. Although the current managing director explains some of the issues, the worker-directors have not had, as they have in some other GLEB-financed firms, any formal training; they expressed interest in the idea of, for example, a weekend school.

They have had one wage rise since the company was set up nearly two years ago: 'we know how the land lies'. Wages are lower than they are in the other factory of the previous owners of the site, to which some of the workers have moved, and a few still are moving. Most of those who decided not to move did so in order to avoid the travel; although a mini-bus is provided, they would have difficulty in getting back if, say, a child was sick, and would have a good deal of extra travelling time. Many have stayed out of loyalty to one another, a commitment to prove that they could make a go of it. They are also working harder. The worker-directors say that they have not had pressure put on to them to ensure that people work harder or to enforce discipline, although the board meetings make it clear to them that a certain output has to be reached. Nevertheless people have been working 'twice as hard'; they are producing more than they were before the redundancies; but they get no extra money for it.

There is however resentment at the fact that management are paid considerably more than the shop floor workers. As some of the workers said: 'I feel that when it's a new company and ...

you're supposed to be all one ... I know if you've got a managerial position you warrant a good wage ... but you can't earn that sort of money until the company takes off ... they have two or three times more (than us) when we haven't got the money, when you're being told some months, look you know, you've got to crack the whip harder. We could have kept asking for more money, but we wouldn't have got it.' Management, they felt, were being paid big company wages, whereas they were not. The new managing director felt that this was indeed one of the problems: when the new company was set up, the people were already in place and doing the same work and they 'were used to big company benefits, big company salaries'. In GLEB however the problem was raised of how you could attract good managers without offering them the sort of wages they were used to; for example: 'Setting up a co-op doesn't solve your problem about attracting somebody with experiences you're looking for and then being able to reward them in a way that the market dictates that you've got to if they don't have some wider commitment to co-ops.'

The workers also described day to day inequalities between managerial staff and shop floor workers: managerial staff don't have to clock in, shop floor workers do. Shop floor workers have to pay for their coffee, managerial staff get theirs free. As one worker commented: 'Little things like that gradually start worming away; they niggle you ... mind you I think people won't put up with it if things go too far'.

The experience of Elco demonstrates that, in spite of GLEB's majority ownership of the company, in spite of the formal ownership share of the workforce and their representation on the board of directors, the actual control of the workforce over major decisions that affect their lives is small. It is less than would be the case in a firm with strong union organisation. Nevertheless the feeling is strong among the workforce that they are entitled to more control, to more information, to more involvement in decisions, and to more equality with management. This is perhaps one measure of GLEB's achievement and a basis for progress in the future.

Although the institution of worker-directors gives workers no independent strength, some strongly organised workers in other GLEB enterprises have felt that having a worker on the board would be useful to them, mainly as an additional means of acquiring information about management decisions. As the convenor in one of GLEB's larger and better unionised companies, Compart (described in more detail in the section on extending collective bargaining), explained: 'In that way you get much more involved in the company's situation. Once you're on the board any future plans being discussed or any cash flow problem or any other matters being discussed, you are regularly involved and you get much more idea. That's why we would like to have a worker-director.'

In several cases the idea that there should be worker-directors came from GLEB and was, initially at least, opposed both by trade union officials and by the workforce. As a trade union official working with another fully-unionised engineering company put it: 'The idea was there before GLEB signed on the dotted line; it was the implementation that took some time because of a reluctance of the shop floor itself to put forward the appropriate sparring partners ... There was the entrenched resentment of selling your soul to the employer. That was primarily the objection on the shop floor: "I do not want to be one of them" ... We had another meeting and spelt out that our ambition was to be one of them, but to be one of them in the name of the people we represented. They they said Tom [the shop steward] should go on. Well we had tried to keep him away from that arena in case there was a time when he would actually come into conflict with the directors. But it was quite clearly the unanimous decision of the shop floor that they trust him and he's the best man to look after us in that board room ... he made it quite clear to the two directors what his role would be, workers' representative, and he'd go back and report to them diligently. [The board] tried to impose on him the vow of confidentiality, but he saw himself as workers' representative going back to the workers, always provided of course that the report of the business that was discussed wouldn't in any way undermine the welfare of the workers. We accepted that, but in the main we felt we were absolutely entitled to report to the workforce and to push the workforce interests on that board, if necessary above the financial interests.'

In the case of another company, an AUEW official explained: 'The stewards were coming to us and saying let's have a look at this, and as a union, we weren't prepared to have a seat on the board, we didn't want to know. It was the policy of our union. Since then the union has said that, although in a normal private company we wouldn't want a seat on the board, there's similar set-ups [to this GLEB-owned company] in Merseyside where we've got seats on the board, so our union said yes, if it's going, take it. So then we put in for it.'

Thus it is clear that, in the view of many trade unionists, and also in the experience of GLEB, the institution of worker-directors can be an adjunct, or supplement, to strong collective organisation among the workforce. It can also be of some use in some companies which are basically owned and managed by GLEB employees or appointees and where owners and managers are sympathetic to the idea of enterprise planning. It can, in normal times, increase workers' access to information. But it does not guarantee that major decisions will not be taken in other places. And worker-directors, as individuals on boards whose management is hostile and where there is little or no trade union organisation, have no power whatsoever.

Co-operatives

In co-operatives formal ownership and control is vested, not in a board of directors on which individual workers may sit, but in the workforce as a whole. Each member holds one vote in general meetings of the workforce, which have the ultimate right, for example, to hire and fire their members, including managers. Around a quarter of the larger firms funded by GLEB are or are in the process of becoming co-operatives or have some aspects of co-operative ownership. GLEB has also funded numerous small co-operatives, many of them in the black communities; co-operatives account for nearly half of all GLEB investments, although for only a quarter of the jobs and a tenth of the money invested. Some members of GLEB's co-operative unit believe that this is the direction in which enterprise planning must go: 'Enterprise planning is a twenty-year route to a co-op'.

The initial emphasis in GLEB was on funding large co-operatives. There are problems associated with small co-operatives, in addition to their limited impact on jobs. Many of the small co-ops in London have grown from the 'alternative culture' of the 1970s; their links with the trade unions and the labour movement were often slight. Trade unions, on their side, have tended to see co-ops as breeding grounds for self-exploitation and to fear that they could weaken and fragment working people rather than strengthening them, although there are signs that this attitude is changing; the TGWU, for example, has recently set up two branches for members in co-ops in East and North London.

GLEB has attempted to overcome some of the problems of small co-ops in a variety of ways. It has provided them with funds for initial investment which are intended to help them not to rely on 'sweat equity investment' — that is an investment only of their very hard labour for low wages (wages are nevertheless lower in the small co-ops funded by GLEB than they are in the rest of GLEB's portfolio). It has encouraged trade union membership in the co-ops it funds and has often been successful in this.

GLEB has also helped to set up organisations to co-ordinate the activities of small co-ops in the hope that this will increase their collective weight in the market. It set up the London Co-operative Enterprise Board (LCEB) to provide funds of up to £25,000 and to co-ordinate the training, educational and marketing requirements of London's co-ops; the LCEB is controlled by representatives from retail co-operative societies, Co-operative Development Agencies (CDAs), the South-East Region of the TUC, the London Industrial Common Ownership Movement (ICOM), and individual co-operatives. It has also funded CDAs, training schemes and a Co-op Marketing Resource Centre. It has promoted federations or networks of sector-based co-ops, including, for example, the Co-op Printing Federation. It has helped to organise shared or integrated premises for co-ops. Finally, it has urged co-ops to expand and has provided assistance for them to do so.

GLEB has been involved in a second type of co-operative which is very different, and which has a longer history of support from the labour movement. This is the conversion of larger companies to co-operative ownership, particularly in cases of threatened closures, or 'phoenix co-ops' where they rise with new life out of the ashes of the old company. When the previous owners and/or managers have been unwilling to work with GLEB, this possibility has arisen in a number of cases though it has not always been realised.

GLEB has been involved in the successful conversion to co-operative ownership of Signwriters, the medium-sized sign-making company discussed earlier. After negotiations with the previous owner had broken down and the company was put into receivership, Signwriters was revived on the basis of negotiations between GLEB and its workforce with the explicit intention that it should become a co-op. A big transformation has taken place, from a conventional, badly managed and non-unionised private company, to a co-operative with full union membership and fully functioning democratic structures. The workers' commitment and self-confidence have greatly increased.

This cannot happen instantly, or as an automatic result of changes in ownership; both workers and managers have worked hard to achieve it. The conversion to co-operative ownership has taken place in stages during which the workers' interest in and knowledge of the financial state of their company gradually increased. Their involvement has led to considerable changes in working practices and attitudes; difficult questions such as the determination of wages have been raises at general meetings; and the questions of the role of the trade union and of management have arisen in ways that are complicated, and that have similarities with the questions raised in more conventional GLEB-owned companies (see next section).

Signwriters has a workforce of around 25 people which is expanding. The workers are mostly skilled sign-makers; there is one woman on the shop floor and several workers of Asian and Caribbean origin. The trade union committee was fully involved in the discussions on who should and should not be taken on in the company. Most of the former management was not re-engaged; the former owner carried on as a sales consultant, on comission, but without a salary. In addition, as one of the workers put it: 'Before, the people who weren't so sure [about the co-op idea] went their own way; it was a natural weeding out process'. He added that: 'None of us were short of a job. Almost without exception we were offered jobs elsewhere. Two or three firms went through the papers; they were like gannets; they wanted to get the people. So very few of us came back just because it was the only employment we could see.' They came, he said, basically because they liked the idea of working as a co-operative.

Signwriters became a co-operative in the full legal sense in February 1987. But since it was set up (including the period during which I talked to the workers and managers concerned) it had an orthodox management structure with the addition of a general meeting of all the workforce which in practice, though not in any legal sense, had extensive powers. Two general managers were appointed from outside by GLEB, in consultation with the workforce. One is in charge of finance and marketing, setting up new systems of financial control; as he put it: 'I have no experience of a co-operative at all; my experience is with making businesses work'. The other manager is an engineer by trade and is mainly in charge of the production side; he also has long experience and commitment in the co-operative movement and he is one of the strongest forces in the conversion to a co-operative. There is a board of directors which consists of the two general managers, two directors from GLEB and the production manager from one of the two floors, who had been closely involved in the union committee's negotiations with GLEB while the company was in receivership.

In addition there is a management committee, whose minutes are available to the workforce. At first, the union shop steward sat by invitation on the management committee. He resigned, however, on the grounds that his two roles were in conflict in particular because he found himself discussing the case of a particular individual who was regularly late for work; the individual then asked him as shop steward to take up his case, but he had already made up his mind on the basis of the discussions they had had on the management committee. He also felt he was becoming inhibited in taking part in discussions at the general meeting.

General meetings of the whole workforce take place once a month. There is an air of compulsion, as one participant put it, about attendance, and in fact attendance is almost 100 per cent. Although there tend to be a few individuals who regularly speak out there has been a gradual increase in participation. They began to rotate the chair; the shop steward was the first to replace the general managers in chairing a meeting; others are scheduled to do so. Some decisions, from the organisation of work to wage increases, are taken by vote. The agenda, the accounts, financial projections, and so on are written up on sheets, displayed and explained by the manager who deals with financial matters.

One of the main functions of the general meeting is in fact to transmit information, in both directions. Under the previous ownership and management there had been little participation by the workforce. As one of them put it: 'we had always suffered because there was no mechanism for people's ideas to be fed back, and so the jobs were not done in the most efficient way; there was no thinking through, the same mistakes were made over and over again, there was no way to avoid it, however small an idea we had. In a co-op there's a way to avoid that situation. It helps to do the work efficiently — which is the most important thing.'

The question of knowledge is also crucial as a source of power for the workforce. As both shop steward and other workers categorically stated, information is freely available, and more is available for the asking. The workforce have been on weekend training courses with their managers and also on courses organised by ICOM (Industrial Common Ownership Movement), mainly to learn financial and accounting techniques. The workers vary of course in how much they are interested. But it is clear that both the shop steward and a number of the other shop floor workers are very interested indeed in expanding their knowledge of the operations of the firm, and that they are aware that this will give them much greater ability to control the decisions taken at general meetings and elsewhere. They are also working hard to engage the interest and commitment of the workforce as a whole. As one of them said: 'It is not an easy process ... old attitudes die hard.' At one general meeting the workers discussed how to organise meetings in such a way that proper discussion of the firm's long-term objectives took place; part of the discussion was about the extent to which all workers should be forced to take part in such discussions. During the course of this discussion, they raised a lot of points about the direction the firm should take, what type of work should be undertaken, the role of sales personnel and whether they wanted a commitment to long hours of work in order to build the firm up, or whether they would prefer a 35 hour week and perhaps less money.

Greater knowledge of their financial situation is expected, by some at least of the managers and workers, not only to give workers more power, but also to create a greater commitment to work. The financial manager remains open-minded on whether this happens in practice. The other manager said that productivity had increased dramatically, though 'some people work exactly as before'. There was 'no room for coercion' by management; the way in which the situation was most likely to change was through pressure from fellow-workers. At one general meeting the workers discussed the best methods of conveying criticisms; people were said to be hesitant to do so openly at general meetings or face-to-face; the meeting voted to set up a group to investigate new procedures by a fairly narrow margin of eight to five.

There was also discussion on flexibility, and some mutual recrimination about whether or not particular skilled workers were willing to spend their days 'drilling holes' when jobs appropriate to their skills were not available. One worker said: 'When we started back we all took on roles which were too defined; we should all muck in.' To which another worker protested: 'Are you getting at me? I'm not willing to drill holes every day of the week; I'd leave if so.' But others protested vehemently that they would do what was needed: 'I'm willing to do anything. It depends what the market wants. I'll drill 500 holes if I have to'. A manager commented: 'There is no doubt that people are flexible, they'll turn their hands to anything. [The previous owner] must be chewing his hands.' The workers then discussed whether, on the basis of an assessment of what type of work was most profitable, the sales people could be instructed to go out and get it, rather than passively receiving orders.

A central and of course contentious issue was and is the issue of wages. When GLEB took over, the basic wage was increased and everyone was put on salary, but overtime was abolished; it has recently been re-started, but on a small scale; overtime is now paid but not at premium rates. The result is that the workers are earning less than before. Most of them are aware that the previous system of overtime payments was one of the major factors in putting the company into receivership. According to the shop steward: 'It was a learning process; we realised we couldn't take on people who did that and survive ... Jobs were not priced including overtime ... but work was strung out so as to get overtime.'

Most of the workers now accept and even appreciate the system of working fewer hours for less pay. Some of them were nevertheless impatient over basic wages. One general meeting demanded, and got, an early date for discussing a rise. Workers complained that the decision had 'been put off and put off', that they could start looking for another job, 'they were not being greedy', the company was within budget. The managing director wanted the decision made when the next year's budget was presented. Finally, the budget was produced and circulated, and a proposal for a five per cent 'cost of living' increase was narrowly accepted by the meeting with two members of the management committee voting against it. One worker complained that: 'The five per cent was presented as a rise but it was actually a cut on living standards.' On the other hand, it was said by management to be 'difficult to change people's mentalities; it's not a question of us as managers "offering" five per cent, we are paying ourselves.' One worker proposed that the 'rise' should be five per cent of the total salary bill but should be given as a flat increase to everybody; this was accepted. The differentials in this company are not wide and are expected to be reduced.

The role of the trade union is of course different from what it would be in a company which is not owned by its workforce. Thus the union has not played any role in wage negotiations. It is hard to see how it could do so in this type of company, given that the distinction between managers and workers is not clear-cut. Although wage proposals are put forward as part of the budget drawn up by management, they and the budget are discussed and can be voted on at the general meetings in which of course the workforce outnumber managers. Other co-ops have had similar experiences; thus for example in Printworld, another medium-sized GLEB-funded co-op (see below, p. 170), the workers said that: 'The kind of things that would be discussed in a trade union shop are discussed in our collective meetings'.

The main role which trade unions do have, in Signwriters and in other co-ops, is in providing alternative procedures to which individual workers can have resource if they do not feel that they are being properly treated by the rest of the workforce, in general meetings for example. Thus, as one of the managers at Signwriters said: 'I fully believe that there should be a trade union; it's easy for forms of victimisation to take place without powers to redress them, if there is no trade union'. The Signwriters workers have grievance and discipline procedures in their job contracts which were drawn up with the help of the Lambeth CDA and a GLEB executive and discussed and ratified at a general meeting; there is a Health and Safety Committee; there is currently no union negotiating committee.

The shop steward at Signwriters has divided responsibilities in ways which are, however, not exclusive to co-operatives (and will be further discussed in the following section). One of the managers actively warned him that if he accepted the invitation onto the management committee, this 'might be seen as a ploy to make him co-operate with management'; as has been said, he decided to resign from this committee because of the ambivalence of his role in a disciplinary case. On the other hand, he himself subsequently proposed at a general meeting that he should be a channel for disciplinary complaints *against* workers and was then reminded that this might conflict with his role in defending individuals. He is one of the workers most actively engaged in attempting to secure the full commitment of the workforce to making a go of the business, and this can mean urging greater effort and the taking of more responsibility.

But in Signwriters the trade union is of course established in a company in which the union did not previously exist at all. Although one or two people said that union membership is little more than a formality, the union is becoming more securely established and is extending its role. Union matters are on the agenda of general meetings.

Four or five workers from Signwriters now attend their local TGWU branch meetings, they produce a local union newsletter, they arrange social evenings with other firms. They have recently elected a second shop steward. There is no doubt that a major part of the change that is taking place in Signwriters is the building of trade union membership and organisation.

One of the most difficult questions that arises, in this as in other co-ops, is the question of specialised management, and of the relationship of management to the workforce. Part of the reason why the union has no very active negotiating role in Signwriters is of course that the workforce not only have a good relationship with their managers, but also feel themselves to be in a relationship of considerable power towards them. This appears most concretely in the legal right of the general meeting to hire and fire managers as well as others, subject to appeal to ACAS, the Arbitration, Conciliation and Advisory Service.

Before it became a co-op one worker considered going along to GLEB and demanding that they should be relieved of the burden of paying the salary of their financial manager, in part because he himself had 'O' Level Maths and had found a mistake in the manager's figures. Another worker said they did not yet know enough to replace this manager; he himself was planning to go to evening classes in accountancy and in due course would like to take on some of the budgetting and accountancy jobs. Since he came from the shop floor, he did not consider that the same problems of separation from the workforce would arise as they would with a professional manager appointed from outside. The workers also argued that this manager was too meticulous; he had drawn up a budget and an accountancy system which was good enough for ICI, and not needed for a company of this size. In GLEB, on the other hand, it was felt that his skills were still definitely needed. They were, however, dispensed with shortly before Signwriters became a co-operative.

This question of specialised management frequently arises in co-ops. For example in Free Wheeler, a company in the music trade, in which GLEB staff have been involved in the reorganisation of the ownership and management structures, the decision was taken that the workforce should have a workers' trust which would own 75 per cent of the company. The workers nominate directors from outside, not, as in co-operatives, elect them internally, but they will have the power to remove them. GLEB staff hope that this will 'remove some of the strains from direct democracy. Free Wheeler has to operate flexibility in a rapidly changing market; it's easier to make the consequent difficult decisions from outside.'

Even a co-op cannot do away with the power financial knowledge gives to managers. This issue has arisen, for example, in Printworld, a successful co-op employing some twenty people in the printing trade; GLEB made it a loan with the prospect of more than doubling its membership through expansion. In theory all members of the co-op make management decisions at collective meetings. In practice people working in administration tend to assume managerial roles on a day to day basis, although there is no formal worker-management structure.

The workers say that they 'understand about cash projections and so on. And we're given financial reports at collective meetings which we can have explained to us if we don't understand them.' At the same time it is acknowledged, at least by one of the two people in administration, that there is an inevitable degree of power invested in the people responsible for financial administration, simply by virtue of the fact that they understand more than the others: 'Compared with when I worked [on the shop floor] I now have much more knowledge of what's going on overall, and therefore more power. But compared with conventional business organisation the use of that power depends on the confidence other people have in me.' He points out that there cannot be watertight checks on how such power is used, but that in a co-op a great deal depends on trust between members.

In Printworld there is uncertainty about what constitutes 'management' and whether certain people can be identified as 'managers'. 'I see you as a manager', one person said, and another agreed; while the worker thus designated disagreed. The uncertainty lies partly in defining to what extent specific decisions not actually delegated by the collective meeting are in fact 'management' decisions, rather than simply day-to-day routine administrative decisions, as those in administration tend to see them.

The workers in Printworld say that 'they are still learning' about management. The two people currently doing administration work have been on a one-week residential course organised by ICOM. GLEB, as a condition of its loan, required an upgrading of management skills through bringing in a management consultant for two weeks. This was justified by GLEB on the grounds that the co-operative was moving into a phase of expansion; but, as a co-op member said: 'We're in a difficult period, because the skills we're being told are appropriate are applicable to bigger companies, but we're just coming into that category'. Thus the tensions remain, and are in fact reinforced by the intervention of GLEB, between the requirements of commercial survival, which appear to demand an intensification in the division of labour, and the aspirations towards democracy and real control by the workforce over 'management' decisions, which imply an attempt to break down the division of labour, and perhaps more deliberate moves towards a sharing of manual and/or routine and intellectual tasks.

These are clearly questions which cannot easily be resolved, either within the capitalist market or in a planned system of organising production and determining rewards. There are gains in efficiency to be derived from certain forms of the division of labour under any system; these have to be set against the objectives of more democracy and more equality. Co-operatives, however democratic and equal their internal organisation, will be subject to external constraints and they cannot be a complete solution to the organisation of production and distribution. Nevertheless they do provide examples of advanced forms of workplace democracy and an illustration of the problems and possibilities involved in building workers' control. Their members are usually committed to a co-operative way of working and feel that their greater ability to control the choice and use of technology, their use of free time, and their working environment in general, improves the quality of their jobs and may even justify some loss of material gains.

Extension of collective bargaining

Traditionally, as has been said, trade unions have not supported co-operatives and have also been wary of any incorporation of workers into management. They have seen an extension of collective bargaining as the means for workers to extend their control over management decisions, by building on their own independent strength. As the Vickers Workers' Report put it: 'The extension of collective bargaining does not threaten the independence of workers' organisations in the way that involvement in participation schemes can'. In practice the distinction is a hard one to maintain: once workers and their unions have more control over management decisions, and especially if they have a share of ownership or a commitment to the survival of their particular company, they are bound to change their attitudes towards its profitability and their contribution to it.

The extension of collective bargaining can barely be said to have taken place in GLEB-funded enterprises, at least in the sense intended by some of GLEB's founders. Workers have not devised alternative production plans and bargained with management for their acceptance, in the same way that some shop stewards attempted to do in the 1970s. GLEB has however been involved in companies in which the trade unions have not only backed the idea of greater involvement of the workforce in management decisions but have also, if not initiated, at least controlled the process. In that sense it can perhaps be said that an extension of collective bargaining has taken place and that, in some cases, enterprise planning has indeed been based on trade union organisation, although not in the forms originally envisaged.

Perhaps the clearest case of an extension of collective bargaining is in Compart, a GLEB-owned medium-sized engineering firm, in which there is a closed shop and well-developed trade union structures. The majority of the workforce is black and they have recently elected a black convenor for the first time. They have the active support of their district official. The first contact was made by this union official who invited a speaker from the GLC's Early Warning Unit to come to the shop stewards' quarterly meeting; that 'gave the workers confidence to look and see the danger signals, the decline, the rundown, redundancies, the nil wage increases ... the factory just gradually dying and going down a hole'. The official and the stewards jointly supported an approach to GLEB, in the face of the owners' lack of interest in the company's survival.

Nevertheless, even in this case, the progress that has been made has depended fortuitously on the managing director's own history. 'I originated from a background almost identical to [the union official's]; I could have gone into trade union, he could have gone into management ... my relationships with him and with the trade union have always been extremely open.' He was sympathetic to GLEB and keen to rescue the company from its owner's neglect. GLEB ownership actually made things easier for

him. But he says: 'I still have difficulty with my managers ...
One of these days that is something that will have to be faced, I
think; GLEB would almost have to have custom-made chief
executives ... I just happen to be a somewhat unique individual.'

When GLEB restarted the company, the union official
recounted how 'we called the workforce together ... We put to
the board that they ought to be seen as a different employer, and
we laid on a champagne lunch for the factory ... Everyone's out
with streamers and drinks, and people bring food in and Indian
samosas ... It was electric.'

The white collar workers are not unionised though attempts
were made to recruit them. The closed shop therefore operates
only for the shop floor and the trade union structure continues
much as it was before GLEB ownership. Each department on the
shop floor has a steward and deputy steward. The stewards sit
on a shop stewards' committee which meets normally every
fortnight, and more often if necessary. The convenor commented
that, under GLEB, the union's facilities and access to management had improved: 'Since the GLEB has taken over, they are
very flexible with us ... if we would like to call a meeting we get
time off, no problem ... The previous owners were a bit different
— private enterprise — but we feel very comfortable under
GLEB. We can see the chairman, who is [a GLEB executive]; it's
very easy for us to approach him, whereas in the past, the
previous owner refused even to see the union.'

There are also fortnightly meetings of a negotiating committee
which has three representatives of the shop stewards' committee
and two representatives of management. The agenda is mutually
agreed and covers the usual trade union bargaining matters such
as piece rates, problems of payments for waiting time and other
aspects of wages and conditions. There is a Health and Safety
Committee and all the usual grievance and disciplinary procedures.

In addition, since GLEB became involved, a new 'plenary
committee' has been set up. It normally meets quarterly and is
attended by the trade union official, the convenor, the chair of
the shop stewards' committee, the managing director, the manufacturing director and the GLEB chair of the board. This committee is thus clearly based on trade union structures. The white-
collar staff are not on the plenary committee because they are not
union members. As the convenor put it: 'There was some complaints to us, indirectly, from the staff side, that we get information and they don't. We told them to join the union ... but

they don't want to.' Moreover, the committee is specifically *not* intended to supplant normal union negotiating machinery. As the union official explained: 'It's not a negotiating committee: it's a consultative body ... it would take a decision that they would go away and look at it and then meet the stewards ... that's the right way; I don't want it to become the negotiating body'. The shop stewards' committee meets before plenary committee meetings and decides the matters is wants put on the agenda: these have included a request for cancer screening, the need to train replacements for the skilled workers who are near retirement, for example by training up women shop floor workers, and other more general questions about the running of the company and about GLEB.

The plenary committee was originally set up as an alternative to the workforce having a seat on the board of directors. Originally the union, offered a seat on the board by GLEB, refused on principle. Subsequently, the reason for not having a worker-director changed to one of concern about the effect it would have on their relationship with customers. Although the union official now says that 'I think it would give us a greater understanding on how decisions are made', he feels that the decision to set up a plenary committee has been 'a very successful decision ... It really is to allow the board to tell us what's happening, what they would normally discuss in a board meeting. To give an input to the board and to senior members of the board.'

The managing director says that the plenary committee partly formalises what went on before GLEB: 'I always had the attitude that I wanted to tell people what we were doing, so I used to hold sort of state of nation meetings with the shop stewards on a regular basis and tell them what was going on. I think they always looked at me a bit sceptically, so as to say, well, "Why is he doing that? I don't think I want to know". Particularly if it led up to a problem, which very often it did. But over the years they became used to it and it was just something which was fairly well accepted. Now, when GLEB took over, we then decided to do it a little more formally, and we put together a plenary meeting.' After these meetings there is supposed to be a report-back by the union official, GLEB's representative and the managing director to the workforce as a whole, although these have been difficult to organise regularly.

There seems little question that both the workforce and senior management are committed to making a success of these arrangements and of the company as a whole. For example, the convenor believed they would succeed in winning orders in competition with Japan. He made it clear that the workers are committed to meeting the necessary quality requirements: 'We are all very much concerned about the quality ... all inspectors have taken extra work without any [wage] increase'. In addition, 'since the GLEB has taken over, there's not been a single walk-out or any problem as far as the industrial relations are concerned. Everything is mutually settled in the plenary committee ... we used to have walk-outs nearly every day ... the thing is, now we are working for ourselves.'

The change of attitude was described also by the union official: 'We've always had a very good union organisation. We've had reasonably good conditions. We got six weeks holiday, under private ownership. That was through brute strength. What did come about [under GLEB] was a tremendous change in the management's attitude, and of our attitude, that everything wasn't a trial of strength. That we could really have consultation. It was very difficult. Difficult for our stewards to get into the right state of mind, and it was very difficult for foremen, traditional foremen ... To a certain extent [the managing director] and I were really pulling strings ... saying you'd better have a word in that foreman's ear because he's threatening to sack our people and that ain't in the game. And ... we don't want an overtime ban because we're trying to collect that order ...' He added that: 'Our whole role has changed. Rather than it being a confrontation situation we're now the opposite. Our convenor is the epitome of that ... he's blowing the embers like, and the last thing in the world he would want is an overtime ban or a work-to-rule ... We've had a few hiccups and said I don't want to do that or whatever, but we haven't worked in a traditional way because we've been trying to nurture this bloody sapling that's growing ... we've let the company do things that we'd never allow any other company to do, because we want to prove it can work ... if the convenor was a shop steward down the road on piecework, he'd be fighting every inch of the way with the foreman, he'd be fighting the governor; his job would be under attack, people would be trying to find ways and means of getting rid of him. What I see there in comparison with the other 140-odd factories I look after ... the factory has as good working conditions as anywhere in the area ... it's got to be saved.'

The comments on the commitment of the workforce are borne out by the convenor. He believes the workforce and the union are more committed to the company than middle management are: 'They are not that much interested to make this company successful'. He gave several detailed examples of middle management holding up production and incurring unnecessary expenses, and of himself trying to chase the works superintendent, and 'that time we lost seven hours production, our members lost £2.85, the company lost — I don't know ...' Workers were saying to him: 'When is the report back meeting ... we will be asking some questions'. They had already raised the matter on the plenary committee and were prepared to call for an emergency meeting. Middle management attitudes were hard to change, thought the union official, who described their obstructive attitude, for example, over a request by the workforce for cancer screening: 'You've still got that type ... I bet twenty years after you achieve socialism you're going to have those types of problems, and there's going to be a bloody capitalist class still there ... so I don't think it's only us: I think our stewards have developed far more than local management; foremen for example; I think there's a bit of resentment amongst foremen that the stewards can go up and find out what's going on'.

The managing director gave a similar account of the changes of attitude. One former manager, he said, had had to go 'because after, in his terms I suppose, fighting the union for so long, he couldn't sit down and say we're going to be much closer and we're going to sit round a table and discuss problems and nothing will be sacred. Problems that come up are faced by both sides although there is, I think, a difficulty with the trade union in this way; they know collective bargaining as a route and they are uneasy and unhappy sometimes when they can't make progress through a confrontation almost.'

The union official is, however, aware that there can be a problem of divided loyalties: 'The [trade union] haven't become a kind of company unit, by no means have they become that. But they can see that they've got an investment in that business, and they want to see it run ... a typical example was last week — usually we shut down for Christmas and it's sacrosanct — they rung up and said, look, our customers have got a big new launch, we can't get enough production out — we want to work; will the union let us? The only condition we laid down was that they had to take their holidays at a later stage, we wouldn't let them take the money instead of the holiday because I just don't believe in giving holidays up to anyone, including GLEB ... Now, we wouldn't have that feeling in any other factory.' But, he says, 'it's very difficult to ride two horses like this.'

On the question of wages, the convenor says that: 'We have made it very clear to our members that it's not an open door. We have to be very careful, first, that jobs are saved ... As far as our wage level is concerned, we have gone through the inflation figures and we have seen what is the climate outside, and we settled for seven per cent increase last year.' The workforce also operates more flexibly and have agreed that management can transfer an operator from one department to another.

The convenor has had some training in matters which are normally a management prerogative, and he would like more. He and his predecessor attended a worker-director course at the TUC, paid for by GLEB. The convenor explained that: 'They have given us a lot of information and ideas about this worker-directorship, and because I was involved in that I've got some idea how to deal with things on a board level'. He felt that since then he had been accumulating knowledge, particularly from the discussions on the plenary committee, but that it would have been useful if GLEB had arranged further courses.

Without more training of this type, it is obviously difficult for the workforce to engage fully in discussions on the fundamental issues involved in the business. The managing director felt that, while some people want to be involved, others 'just want to have their wage, do their job, in reasonable conditions, get a bit of overtime.' The plenary sessions tend to focus on wages policy and matters that affect the workers' day by day existence. Fundamental questions that affect the company's future are also raised at these plenary meetings, and by the managing director in discussions with people on the shop floor, who, he says, 'display a willingness to talk about that, and cannot understand why certain things are happening'. He also acknowledges that management can learn from the workforce: 'Very often they can perceive things that management don't know about. I know from the shop floor that one used to think, do they really not know what's going on? And it's only when you get into a managerial position that you realise that you don't know what's going on ...' He himself had some back-up from GLEB through one GLEB project executive with a commercial background who 'is extremely helpful and very supportive in times of difficulty'.

It is difficult to combine the structures a workforce needs to independently elect its own representatives to pursue their interest as workers with those required to involve workers' representatives in enterprise planning, especially where they need management training. Some have argued that the attitudes and even the abilities required in the two cases may be different. But both the union and GLEB executives considered it important for the industrial democracy structures at Compart to be based on the union structures. If people are elected separately for the two functions, there is a danger that the representatives on the enterprise planning committee (or the board) will become cut off from the shop floor. Difficult though it is for workers and their unions to 'ride two horses' it is probably essential for industrial democracy that they should. And in fact it is clear that, as has been said, the trade union's attitudes have changed a great deal. Moreover, training for enterprise planning matters should ideally be available for the workforce as a whole, and there should, at least, be a gradual build-up of knowledge among the workers.

The question remains whether the experience in this company has had the effect of weakening or strengthening the union. The union official, after describing the willingness of the company to make improvements in the situation of the workforce, says: 'That goes onto another thing — the whole question of trade unions, the usefulness of trade unions once you get that situation.' He believes this is one reason why it has been impossible to recruit the white-collar staff. Clearly the trade union is not as combative, and possibly not as strong, as it once was. But then, there must be few medium-size manufacturing firms in London in which that is not the case in the current political and economic situation. And the official believes that it is right for the stewards to 'play it that way' and for the convenor to say of workers' demands at, for example, the plenary: 'Just leave it ... they can't afford it.' He concluded: 'If we're really serious, I'll tell you what, I've learned so much through this exercise, about how people think, how I think, how shop stewards think, how workers think — if we're really serious about changing society and bringing socialism or something like that — the whole role of trade unions is going to change isn't it?'

GLEB has invested in another medium-size firm, Universal Books, in which, as a GLEB executive put it, 'trade unionism seeps from their bones.' The workers, who are both women and men, white and black, are members of SOGAT. As one of them explained, before GLEB bought the company the union already had considerable control over production 'through the normal bargaining situation. If we didn't like the way management wanted the job done we would argue. If there was a difficulty management would come to us to sort it out. We strove for control ... We achieved a lot. For instance, shop officials would be shown the accounts. We were consulted over changes in working practices. When we moved from one factory to another, we actually organised the move; we laid out the factory.' As a GLEB executive put it, the Father of Chapel (FOC) 'was known as the governor, his deputy FOC was known as the mini-governor ... he could cause strikes on hot days, and get ice cream and salt tablets and orange juice'.

But the problem was 'the company was being sold under him ... he'd been out-manoeuvred by capital'. As the FOC says, the company had been virtually asset-stripped by its previous owners. Powerful though the union's industrial clout had become in the 1970s, it was powerless to resist this process. Moreover, unlike in the previous case, this company has not had until recently local managers who were either competent or willing to work with the trade unions in any constructive way. The management situation was in fact so disastrous that, late in 1985, as in at least three other major GLEB investments, GLEB had to send one of its own executives into the company as a full-time managing director; the improvement was impressive.

When GLEB was first approached, the company was in liquidation. One of the local managers had seen an advertisement for GLEB in the SOGAT newspaper. 'After the closure,' says the FOC, 'we all rushed over to GLEB ... I did most of the explaining of the history ... in the initial stage of the negotiations I was very closely involved. We put together the prospectus for the company, in conjunction with the local management. This included the number of people, the wages, future sales and accounts.' As part of its appraisal of the investment, GLEB also asked the workforce about the state of machinery and used this information in its negotiations over acquiring the company. During the time it took for GLEB to make its appraisals and for its management committee and then its board to accept the proposal to buy the company, the workforce was kept together by the union; they held weekly meetings in a nearby canteen. GLEB executives said to the union that if key people got jobs elsewhere, 'then we just wouldn't have a company'. It was a sign of the 'strength of the union tradition and belief' that the workers were in fact held together; in addition some of the male shop floor workers were able, as members of SOGAT central branch, to get temporary evening work on Fleet Street.

There was some discussion among the workforce on the type of ownership under which the company would be set up. One FOC says that he definitely believed it should be set up as some sort of co-operative, but: 'The sad thing is that we all had different views about how it should be. We lack direction within our own chapel. Some people thought that owning the company ourselves meant becoming a shareholder and marching around the shop floor with a share certificate. I always saw it as a collective responsibility, as a way of bringing things together and working towards a common aim, a proper co-operative. We'd lay aside all our discriminations and old prejudices ... at our meetings I said that women would learn to work on men's machines and men on women's. The aim was that we'd all be on the same level as far as wages and skills were concerned ... There wouldn't be a management: the management would be all of us working together. I understand and accept there have to be people who show direction, people in responsible positions. But ultimately management, the shop floor would be all in the same union, working together for the same aims ... In my view we would either elect or appoint management; we would negotiate with them a form of working arrangement by which they would work efficiently and productively and we would abide by agreements, on discipline or whatever. I still believe this could be the case today. It would mean recognising there are some skills outside the company which we have to go out and get, sales, administration, accounts ... people could be brought in, provided with a framework, convinced of our way of working.'

The company was however set up with a majority of shares owned by GLEB; the national union, SOGAT '82, owned a portion of them and the local union chapels have small shareholdings. It has a conventional management structure, with a board of directors and a management committee. GLEB has two directors and it appointed a non-executive chair, a retired businessman with knowledge of the industry; SOGAT '82, as a national union has one director; two local managers are on the board; and there is one worker-director representing the chapels. The workers at first, as a result apparently of a manoeuvre by the local managers, elected a foreman to go on the board: 'It's happened in [other GLEB-funded firms]: the workers ditch their old militant shop stewards and vote for the foreman who seems more intelligent, more articulate.' But GLEB then did its own manoeuvring; the vote was re-taken and the (then) FOC was elected, even though GLEB 'pointed out the conflict that could arise if the FOC was also the worker-director'.

The current FOC thinks there should have been two or more worker-directors, in particular so that more workers can get to know how the company works, and certainly the FOC's position on the board appears quite isolated. He also believes that one reason for the union's weakness on the board was its lack of credibility: 'We didn't achieve production targets; this came back to the board and the chapel got blamed.' At board meetings the FOC was expected to explain why the targets had not been met and he was then told 'we rely on you' to ensure that the performance of the workforce is improved; in this situation he 'got riled', and said for example: 'just you try meeting those targets on those machines.'

GLEB also instituted a management committee, with two representatives from management and two from the workforce. Previously, according to a GLEB executive, 'the chapel would insist on various things ... their branch officials would come down ... management didn't attempt to bring the workforce into the reasons why they had to do these things ... so it was a typical British company. Management demanded the right to manage which didn't include involving the workers. The workers themselves reacted in the usual alienated bloody-minded way workers react when they're put in those positions ... these antagonists are now supposed to sit down in this management committee every Monday morning ...' The workers' representatives on the management committee were again the FOC and MOC. It seemed clear that there could be a danger of setting up rival sources of power.

Management and the workers' representatives report back to the workforce as a whole, although not, in the FOC's opinion, enough: 'Management should be more accountable to the workforce. There used to be a lot of meetings, but irregular, a hotch potch. Then they took place once a week after work. These worked in the sense that workers got proper report-backs. They got information but it wasn't going anywhere. We had no control over the sort of work we did, so people felt we couldn't increase productivity easily. But I felt we should do our best to prove ourselves in our domain and *then* we could be in a better position to control the sort of work we did.'

The FOC blames the workers' failure to meet production targets on a lack of direction from GLEB; in effect on inadequate local management: 'The first few weeks were electrifying. The energy was incredible. But there was nobody directing. The energy was going off in all directions. People would offer to work on Saturday for nothing, others were saying I'll turn up the machinery fast ... We had all been given the idea it was our company and we could do what we liked, provided we achieved the results. I'm not sure everyone was taking seriously what it was about; it wasn't just a matter of here's the money, do what you like ... there was a feeling that the situation was completely open. The new purpose of the company hadn't been explained' (although the FOC did go on a course on industrial democracy, where he learned more about GLEB). Not much thought was given to how to establish work discipline, he said, and not everyone was committed to the idea of co-ops. 'The phase of directionless energy was followed by demoralisation, a diffusion of energy ... In some ways it was GLEB's fault, we had a good GLEB support worker, but that's the only support we had.'

But, partly because of unresolved and acute local management problems, GLEB's project executive, who is himself a former print worker and a member of the craft print union, the National Graphical Association, became increasingly involved in day-to-day management matters, and eventually he went to work in the firm full-time. He confirms that when GLEB first re-started the company 'it was very good', but then 'they got into the bad old ways. People actually believed that as long as GLEB's there in the background, like a fairy godmother, that the bad day would never come and their jobs would be all right.' The company was losing money: 'Some of it's down to bad materials, machine breakdowns, there's always a reason ... But quite a bit of it's been down to the workforce attitude where people have thought, it's just another job; they haven't made that transition ... their alienation hasn't dropped to the extent that they recognise they're working for themselves, that there isn't a governor, so they begin to see me as the governor; I became the devil personified ... I said I'm not your governor, you work well or not well, you don't please me or displease me, you do it for yourself.' He was doubtful about how far they would change: 'it's a generation literally before you've got a different type of worker ... we need the new worker ... people weren't working to their best ... people are hanging back for overtime'.

The question of further GLEB funding then came up; a critical paper had been written for presentation to the board: 'I had to call a meeting of the workforce and say, your time's up, you've had it ... I know it's not all your fault ... but ... I could have got you half a million if you'd only just got the work out on time.'

He asked them to stagger their holidays; they refused. 'We were so far apart, I was sort of hitting my head every so often and saying, where are we failing to communicate? ... We tried everything ... I said: organise your own work. We had them elect section leaders in their own areas ... it was just nonsense'. Eventually there was a change of attitude. 'It was like a sort of confessional.' The workers agreed that there were slackers; with the agreement of the SOGAT director, some redundancies were made; the union chose who was to be made redundant. The workers agreed to work over their Christmas break.

There were also considerable disagreements over wage rates. As the FOC explained: 'One factor in our love-hate relationship [with GLEB] was an argument over equal opportunities. April 1984 was normally a time for our pay review. The chapel elected not to have any pay review; it decided this, with SOGAT's support, without any suggestion from GLEB. But certain sections of the factory were paid a machine rate; this was mainly men. GLEB found this divisive and wanted to equalise rates and abolish machine rates. They also wanted to bring in training for women on the machines. At first this was worrying for the male members and some women; it meant some men going for two years without an increase.' Nevertheless, GLEB finally obtained a phased abolition of machine rates. The GLEB executive who negotiated the change commented: 'These people were on pretty low wages anyway; it's no good for men to say machine money is unfair, if you're living up to machine money ... At the same time it *was* unfair, and we couldn't give everyone machine money, which was what they were suggesting ... it would have wrecked the company. So, we had this battle ... with me saying, look the money [from GLEB] is not going in ... As a trade unionist of course I did have grave fears that I was acting as management would do ... there I am doing the sort of things that years ago I would have brought people out on strike against ... so yes, I had doubts, and still have doubts, am I a lackey of capitalism, is it possible to work within the system, should we sort of start passing out the Kalashnikovs ...?'

And yet, in this company and in many others like it, the workers' tradidional trade union militancy had not been enough to save their jobs: 'the wheeling and dealing was being done elsewhere, and the workforce didn't have the skills to operate on that level, and that's where our movement lacks those skills and that's why we've gone through a learning process, people like me, and we need those skills. We need to be able to put together companies; I can now put together companies; I know where to find headhunters and all that sort of thing ... It's easy to pass rhetorical resolutions about taking over the commanding heights, but we take them over, and who the bloody hell's going to run them?'

Equal Opportunities

Universal Books was one of the cases where GLEB successfully used its leverage in a firm to make a major improvement in equal opportunities for women workers. The guidelines which the GLC set for GLEB state that 'GLEB will ensure that the needs of women and ethnic minorities are recognised.' And enterprise planning was intended to be the principle means by which this commitment to equal opportunities would be implemented. Universal Books offered an opportunity to follow up this commitment. As a result of GLEB's intervention this firm in the traditionally male-dominated print industry now has an agreement for women to work on machines and at rates of pay traditionally reserved for men. This meant pressing the workforce to accept a new flexibility in what they did. A GLEB executive described the process: 'I was determined that we weren't going to walk back into that factory with all the old bad habits, so a condition was that ... there should be an equal opportunities flexibility agreement, that allowed for women to be trained for the skilled areas, and the flexibility would be on two levels at first: it would be immediate on levels where there was no great skill required ... in the past the men would stand around, the women would be working like slaves, when the men could just have walked five yards. The same was partly true in the men's areas, because all the women could do in the men's areas was take off the end of machines. But when the women were slack there was no reason at all why they shouldn't be over there learning, picking up things from the machinists. So the agreement was first of all that that sort of flexibility would take place straight away, unless there were real, physical or whatever reasons against it; and if anyone refused they would be disciplined ... and the second level of flexibility was that the training take place and the women get into the skilled areas ...'

At first there was a majority, both men and women, against the changes; it was only after it was made clear that they were a condition of GLEB funding that the workers voted to accept them. And of course, in this case, the changes were expected to decrease costs rather than increase them. Subsequently, GLEB 'got through a clause of equal voting: if there were twenty men at a meeting and fifteen women, five men would not vote ... so the women wouldn't be swamped every time.'

This story, one of very few successes, contains a number of lessons about enterprise planning and equal opportunities. The first is the element of compulsion by GLEB involved. In this case, GLEB used its control over finance to pressure the workforce into agreeing to major changes in women's work opportunities. In too many other cases, equal opportunities considerations were never raised within the tripartite enterprise planning process, which did not represent the people whom equal opportunities policies were intended to benefit. Trade union organisations all too often did not represent the specific needs of women and black people. When the survival of the firm was at stake, management, unions and GLEB itself were compliant in ignoring issues such as hiring or training or promoting black people and women, arguing that it would be 'disruptive' to the immediate task.

One example where a plan for equal opportunities was never raised was the £1.5 million investment in Cabinet Designs Ltd, intended to be an exemplary investment and a key part of restructuring an industrial sector; the plan for this enterprise contained no proposals for extending equal opportunities, nor indeed did it allow for much trade union involvement. In one clothing firm where most workers were women, the representatives on all three sides of the enterprise planning process were male.

One of the two GLEB staff members hired, rather late on, to promote equal opportunities in GLEB work, rapidly came to see equal opportunities as an issue quite separate from enterprise planning. She argued that: 'Democracy within one enterprise can run counter to the democracy of public accountability ... enterprise planning is a consent-based exercise, but members of certain categories are absent and cannot participate in a voluntary, negotiated process. If equal opportunities are predicated on enterprise planning, this is discriminatory: people who are already in a good position are to be asked whether they agree to others being brought in ... This does not mean that you won't sit down and try to persuade. But GLEB should say, we would rather you did it voluntarily, but if you won't, you must do it anyway. There must be an element of enforcement.'

That element of compulsion was certainly present in the Universal Books case. In many other cases GLEB showed no such commitment to equal opportunities. There were a number of reasons for this. One was a general lack of knowledge of or commitment within GLEB to the question of who got jobs, as compared to trying to expand or defend the numbers of jobs in London. GLEB's Board of nine people had one black member, and two women: until 1984, there were no GLEB staff with the brief to promote equal opportunities. By late 1984, only four GLEB professional staff were women, two working in the co-op unit. No directors of GLEB's divisions were women and all were white. Individual Board members found it difficult to get the issue discussed seriously. The GLEB funding agreement set out an elaborate structure of 'premia', additional funding for firms employing women or people from ethnic minorities, taking on apprentices or providing nursery places, and these were intended to influence the pattern of GLEB investments. In practice, except in the case of co-op investment, the premia were not used, partly because GLEB never reached the limits of its funding possibilities, where it would have been making choices on these grounds. And the efforts of individual GLEB staff to push for equal opportunities policies in GLEB firms were not reflected in GLEB's general aims, corporate plans, or enterprise planning practice.

While there was a problem of commitment to the issue, there were other serious problems built into the idea of requiring an investment board to pursue what came to be seen as 'social objectives'. The GLC required GLEB investments to become profitable after two years — the 'commercial objective' — and this could conflict seriously with social aims. Equal opportunities cost money — for training, reorganisation, wage changes, alterations to the buildings for people with disabilities, let alone nursery provision — and, as one Board member put it, it was initially assumed without explicit discussion that 'the firm would pay'.

But many GLEB firms were in no position to pay, even had the will been there. One example of the conflict between saving jobs and improving the quality and availability of jobs comes from engineering. It was an engineering firm made up almost entirely of white male skilled engineers. GLEB made an agreement with the firm that half the next intake of apprentices would be women and at least 20 per cent from ethnic minorities. However just as the agreement was to be publicised, a financial crisis in the company led GLEB to freeze the number of apprenticeships.

Other firms were rarely in a position to begin to make such choices. The kind of firms which came to GLEB were generally not the potentially successful, well organised firms employing skilled labour, simply in need of reorganisation. Rather it was the marginal firms — and worse — that came to GLEB for support. It was the small clothing, food and light engineering firms, sometimes owned by members of an ethnic minority and employing a lot of women. Indeed 40 per cent of employees of GLEB firms turned out to be women. But almost without exception they were in low paid jobs with few skills or prospects for improvement. And the crisis in their industries was so serious that rescue plans could sometimes make the quality of jobs even worse. Cossett, a work wear company which GLEB took over in its first year, was just such a case. Here GLEB's survival strategy involved the de-skilling of women's work (turning it into repetitive work on one component only, rather than work on the product as a whole). Job content was determined by market conditions. GLEB tried to gain some kind of leverage over market forces in the clothing industry — a sector where women were losing jobs at a particularly rapid rate — by encouraging the most progressive and least antiquated to expand. When this failed they decided to refuse any further clothing projects. This meant in effect that they had decided that they could not intervene successfully in one of the major industries employing women and ethnic minorities in London.

From 1983, there was increasing pressure on GLEB from within the GLC to develop more effective equal opportunities policies. Both women and black officers working on these issues within the GLC found it difficult to exert pressure for change, given GLEB's autonomous position, and despite the principle that the GLC set GLEB policy guidelines. One result of these efforts however was a paper which the GLC's Women's Employment Project Team took through the Industry and Employment Committee. This reported critically on GLEB's progress towards equal opportunities, and recommended that GLEB insist that all firms meet minimal equal opportunities standards; that they develop training programmes and policies on working hours and above all that as a priority they appoint some staff whose job was to promote equal opportunities in GLEB firms. Until that point there was no-one in GLEB specifically with responsibility for equal opportunities; a contrast with the GLC which created several senior posts with this responsibility. As a consequence the latest appointee — a woman — was asked to add an equal opportunities brief to the trade union liaison role for which she was appointed. She quickly found that she had insufficient power to do her job. However she set to work to gather the basic information that would enable her to identify problems and opportunities. Even this basic information took nearly a year to gather.

At the same time a staff member was appointed in GLEB to work on equal opportunities for black people. Pressure for opportunities for ethnic minorities had centred on the level of investment for GLEB in black-run firms and firms employing black people. It could be argued that GLEB's support for larger firms in which there was a strongly organised black workforce or in which such organisations could be built was of greater significance for equal opportunities than the promotion of new black businesses. But the GLC's Ethnic Minorities Unit pointed to black businesses or co-operatives which had been turned down for funding, and argued that, since both management and unions discriminated so widely and systematically against black workers, GLEB's commitment to equal opportunities had to take the form of much greater funding of black-run businesses as well as support for ethnic minorities employed by predominantly white-owned businesses.

Jay Thakker, the member of the Ethnic Minorities Unit who was appointed to work on equal opportunities, found the task extremely difficult, if not impossible. For a start he had three jobs to do at once: monitoring equal opportunities in all the existing GLEB projects which were not co-ops; running an investment project giving interest-free loans of £5,000 to black businesses, including co-ops; and supervising a scheme to provide black businesses with advice. He found that GLEB's track record in investing in black businesses, in improving the conditions and opportunities for ethnic minorities in existing GLEB companies, and even in GLEB itself, did not provide a firm foundation on which to build. GLEB itself employed a significant number of black people, but the majority of them were clerical workers, cleaners or people who served out the food in GLEB's restaurant. There were only four black professional staff throughout its life under the GLC (and this has not been improved on since), none of them were in the co-op division. A great strength of the co-op division was that it was staffed mainly by people with detailed experience of co-ops yet none had detailed knowledge of the specific importance of co-ops in the black community. Of £5 million spent on co-ops during the lifetime of the GLC's GLEB, only £200,000-£300,000 went to black co-ops. The extent of the missed opportunities can be gauged by contrasting this record with that of the London Co-operative Enerprise Board, set up by GLEB in 1985, with black people well represented on the board and the staff: around 40 per cent of its funds went to black co-ops. As far as conventional black enterprises were concerned, money was invested through the investment division, but often without the rigorous evaluation and criteria which GLEB applied to many other companies. For instance in several instances enterprise planning was allowed to lapse and no effort was made to bring in the union; the follow-up to encourage, monitor and support improvements was weak to non-existent. It was as if it was enough that it was a black enterprise. The record on improving conditions for black workers in GLEB's large investments was uneven. On several occasions the problem was a defensive and patriarchal employer who made union access to 'his workers' extremely difficult. In at least two such instances GLEB worked closely with the unions and using its bargaining power made some progress. On other occasions, particularly where black workers were a minority, Jay Thakker found it difficult to get involved so he could not suggest the sort of improvements, for example in training, which GLEB could make a condition of their financial support. Sometimes departmental jealousies stood in the way. On the other occasions, it seemed to Thakker that GLEB executives were not prepared to upset their relations with union officials by 'raising difficulties'.

GLEB executives vary in their acceptance of these criticisms. However, two things are clear. First, neither the Board nor the management committee had a substantial discussion of the specific economic problems and opportunities faced by the black community or by the problems raised by racism in the companies in which GLEB was investing. Secondly the equal opportunity officer was not in a sufficiently powerful position within GLEB to bring about change.

There are then several issues about equal opportunities which emerge from GLEB's experience. Was the central aim to increase the number of jobs for women and black people, or was it to improve quality as well, and what happened if these two aims conflicted? Should an enterprise board hold investments in firms which were lousy employers just because they employed desired categories of people?

Enterprise planning as a vehicle for equal opportunities anyway turned out to be enormously problematic. Women from the

GLC's Womens Employment Team suggested that women and ethnic minorities be represented directly in the process of drawing up enterprise plans and that women's meetings be held in work time. The equal opportunities officer who was eventually appointed did arrange for such meetings to be held but this was too late to have a significant impact.

If enterprise planning and equal opportunities were treated as separate issues, however, they still raised similar problems. Both were costly. Some argued that these costs were transient. Equal opportunities would reduce costs in the long run: investment in the training of women would for example increase the pool of skilled labour and reduce its cost; and this was just the sort of investment that GLEB was set up to foster to counter the short-time horizon of banks and other financiers. Alternatively it might be possible to set new standards of conditions for an industry. For instance if the subsidy were used to improve opportunities through training, childcare and shorter working hours, then other firms would not be undercut and the example set by GLEB firms might lead workers elsewhere to demand similar facilities. Thus the quality of jobs would be improved without a loss of jobs. This strategy required a long-term view and it required a greater level of subsidy linked to achieving specific improvements in the quality of employment.

Finally, a different argument accepted the necessity of subsidy to quality of employment and viewed it as very long term: in effect public sector holdings in the private sector for the purpose of long term social plans. This led people however to question whether in that case an enterprise board was the right vehicle for such public grant finance.

While these arguments went on, however, the public debate with government centred on 'the numbers game'; how many jobs and at how low a cost. Yet equal opportunities and enterprise planning experiences, both focussing on the quality of jobs lead those involved to question why a low cost per job should be a desirable objective in itself for public authority investment.

Conclusions

Industrial democracy is central to the purpose of GLEB. Although much emphasis has been put on the objective of creating jobs, it could be argued that, in a recession and without increases in overall demand, jobs created or saved by GLEB will be at the expense of jobs elsewhere. The justification for GLEB's existence must primarily be that the jobs it creates and saves are better than jobs elsewhere and, perhaps, that jobs in certain parts of London are disappearing at a catastrophic rate and at high social cost. An important part of this justification is that they provide an experience of workers' control.

Any process of building socialism must involve the democratic control of the economy by the working class. The extension of democratic control within the workplace will be part of this process. It is unlikely to take place overnight. It is therefore important for workers and the labour movement in general to gain experience about the problems of running industry in advance of any radical changes in ownership, and GLEB has made a contribution to this experience.

GLEB is not necessarily the best instrument for achieving this goal. It could be argued that the GLC, in its endeavour to extend workers' control, could have put the resources available to it to better use. It could perhaps, for example, have used them to extend municipal ownership. Part of the argument of the founders of GLEB was that it could spread its resources more widely by making loans or taking a small proportion of the equity in private companies, and thus give itself leverage to back the interests of workers in wider sections of industry. In fact GLEB ended up taking over a number of the companies it invested in; in 1985 GLEB had virtually full ownership of around half of its larger projects; a further quarter of them were co-operatives. Given the limited resources of local authorities, neither municipal ownership nor the activities of local enterprise boards can have more than a limited impact on the industries in their area. GLEB, and the workers and unions it has worked with, have at least attempted to become involved in issues at the eart of the problems of industry in London.

As the following chapter describes, GLEB hoped to demonstrate ways in which sectors of London's industry could be restructured in the interests of labour. Without government backing, this was probably an impossible task; it was made more difficult, in particular, by GLEB's lack of compulsory powers in relation to profitable firms. In the absence of such powers, and also because of GLEB's commitment to saving jobs, GLEB responded to requests for rescues of some medium-size manufacturing firms. Especially when these requests came from trade unions, these have provided the best prospects of gains in workers' control on which the labour movement can build. They can be made viable, but only with large commitments of resources and time. The tragedy will be if the abolition of the GLC and the contraction of GLEB lead to the abandonment of these enterprises, the loss of this experience and the bitter dis-illusion of their workforces.

The fact that GLEB was set up at a time of high unemploy-ment and harsh government policies has driven home the lesson that the interests of the working class cannot always be defended by traditional trade union bargaining methods. In the 1960s and early 1970s, it did seem as though the power of the workers could be extended through their unions into areas of manage-ment prerogative. It is clear now that it is difficult enough to set up any form of trade union organisation in many sectors of London's industry, let alone to use this organisation to deter-mine the policies of management. Changes in both ownership and management are required. GLEB ownership in turn has in some cases not ensured that any changes in the internal organ-isation of enterprises take place, and the institution of worker-directors is of no use in the face of hostile management and weak trade union organisation.

One of GLEB's biggest problems has, not surprisingly, been with management, not least because the firms needing rescue were often those with the weakest management, or came from sectors with a long pattern of poor management. It has had to deal with managers who are incompetent, unsympathetic towards the workforce, and at times dishonest. Workers and their unions have often had a clearer understanding than GLEB of the weaknesses of management and/or owners and have been astonished by GLEB's willingness to 'go along with them'. Yet GLEB has found it difficult to replace them, and there is general recognition that certain specialist management skills are required. One of the clearest lessons from GLEB's experience is that it is necessary for the labour movement to provide training in these skills on a large scale. Both the companies funded by GLEB and GLEB itself have suffered from a lack of individuals who possess both adequate commercial skills and a commitment to GLEB's wider political objectives. Moreover, this training should of course not be available merely to the individuals who run businesses and to GLEB staff but to workers in general, who need to understand the processes of management in order to control them.

GLEB's experience does not only show that trade union

organisation, however strong, is powerless on its own to defeat threats of closure by capital. It also shows that, even in enterprises which are owned by GLEB, there is much need for strong collective organisation of the workforce on which to build genuine, rather than symbolic, extensions of workers' control. This does not mean that GLEB should neglect sectors in which trade union organisation is weak or non-existent; merely that, in such sectors, trade union organisation has to be built before workers' control can have any meaning.

There remain questions on the role of trade unions which are hard to resolve. The purpose of some management and Tory proposals for worker participation schemes is in part to undermine and weaken union organisation. Many trade unionists shun any involvement in management out of fear that such involvement will mean that they adopt the point of view of management and neglect the interests of the workforce. It is possible to argue from different points of view that the brutally antagonistic behaviour of much of British management, their scorn for working people, is one of their clearest failings; as one GLEB executive commented, referring to his hope that GLEB could recruit sympathetic managers: 'There's every reason to be able to prove to people that it makes sense to have worker-directors, it makes sense to tell people what's going on, it makes sense to listen to what people are saying, because it's better management ... good managers do it anyway'. But whether this amounts to more than better management of capitalism is another question.

There is in fact considerable ambivalence about what enterprise planning, as practised by GLEB, is meant to achieve. For example, although in some cases GLEB's intervention on behalf of the workforce has led to wage increases, in other cases the workers' greater knowledge of the financial situation of their enterprise, and their commitment to its survival under new forms of ownership and control, has undoubtedly made them accept lower wages — as is classically the case in co-operatives. More generally, it has often led workers to work harder, to adopt more flexible working methods and, as it was intended to do, to become actively involved in improving production methods.

The major difference between most GLEB projects and conventional private sector firms, and the reason why unions such as the AUEW and SOGAT have become involved in and supportive of the experiment, is of course that enterprises are wholly or partly owned by GLEB or their workforce. Any profits that arise from the workers' greater effort and commitment are not privately appropriated, or not to the same extent. In some cases, GLEB executives, union officials, shop stewards, managers and individual workers have united to persuade the rest of the workforce that their different situation requires a change of attitude towards their work. Former shop stewards have resorted to the clock to discipline their members; in other places the workers have pressed for greater discipline; others complain that 'there are people down there who still operate on the basis of sticking the *Sun* up their jumper and hiding in the toilet ... we have to convince people that they've got to make that transition.' In a co-operative, a worker who refuses to run a machine is 'literally stealing the bread out of other workers' mouths'. Much the same issues would arise under socialism.

Moreover GLEB, unlike the Tory proponents of 'industrial democracy', usually insists that extensions in workers' control should be based on trade union organisation. In these sorts of situations, union officials and shop stewards fully accept that the role of the trade unions is changing and that it will have to change more in the future. The problem remains of how to reconcile their role of defending the interests of the workforce, both as individuals and collectively, with their role in running the enterprise. In a co-operative, the clearest role for the unions is usually to provide an external means of resolving individual questions of discipline and grievances which the co-op has been unable to resolve internally, and to ensure that individuals have some protection against victimisation by their fellow workers. The unions may be involved in giving assistance on health and safety matters. But there is virtually no role for them in, for example, wage negotiations; these questions are resolved in the co-op's general meetings. In firms which are owned by GLEB and have a more conventional management structure, the trade union does retain a role in negotiating for improvements in workers' wages and conditions, as it would under a system of full public ownership. But the unions are certainly not out for all that they can get out of a hostile management, in whose problems they have no concern.

GLEB's intention — not always fully adhered to — is that the unions, generally through their elected shop stewards, should progressively gain greater control over management decisions. The mechanisms used have been trade union representation on management committees as well as on boards of directors; sometimes separate 'enterprise planning committees' have been set up with the idea that these will provide a consultative framework, and that the issues raised will then be taken back to the union's negotiating committee for decision. In all of these cases, the union is expected to play an active role in the survival and progress of the company, which may mean that it accepts changes which amount to cutting labour costs, such as the elimination of overtime, more flexibility, and even redundancies. At the same time, it may win improvements, such as harmonisation of conditions for staff and shop floor workers and, of course, complete acceptance of the need for time off for union meetings.

The extension of the workers' and their unions' control over the wider matters of enterprise planning, such as financial and accounting matters, future marketing strategies, new equipment, and so on, has fallen short of expectations. Financial matters tend to be raised in relation to how much the company can afford to pay in wages; and shop floor workers of course have much to say on the type of machinery that is needed. Both managers and workers sometimes express regret that the workforce as a whole is not more interested in making use of the new access to information and the possibility of control. It is partly a matter of training; workers cannot be expected to make much of an input in financial, accounting and marketing matters, unless they have the chance to learn about them.

Some people are sceptical, more generally, about whether people actually want to have more control over their working situation. The evidence from GLEB-funded firms is that there are workers who do not at first make full use of their access to information and others who do not feel they are getting enough and who would welcome more training to enable them to participate more. It is undoubtedly partly a question of time, of building up knowledge and confidence. There have been several cases of a gradual extension in the amount of participation by the workforce at general meetings. It takes time to change attitudes on all sides. Patronising attitudes by management are not conducive to open discussion. In one GLEB enterprise, the workers actually feared victimisation by middle management if they were too outspoken. The experience of GLEB demonstrates that, given time and the right structures, workers and their unions welcome the opportunities provided by an expansion in democracy in the workplace.

These are broad and general questions, common to most experiments in industrial democracy. The GLEB experience provides some more particular lessons. One is that there needs to be a much stronger insistence on and monitoring of the 'social' objectives, including its formal commitment to equal opportunities, than was the case in GLEB even when it had relatively ample resources compared to other enterprise boards and local authorities. This problem is likely to become even more acute with the reduction in the resources of GLEB following the abolition of the GLC. In addition this monitoring could and should take place much more clearly in conjunction with a shop floor and trade union view of what needs to be done and with more control by them over funding decisions by GLEB. Funding decisions need to be based more explicitly on the achievement of certain social objectives. These may, in future, be embodied in separate 'Social Plans', so that the goals and their costs can be clearly determined and accounted for, and funds allocated specifically to them. One of the most important and neglected of these costs is the cost of training. If workers' control is to become a reality, much more training is needed. The following chapter also demonstrates the value of funding sector-wide forums and education for trade unionists.

But if this work is to take effect and the experience is to be built upon, there is a great need for more long-term security and more assurance that the workers' commitment will in fact enable them to keep their jobs. If, on narrow commercial grounds, GLEB's larger investments are allowed to collapse, this will be a tragedy. A union official, asked what he thought is the attitude towards GLEB of the workers in one large GLEB-funded firm, the great majority of whose workers are Asian, said: 'They really appreciate what's been done. But they're very concerned about what's going to happen after the GLC ... They've gone through a terrible nail-biting exercise, and then got onto cloud nine, and now they're back into a nail-biting exercise, and they're worried sick ... I'm concerned, it can almost become an academic exercise if we're not careful ... We've come on, we've proved it can work and we're going out now, and we can quote it as an exercise. But our people, they ain't going to use it as an exercise. GLEB has got to understand that people's hopes have risen and you can't smash them on the rocks now. They've really got to have a secure future ... I want to know what their plans are ... Otherwise it could all end up as an academic exercise with them saying, well, if we'd had a Labour government it could have continued but hard luck, two hundred are all sacked and two hundred have got very bitter now. It would be a bloody tragedy for that to happen.'

7

Socially Useful Production: Policy and Practice

'We shall assist groups of workers seeking to develop alternative forms of production, with finance, with premises or in other ways.' This was the manifesto commitment to promote socially useful production. A bold commitment for a local authority, albeit one of the biggest in the world. A report to the Industry and Employment Committee spelt it out: 'Socially useful products,' it argued, were 'products which assisted human beings rather than maimed them; products which were produced in ways which conserved energy and raw materials rather than wasted them; and products whose manufacture, repair and recycling was carried out by non-alienated labour.'

In one sentence, then, the manifesto was in effect taking on the whole military-industrial complex and the capitalist organisation of work. It is perhaps not surprising that the practice should fall short of the intention!

In one sense the whole of this book is about struggling for socially useful democratically controlled production. The term 'socially useful production' is often used as a short hand for an alternative to capitalist production; it sums up the principles we would like to see behind a socialist economy. But it also has a more specific meaning referring to actual products and production processes, indicating that some are more socially useful than others and that there are social values in the choices which designers and producers make. The wider implication is that we cannot treat technology as neutral; that if we are concerned to change the way the economy is organised we should not limit our attention to the way that technology is applied. Rather we should question and explore alternatives to the design and development of the technology itself.

This critical approach to technology gained political force originally from the shop stewards' combine committee — a committee covering all the unions at the plant — at Lucas Aerospace. Their detailed plan for converting their plant to make socially useful products was a response to the problem of growing structural or technological unemployment. In their advanced engineering industry, the cause of unemployment was not so much a fall in profits or a contraction of demand but the increasing displacement of labour by advanced capital intensive technology combined with the absence of mechanisms for reallocating the free labour.

Much of the impetus for the combine committee's plan came from highly skilled designers and shop floor engineers who had built up strong company-wide trade union organisations with representatives of every part of the workforce. For the first time in their lives (that was the early 1970s) they faced the prospect of 'redundancy'. They had immense confidence in the usefulness of their collective skills and would not accept that these skills were really redundant. The prospect of government support gave them the incentive to demonstrate with detailed product design and prototypes the social uses to which their skills could be put. In the end the government backed off and Lucas management refused seriously to negotiate over the plan. However the ideas spread.

The left Labour local authorities of the early 1980s, notably the GLC and Sheffield, were probably the first public authorities to take this idea on board and commit resources to exploring alternative products and production processes as a central part of their economic strategies. The GLC embarked on this exploration from two starting points. On the one hand, through setting up the Greater London Conversion Council, it started from the desired aim. On the other hand, through GLEB's technology networks, it started from the technologies themselves.

The two experiences make distinct stories which we tell below. But both were affected by a common industrial and political context very different from that in which the Lucas Aerospace stewards were working: the decimation of manufacturing industry, in which one of the very few expanding sectors was defence; low levels of confidence and organisation in the trade unions; a hostile government. This meant that the ideas of socially useful production often lacked an active workforce to generate pressure and ideas. There were exceptions, such as on the issues of energy around which a movement had developed independently of the upturns and downturns of trade union strength.

The Greater London Conversion Council

The Labour administration that took over County Hall in 1981 did not need convincing that arms conversion — switching defence production to commerical and civilian manufacture — was politically sound. Any Labour government committed to cutting the defence budget or to pursuing a non-nuclear defence strategy would need to be able to convince workers in the arms industry that they would not be left jobless.

The problem with translating support for arms conversion into practical alternative plans for defence plants in Greater London was that the incumbent Conservative government, far from reducing defence spending, was pledged to do just the opposite. Until 1986 the defence budget was rising in real terms every year. That meant the electronics and aerospace companies in the south-east dependent on defence contracts were doing very well compared with the rest of manufacturing industry.

From the start, it was likely to be an uphill struggle to convince workers in defence plants that they should be concerned with drawing up plans for alternative products. Apart from the problem of what products they could make that would sell during a recession, there was little incentive for workers in relatively secure jobs to worry about a future when defence spending might be reduced. The GLC was to discover from research commissioned from Sue Willet, then at Birbeck College, that at Thorn EMI, a major defence contractor, it was the company's civilian work, rather than its military production lines, that was at risk.

The first aim was not to create or preserve jobs, but to prepare the way for reducing London's dependence on arms manufacture. As the initial outline of the work put it: 'If peace, disarmament and jobs is the goal, conversion planning is an indispensable tool in achieving it.' Bill Niven, a former official with AUEW–TASS, the largest white collar union in aerospace, was appointed part-time to develop this work. At the time he was working on defence policy with Mary Kaldor at the Science Policy Research Unit at Sussex University.

Niven had already put a great deal of thought into the kind of structures a sympathethic government might provide to enable defence plants to switch to civilian manufacture without any major dislocation of jobs. In his design, a special unit at government level would direct resources through regional conversion councils. Workers would be involved in drawing up plans through local use committees set up at defence plants. Part of this thinking provided the basis for the strategy he proposed to the GLC. There was to be a London conversion council, which would draw together academics, trade unions, representatives of the peace movement and the defence employers. The second practical strand to the work was to be the identification of sites where defence workers would be willing to be involved in drawing up plans for arms conversion. The first report to the industry and employment committee stated: 'In London there is a need to develop particular plans for particular sites. This work needs to start from the interests of the workers immediately affected.'

By October 1983 Niven had produced an analysis of the defence related industry in the GLC area. He estimated that some 49,100 jobs in Greater London depended to 'a greater or lesser extent' on defence spending, about seven per cent of manufacturing employment. In addition, there were 24,612 Ministry of Defence industrial and non-industrial civil servants, plus 14,534 in the armed forces, producing a grand total of 88,246 jobs dependent upon defence spending. Niven estimated that jobs in defence would be likely to see a further decline of 15,750 between 1984 and 1988, but his projections were based on extrapolations from national trends and were not based on an analysis of the prospects for London's defence manufacturers.

Niven concluded: 'There is an urgent need to begin preparing detailed proposals for technology transfer, the development of alternative non-military products and alternative markets, all of which act as a safety net and assist in smoothing industrial transition, if and when, defence spending is reduced.' The first potential site for an arms conversion project was also identified in the report. In July 1983, three months before the report was presented, the workforce at London's largest single defence plant — the Kingston-upon-Thames site of British Aerospace — went on a day's protest strike. They had heard rumours that the plant was to close and production moved to the BAE site at Weybridge. The Kingston plant employs about 3,000 people and produces different versions of the Harrier jump-jet and the Hawk ground attack/trainer aircraft, which can carry Sidewinder missiles. The GLC had links with Kingston through John Page, a lecturer at Kingston Poly, who was to join the conversion council.

At the time, GLEB was contacted and a provisional paper identifying possible new types of product was drawn up, but the GLC did not appoint a full-time researcher to get a project underway at Kingston until October 1985. By then the GLC had only another six months to run. When Bernard Harbour, a graduate in peace studies from Bradford University, arrived to begin work not only was the GLC's time running out but the situation at Kingston had changed dramatically. The plant had orders for fighter Harriers for the US Marines and GR Harriers for the Ministry of Defence. The future of Kingston appeared assured for at least the next five years and the shop stewards were no longer interested in being involved in an audit of the skills of the workforce; nor did they want British Aerospace to know the project was even being considered for fear that might give the impression they were not committed to the industry. They didn't even want their involvement to become known on the shopfloor.

It was the changes in the order book that effectively doomed the project. According to Harbour: 'The people at Kingston want to make fighter aircraft. If it is a question of making nothing or making alternative products then they will make alternative products. There isn't any commitment to conversion. It is a fallback position.' Harbour did go on to carry out research into the aerospace industry, with particular reference to British Aerospace and the Kingston site. It will be useful to the unions in the industry, but it was not what he had intended when he took on the work.

The body responsible for directing the conversion strategy was the Greater London Conversion Council, set up in 1982. The membership of the council was decided by Niven in consultation with Kaldor and Murray. He was keen to see representatives from the academic world, from trade unions, the defence employers, the churches and the peace movement. Niven was particularly pleased to have Brian Slade, the principal procurement officer for aerospace at the Ministry of Defence, on the council. (He was a churches' representative.)

The intention was to have a broad-based body that would command credibility. Niven was disappointed when the defence employers rejected his offer of three seats, but he wasn't surprised. Organisations such as Electronics for Peace, CND and the

British Society for Social Responsibility in Science did take up seats. The union seats were taken by full-time officials, who, it turned out, had little time to spare for its activities. The body that emerged was the kind of committee that is immobolised by the differences among its members. Mike Ward, the chair of the Industry and Employment Committee, takes the view that the council brought together people with different points of view in order to work through the problems of arms conversion. The people on the committee ranged from complete disarmers and pacifists, to people who were nuclear disarmers, but supported conventional weapons — the whole spectrum of different positions.

According to Ward, the national trade union figures on the council were looking for an argument about creating jobs nationally and were prepared to support the conventional weapons policy. They were not very closely linked to the people working in defence establishments in London concerned about the long-term future of their jobs, but fairly sure that orders in the short term were there.

Others who were drawn into the work of the Conversion Council say it amounted to a collection of notables who met to discuss 'this great issue'. The failure to direct any practical work meant it quickly became a talking shop only and people drifted away from it. In May 1984 the Labour Party's defence spokesman, Denzil Davies, attended the Conversion Council and there was a high level debate about the future defence intentions of a Labour government. But from then until November 1984 the council did not meet again.

Prior to that meeting the Industry and Employment Committee approved a budget for organising a conference for defence workers, but pressed by Conservative councillors, the funding was conditional on also organising a conference for defence contractors. The conference for defence workers took place in March 1985, but the attendance was disappointing. In total, apart from the speakers, about 45 people turned up to listen, and of them perhaps half a dozen were from defence plants.

By the time the contractors' conference took place in November 1985, Niven was employed only to carry out research on a consultancy basis. He had already done part of the organisational work for the conference — amongst others, he had invited Inga Thorrson, a well-known disarmament expert, who was flying in from Sweden, where she was Under-Secretary for Foreign Affairs. Five months before the conference, in June 1985,

Liz Gamlen had been appointed as the full-time conversion worker. An engineer who had done an MA in Peace Studies at Bradford University and had worked voluntarily for CND, Gamlen spent her first months getting out the invitations to the conference. No defence contractor would agree to speak. And out of an invitation list of more than 300, an attendance of 68 was not particularly impressive.

The Thorrson contribution — on Swedish plans for a central conversion fund and the creation of conversion funds at defence-related plants — upset at least one of the contractors, who objected that he had attended to discuss the defence industry in London and not to talk about disarmament. Although the conference report makes interesting reading, no-one had expected to get any mileage out of involving the employers.

Technology Networks

The clearest commitment to socially useful production was through the establishment of five technology networks, intended both to service the needs of groups of workers seeking to emulate the Lucas example, and to provide an experiment in community-based technology transfer. These networks aimed to draw on resources in polytechnics and colleges in London, and to draw together unions and users. Despite problems similar to those found in arms conversion, of lack of an active industrial base, and despite problems in securing community involvement, the 'technets' developed and grew from an initial base in community campaigns and individual inventors. Also networks were set up in the hope that the example itself would help to stimulate the input — what Mike Cooley referred to as 'technological agitprop'.

The outlines of the GLEB's technology policy were set out in July 1982 in a GLC Industry and Employment Committee policy document which developed an earlier policy decision to set up a number of technology networks involving innovation centres, product banks, machinery and production equipment banks, as well as technical support and advice units.

Objectives

In making the initial funding for this available, the paper proceeded to set out five objectives:

1. The urgent need to address the problem of technological change and the dramatic restructuring of London industry. An example given was the way that the introduction of first-generation electronic systems had caused major job losses in the electro-mechanical engineering industry of North and West London. Clearly, any strategy for creating jobs in London had to include a policy for the appropriate harnessing of new technology.

2. Such technology should build on the existing skills of the workforce. Makers of numerically-controlled machine tools in the US had recommended that they be worked by operatives with a mental age of twelve. But work on a 'human-centred lathe' conducted by Professor Howard Rosenbrock at the University of Manchester Institute of Science and Technology (UMIST) had shown that new technology could be designed and applied in ways that enhanced existing skills.

3. The introduction of new technology should be planned so as not to reduce overall employment.

4. New technology should 'meet social needs'. This was defined as follows; 'that in manufacture and in use it conserves energy and materials; that its manufacture and repair, and the recycling of its products can be carried out by non-alienating labour; and that its production and its products should assist human beings rather than maiming them'.

5. On this basis new technology should be fostered, but with a commitment to those 'alternative' applications which 'enhance skill, economise on non-renewable resources, increase long-run employment and meet the needs of working people as consumers'.

Principles

In pursuing these objectives, GLEB was to follow two main principles. First, the workforce and the community were to be seen as a major untapped source of product ideas; specific reference was made to the Lucas Aerospace workers corporate plan, and to other initiatives in Vickers, Metal Box, and EMI, as well as to initiatives by Hamburg shipyard workers and Bremen aircraft workers, in all of which large numbers of product ideas had been put forward from the factory floor. Reference was also made to the large number of product ideas in the R&D departments of larger companies which are not taken further because of lack of risk capital or cutbacks in R&D budgets.

Secondly, London's three universities and seven larger polytechnics were to be seen as themselves a major scientific resource, larger than those of any multinational corporation. This asset was under-used. A number of science parks were recognised as having gone some way to remedying this. Special reference was made in this connection to South Bank Polytechnic and its proposed Technopark. But, it was claimed, there had been no community involvement, and fostering this was seen as 'one of GLEB's principal tasks'.

An example had been set by the Lucas Aerospace Combine's work on alternative products. They had set up links with North East London Polytechnic, with whose equipment, space and advice they had built the prototype Road-Rail bus.

Proposals

It was therefore recommended that GLEB should implement this policy through the establishment of Technology Networks. These would be linked with existing polytechnics or university colleges, with 'user-friendly' access points for members of the public. They would also include enterprise support units offering technical production, marketing, and planning advice. Appropriate access would also be provided for people in the community to university and polytechnic facilities for their own research and development needs. Facilities would be spread round London rather than being concentrated in one place. And the networks would encourage student projects on relevant products and projects. Specialisms would also be encouraged depending on special expertise of the associated academic institutions. The networks would also contribute to a 'product bank' providing a return for the networks on products originated by them or their facilities as well, where appropriate, as a 'machine bank' of second-hand machinery refurbished as part of a training programme and then made available for co-operatives and other appropriate groups. The networks were also required to involve community groups and groups concerned with alternative technology in their management and day-to-day operations.

The policy therefore envisaged a three-way 'networking' between the public, including both trade union and workplace groups, community groups, and individuals; academic institutions, and individuals; and resources, in terms of buildings, equipment, and specialist staff. The sources of inspiration were clear, but diverse; the Lucas plan, the role of CAITS in assisting the Lucas combine, and the Netherlands Science Shops were among the influences most widely quoted. But the specific combination was new, and the work had therefore to proceed without precedents or rule-books to which to refer. And, as with everything to do with the GLC experiment, the inexorable background of shortage of time, pressure for results, and the constraints of bureaucracy took their toll. But the history of the five networks has interesting lessons for others trying to create a more socially desirable technology policy. And, furthermore, by adapting to the need to bring in revenue, and by finding other grant funding, several networks survived the end of the GLC.

The Five Networks

In the first three financial years, a total of £5.6 million was allocated through GLEB to its subsidiary Technet Ltd, for setting up and funding networks. A total of five networks were established. Two were geographically-based; the London Innovation Network (LIN) in North-East London, linked with North London Polytechnic and Thames Technet, linked with Thames Polytechnic. The remaining three were product- or service-based; the London Energy and Employment Network (LEEN), set up with help from Central London Polytechnic and South Bank Polytechnic; the London New Technology Network (LNTN), involving academics from Imperial College, City University, Polytechnic of Central London, and St Thomas' Hospital; and the London Transport Technology Network, which has close links with the Polytechnics of Central London, City of London and the South Bank.

The five networks were very diverse from the start. Different emphases emerged in their work depending on who was involved and the focus of activity. Looking at a number of these different activities, some not foreseen by the GLC or GLEB, demonstrates the achievements as well as the problems and frustrations of those involved in the networks.

Development of New Products

As the policy document shows, the development of new, socially useful products was seen as a central activity of the networks by those who dreamed up the idea. And all the networks did some of this. A stream of socially useful products and services resulted, many of which have gone into production, either through the creation of new enterprises or by placing in existing ones. In many cases, the input from community or trade union groups, or from members of the public was crucial.

One of the networks which concentrated most on product development was The Innovation Network (LIN). There, a group of local carpenters developed the Playbox, a neatly-crafted nest of interlocking storage play equipment ideal for use by playgroups, creches and nurseries. The brightly-painted components stack into a base with wheels and come apart for use as see-saws, rocking horses and other play equipment. Orders were secured from a London borough and the furniture union FTAT was able to find a London firm interested in producing the product, thus safeguarding existing jobs. LIN was also able to help develop a new product, the 'disability bus', which became the focus of a successful campaign for London Transport to adopt it on certain routes, thus transforming the lives of many Londoners with disabilities. John Butler, at that time the workshop manager at LIN, recalls the experience:

> What it is simply, is a wheelchair lift, a ratchet lift like you see on the backs of lorries. The person just gets into the lift, onto the bus, and clamps are provided to clamp the thing down. I was working the weekend we assessed it and it was fantastic. We had people who hadn't been on a bus for thirty or forty years, there were even one or two people who'd never been on a bus because they'd been in a wheelchair all their lives and they just could not get on a bus, and they all thought it was fantastic.
>
> There were people at Ladystar House, a residential place for severely retarded people, basically their only outing had been a walk round the grounds and onto the roundabout at the Green Man with the cars and bikes, and now they could actually get on a bus and be pushed around the Stratford shopping centre for a few hours and actually get into a visual experience. And they'd come back and say it was much more exciting for them than looking at the same four walls that they'd been looking at in some cases for twenty years.

Other projects came from individuals who came into the network buildings with their own ideas, some of them apparently eccentric. Mary Moore, the 'front of house' contact person at LIN, comments:

> Some are definitely whacky, but how do we judge? One thing that helps is where the idea comes from; for example, one man approached me with an idea and a rough prototype for an onion peeler. The idea came from his companion who worked in school

kitchens. She came along, discussed the need with us and from her experience and that of many other women, we could see there was a need.

John Butler recalls other cases:

We found it was the individuals who came in with ideas, half-baked ideas. We loved it. There were several perpetual motion machines. One bloke with a camera for one-armed people who showed me dirty photographs and things like that, all sorts of loonies, but anyhow we had some good ideas, and the ideas tended to come from individuals.

Other networks were less focussed than LIN on product development, but they all did some. Transnet was involved in the disability bus; it also worked with South Bank Polytechnic on developing and fitting to lorries the 'hush kits' required by the GLC Lorry Ban for vehicles with permits to travel in London at nights and weekends. The energy network, LEEN, included a number of groups using its workshops to develop new, useful and potentially marketable products in the area of energy conservation and renewable energy sources. It is a long road though from having a good idea to creating jobs in London by producing a new product. Susie Parsons, LEEN marketing manager, reflected on some of the difficulties:

There are a lot of problems in further development of products. There is a long lead time. For example, we are developing a user-friendly central heating control, and that's behind schedule because the people who were making the essential microchip for it failed to deliver on time ... now i would always assume that people won't deliver on time.

Learning to choose products takes time. 'We started off looking at any kind of energy-saving products. But we've now homed in on micro-electronic products because they seem to be the ones we do best, and there's a market.' Lack of commercial experience was a problem too. 'When we started off we weren't very good at marketing.'

Finally, investment is difficult to finance: 'We don't have the money to set up manufacturing operations ourselves. And without the resources to manufacture it, you're stymied. You sell it to someone who might be manufacturing it in Glasgow, which is no help to London's economy.'

Service Provision

Partly in the light of these problems, many people involved in the technology networks quickly came to the conclusion that they had other useful roles besides product development. One of these was the use of existing technology to provide services to people, and helping people to understand and use existing technology more effectively. Peta Sissons, the GLC officer on the LEEN Council, had worked for a number of years on housing, spending two years, for example, coordinating the anti-dampness campaign. She had a particular commitment to using the technology networks as one focus for 'using state resources to strengthen campaigns and local organisations'. She saw energy as a good focus for this: 'There's a tremendous amount of research around on energy and energy conservation. But day to day, people are facing these appalling living conditions, and were beginning to organise or had organised for some time and got nowhere. So how could we use resources from the state to strengthen those local campaigns?' LEEN tried a number of tacks. One was supporting the development of local energy plans, 'not a grand plan ... a process of people developing an alternative to the policies they're faced with ... bad housing, and heating problems and bills they can't pay'. The people working on the local plans did a mixture of organising, and research, and work for individual tenants groups. The workers have done energy audits with tenants groups, undertaken surveys of estates to see if they could be classified as hard to heat under DHSS rules, and provided individual advice.

Much of the work has focussed on local councils, both pressuring them and working with them to improve their energy conservation work. A lot of GLC and ex-GLC tenants saw an irony in this:

> They were fighting in many cases against the GLC as a housing authority. There is a conflict between one part of the state handing out money to independent organisations, and another part of the state as the housing authority producing those bad conditions people are fighting against.

LEEN did not succeed in having much influence on the GLC Housing Department. But it did increasingly work with, as well as pressurise, local boroughs. It has helped to draw together people in different council departments whose work affects energy conservation; for example, it helped Hackney set up a working party on energy conservation which includes some tenants. By 1986, LEEN had formed links with six boroughs, and were providing services. They teach London borough workers in housing and benefits to give energy advice; they set up and help run a technical advice service and do surveys of office blocks or housing blocks; they run a tenants insulation service, and have, for example, put in efficient draughtproofing in a tower block owned by Hackney Council.

Other networks also provide services, funded in various ways. John Butler of LIN provided another example of a service, promoted by a campaign, which has secured outside funding:

> We set up the mobile repair service in Islington, which specialises in electrical work, going round making repairs for pensioners and disabled people in Islington for a flat rate of £1 plus the cost of materials. That's still going, it's been funded by the Department of the Environment, partially funded by Islington at the moment, and there's a lot of interest from other boroughs. It even made Thames TV on a Friday evening.
>
> The idea came from a meeting we had a with a group of people representing the disabled. And their concern was the kind of thing many people can't do, changing a plug, or if something goes wrong with a kettle or a toaster and you get somebody in and the call-out fee is £15 and people can't afford that. From that we did a kind of survey of various disabled people's organisations in Islington and the one thing that came out on top was the idea of someone going round in a van ... and carrying out this work. So we put forward a paper and got Islington to fund it, and we made sure all the pensioners turned up and made sure the council would have been embarrassed if they'd said no. It worked.

Relations between Networks and Trade Unions

The founders of the networks had seen the trade unions as a major source of product ideas, and of organisational strength to get those ideas put into practice. As with arms conversion, this expectation ran into problems with the structure of London industry, and the pressure the unions were already under. Relations with the unions were more problematic for the networks than expected, and had to be built up slowly. John Butler commented on one set of problems: 'The original idea was that we'd open up this workshop and then there'd be all these fitters queueing up every night to use the workshops for their ideas, but you see it's not as simple as that. For most people who spend their day working on a lathe or a milling machine, the last thing they want to do is to go and work on it in the evenings.' In the absence of any mass industrial struggles over jobs to which a GLC-backed re-run of the Lucas experience might have seemed relevant, trade union routinism prevailed. As one GLC officer involved in the early preparatory work put it:

> The trade unions have no easy way of seeing what the networks are about or being involved in any official way. Even though any number of the individuals who are involved in the network may be active trade unionists, they're involved as individuals because there's little foothold for the trade unions to say, ah this is a thing which we do because it's recognisably part of trade unionism.

In the transport area however, where there were in the early 1980s well organised groups of engineering stewards in public transport, already working with the GLC on trying to save transport engineering in London, those local authority-union links were the basis on which the network was established. The GLEB Technology Division were already working with the bus engineering stewards in 1983 on trying to develop alternative and additional work for the Aldenham bus works. The chair of the Joint Works Committee joined the network council at the start, and the network continued to support the engineering unions after the formation of LRT.

In particular, Transnet was able to help with continuing work on possible alternative employment for the maintenance depots at Aldenham and Chiswick. A detailed report identifying potential markets and likely rates of return for alternative products and services was produced for the unions. This led to later requests for assistance when LRT announced plans to introduce electronic ticket machines to replace the existing electro-mechanical equipment. This threatened a progressive reduction of work for LRT's Effra Road ticket works in Brixton. With the agreement of LRT management and support from Lambeth Council, Transnet was asked to work on a survey to identify possible alternative employment.

In energy, relations with the unions were more problematic. The network built its strength in the area of tenants' associations in public housing. While the LEEN council could see that there were links to be built with the unions, especially in the Direct Labour Organisations, based on the attempt to create 'jobs from warmth' (insulation, heating, energy conservation, perhaps in the long run combined heat and power), in practice those links were created only slowly. Peta Sissons recalled some of the difficulties:

> There was an interest from the Trades Council and from some NALGO members. They could see this was a sensible thing to do, linking living conditions and job creation. But the DLO was fighting just to defend itself you know. People were not even considering the possibility of new jobs.

There has, however, been growing interest from the unions at different levels in LEEN. Susie Parsons commented that some trade union organisations are members of the network, and unions have backed individual initiatives: 'The London Energy Action Plan is backed by NALGO. [But] I wouldn't claim that the broader trade union movement knows much about us. The only way you can change that is by talking to people .. making contacts.' LEEN has run workshops and discussions with trade unionists on energy conservation and nuclear power: but not only is the process slow, they are also of course faced with a divide in the trade union movement on the issue of nuclear power. It is a somewhat similar divide to that facing Transnet on the issue of private road transport versus public and rail transport.

Creative Tensions

From the start, there were inherent tensions in the technology network concept, and those involved — users, members, workers, GLEB executives — took the brunt of these. GLEB, for its part, put an increasing emphasis on commercial skills and product development, worried that money might be wasted, and the networks not survive, if products were not produced and marketed fast enough. They saw the products themselves, as providing a sort of 'technological agitprop' capable of stimulating a further input by example. They argued that such practical demonstrations of the potential for socially useful job creation had to take priority over open-ended outreach work.

GLEB saw that this project-related approach jarred with the community orientation of some Technet staff members:

> You were putting technology networks, which were felt by the people keen on the idea to be to do with resourcing and supporting a particular kind of political struggle, and putting them into an environment to do with capital investment. That tension has bedevilled the networks throughout their existence. And I think it was never

fully accepted or felt by the people in the networks that this mainstream process of capital investment had much to do with what they
were being paid to do!

Network staff, members and users, however, take a more complex
view than this. They acknowledge the importance of commercial
skills, and of having a plan of development of the networks. But
they see on the whole a too early concentration on new products
as counterproductive. What GLEB calls 'outreach', they see as
the essence of networking, and the factor which can in the end
generate the real innovations. While recognising the tensions,
they see them as creative: the only way to democratise inputs to
technological development. And the London boroughs and other
funding bodies have implicitly agreed, by funding the networking and advice work, for example of Transnet.

The networks have therefore implicitly rejected GLEB's sharp
distinction between product development and manufacture —
revenue generating work — and advice, outreach and campaigning — not revenue generating. On the contrary, they have looked
for a range of funding sources for different types of work. LEEN
for example, in addition to work with local authorities and tenant
and community groups, also developed projects aimed at the
private sector, on the basis that energy-saving consultancy services could be more than self-financing for the clients. Though
LEEN's work lay mostly in the provision of services rather than
the development of products, it was able to turn this aspect of
advice and consultancy work into self-supporting or revenue-
generating activity, to the point where it was meeting some 40
per cent of its costs and had an ultimate perspective of self-
sufficiency.

Much of LEEN's funding however, like the other networks,
comes from the public sector. In different ways, the networks
have all been pushing for a 'social market' for new products and
services funded by the public sector, and they have demonstrated the potential for this. One example is in products to help
those with disabilities. A local trade union conference organised
at the beginning by LIN had identified these as a major focus of
local concern. A range of products for the disabled were
developed through LIN. One, the Cloudesley Chair for the disabled, originated from a student project by Kanwal Sharma at
the London College of Furniture, and could be promoted as not
only better able to meet the needs of disabled children than any
chair already in use, but also as being cheaper.

Other examples are in links between training and product development. Technets were able to house projects which dovetailed with their own work and widened the range of facilities they were able to offer to the community. Thus the London New Technology Network housed a course, part-funded by the European Social Fund and the Greater London Training Board, to train women in micro-electronics engineering skills which have till now been an almost all-male preserve. Trainees could gain experience working with the dozen or so start-up businesses housed in the LNTN building. Also housed in the building as a component part of LNTN was the Minorities Information Technology Awareness Group (MITAG), providing minority groups with Information Technology training, as well as organising workshops and training. In the end, it is the networking and outreach roles which are crucial to creating new directions in technology. Mary Moore of LIN brings out the reasons why the definition of what is 'socially useful' itself presupposes an input that cannot come from conventional product development processes, and which requires a continuing community involvement:

> If you talk about social usefulness then that involves a commitment to making sure that what you do is going to be of real use to the intended users which means somehow getting them to take part in the design process rather than just pop in with a product when you've produced it. If we couple that with the idea of 'technological agitprop' then people should also learn to do more things, to become more powerful and competent in the process of creating a new product. So you wouldn't just market-research a new product, which puts users in a passive role. You'd actually get them in the workshop and enable them to learn more about how such things are made and designed and repaired and modified. That's part of the commitment to socially useful production.
>
> Imagine we are going to pursue the idea of producing a piece of anti-sexist play equipment that will be made in plastic with electronic circuitry. We need to find out if other people involved in childcare believe there's a need for it. We will want to explore with them as feminists the anti-sexist content of the idea. Then we need to involve technical people, engineers and designers, to look at the practical possibility of making it. We need input from the people who know about the market for play equipment, and from people who know about the appropriate production processes, and what manufacturer could take it on. You will not find this group coming together naturally after a CND demonstration or a football match, for a quick drink or an exchange of ideas.

8
Planning from Above;
Planning from Below:
A Case Study*

The Problem Of Leverage

The problem for a local authority with industrial ambitions is its weak leverage over the national and international forces shaping the local economy. 'Spitting from a helicopter and thinking you are watering the gardens of London', commented Robin Pauley from the *Financial Times*.

It is partly a problem of funds, or rather lack of them. Many corporations spend well over GLEB's total annual budget of £40 million on one investment in one factory. It is also a lack of power: local authorities have no power to take over private companies unless they are for sale; they have no power to influence international trade; no power to plan major public purchasing beyond their own. In other words they lack the power to influence the economic environment of the firm.

If the economic leverage of local authorities is so negligible *can* their 'intervention' in the privately owned, market dominated parts of the economy be anything more than spitting from a helicopter? Can their investments, usually in companies vulnerable in the first place, be protected? Can they avoid one jobs rescue causing job loss elsewhere? Can any of the strategic and social improvements that they intend to make through their investments, have a wider positive impact on the industry?

*The names of GLEB investments in this chapter are fictitious.

215

Following The Industrial Links

For the GLC and GLEB, as for any local authority, a realistic answer to these questions needed a wider, strategic view of each industry. Without such a view they undoubtedly *would* be spitting from a helicopter, with illusions of rainfall. With relatively limited resources, the GLC's only chance of effectiveness was to select particular points of leverage where its limited powers could be used to maximum advantage and to find allies with whom to pull these levers. This required a picture of the workings of the industry as a whole. And this meant more than a view of the production side of the industry. It meant tracking down the complex web of economic connections linking production, distribution, supply, related services, associated industries, the government and international markets — for a start! Such an overview of the industry, or to use the jargon, the 'sector', would help a local authority to identify the points of possible leverage and to find allies.

But there is no one way of following through the threads of an economic sector. Your starting point and your purpose in following the threads will influence the overview you end up with. The GLC had two purposes in its intervention, through GLEB, in the private sector: two purposes that were, in GLEB's approach, inseparable and yet in constant tension.

First, its purpose was to transform the company, and if possible the appropriate sector or sub-sector, to achieve viability and lasting competitive strength. The GLC's guidelines for the funding of GLEB included the condition that companies receiving GLEB loans must break even after two years. In fact this relatively stringent condition (several merchant banks offer more generous terms) was not strictly adhered to although as the abolition of the GLC, and therefore the cut-off of major funding, drew near, commercial vaibility became the dominant consideration.

GLEB's second purpose was to achieve this transformation in a way that would benefit working-class people both in production and in the community. The intention was that Enterprise Planning would be the means towards this second objective, at least as far as the individual enterprise was concerned.

In an earlier chapter (on Enterprise Planning) we have seen some of the tensions between these two objectives within individual GLEB investments. They were clear too when GLEB developed its investment strategies for whole sectors.

London Furniture workers report on
the collapse of their industry and spell out
what should be done to save it.

BENEATH THE VENEER

Cover: Peter Kennard

In the popular planning workshops, workers had a chance to examine their industry and spell out what should be done to save it, publishing this book with their results for both local authorities and their union to learn from.

The Furniture Industry: A Tale of Two Strategies

There were few recent models of industrial strategy from the point of view of labour on which the GLC and GLEB could draw. In 1945 the Confederation of Shipbuilding and Engineering Unions drew up a trade union 'Plan for Engineering'. And the Miners' union, the NUM, has a strong tradition of developing its own strategies for the coal industry. The Communist Party in the 1950s used to have commissions on different industries made up of trade unionists from the industry concerned plus sympathetic

economists who would draw up strategies for a Labour government and the unions to carry through. But beyond such sporadic
initiatives the only sustained involvement by trade unions in
industrial strategy has been on a tripartite basis (that is with
employers and the government) through the Nation Economic
Development Organisation, NEDO. Trade union representatives
— usually overburdened national officials or researchers who
service several committees — attend the Sector Working Parties
and feed in specific policies, but the strategies these SWPs produce normally represent the lowest common denominator of the
three sides. Policy making on industrial issues within the labour
movement itself, both the Labour Party and the trade unions,
concentrate almost exclusively on *institutions* and structures (the
relations between different ministries, the need for various
investment banks/boards, the role of NEDO etcetera). It rarely
involves strategies for particular sectors of industry.

Consequently the GLC and GLEB had to experiment. As far
as the private sector is concerned, their 'experiments' in the
furniture industry are particularly interesting to explore and
especially likely to generate lessons for the future. The reason for
this is that two relatively coherent approaches were attempted.
They involved very different processes — one gleaned its information mainly from interviews with management; the other provided a forum and stimulus for the trade unions at shop floor
level to develop their own strategy — and they led to some
different perceptions of the industry and to conflicting views of
particular investments. Another reason for interest in the GLC/
GLEB's work in the furniture industry is that a distinctive feature
of GLEB's investments in the furniture industry is that they were
chosen on the basis of the strategy. Investment was consciously
an instrument of strategy. In many other sectors, strategy tended
to be more a rationalisation of investments made at an earlier
stage, and only latterly a guide to the development of these
investments. A look at the experience in the furniture industry
consequently provides the best example of the connection
between strategy and practice.

The other reason why the contrasting 'experiments' in the
furniture industry are especially interesting — a reason which
maybe also explains why the approaches are relatively coherent
— is that compared with many sectors it seemed a particularly
favourable one for GLC/GLEB involvement: middle-size companies, over which GLEB potentially had some leverage, pre-
dominated; the industry had a potential, underused advantage in

London's design skills which GLEB could strengthen; and workers were organised through a single industry-wide union which welcomed wholeheartedly the GLC's political initiatives.

Moreover the London furniture industry posed a challenge to the idea of a strategy for labour. Capital's strategies internationally had almost rased the industry to the ground. In North London in 1981 only four major factories remained. In 1975 there were nineteen. Clearly, traditional policies, based mainly on subsidising existing management, would do no more than delay total collapse. A radical new approach was, and still is, needed if the industry is to be saved.

The two approaches, for viability and social benefits, were both committed to meeting social as well as commercial objectives. But with the former the objective of competitive success was the prime focus, and assumed that the needs of labour, and other social objectives would be attended to at a later stage. The other brought the needs of labour to the forefront and treated viability as a constraint.

Background

The decision by the GLC to develop a strategy for the furniture industry was in part a result of trade union pressure. This grew in the aftermath of an early GLC involvement with the industry. One of the first initiatives of the new GLC Industry and Employment Committee was to rescue one of the largest furniture companies in London: Austinsuite in the Lea valley. It was a classic rescue. A collapsing family firm in the hands of an incompetent heir, 200 jobs at risk, the banks not interested unless public money or some other guarantee was assured, and a committed Labour authority, lacking a wider strategy but determined to do something.

The rescue, involving a takeover by a neighbouring company, was successful at the time (four years later it went into liquidation). But leading shop stewards from the furniture and timber union, FTAT, in other similar companies sounded a note of caution. Brian Ashton, convenor at Stonehills, for example: 'We were fully behind the Austin's rescue. It was a real ray of hope for us. But it was unfair to move into one company which could put others into jeopardy, without discussing through the implications with all concerned. Also we felt certain that the governors would be quick to take advantage of the GLC's generosity.' FTAT convened a meeting for officials and leading stewards to meet Mike Ward and Industry and Employment officers, and press on them the need to take an industry-wide view. They did not need much convincing, it was already their general intention. But the union pressure added an extra impetus to put particular resources into both a study and strategy for the furniture industry and once this was done, into further investments. This led to the first approach, the strategy carried out by officers from GLEB.

GLEB's Strategy: The Process

The intention of the two GLEB officers, Mike Best and Steve Baker, was to investigate the markets, the technologies, the company structures and strategies, in London and on an international scale. They interviewed managing directors, consultants, lecturers at the College of Furniture and the Furniture Research Association.

They wanted to find out why the furniture industry was so weak in London when the Italian, German and Scandinavian furniture industries had been able to compete so successfully — and virtually eliminate the London industry in the process. What were the strengths and potential strengths on which the London industry could be rebuilt? And what were the points of leverage by which GLEB could make a contribution to this process, if only by setting an example?

With headlines about 'Red Ken' dominating the London press, GLEB's initial approaches to management were met with some scepticism. However, before long, it was they, the managing directors, who wanted to see GLEB. They even wanted to use Mike Best as *their* consultant. The story goes that he had to change his telephone number to fend off calls from desperate furniture employers! The reason for this rather unexpected response lies in the dire state of the industry in Britain. 'The market suddenly and unexpectedly fell away. It was like going over a cliff', the managing director of Sleepeezee, a subsidiary of an American multinational with a factory of 200 in Merton, told GLEB. They had neither a clear explanation as to why they faced such a crisis nor a strategy for survival — beyond continuing more desperately than ever with their existing, disastrously short-sighted, strategies.

For some time the main manufacturers had been trapped in the incestuously competitive world of the London furniture industry, lacking any direct contact with international markets. They have been dependent on and dominated by the retailers since the sixties, when the main manufacturers invested in volume production but failed to establish their own means of mass distribution. The retailers adapted to changing markets by switching to international suppliers or by forcing domestic suppliers into a downward spiral of price competition.

Mike Best and Steve Baker provided managers with information about wider international market trends. This was one reason for these managers' interest in the GLC's survey, if not in its conclusions. There was another vacuum on the employers' side which the GLC's survey momentarily filled. The industry is extremely fragmented, mainly because of the cut-throat conditions just described. No organisation provided a coherent overview of the industry. The British Furniture Manufacturers' Federation, never strong, except perhaps in immediate post-war years, has been weakened further by the Conservative Government's employment legislation which made national agreements on minimum conditions voluntary. Many companies consequently withdrew from the Federation in order to evade pressure to abide by national agreements. (One such employer, Silentnight in Lancashire, provoked a strike which has gone on now for over a year. The main shareholder/manager refused to pay the national minimum, pleading lack of funds, and meanwhile creamed off the profits for his personal use. When the majority of workers went on strike, he sacked them.) The discussions with Mike Best and other staff from the Greater London Enterprise Board provided panic-stricken employers with some wider bearings.

GLEB's Strategy: The Conclusions

The GLC/GLEB strategy argued that the best way of overcoming this fragmentation and enabling London's furniture industry to be more responsive to the international market would be to form an industrial district of complementary enterprises which shared common services. The strategy emphasised the need for co-operation between firms which would lead to complementary product ranges and to certain shared marketing and design facilities. This was the advantage of industrial districts. Industrial districts in Italy were an important model.

The strategy saw the role of GLEB as being to stimulate, fund and encourage such collaboration. Only public sector funding agencies could provide this role. British banks tended to reinforce the short-term, price competitive approach of the majority of companies. GLEB suggested the kind of market and production strategy that such an industrial district should pursue. This is the most innovative and potentially controversial part of the strategy. Mike Best's studies of the furniture industry internationally indicated that an industrial revolution was taking place based on the introduction of the computer to production and distribution. Although this was general in manufacturing, it was particularly marked in a fashion-based industry such as furniture.

Computer controlled shaping, boring and routing machinery, computer aided design, and retailing linked by computer to production, have completely transformed the economics of short-batch design-led production. It makes it economic for a company to produce batches of forty different designs and to change them every year, where before it was necessary to continue for years doing long runs of the same twenty designs. These developments could almost wipe out the London furniture industry with its volume production and lack of design, on the one hand, and on the other, its costly craft-based reproduction furniture. GLEB's strategy suggested points of leverage to encourage sub-sectors of the industry to make the leap into 'flexible manufacturing', as the new systems are generally described, and to do so in a way which enhances the skills, conditions and control of those who work in the industry.

The leverage was to be through a combination of highly selective investment and the funding of shared support services in technology, design and marketing. The provision of design support is crucial to the strategy; for without very good design the potential of the new technology is wasted. In each investment the Enterprise Board was committed to exercising its leverage in ways which improved workers' conditions, strengthened the trade unions and extended trade union bargaining where posible.

Here then was the GLC's first approach to a strategy for the furniture industry, and in particular for GLEB's intervention. It did not involve any extended contact with shop floor representatives of FTAT, though there was regular liaison with national regional officials. The detailed company information came from direct contact with management.

GLEB's Strategy: The Practice

The strategy led GLEB to make two major investments: one was in Cabinet Designs (CD) Ltd, a volume manufacturer, employing around seventy people. The other was Repro, a reproduction company employing around thirty people. We will tell the story of the investment in Cabinet Designs because this is the investment over which there were some differences of opinion between GLEB and the shop floor trade unionists who developed their own view of the industry.

Between June 1984 and June 1985 GLEB invested £1.5 million in CD in two stages. GLEB saw CD as a point of leverage for restructuring the panel sector of the industry. Its advantage from this point of view was that it had the highest annual turnover per employee of all London panel producers. And its owner/manager seemed sympathetic to GLEB's objectives and was approved of by Ben Rubner, FTAT's General Secretary.

GLEB's general aim described by Mike Best was to provide CD with the breathing space to 'wrench itself free from the old forms of competition — cost cutting with standardised mass production — and into the new forms of competition — flexible, specialised, batch production'. At first it invested £500,000 to help CD make this move. Such a move would, according to GLEB, require a 'strengthening of management especially in building up design and marketing skills, a change in the production process to enhance flexibility and allow for skilled labour inputs; commissioning market research to guide designers and the promotion of product development with maximum participation of different sections of the workforce.'

Prior to making the initial investment GLEB commissioned an accountant's review of CD's accounts. According to this review CD had broken even in the previous six months and would continue to do so for the next six months if there was a high level of production output, and a continuation of the current order level. GLEB bought 40 per cent of CD's voting shares. The owner and his family retained control though, with the proviso that if cumulative losses exceeded £300,000 control would shift to GLEB. But CD's order book was already declining even as GLEB invested.

The GLEB investment was absorbed by debts before the restructuring plan even got off the ground. The only moves that could be made towards restructuring were the comissioning of market research, interviewing potential sales managers and recruiting a management accountant and an experienced German production engineer to enable the owner himself to spend more time on sales.

The market continued to decline. GLEB believed that the company's short term as well as long term future depended on diversifying markets. GLEB made a further investment of £600,000. £350,000 of this enabled CD to take over a neighbouring company, Tottenham Furniture, which was about to collapse. Tottenham had sales outlets which would diversify CD's customer base. The rest of GLEB's funds were for working capital within CD. Designers were employed, exhibitions organised and other moves were made to improve CD's ability to produce and distribute for the independent retailer market.

Orders to the independent retailers grew, but to the traditional outlets they collapsed. In mid-June, the new management (employed by GLEB) at CD asked GLEB for more money. GLEB did not give the full amount, but provided £300,000 to keep the company from receivership while it assessed the new management's plans, including a move into retailing.

Before such an assessment could be completed the new auditors that went into the company when the new management took over, found that the losses were larger than originally realised. The managers appointed by GLEB recommended that further investment would be unwise. CD went into receivership on 30 June 1985.

The lessons that GLEB officers involved with this investment draw are radical. They argue that in retrospect a change in power relations was needed both between workers, staff and management and across the different functions of management. Such a shift would give more influence to design and marketing as well as a closer relationship on the shop floor between planning and designing on the one hand and production on the other. They questioned whether in fact that was possible in CD. CD, argued Mike Best, was too production oriented. Its relative efficiency in production perhaps created an inbuilt bias towards price cutting competition. This reduced profit margins and thus ran down the resources available for the move to a more flexible, customer-oriented strategy.

As we shall see later, the lessons that the FTAT shop stewards drew from this experience also concern power and the character of management. They argue that if GLEB had involved them more in the first place they could have provided this insiders' understanding of the character of the management team and the implications of his power, before GLEB made its investment. But before we come to their assessment of this particular investment let us describe the process of their strategy making and the wider conclusions they came to about the industry as a whole. Their assessment of CD follows logically from their wider view.

Furniture Workers' Strategy: The Process

The second approach started with meetings of shop stewards and officials from FTAT. The purpose of the meetings was to prepare a trade union view of the industry, and proposals for what the union, the GLC and a future Labour Government should do. They intended to make an assessment of the GLC's strategy and GLEB's investments as part of their own report.

Four day-long workshops of fifteen or so stewards took place. The shop stewards were recruited through the FTAT District Committee, who sent details to all East London/North London FTAT branches. The workshops were led by a TUC tutor, Mary Davis, from the Trade Union Studies Centre, South Bank Poly. Several workshops were attended by GLEB staff responsible for furniture investments. On one occasion the worker director and father of the chapel in the print union SOGAT at the GLEB-owned bookbinding company talked about industrial democracy.

At the fourth workshop a steering group of nine stewards was elected to report back to the full workshop and possibly to a London-wide meeting of FTAT stewards and officials. This steering committee had eight day-long meetings, including a visit to the London College of Furniture and to Rye Machinery, High Wycombe, a woodcutting machine tool company. There were discussions with a health and safety inspector, with a member of a design co-operative, with Ben Rubner, the General Secretary of FTAT, with several GLEB executives including one on the board of Cabinet Designs, and with the GLC's Chief Economic Adviser. I acted as the 'scribe' for their discussions.

The Workers' View: What's Wrong with Management

The steering group started with the issues that, as shop floor representatives, they were most familiar with: conditions, including health and safety, wages and new technology.

These are some of their comments on health and safety drawn

from an article they wrote for the FTAT *Record* summarising their investigations:

'One thing is very clear: working conditions in our industry are very poor indeed.

'Judging by the workshop reports toilet facilities range from non-existent to barely adequate. Management's view appears to be that if they provide decent toilets workers will spend more time in them. Dirty walls, broken bowls, cracked sinks, leaking urinals, no handles on closets and no bolts on doors. These are the conditions in most of our factories.

'Management argue that workers create these conditions themselves, so therefore there is no point in providing toilet facilities similar to those in the offices. This view is clearly unacceptable . . .'

'In many of our factories we have to take our meal breaks surrounded by dust and dirt. Not many companies have made any real effort to provide canteen facilities, or at least an area away from the working environment with table and chairs, so that you can sit and eat your meal in dust free conditions.'

'Noise! Perhaps the major problem for us all. Without doubt noise levels in all woodmills are far too high. Tests taken in one large North London factory recently showed that industrial deafness is becoming a real problem.

'We all know that the "acceptable" threshold of 90 decibels is too high anyway. But there are many things companies can and should do to reduce noise even to this level. Manufacturers of the machine tools should build noise reduction into their design.'

'Dust! In an industry that creates so much dust, we find our workers are faced with yet another health risk.'

They drew some more general conclusions from these and other findings:

'These working conditions tell us a lot about management's attitudes: their lack of concern for their employees, their obsession with costs and their reluctance to move along with the times. In our view, the state of the toilets is an indication of the state of the industry!'

They also made some recommendations:

'a) Local or national authorities investing in or taking over furniture factories could help to make them cleaner, safer, healthier places to work. They should use their bargaining power to support trade union demands to reduce dust and noise and improve toilet and canteen facilities. They should insist on a health and safety committee and on time off for the trade union training necessary to make it effective.

'b) Local authorities should provide funds for technical and scientific facilities — "hazard centres" — to provide trade unionists with the information and the advice they need on work hazards. These could make use of the resources of Polytechnics and Universities.

'c) Health and Safety legislation should impose conditions on the manufacturers of wood working machines, as far as noise and other risks which could be avoided by a health and safety conscious approach to design.'

A major section of their report is an investigation into the behaviour and character of management. They introduce a detailed documentation of the failings of management with the following:

'The first task of management is to manage production; yet in our experience in the furniture industry management show a careless attitude to the details of production as long as the flow is being maintained. Management fail to follow through suggestions you make. Management fail to come back to you on a problem that needs to be sorted out.

'Take waste for example: the wastage on a day to day basis is tremendous and management rarely comes on to the shop floor to see why there are so many returns.

'All too often management fails to discuss new methods of production with the workers. This means that there are many occasions when a worker can forsee that a new method will break down — and yet when this happens management do not accept responsibility. That it's their fault. It's always the worker's fault.

'In one factory management has introduced the Japanese method of monthly quality circles. But these are on management's terms and people do not trust them. After decades of treating workers with utter contempt, it is not surprising when workers respond in the same way. The only time the management seem to be a little human is when it needs a favour.

'In our experience the majority of management are devious and underhand. Management assumes that it can misinform us and that we will not realise what it is up to.

'As long as there are profits and orders management is satisfied and complacently rejects improvements in design or the idea of ploughing some of the profits back into the business. Managements are riding high at the moment on a government which is just made for them. Until Thatcherism is defeated, management's attitudes will not change.'

They are critical of management's long term view of the industry, or rather their lack of it:

'Management's labour policies in the '50s and '60s were very short-sighted. When they moved into mass production, flow line systems, they increasingly employed unskilled labour and made no provision for training or apprenticeships. The result is that skilled labour is scarce just when management need more flexibility and when new technology opens up new possibilities for the skilled craft worker, possibilities which would also improve the market position of the company which recognised them.'

They also recognise that as union members they got drawn into management's way of looking at technology. They defended their members' immediate interests but they did not think long term:

'Though we accuse management of a "head in the sand" approach, we too, in the rank and file, have been complacent. We accepted the deskilling, we agreed too easily to use the multi-operational machinery, the quick drying glue method, the warm air drying tunnels and the plastic fittings.

'Now we face a new phase of technological change: the computerisation of production. We have not seen anything compared with what is in store for us. Therefore it is important to act now.'

Workers' Proposals for Change

After their visit to Rye machinery they had an extensive discussion about what a trade union view on the new technology should be. A shorter working week was high on their agenda. So also was the issue of skill.

'The other double-edged aspect of CNC machines concerns the skills of those who use them. They could be introduced in a way which takes the skill away from the operator into a programming office away from the shop floor. On the other hand they could be introduced in a way which extends the operator's capacities with training to programme the machine and to work with designers on modifications which would apply to batch production. They could enable the highly skilled craft worker to play a significant role in the industry once more: the machine could be set up to do the basic pattern, leaving the engraver to add the extra touches which would produce an economic, "up market" product.

'At the same time as bargaining to retain and extend our skills we would need to be flexible, to be multi-skilled and to broaden our horizons not only within our own crafts but in the industry as a whole. We must negotiate training schemes for ourselves otherwise we will be ourselves out on a limb.'

They made the following recommendation:

'a) We need to negotiate new technology agreements in which:

    i)   We are consulted before changes take place.

    ii) We are able to negotiate over management's future investment plans.

    iii) There is a proper period and scheme for retraining with no loss of pay.

    iv) That computer programming is done on line, by or in close collaboration with the craft worker.

    v)   There is a shorter working week (or working day, depending on what the members wish) with no loss of jobs or pay. Other forms of extra time off should be investigated e.g. paid sabbatical leave, early retirement.

    vi) Equal opportunities should exist for everyone.

    vii) All new equipment is investigated by the Health and Safety Committee.

    viii) There is no change to the status quo without a negotiated agreement.

'b) We would argue that public authorities investing in the industry support this approach and do what they can to help with training schemes.

'c) We believe they should provide funds specifically to enable companies to invest in the new technology, but they should make these funds conditional on the management making the above form of technology agreement.

'd) Public authorities can also help to provide trade unionists with access to the new technologies in order to understand their dangers and benefits before they are introduced into particular factories. GLEB's technology networks have this potential but it is a facilitiy which needs to be made far greater use of by the trade union movement. Too often we are caught unawares.'

Knowledge Of Production

The FTAT stewards' report showed, as one would expect, an

immensely detailed knowledge of the production process. Such knowledge would clearly have been extremely useful for GLEB both in drawing up its strategy and in running the particular enterprises in which it invested. Certainly, the more sophisticated private management realised its value in a limited and contained sphere when they set up Quality Circles. But stewards dealing with one such management, at Nathan's, reported that this kind of brain picking without power was not having much success.

'Most of the guys just don't want to know. They don't want the half an hour paid time off for the meeting; they want to carry on working. They don't want to divulge the information that they've accumulated over the years, for the company's benefit when they are doubtful whether it woud be in their benefit. Their biggest fear, quite rightly, is that management are trying to do away with jobs in a devious way.'

The stewards from Stonehill's described how they used their knowledge of production in wage bargaining: 'When we go in for a wage rise, management's first reaction is always, "how can it be funded?" We always have answers to that based on our knowledge of production and the opportunities they have missed and the wastage they have allowed.'

Design

Design was an issue where they could see management making fatal errors:

'The designers are not given any scope to design. In a lot of cases they are given designs by other companies, told what the product has to cost and asked to modify an existing design. Sometimes the design even has to be determined by how many units have to be in a load. One member of the group gave an example of this: "We had a design of a wall unit and they could only get X amount on to the lorry. They had to change the design so that they could get more on."'

They agreed with GLEB that the other pressure against good design are the mass retailers, Queenway and MFI. 'The leeches of our industry', they called them. They did not think they could do much about design directly through the union. Because of the low priority put on design by the major companies, most designers are freelance and rarely stay long, or they work in small, specialised firms. They are not in the union. It is not like engineering companies such as Lucas Aerospace where high level design is an integral part of the business and designers are well organised. The Lucas model of trade unionists in the company developing alternative products was not therefore appropriate for the furniture trade.

The FTAT stewards also believed the problems facing furniture workers in London could only be understood in relation to the furniture industry internationally. They intended to visit furniture factories in Europe and compare notes with furniture trade unionists there. (Italy was the favourite spot!) The GLC would have paid for the visit, with some back up on the organisation from FTAT. But with the pressure of GLC abolition the visit never got arranged, and the stewards made do with several discussions on the issue, including one with Robin Murray from the GLC.

At first they had a simple answer to the problem of international competition: import controls and subsidies. This is FTAT policy. But put forward as the central thrust of a strategy it has acted as a block to thinking any further; in particular to thinking about transforming production itself. After lengthy discussions the steering group modified, or rather developed its view. As they said in their report *Beneath the Veneer*:

'At this first meeting we believed that the only solution was import controls and or subsidies. The discussion at our second meeting led us to believe that such policies were not enough. They need to support a deeper strategy for production itself, including the control and direction of the industry. Otherwise they would merely provide a support for the present management with all its incompetence and lack of care and imagination.'

Import controls and subsidies on their own would stave off the problem, they decided, not least because of a larger crisis in the international economy.

'In countries such as Britain, Germany and Italy it is a crisis of profits. Governors and governments are trying to get out of it either by directly undermining the strength of labour and/or by increasing productivity through introducing new technology at the expense of labour. In poorer countries like some in Eastern Europe and most of those in the Third World it is a problem of debt, of obtaining the hard currency (i.e. dollars, deutsche marks or pounds) to make the repayments required by Western banks and governments. It is this desperate need for hard currency which leads these countries to subsidise their export industries, like furniture, or in the Third World to increase the price of raw materials or start to manufacture and export components themselves.'

As a long-term solution, they said, import controls would provoke retaliation and an even worse financial crisis: working-class people in the West would suffer but the economic misery in countries such as Poland and Ethiopia would be even worse.

'On the other hand we believe it would be possible to introduce import controls as a means of protection — and therefore for a limited period — while carrying through a radical transformation of production. The government would need to coordinate with labour movements in Europe to minimise the likelihood of retaliation. To achieve the rapid transformation needed to lift the furniture industry out of its present crisis, the government working closely with FTAT representatives at all levels, would need to direct the computer technology which is now sweeping through the international economy, in new ways. For this it would need to make available massive investment funds specially for designing and introducing the new system on the basis of technology agreements we suggest elsewhere.'

They spelt out the implications of their conclusions for Government action. There should be temporary protective measures including import controls and public investment to pay for the introduction of computer based technologies, and a government scheme tieing increases in demand with increases in employment, perhaps in the form of a special rate support grant for local authorities for them to intervene in industry on condition the investment preserved or created jobs. They also proposed government guidelines to regulate the mark-up of prices by retail outlets, and a system of monitoring whether extra revenue was reinvested in the company rather than lining the employer's pocket.

Joint work should be started now,' they concluded, 'by the trade union, local authorities and the Labour Party nationally on the details of an alternative strategy for different parts of the furniture industry, including the international dimensions of such a strategy. We hope this report provides a local beginning of this process.'

The report proposed two areas of further work by FTAT and the Labour Party or by Labour local authorities: what forms of public ownership and industrial democracy — both at a company and a sector level — would be best for workers and consumers in the furniture industry and what form of competition and cooperation between companies in any one region should this involve? Secondly, what kind of co-operation needs to be built between furniture industries on a European scale? The report also made recommendations for local authorities, drawing from the lessons of GLEB.

Workers' View of GLEB

The GLEB experience was a major impetus to the workshop discussions. By the time the workshops started, GLEB had produced its strategy paper and made several investments. Workers were angry they had not been consulted — they blamed their union as much as GLEB. They were keen to react and to give their opinion, not just as workers, but as ratepayers and as supporters of the Labour GLC. Discussions quickly moved on to issues of policy.

The debate about GLEB began when Steve Baker came to an early meeting of FTAT stewards to answer questions. He was given a rough time — all taken and given with good humour. The questions focused on how GLEB takes its decisions: 'Every governor is a crook. How does GLEB find out what the government is up to?' They went on to ask who GLEB consult: 'Do you know what the latest technology is? Would you take management's word for it? Why haven't you involved us?'

Then they asked what sort of people work at GLEB. The stewards interrogated Steve Baker about his own experience: 'Have you worked on the shop floor? If management took you round the shop floor and told you about the machines, you would believe them wouldn't you, because you haven't had any experience on the shop floor.'

They were sympathetic to what GLEB was trying to do:

'At the end of the day GLEB is a good thing, but I'd like to have the stewards from Cabinet Designs here and find out exactly what their experience has been and what contract they've signed.' But they were wary. They wanted to find out more and to be in a position to propose as well as to criticise. Moreover they assessed GLEB as ratepayers, as contributors to GLEB's money: 'It's bad management that has caused the crises, yet the danger is that our money is used to prop it up. This is where the workers need a lot more research before we get involved in this.'

In the light of what they knew about the management of the industry they considered some of GLEB's proposals unrealistic.

As one steward put it: 'The GLEB proposals are like a fairy story. They are wonderful but just couldn't be carried out with the present governors.' Someone else expanded the point: 'GLEB isn't powerful enough to get them to co-operate in the way that is necessary, unfortunately. The employers won't get together. We work for one of the better governors. But he enjoys firms going broke. He rejoices when his cousin goes out of business, literally.' While they shared GLEB's analysis of the problem they felt that their proposals underestimated how entrenched the employers are in their approach.

Some felt that GLEB should not invest in individual companies, because their resources are too limited to have an influence on the sector as a whole. Rather GLEB should concentrate on providing common resources like marketing and design and working with the unions on bargaining strategies over new technology and early warning of redundancies. Others argued that GLEB should concentrate on small enterprises with a good record, help to promote co-operation between them and encourage their workers to join the union.

A point on which everyone was agreed was 'the need for GLEB to consult more widely amongst trade union representatives both on its general strategy and on particular initiatives. It is important to talk to the trade unions in the factory, not only the area officers. We know our governors. We know how to assess what they say. Also in many factories we more or less control production. Management come to us when they want a problem sorted out. We can tell when things are going wrong. We realise that GLEB do have a policy of working with shop floor representatives but in our experience this has not always been a sufficiently high priority.'

These points are illustrated vividly in the workers' assessment of the CD investment. Their general conclusion was that GLEB had been too passive and trusting of the owner and his management team. They agreed with the view put most strongly by one of the foremen from CD who came to a special discussion of CD after it had collapsed: 'Do you know what should have happened? And I'm speaking with hindsight. GLEB should have moved the owner from MD, sacked the production manager (the owner's brother-in-law) and they should have put in the MD from Tottenham to run the sales side; and one of the blokes from the shop floor, one of the foremen, to run production.' The foreman had an interest in this argument, but the stewards agreed with him. One of them added: 'After all, we and the foremen have been running the factory for the last four years. We haven't had a proper manager all that time. Just the Tottenham MD and occasional consultants from Germany who come and go.' It is interesting that other furniture companies were quick to snap up two of the CD foremen as managers when it went into receivership.

GLEB had also concluded in retrospect that what was lacking was a radical change in power relations. But they despaired at how this could have been achieved. The implication of the workers' lessons is that if GLEB had treated the union — shop floor and staff — as a more active, positive ally — its only ally initially — it could have been the force that made the shift possible. Formally of course GLEB did involve the union, but for much of the time it *was* predominantly formal. The one real gain in union strength which GLEB made possible was the unionisation of the staff. Otherwise enterprise planning meant little.

It was not that GLEB did not care about the workers. Rather the architects of the new strategy of flexible specialisation tended to assume that the benefits for the workers and the increase in their power would come *after* the shift to flexible specialisation. What comes very clearly out of the discussion with shop stewards, on the other hand, is that a new relationship with the unions could have been a *means* of making the shift. That meant changing power relations while the old form of production still existed. It meant basing GLEB's intermediate strategy on the trade unions' knowledge and control of production, as well as on GLEB's overview of the market shifts. The insights of the overview and of the 'underview' were both necessary.

Treating the workforce as allies, rather than potential beneficiaries, might also have improved CD's immediate market position. 'We could have told GLEB that furniture was going out so bad that we were losing orders because of it,' said one foreman. 'A couple of minutes more on the job in the mill alone would have improved it.' And in terms of quantity: 'You can take it from me there were ways and means of increasing production on them lines. The scope for improvement was incredible. But to get more production you've got to become a friend of the men, right? You've got to treat the men as men, with respect. There was none of that there.'

The FTAT stewards' recommendations drew one central lesson from GLEB's involvement in the furniture industry in general and CD in particular. They emphasised the importance of a direct, close working relationship between the public authority and the shop floor representatives of the company in which they are intervening — with sufficient resources for time off for the workers' representatives and educational back up. Across the industry, they thought the trade union should be consulted on investment decisions just as it was, by law, on health and safety. 'Discussion with management and trade unions to draw up an industrial strategy should go on in parallel,' though the initial framework should be discussed first with the unions. The public authority cannot be neutral.

Comparison

Here, then, were two different ways of developing an industrial strategy. One an 'overview' identifying trends and structures through study and investigation, the other an 'underview' gained by exchanging experience, reflecting on it and going on to discover trends and to analyse behaviour and character. This 'underview' provided a degree of detailed insight into the character of management in the London furniture industry which could only come from the inside, as well as knowledge of the details of production — and the written report can only be the most superifical indication of a knowledge which is by and large practical and tacit. Lacking this knowledge, GLEB's investment was not used effectively.

One obvious lesson would be that the GLC-sponsored workers' investigation of their industry should have gone on simultaneously with the GLEB/GLC study of management strategies and market and technology trends. When the FTAT stewards put this to Mike Best, he was sceptical about any direct trade union involvement with the GLEB interviews. One steward put it to him: 'Our governors are not telling you the truth. If we were involved we could tell you.' (This became a constant theme — if only GLEB had talked to us, they would have known ...) Mike: 'They wouldn't talk to me with you there.' 'They would,' came the reply, 'we'd make sure of that'.

In the case of the well-organised workplaces, this was not bravado. But there are many furniture factories where the workers would not have had the clout to insist. In such cases local authority officials could report back to the stewards after any interviews they have with management, rather like health and safety officers should report to the shop floor representatives when they come to investigate a company.

Conclusions: A New Approach

A method of developing industrial strategy which based itself on constant involvement with the union, shop floor as well as full-time officials, but investigated the overview of management's strategies and market positions would itself help to change the balance of power, even before any public authority investment. The process of the investigation and making policy would thus become explicitly political. The experience of the FTAT/GLC workshops, in spite of their limited role in GLEB's decision making, points to the potential of such an approach to industrial strategy, especially for Labour local authorities, in several ways.

The workshops had a limited influence on GLEB but they did provide an opportunity for stewards across the main furniture factories to meet and exchange information and advice, including trips to the more poorly organised shops. FTAT's structure contains no such forum on a London-wide basis, not even the kind of gathering which the AUEW's shop stewards' quarterlies provides (or used to provide) in many areas. In the past, branch meetings were the occasion to hear reports from different factories. But, as in other unions with a geographical branch structure and with the introduction of the check off system, members no longer need to attend to pay their dues and meetings often consist only of branch officers plus one or two highly committed members. The life blood of the union has gone. It's no wonder that stewards become isolated. The occasional visits from a full time officer cannot substitute for a regular direct contact with other shop stewards.

There used to be an unofficial London-wide FTAT shop stewards' body which met on a Sunday afternoon. It collapsed some years ago but one of the proposals from the GLC/FTAT workshops was to re-establish this forum with official support. One benefit of the workshop discussions was to enable people to see particular, apparently fragmentary developments in their own workplaces in a wider context. It was like piecing together a jigsaw. And information fed in by GLEB or the GLC, gleaned from interviews with management or studies of the European industry, would sometimes provide missing pieces. In effect this provided stewards, and the full-time officials who occasionally attended, with a kind of early warning system. It increased their confidence because they knew better what management was likely to get up to.

The potential of this became evident over new technology.

Normally trade unionists can only react though the changes they face could transform their conditions and future prospects. They have few resources to investigate, let alone challenge, a technological innovation and suggest the alternative ways in which it could be directed. However joint trade union and local authority work on industrial strategy can look beyond the conventional bargaining subjects to the technologies being introduced and the alternative options for their design, development and application. The GLC/FTAT workshops began to do this with their visit to Rye machinery and discussion with staff from GLEB's New Technology Network. This was only a beginning though some of the stewards felt they understood the options several steps before management had made its decisions — but their potential was as part of an alliance between a Labour council and the unions to impose an accountability on management for what they were doing to the industry.

Public Scrutiny

A local authority can only enforce accountability over an industry indirectly through spreading information, and encouraging scrutiny and debate. This can strengthen union arguments, especially at a time when purely industrial bargaining power has been eroded. Public scrutiny and pressure on owners and managers can strengthen union attempts to improve conditions and press for investment. And public debate helps unions press for the sort of strategic transformation which only national political action can bring about.

Trade Unionists As Producers

The problem which led us to examine the two approaches to the furniture industry was the local authority's lack of leverage over the forces shaping the local economy. The experience of GLEB strategy and the trade union criticisms of it point at least to part of the answer: leverage over economic forces needs not only power from the outside but also power within production; for a Labour local authority committed to saving jobs and improving their quality and conditions that means power based on the workers. In fact the lack of such power can undermine the best laid schemes for public funding and purchasing. Some of GLEB's experience with CD illustrate this. Power within production requires an ally amongst the producers. And a Labour authority that has not built a detailed working relationship with the workers at all levels, is in danger of relying on management whatever its good intentions.

The idea of a direct working relationship between a public authority and shop floor representatives for the purpose of transforming production is new and difficult to put into practice. One problem is an inertia in relations between a Labour authority and the trade unions, especially private sector unions. To a large extent both 'wings' of the labour movement, political and industrial, take a relationship for granted. But normally the relationship is passive; indeed, it is more a historic settlement over a division of functions than a working relationship. Our argument here challenges this passive division. It does so not by upsetting the traditional independence of the trade union in wage negotiations, but by working with trade unionists as more than wage earners, as producers with knowledge and potential power over their work, and concern about its purpose and future.

If trade unions are to expand their traditional function, especially at a time when they find it hard to maintain even that, they need considerable political support. In hindsight we would conclude that the GLC/GLEB should have put more resources into providing such support, even at the expense of funds and staff for investment. Moreover the research we carried out should have fed more directly into union education and policy making, rather than being intended purely as a guide to GLEB investments.

One idea on how to do this was for trade union resource centres for specific industries, for instance clothing, furniture, and print. Such initiatives are more than simply 'supporting the unions'. They help to create the kind of alliance within production which is, I would argue, a precondition for public ownership providing any effective leverage over the local economy.

9
Labour's Plans for Construction: The GLC as Client and Employer

Construction is always an important political and economic issue in elections, even if it is not always an explicit one. The construction industry itself is a sensitive barometer of the economy — it responds quickly to recession and reflation. A future Labour government promises to pump money into this sector because it creates jobs quickly — quite apart from the need to deal with the levels of homelessness and the dire condition of much of the country's housing stock and infrastructure.

However construction workers will be the first to tell you that simply throwing money at the construction industry without having a strategy for the industry will not be enough. The circumstances and conditions under which investment in the construction industry takes place are particularly important because of the nature of the industry itself: labour is highly casualised with very little strong trade union organisation.

Our experience at the GLC also shows that throwing money into the private or public sector of the industry without having an employment strategy is likely to make working conditions for building workers even worse than they are now even if more of them have work. This is because a higher proportion of the new jobs will be casual, 'on the lump', further decreasing the proportion of directly employed workers in the industry. This will make any attempt to rebuild trade union organisation and improve working conditions in construction even more difficult.

Moreover, in its present state, the construction industry could probably cope with no more than a 3% increase in annual investment, because there will be neither the organisation nor the

Credit: John Sturrock/Network

Safer working conditions on construction sites have been part of Direct Labour Organisations' aims since 1892. In the 1980s construction workers are having to press the same demands.

trained building workers or other technical staff to meet a larger increase in demand. This is despite the fact that 3% growth is very slow when compared to the slump experienced in the last decade.

In the last two years before abolition the GLC was 'throwing' £300 million a year into the construction industry. This means that the successes and failures of Labour policies in the last five years of the GLC need to be understood, and in particular, who benefitted more from them: building workers, or their public and private sector employers?

What Labour had to Face in 1981

The GLC's strategic role in London's construction industry had been in serious decline throughout the previous Tory administration led by Horace Cutler. Most of the GLC's massive housing stock of some 224,000 dwellings had been, or was being transferred to the London Boroughs. With the housing went the building workers who maintained the housing. This fact aided the second strand of Conservative policy — the destruction of the GLC's Direct Labour Organisations.

There was nothing new of course about this second strand — it was part of a struggle that has been going on for nearly 100 years. For it was the London County Council — the forerunner of the GLC — that formed the first Direct Labour Organisation in 1892. It was formed, as were those that followed it, in response to the failure of private contractors to provide an adequate service to local authorities, and in response to the growing trade union organisation within the construction industry and their demand for fair wages and conditions.

The success of the DLOs provoked successive attempts by private contractors to restrict their activities. In 1908 the contractors' supporters — the 'Moderates' — won control of the LCC and sacked its 3000 building workers. After the First World War, many new local authority DLOs were set up to build council housing. Each time the construction industry hit recession, as in 1927, and in the late 1950s, new attacks were mounted on building by direct Labour. Despite this opposition, the scale and number of local authority DLOs grew to a peak in the late 1960s, when the LCC employed over 6,000 people in maintenance work alone out of a national total of 200,000 DLO workers, before the next slump provoked the next attack.

During the 1970s the GLC/ILEA was the largest local authority building employer in the country. In 1977, at the start of the Cutler administration, they employed over 5,000 building workers — 4,000 maintaining houses and schools and 1,300 building new housing. By 1981, when Labour took over County Hall, two thirds of these had gone — through 'natural wastage', compulsory transfer to the boroughs and redundancy. The other major problem Labour had to face was the Local Government Planning and Land Act with its requirements for DLOs to 'compete' with contractors and achieve a 5% 'profit'.

Labour's Manifesto Plans

There were 3 main areas of policy affecting the construction industry in the 1981 Labour Party manifesto for the GLC, all influenced by discussion with the construction trade unions.

(1) The formation of London Community Builders, a new GLC/ILEA DLO made up from what remained of the ILEA Architects' Branch, the Housing Maintenance Branch and the Construction Branch. London Community Builders was to aim to carry out virtually all the GLC's and ILEA's maintenance work and win in open tender 50% of the Council's capital building programme, that is, its new building work and major improvements. It was to tender for work for the London Boroughs and be able to provide a comprehensive building contract service — from design to completion. It was also to provide good employment conditions and establish equal opportunities for women in building trades traditionally dominated by men.

(2) The use of the Council's economic power to ensure that private building contractors followed decent employment policies: Contract Compliance.

(3) Investment in London's building stock and industrial infrastructure through improvement work on housing estates transferred to the boroughs, new housing, small factories, workshops and warehouses, fire stations and schools, and investing ratepayers' money in improving London's Underground and local British Rail stations.

London Community Builders

The nucleus of London Community Builders was the Construction Branch of the existing Housing Department. 'C' Branch, as it was known, had been the main target of the previous administration's job cutting. The fact that any organisation remained at all in May 1981 was due to the efforts of the trade unions in resisting job losses and what was, in effect, a privatisation programme. It was understandable that the stewards in 'C' Branch saw the new Labour administration as a lifeline, at a time when they were completing the existing housing contracts they had at Bayonne Road in Fulham and Piggott Street in Bow.

'Without the return of a Labour GLC we were faced with the dole queue once our existing work was completed. The Tories were determined not to let C Branch have any further work even when we tendered successfully in competition with private contractors,' a steward remembered.

Under the new Labour administration, the rundown of 'C' Branch continued, the intention being to transfer building workers to the LCB as work for them in 'C' Branch dried up.

But there were problems from the start, and the trade unionists involved feel that from the start there was a problem of commitment of the GLC officers to the new organisation, and a lack of belief that it could succeed at the scale planned for it.

A conflict between the trade unionists and the new administration quickly emerged, when the councillors, on the advice of officers, continued with the voluntary redundancy scheme and attempted to speed up completion of the largest contract at Bayonne Road, by introducing private contractors to carry out the work. The building workers at Bayonne Road resisted this, even when the recently elected Labour councillors came to a mass meeting and attempted to persuade the workers to accept the private contractors. The attempt only stiffened the resolve of the workforce to insist on direct labour on the site, and eventually the Council was forced to recruit further labour and also 'borrow' workers from the local borough building force.

It is fair to say that an important reason for this ill-judged intervention by councillors was their inexperience in dealing with the senior officers of the Housing Department who ran 'C' Branch and who expected to continue running it in the way they had under Cutler, but it also indicated the shape of things to come.

London Community Builders was set up in 1982, and was to

amalgamate with the ILEA DLO based in the ILEA Architects Department. But this amalgamation never took place, and the GLC and the ILEA continued to maintain 'separate' DLOs. The background to the abandonment of this part of Labour policy is best explained by shop stewards from the two organisations:

> There was definite opposition from ILEA councillors themselves although it was a manifesto commitment. The objections originated with management in the Architects Department who went to counsel to get a ruling whether ILEA was part of the GLC! They also claimed that, because of the requirements of the Planning and Land Act, any 'losses' made by any part of an amalgamated organisation would threaten the future of the whole. In fact as ILEA was a Sub-Committee of the GLC, as far as the law was concerned we were one organisation anyway.
>
> LCB shop steward

> I don't think our management ever wanted to participate in LCB in any way. Their position within the Architects Department had been well established over the years. For us, the pay and conditions in LCB were better than ours, but while discussions went on about amalgamation, there were no negotiations about wages and conditions in the new organisation. In the end, because of this, and because the management told our members that their losses would threaten us, our members rejected the idea of going into LCB.
>
> ILEA Shop Steward

Despite the obstacles London Community Builders did trade 'profitably' during its existence but it never grew as had been hoped. While the formation of LCB eventually brought about an increase in the amount of maintenance work carried out by direct labour, new building work was restricted by a self-imposed limit on the scale of work for which the LCB would tender. Opposition within the GLC continued to be a problem too. As one steward described it:

'I think there's been a deliberate practice to try and keep down the level at which LCB tendered for contracts. I don't think it was policy at member [that is, councillor] level, but a decision by management on what they thought we could really cope with. Also a lot of work wasn't being offered to us because officers in one department weren't co-operating with the LCB management until the stewards opened lines of communication between them. That didn't happen until early 1984.

'Up until then, the architects obviously knew we existed but they seemed to regard themselves as the professionals who could carry on in their own sweet way regardless of any policies that are laid down by the Council.

'The officers steered LCB into being essentially a maintenance organisation. If the councillors had gone into it more deeply, more of the work might have come our way.'

The total turnover of LCB in 1983/1984 was approximately £23 million. Of this, £14 million was spent on work carried out by council employees. The GLC/ILEA spent approximately £230 million on building works in the same period.

The other issue for building workers was that of pay and conditions. While there were no specific manifesto commitments to building workers, and while they were not the lowest paid manual workers, building workers expected a better deal from the Labour administration. Building workers could potentially benefit from commitments to create common pay scales and conditions for white and blue collar workers: in addition there was an outstanding issue of a new national agreement on bonus payments. The Labour Councillors accepted the arguments of their senior management that it would not be legally reasonable to incur additional expenditure by improving pay and conditions (such as sick pay, holiday pay, London weighting etc.) without any external reason or pressure. The lawyers argued that unless the GLC could demonstrate either a clear benefit to the Council, or that they were responding to the pressure of industrial action, any improvement in the pay and conditions of building workers would be unlawful! (Chapter 4 discusses the councillors' response to this advice.)

At the time that Labour took power at County Hall, the construction trade unions had also negotiated with the local authorities' Joint Negotiating Committee a national increase in the 'bonus calculator' (the amount that determined how much bonus would be paid for a particular task). The employers had decided that the increase should only be paid to workers operating bonus schemes that had been reviewed, and judged 'satisfactory'. GLC officers instituted a review which held up the payment and meant that GLC building workers' earnings were lower than those of building workers in some other London Boroughs.

'The officers in the GLC and ILEA dreamed up all sorts of reviews and wasted hundreds and thousands of pounds in preventing us from obtaining the new bonus calculator. We still haven't got it 5 years later. The ILEA threw out a bonus scheme for small works on the recommendation of officers', said one steward.

The policy of harmonising pay and conditions for manual and white collar workers yielded one change. In return for accepting pay cheques instead of cash, building workers received an additional payment of £6 a week. But big differences remained between white and blue collar workers.

It has to be said that, had Labour not been elected in 1981, the Conservatives would have destroyed the bulk of the GLC's Direct Labour Organisations. However, it also has to be said that the Labour administration did not live up to the expectations of the GLC's building workers. The jobs of those that remained were preserved, but little else changed. The division between GLC and ILEA building organisations exacerbated division amongst its building workers and weakened them organisationally. This suited the management — it may have suited some of the councillors.

The manifesto commitments on improving the housing stock, and building new housing, factories and fire stations benefitted the private sector of the construction industry more than the public sector, although this investment clearly provided jobs — around 13,000. Another area of policy — Contract Compliance — was designed to change the quality of those jobs.

Contract Compliance

By the time that the GLC was abolished its Contract Compliance initiative had been operating for three years. What effect have these policies had on the construction industry in London?

Before we look at this we need to take into account the present state of the construction industry. It is an industry in which, in the private sector, 50% of workers are now self-employed and a very low proportion of the employed workers are members of a trade union. Trade Union activists are victimised for demanding rights and facilities taken for granted in other industries. The sub-contracting system has large numbers of small employers. The large employers have all reduced their labour forces, relying on casual labour and the sub-contracting system to regulate their labour pool and ensure that they do not carry workers who may be 'idle' for periods when the employer's workload is low. The death and accident rate in the industry has increased even though numbers employed in the industry have fallen dramatically because of the recession and the cuts in public expenditure on housing and other capital projects. The traditional apprenticeships in the industry are disappearing and are being replaced by YTS training.

The Labour GLC manifesto called for the creation of a code of practice which would eliminate the 'lump' — the system of sub-contracting and self employment. The code would cover health and safety, wages and conditions and trade union rights. This policy was a response to trade union demands that private contractors and Direct Labour Organisations should compete on genuinely equal terms: terms which included decent employment conditions for building workers. It was also a recognition that the GLC could use its economic power as a purchaser in pursuance of social objectives.

One particularly strong influence was that of the 'Contract Compliance' policies developed in the United States in response to the Civil Rights movements. The purpose of these policies was to ensure that Federal spending was not directed into companies that practised discrimination in employment and promotion against women and black people, but instead would be an economic force promoting equal opportunities.

Contract Compliance, then, was simply an extension of existing contractual powers — but with an ideological difference. Contractors who wished to carry out work for the GLC had always had to meet financial and technical requirements — in other words to show that they were capable of carrying out the work and were financially stable.

The Construction Industry Contract Compliance Unit brought additional powers into play: contractors now had also to demonstrate that they had adequate health and safety policies, as required by law, and their pay policies were scrutinised. They were to adhere at least to trade union rates of pay and to operate the negotiated holiday and sick schemes, or comparable schemes.

Some of these requirements arose from new council powers agreed by the new Labour administration. The rest resulted from an attempt to use powers that that had existed unused for decades. The two most significant existing powers were:

(a) The 'Fair Wages Clause' — a clause written into all GLC contracts which demanded that private contractors pay wages not less than those agreed in negotiation between employers and trade unions;

(b) Powers to control through contract terms the use of sub-contractors on public sector sites.

To these were added requirements that contractors:

(a) meet their obligations under the Health and Safety at Work Act;

(b) be members of a recognised employers' association;

(c) comply with the building employers' declaration of intent on direct employment of labour as opposed to the use of self-employed labour;

(d) use 'labour-only' sub-contractors (the small contractors who are the basis of the 'lump' system) only with the approval of Council Members;

(e) be able to demonstrate to the Council that their employment policies were being brought into line with the Race Relations and Sex Discrimination Acts.

The GLC divided its contract compliance activities between two Units: the Construction Industry Unit which dealt with all the construction issues except (e) above and the Equal Opportunity Unit which dealt with equal opportunities compliance by suppliers of all goods and services to the GLC and ILEA, including construction contractors.

The GLC and ILEA had an Approved List of Constructors for construction work. The Contract Compliance Unit began by sending these contractors a detailed questionnaire on their employment policies, including Health and Safety, employment and training policies. Subsequently firms with over 50 employees who met these requirements, were then asked for information on their equal opportunity policies and the profile of their workforce by grade, gender and ethnic origin. Those contractors that failed to complete the questionnaire were in principle to be removed from the Approved List. Those who were willing to meet the Council's objectives were, if necessary, to be given advice and assistance in doing so, by the Contract Compliance Units.

On the basis of this information, the practice of the contractor then had to be monitored while the contract was carried out. Unit workers made random on-site checks, looking particularly at health and safety practices and sub-contractors and, in some cases, cross-checking through inspection of company wages books. Where there were breaches, contract compliance staff were to try to negotiate changes in the contractors' employment policies, and to warn the contractor of the consequences of not changing them.

When the policy was put into practice a number of constraints soon appeared. First the ability of the GLC to impose conditions on employers in respects of trade union rights was severely limited by the 1982 Employment Act. This specifically forbade local authorities from requiring their contractors to use only trade union labour. This meant that the GLC could only impose vague requirements that trade union officials should not be prevented from communicating with building workers on GLC building contracts.

Second, Technical Officers within the GLC were generally hostile to the policy as an 'interference' in their area of responsibility. The officers responsible for carrying through the policy — the Construction Industry Contract Compliance Unit — were put into the new Industry and Employment Branch. Their job was to monitor contractors' employment practices, but it was necessary to monitor the technical officers as well, a job better done from outside the Architects' Branch. A measure of the initial hostility they faced was their nickname among one group of Architects — 'The secret police'. One contract compliance worker said, 'I recall talking to one architect about a contract he was supervising in which there were at least three unauthorised sub-contractors on site. His response was that he didn't care who carried out the work, or how they were employed, so long as the work was carried out to his satisfaction. Behind his desk he had pinned a postcard of a Berthold Brecht poem — "Communism is Simple" ...'

Even where architects were more supportive of the policies, very little responsibility for implementing them was taken within the main Departments using private contractors. The new contract conditions were seen as peripheral to the task of getting building works successfully carried out rather than as an integral part.

The third problem, however, lay in the central aim of the policy: to persuade employers to change their ways and become 'good employers'. This led, ironically, to a reluctance to use the Council's power to remove contractors from the Approved List when bad practice was found. Senior officers in the GLC refused to countenance the removal of some major contractors who had failed to supply the Contracts Compliance Unit with information on their employment policies and one GLC councillor said he regarded each contractor removed as an 'expression of failure'.

The most common breaches of Council conditions found during site inspections were in the unauthorised sub-contracting of work and the use of self-employed labour. Nearly half of the GLC's sites that were inspected in the first year had these problems. In some cases entire contracts were found to be sub-let to another unknown company without the knowledge of the architect.

Worse, while some employers who adamantly refused to provide information or co-operate could be removed from the list, those who 'co-operated' but did not in fact comply still remained. At first, when lump labour was found on their sites, contractors would undertake to reduce their use of sub-contractors and increase their use of directly employed labour, but they would revert to their old practices when they thought the spotlight was on another contractor. One major contractor did eventually withdraw from the GLC's Approved List rather than directly employ workers to carry out contracts. Another contractor however eventually instructed its site staff not to talk to Contract Compliance officers but to refer them to the company Industrial Relations officer. The site workers for this company were freely admitting to the GLC that their employer was not complying with the Council's contract conditions, at the same time as the company was claiming to hold special training sessions on the GLC's policies for its contracts managers!

The root of the problem was that with the exception of equal opportunities policies, the employers were used to dealing with the other questions raised by contract compliance, since they were the every day concerns of white, male trade union officials in the industry. Consequently the large employers had already developed sophisticated systems for deflecting and absorbing pressure in this direction.

This led to an apparent divergence of opinion between Labour councillors at the GLC and at other local authorities. While many Labour authorities were keen to take up the contract compliance initiative, they saw it primarily as a means to defend their Direct Labour Organisations from the sustained ideological onslaught of the Government and the private sector, and not as a means of intervention in private sector employment.

The Tory Government sees the link between contract compliance and privatisation quite clearly. Their plans for extending their privatisation policies beyond construction work include introducing legislation to limit the conditions that local authorities can impose upon private contractors. This fits in with the 'free market' philosophy, but it also illustrates the power of the employers' lobby. Further privatisation means big profits for those companies involved in contract cleaning, catering, refuse collection and construction and it is these sectors which have been lobbying hardest for these restrictions on local authority powers.

The response of building employers to contract compliance has been predictably hostile and unco-operative. The worst hostility was directed towards the equal opportunities policies, although these, like the more familiar policies on pay and working conditions, demanded no more than that employers meet their legal responsibilities and the terms of their agreements with the trade unions.

It was therefore difficult for the employers to find legal objections to the contracts compliance policies but they did object vociferously to the willingness of the GLC to intervene in the private sector at a time when the trade union movement was too weak to resist the effects of the recession and the 'free market' philosophy that promoted the sub-contracting system.

Even so the policy did force hundreds of contractors to re-appraise their policies and attitudes towards health and safety, holiday and pension arrangements and employment policies. Some have improved their provision. And a few have started to reassess their policies towards the sub-contracting system and the use of self-employed labour and are even starting to change long-standing practises which discriminate against women and black people.

Furthermore, the ILEA has taken over both Contract Compliance Units from the former GLC so that the progress made so far has not been completely lost. Although the scope of ILEA construction is limited, other London local authorities have now set up Contract Compliance Units.

None of the work, however, has brought any fundamental change within one of the most hazardous and most casualised industries in this country. There are few pressures for improvement. The Health and Safety Executive lack the resources to police safety practices, and trade union organisation within the private sector of the construction industry has become progressively weaker in the last 10 years. The Government is considering reducing Health and Safety controls on small employers (which included the majority of building employers). If they restrict the ability of local authorities to include social objectives within their contracts, this can only make a bad situation worse.

In this environment what progress that has been made through contract compliance policies would take far less than three years to disappear. The willingness of Labour controlled local authorities to continue and develop these policies in London will have a crucial effect upon building workers in both the public and private sectors.

But it is also important to recognise that contracts compliance policies as presently implemented have not succeeded in increasing the confidence and ability of workers to organise and to fight for these policies themselves. This is partly because present contract compliance is oriented to promoting 'good personnel' practices: rewarding the 'good' employer and penalising the 'bad'. The effect has been that while trade unions — from shop stewards to national executives — support Contract Compliance and are demanding the implementation of the policy at a national level, once the policy is put into practice the trade union role in it easily becomes marginalised. There is therefore a danger that such policies could be seen as substitutes for helping to rebuild trade union organisation in the industry. In nearly two years of site monitoring of GLC and ILEA contracts ranging in value from £20,000 to £20,000,000, contract compliance workers only encountered two shop stewards. This is a measure of the depth of the crisis in trade union organisation in the industry that needs to be addressed.

Contract Compliance came out of a genuine desire to improve conditions within the construction industry, rather than forming part of a strategy of intervention in the industry based in helping workers to organise for themselves. The GLC policies on Contract Compliance and Direct Labour Organisations could only have a limited effect on problems which partly arise from organisational and political weaknesses within the construction industry trade unions.

When building workers do develop their own strategies for their own industry, then the incentive to struggle for the implementation of that strategy is much clearer. Here the GLC did attempt to promote such strategies, by creating opportunities for building workers to have their own in depth discussions through workshops organised by the Popular Planning Unit. These workshops produced some ideas and proposals which are in sharp contrast to what the GLC had in mind:

'There should be a National Building Corporation run by a board who are elected every three years, as representatives from Regional Boards and Government ministries. It would work in conjunction with a National Loans Board which would give loans for house building at very low interest rates. The National Board would lay down guidelines on standards of work, health, safety and welfare, contract compliance and training. The Regional Boards, who would elect representatives to the National Boards, would consist of representatives of Trade Unions, Local Authorities, Tenants' Associations.

'At local level would be the DLOs themselves in a new form. They would be run by Works Committees. The Works Committee would be made up of workers' representatives elected through their Trade Unions and representatives of management. The Works Committee would be responsible for the discipline of workers and management, for production and training. The same principles would apply on building sites themselves.'

In other words, building worker trade unionists see the public sector as the way forward, not a private sector with 'enlightened' employment policies, which is what contract compliance is all about. This means that their major political concern is how to strengthen and improve Direct Labour Organisations. This does not simply mean trying to persuade a future Labour government to remove the restrictions placed on them by the Tories. The way in which they have been run and by whom is just as important a problem. One shop steward put it succinctly during the Popular Planning Unit's workshops:

'Suppose we all agree about the need for people who believe in DLOs to manage them, and that they've got to be both expert in the industry and politically committed, then the problem is where are these people? Obviously they're amongst building workers, but then maybe UCATT with the Labour Party should be doing some sort of training in committed management because I shouldn't think there are many.'

If the GLC had paid more attention to its own building workers and developed the forms of industrial democracy the manifesto referred to, and if they had really confronted the importance of having managers who were politically committed to improving and defending Direct Labour Organisations, far more progress might have been made in dealing with the problems of the construction industry. The five years of the last GLC administration was not long enough to solve the problems of the industry, but one is left with the unsettling conclusion that, at abolition, the industry appeared largely untouched. Without a determined national strategy, that's the way it could remain.

10
On the side of the Workers? The GLC and Transnational Firms

There's no interest on the shop-floor, everyone is resigned to their fate (redundancies), they've been soaking up the media for all these years. The stewards, even the very active ones, have so many doubts and uncertainties. It would be so easy to tell the membership what most want to hear, i.e. that they should take the money and run, but experience and common sense means that you have to keep going. We're in a very awkward position, and the boost in morale for the stewards attending the meetings is essential.

In March 1986 the giant UK/Dutch company Unilever announced that 600 jobs had to go at its London subsidiary plant, Van den Berghs & Jurgens. The workforce were quite unprepared. They had become used to the security of their work; they made margarines, spreads and other oil and fat products and their market had seemed relatively immune to the ravages of Thatcherite economic policy. Safe in their employment many had taken on large mortgages and new cars and were content with their unions' role inside a highly paternalistic company.

But when the shock announcement of redundancies came, they also knew they were only a small part of the worldwide empire of a powerful company. Unilever employed over a quarter of a million people altogether; their families, communities, suppliers were also dependent on the huge transnational which, in 1985, had made profits of £950 million. What could one London workforce do against this power? It had already seen from a distance the decimation of much British industry and, just down the road at Wapping, the fate of the News International workers trying to fight another transnational company. The numbing sense of powerlessness amongst the workforce is perhaps the transnationals' most effective weapon.

And what could a local authority, with no statutory powers over such a company, do to help protect the jobs of its community? The GLC knew that its commitment to increasing employment in London could be rendered hollow by just a handful of companies shedding jobs or moving production elsewhere. Exploring ways of helping workers in London plants of transnationals to defend their jobs was one of the biggest challenges to the Industry and Employment branch. This chapter looks at what it was able to do in a situation where it had few, if any, legal powers of intervention against the most powerful economic organisations in the world.

The Power of Transnational Companies

Over the last twenty years or more, transnationals have made full use of containerisation, air freight, modern telecommunications and new technology to develop truly international systems of production. (One transnational manager recently claimed that the spread of international direct-dialling telephone networks had more impact on their capacity to organise internationally-integrated management of production than any other single factor.)

This has enabled many transnationals to establish portable factories: they can set up, and close down, production at any site where they can exploit local conditions of weak trade unionism, low wage rates, state grants and subsidies, 'stable' favourable political conditions, access to local markets and other factors in the search for maximum profitability. They have an unprecedented flexibility and mobility.

This has created a new international division of labour — a world-wide 'dutch auction' in which labour, local and national governments bid for the investment prizes held out by the transnationals. In some industries (notably textiles, electronics and the auto industry) workers in, for example, the USA, South Korea and the UK are forced into direct competition. The integration and dependence of each plant and each market in a truly international production process makes local or even national trade union action highly vulnerable. The company is able to play factory against factory, plantation against plantation or country against country.

There is no political power on earth yet able to control multinational companies. The GLC realised this and decided to put its small resources instead into the defence of jobs through helping to establish information and contact between trade unionists on an international scale.

There is no political power on earth yet able to control companies like Unilever, even if they had the political will to do so. The transnationals play off governments who compete for new investment with grants, tax concessions, free or subsidised land (or even complete factories), cheap labour and compliant trade unionism. The only possible bargaining strength for national governments is the power to grant access to domestic markets. Few single national markets are large enough to carry sufficient bargaining power in isolation, however, and even where they are, international trade regulations can inhibit them from using such bargaining power.

For those concerned with creating jobs, preventing redundancies or improving working rights and conditions, this has become one of the most pressing questions. Transnationals dominate the London economy. Of the top seventy five manufacturing companies, seventy two are transnationals.

The policies and strategies of transnationals have been a decisive factor in the loss of London's jobs. Ken Livingstone presented a report to the GLC on transnationals in 1984, claiming that the number of manufacturing plants in London with more than 500 workers fell from 273 to 221 between 1973 and 1978, but by 1982, there were only seventy five of these plants left.

Obviously a good number of these closures were due to the collapse of family firms, or relocation to green-field sites elsewhere in the UK, but overall, the greatest worry was the extent to which major restructuring decisions were being taken at a supra-national level. The future of London employment is in the hands of institutions well beyond the reach of conventional local authority economic policies.

By far the largest employer in London, Ford Motor Company, shed over 10,000 London jobs between 1979 and 1984. The work went to Germany, the USA, Japan and elsewhere. Kodak, another US-based company, employed 8,000 people in 1973. Half of those jobs had gone by 1984, with the prospect of more disappearing to the USA as the European operation is wound down.

Such job losses have far-reaching consequences — not just on direct employment in the transnationals, but on many more jobs in dependent companies, local businesses, and indeed entire local communities. Steve Hart, a TGWU local full-time officer responsible for Ford Dagenham, reflected on the wider impact of Ford job loss.

'Fords haven't been taking on new labour for six or seven years, when it used to take on thousands of workers every year. I am sure that that has had a dramatic impact on youth unemployment, and in particular on black youth unemployment in areas in London like Tottenham, Hackney and Brixton. That obviously has an impact. Without a doubt, seven years ago a number of Broadwater Farm youths would have had a job at Fords, or they would have been through the Ford sausage mill for a year or so, which would have had an impact in all sorts of ways.

'Though it's by no means ideal work to do, at least you're in a big place, you're in contact with lots of people, and contact with organised trade unionism. Whereas the only jobs that people can get now are intermittent and un-unionised. You can get a little bit of casual work, and never come into contact with unions.'

The new GLC administration believed that a policy of defending jobs in London must involve strategies to counter the global restructuring and UK job destruction of these giants. At first sight, it seems impossible. The idea that a local authority (no matter how large or well-resourced) can seriously hope to tackle some of the world's largest corporations seems somewhat idealistic.

Traditionally, local authorities and national governments have accepted or have been forced to accept the logic of competition for transnational investment. Millions have been spent by local development corporations, regional industrial regeneration projects and others on lavish public relations exercises, advertising campaigns and entertaining potential investors. The Tory GLC for instance spent £80,000 per year on advertising in New York, including publishing glossy brochures proclaiming the benefits to investors of London's low wage economy. Tables showed wages in London as the lowest of any European capital except Dublin.

Recent examples include the Northern Development Company — set up by the Northern Region Councils Association with the support of the TUC and CBI and a budget of half a million pounds — to conduct a thorough exploration of the Far East for new investment. Before it even starts, it is having to compete with the established North of England Development Council with its permanent offices established abroad as 'embassies for development', and county councils such as Durham going it alone with their own plans. The company was deliberately set up to compete with the Scottish and Welsh development agencies in the battle for international investment.

The GLC quickly recognised that even with maximum commitment of funds, it couldn't even make a dent on transnationals' policies through investing in companies itself.

Mike Ward, Chair of the GLC's Industry and Employment committee, explained: 'We might have had £20 million a year, we might have had £30 million, we might have had £100 million a year, but even that, even if we'd blown it all on one company, would not have been a major decision-making factor for the large corporations.'

There was no coherent strategy for tackling transnationals. There were however a number of traditions, principles and rules of thumb which were brought to the GLC and formed an overall framework which helped form the foundations of transnational policy.

These beliefs included a commitment to ensuring that economic development in London was not to be at the expense of other areas of high unemployment in the UK, an emphasis on working with the trade union movement at rank and file level, and a willingness to explore and experiment. A further important element was the GLC's general emphasis on the specific predicaments and needs of black people and women.

From the outset, the GLC drew much from the experience of a number of organisations which had been working on transnationals for some time, notably the UK affiliates of the Transnationals Information Exchange — Europe, an Amsterdam-based network of resource, research, and information centres. These included the Centre for Alternative Industrial and Technological Systems (CAITS), Counter Information Services (CIS), International Labour Reports, Conventry Workshop and others, all of which had considerable experience of work on the problem of transnationals — whether through research, trade union education activity, or practical organisation and assistance in helping to create international links between transnational workers. At a later stage, the GLC directly funded the establishment of the Transnational Information Centre — London (TICL), which helped to strengthen this work.

This loose network of local trade union resource centres and research groups shared a broadly common approach to working with the trade union movement in general, and to the problems of tackling transnationals in particular, which had considerable influence over (and involvement in) the GLC's work.

The core of the approach lay in a rejection of the rhetoric and ritual which had so often passed for international trade unionism in the past. Instead, any effective defence against transnational employers had to be based on the international free flow of information, contacts, and ideas between shop stewards and lay trade union members in the transnationals.

Before the involvement of the GLC, some of the resource centres already had invaluable experience in assisting transnationals workers with company research and international contacts — on very limited resources — particularly through the Transnationals Information Exchange network.

The role of the local resource and research centres was — and still is — to help with company research, contacts overseas, the production of newsletters, reports etc., organising (and raising money for) international meetings and delegations, and with the technical problems of foreign language translation. The direction of the work, and the development of strategies and policies, had to be generated from the stewards themselves.

There had been inevitable disputes and conflicts between some of the research organisations and the formal structures of the trade union movement when the positions taken by local stewards developed independently of the national policies of the unions. The conflict was not uniform although the TUC for instance had been trying for years to discourage support for such centres. Often this has reflected the much older running disputes between the TUC and the more innovative Trades Councils — some of whom were responsible for establishing resource centres.

There are, however, particular conflicts which arise when tackling transnationals. The emphasis on developing direct international links across plants and across communities cuts across established national and international trade union structures. The predominant official trade union policies towards transnationals are focused on lobbying and campaigning in the UN, the ILO, the EEC and elsewhere for international 'codes of conduct' for transnationals, the insertion of 'social clauses' in trade agreements, rights of access to company information, and controls on international trade and the transfer of capital.

In the meantime, trade union hopes rest on the development of an international bargaining strength by the international trade secretariats (ITS) — bodies set up to tackle transnationals. The ITSs are federations of national trade unions with membership in particular trades or industries (the International Metalworkers Federation (IMF), the International Union of Foodworkers (IUF), the International Chemical and Energy workers Federation (ICEF) etc.), some of which have their roots in the nineteenth century. Those with members particularly affected by transnationals have developed 'company councils' over the last ten or twenty years, which attempt to co-ordinate company information, and organise regular meetings and conferences for the national union negotiators responsible for the particular companies. The long-term objective has been to build international collective bargaining agreements with the companies, and to co-ordinate claims on wages, working-hours and other conditions.

At the shop-floor, however, few stewards are likely to have had any contacts with an ITS, if they've even heard of it. The official channels of communication are very time-consuming and cumbersome. Playing strictly by the book, the local stewards' committee — if it had decided to seek contact with workers in plants of the same comapany overseas — would typically have to contact their local official, who would contact their national official, who would have to contact the relevant ITS. The ITS in turn would have to contact their national affiliated unions overseas, and run the procedure in reverse. If the political will is there at each stage of the process, with luck the stewards may achieve the overseas contact — after a few months.

Even this assumes a great deal. The ITS very rarely accept affiliation from national unions associated with the communist-led World Federation of Trade Unions (WFTU), or more often *only* accept affiliation from members of the International Confederation of Free Trade Unions (ICFTU) — the western international trade union organisation dominated by the TUC, and the national centres in West Germany, USA and elsewhere.

This ensures that some major unions overseas, where the trade union movement is divided, are excluded from the councils — the CGT in France, or the CCOO in Spain for example, both of whom have a substantial membership in transnationals. Thus the meetings often have no representation from key plants. It should be emphasised that this problem is not necessarily the result of bureaucratic manipulation — the ITSs themselves have no rights to decide who should form delegations to the company councils — it is up to their national affiliates, and the political divisions between the rival unions at national level are often extremely bitter.

The possibility therefore of cutting through all these obstacles to international co-operation by making *direct* links with workers in plants overseas owned by the same transnational has attracted many rank and file trade unionists. Although there were indeed some major conflicts between the traditions of the formal union structures and some of the ideas generated by the networks of 'outside' organisations, in reality there was much genuine co-operation and mutual support between local researchers and activists, and officials at local, national and international levels — including within the ITSs. Moreover, the research and resource activists have learnt through necessity the political sensitivity and subtlety needed if such international trade union work is to be valuable and sustained. Once the GLC decided to take on the problem of the transnationals, there were a number of people and organisations around which had sufficient experience of international work and of good relations with the union structures to apply their knowledge to the problems of transnationals in London. Now they had considerable resources at their disposal.

Credit: John Sturrock/Network

The Dagenham plant.

The Kodak Initiative

The GLC took its first international initiative in supporting workers in transnationals in 1983. The company was Kodak and the Communist Party-controlled local council at Val de Marne near Paris was concerned at Kodak's threat to move its factory from Vincennes in their area to a green-field site in Burgundy. Knowing that Kodak had a similar plant in Harrow, North London, Olivier le Brun — working as a consultant for the Val de Marne council — contacted the Industry and Employment branch at the GLC, suggesting that was the potential for joint action between the two councils on the company.

Robin Murray, the GLC's Chief Economic Advisor, quickly took up the suggestion and met the French council. They agreed on a jointly-organised conference of Kodak workers from Harrow and Vincennes to be held in June of that year. On contacting the workers at Kodak Harrow, the GLC learnt that Kodak was planning to move from Harrow to a green-field site in Nottinghamshire. In both countries, Kodak was seeking to play the workforce of the home country against the other; in both they were actually relocating to green-field sites with much reduced workforces; and in both Kodak were taking the research, innovation and development out of the European plants back to the parent company in the United States.

Kodak management was clearly planning at a world-wide level, and effectively running a 'European Board'. Yet they refused to acknowledge such a structure. They referred unions solely to local or national management on the grounds that each national board is autonomous, and therefore runs its own affairs. The Kodak workers called this the 'black hole' from which European policy directives and decisions emerge while all attempts at contact simply disappear without trace.

After the Val de Marne-GLC conference in June 1983, the Kodak workers declared: 'This is a situation which the European trade unions must grapple with as a matter of urgency. As the process of rationalisation on a European or even world-wide scale continues, we cannot be content to have our views reported second-hand at the European level by those national directors who happen to form part of this remote body.'

From the first conference, a organisation was formed eventually embracing other countries and other plants — with its own newspaper: *Viewfinder*. A series of meetings and conferences increasingly stressed the need for European unity (including ideas of unity of management and unions) against the parent company, Eastman Kodak in the USA, to protect European research, development and new investment.

Following from these immediate concerns of rationalisation and the future of research, the Kodak stewards began to focus on the demand for direct negotiation between European workers and European management.

Tony Barnett, representative from the Union ASTMS from the Harrow plant: 'The organisation of Kodak workers has got to be in a position where it can talk to European management, it has got to be in a position where it knows European management is actually on the side of the European workers in that they are trying to get more work into Europe, that they are not just a puppet management, which is sort of asset-stripping Europe — getting as much as they can out of Europe for the next ten years, and then going elsewhere. I think we need European management to be on the side of the Europeans.'

The GLC backed up the workers' demands with support at a local level — particularly through the establishment of the Harrow Trade Union Resource Centre — and at a European level through work with the EEC and the European Parliament, applying lobbying pressure attempting to force Kodak to negotiate on a European-wide basis.

The Ford Inquiry

Ford is not only London's largest transnational, it is the third largest in the world. At one time, Ford Dagenham, in East London, employed 32,000 people producing 620,000 cars each year. As with Kodak, Ford in Europe is organised as one unit — only on a massive scale. It has 14 European plants — resembling one huge factory. At any one time Ford has more than 1500 containers and rail wagons in service in Europe, and more than 12,000 tonnes of components in transit between plants. In London, Ford had been continuously reducing jobs since the 1970s. Between 1979 and 1984, over 10,000 jobs were lost — then the company anounced the closure of the Dagenham foundry with the loss of an additional 2000 workers.

Ford workers are traditionally some of the best organised and most militant in Britain. Along with the workers at General Motors they have also taken the lead in attempting to develop international co-ordination between shop stewards. Although shop stewards from Britain, Holland, Germany and Denmark had some informal contact by the early 70s, when in 1977 Ford workers in Belgium struck for a 35-hour week, management increased production at Dagenham. They broke the Belgian strike. British workers resolved that they would not be used in this way again, and the drive to build international links began in earnest. An international combine committee was convened attended by plant representatives from Denmark, Spain, Holland, and Britain. It was developed from there, as an organisation of lay delegates. In Britain, this meant the combine had to spend years overcoming resistance from the official structures of the unions.

It was not until the 1983 meeting of the Ford of Europe Workers' Committee, supported by the GLC and held in Spain, that British convenors attended. By 1984, recognition of the value of the combine had developed sufficiently for an international meeting to be hosted by the Ford UK National Convenors' Committee, with financial help from the GLC and Merseyside County Council.

The GLC was able to move quickly partly because one of its staff, Alan Hayling, had been a line-worker at Ford Langley, and had played an important role in the development of the combine. Hayling successfully recommended that the GLC allocate substantial resources to assist the convenors' committee, working closely with the Centre for Alternative Industrial and Technological Systems (CAITS), to plan the first genuinely world-wide Fords conference. It was held in March 1985. Earlier conferences had been overwhelmingly European. This time there were also delegates from Brazil, Malaysia, South Africa, Australia, New Zealand, USA, Canada, and Japan. Major progress was made in building an international strategy — centred on a world-wide reduction in working hours, and a potential agreement to prevent strikes in one country being undermined by increased production in another.

Although these conferences eventually had the support of the British unions, relations with the relevant ITS — the International Metalworkers Federation (IMF) — remain extremely difficult. The major conflict arose over the policy of the Ford meetings, supported by the GLC, in choosing to invite lay delegates from Ford plants from communist and independent unions, as well as from unions affiliated to the IMF. Ford workers from some countries, where genuine trade unions are suppressed, were invited through other unofficial organisations.

It was seen by the IMF as a major threat to their own structure, the Ford Company Council, which of course was composed solely of IMF affiliates, and almost always attended by full-time officials. IMF anger was particularly directed at the TGWU, whose General Secretary, Ron Todd, had been a Ford union representative for many years. The IMF went to the extent of sending telegrams to the unions in the USA imploring them to boycott the 1985 conference on the basis that it was a communist union gathering. Delegates attended nonetheless, and Todd vehemently denied the accusations and defended the TGWU's support for the event.

'When I was Ford steward the official line of the union was that it was against combines. Whether the officials like it or not, workers in a multinational will see the need internationally to get together with their colleagues in other plants around the world. My argument has always been that if there are going to be such combines, they should be embraced within the official structure of the union.

'The part that I cannot reconcile is this. Take for example a meeting of representatives of all Ford plants to discuss Ford's corporate strategy in Europe, and the relative part we play in any particular plant. For someone to then say that we'll meet the workers in Germany, we'll meet the workers in Spain, we'll meet the workers in Britain, but we cannot meet the workers from Bordeaux because they're members of the communist union (CGT) to me is crazy.'

Support for the Ford convenors and shop stewards represented the largest single investment made by the GLC in the transnationals work. Apart from grants towards the conferences, considerable resources were ploughed into shop steward seminars, the production of materials for union distribution, and most ambitiously, a major public inquiry held in early 1985.

This was the first event of its kind run by a local authority. The GLC had already organised a public enquiry into the privatisation of British Telecom in 1984, but this was the first time a local authority had publicly questioned the affairs of a private company. It prompted Ford Europe's Vice-President to comment: 'We do not accept that such sweeping enquiries into the operation of Ford or any other company are a proper function of a Local Authority . . . I believe there is an important issue here.'

The Inquiry was preceded by a large research project, involving independent research oprganisations (such as the Trade Union Research Unit at Ruskin College), trade union researchers, and academics. This formed the basis of the GLC's own submission of evidence, and provided support for the unions' own case.

The Inquiry centred round three days of public hearings, and on written evidence presented before and after. Although the inquiry was established and sponsored by the GLC, the Panel of Inquiry was entirely independent, indeed vociferously so. It was chaired by Alan Fisher, the ex-General Secretary of NUPE, and included Michael Barratt Brown, Dr Manfred Bienefeld, Colin Prescod, Professor Hilary Rose, and Carole Tongue MEP.

The GLC, through Robin Murray, put forward proposals for a 'European Jobs Code', which could specify employment levels, wage levels, working hours, health and safety conditions and provision for equal opportunities at a European level. No car would be allowed to be sold or produced in Europe unless its conditions of production conformed to the code. Such a code would provide a mediun-term strategic focus for unions, local authorities and national and European government bodies, and could be pressed through collective bargaining, supported by national legislation.

New forms of 'planning agreements' were proposed — modelled on the Enterprise Planning Agreements negotiated in companies in which the Greater London Enterprise Board have invested. These are seen as more radical forms of the proposals of the 1970s Labour Government, in that the unions would have much greater power. There were also proposals for 'Development Agreements' to ensure that UK or European plants have a full share in new investment or new technological developments. These ideas were linked to the need for strong law to ensure workers' rights to information disclosure by the company — an extension of the so-called 'Vredeling Proposals' put to the EEC. The inquiry looked at some depth into international trade union action and the potential role of local authorities in supporting such activity. The report from the inquiry panel stated: 'Most British unions have limited resources and would find it hard to sustain the sort of research and international co-operation activities that are needed to combat giant transnationals. Even so, the unions can be criticised for their neglect in this vital area. The next step in international action on Ford must be the development of an effective communication network for exchanging information and ideas between plants around the world ... Local authorities can play a vital seed-corn role in helping to finance the development of these networks.'

The report also gave much attention to the possibilities of

international links between local authorities: 'It has now become widely accepted that communities that are to be affected by major developments such as roads or power stations have the right to the fullest possible inquiry into those decisions, including the wider questions of government energy or ecology policies. In the same way, we believe that communities threatened by massive job loss should have the right to the fullest possible information on the decisions that produce it, and that such accountability is a proper task for local authorities to address themselves to.

'If local authorities are to take their role in this process seriously, there is also a need for them to develop much more systematic national links with other host authorities in Britain and Europe who face similar problems. In particular, this could help to withstand Ford's attempts to set up situations of competitive bidding between regions.'

The most important discussions in the inquiry, however, related to trade and protectionism. This was an urgent and controversial debate for the unions and stewards in Ford, some of whom believed, especially in Britain, that national trade restrictions were an essential defence against the powers of a transnational company. The pros and cons are carefully laid out by the report from the panel, including the possibility of weaker and uncompetitive domestic industries hiding behind tarriff walls, freezing of employment patterns and retaliation by trading partners. Although the panel seem reluctant to come to firm proposals, the consensus was clearly to reject unilateral UK action in favour of a form of European protectionism — particularly directed against Japan: 'For instance there could be European-wide agreements on the use of measures of national protection in order to align more closely levels of production of a transnational in particular countries with their overall market share in that country.'

Other Transnationals

Ford is not typical of all transnationals operating in London. Amongst other things, its managements clearly have little national autonomy, it produces a very limited range of products, and it has a relatively highly organised and experienced trade union organisation, with a well-established national bargaining structure. Stewards have also had experience in international contact at rank and file level, both through the official structures (International Metalworkers Federation, etc.) and through the activities of the 'Combine'. When the GLC began to initiate work on other transnationals, it rapidly became clear that the Ford 'model' could not simply be applied to other companies.

The day-to-day work of the GLC on transnationals concerned a wide range of industries and companies: Philips, Citibank, Pritchards, GEC, Hoover, Heinz, Lucas and others. The work involved a large number of trade unions, local trade union resource centres, research groups and campaigning organisations.

Each company and each workforce needed a different approach. Some involved very weak trade union organisation with little or no experience or willingness in international organisation. Each project involved considerable resources: research, publishing, organising meetings, translating, or exercising GLC's lobbying and public relations skills etc.

A strong contrast to the Ford 'model' was provided by the work on Unilever. The company has a deliberately low corporate profile — so successfully that a majority of people employed by Unilever don't know the real nature of their employer, or the source of management decisions. There is an extraordinary variation in the level of union organisation from plant to plant, with a wide range of different pay scales, production processes etc. The GLC organised seminars, through the popular Planning Unit, for stewards from different factories.

The problem faced here was the need for very basic organisation and education — most of the stewards having no experience of contact with other Unilever workers, other than perhaps with those in the same subsidiary (Brooke Bond Oxo, Birds Eye, Walls etc.).

From the outset, GLC staff and trade union activists agreed that the Unilever work required an open approach to the trade unions at official and senior levels. Whilst the emphasis was still firmly with the shop floor, it was recognised that official support was needed to recruit stewards to the seminars from a wide range of plants. The first task was simply to form a full list of Unilever plants in the UK. No union had such a list. As in all the work, it was important to ensure the continuation of the work after abolition. The 'planning group' involved both shop-stewards and full-time officers, along with GLC staff.

There was regular consultation with the International Union of Foodworkers, where the staff were keen to support the development of a national forum for Unilever workers from all the relevant unions, which could in turn strengthen the IUF's international meetings on Unilever.

The Popular Planning Unit handed over responsibility for the Unilever seminars programme to the Transnationals Information Centre in 1985, and a formal planning group was delegated from the second seminar to supervise the day-to-day running of the programme. It was highly significant and unusual that this group, serviced by an 'outside body', and with no official trade union credentials, sustained and expanded the support of the key national trade unions concerned (notably the TGWU and USDAW), whilst retaining the central principle of shop-floor control.

The seminars themselves by necessity concentrated almost wholly on basic domestic issues (wage rates, overtime, health and safety etc.), although good links were developed with the International Union of Foodworkers, Dutch plants and the COSATU-affiliated union in a South African plant. The programme has (at the time of writing) a good chance of continuation beyond abolition, possibly under the wings of the unions' own regional education departments.

Issues Raised

The work on Ford and Kodak dominated GLC's transnational policy, and formed the basis of the GLC's formal public statements and the treatment of transnationals within the London Industrial Strategy.

Livingstone's report on transnationals — prepared by the staff working with the trade unions in transnationals — was presented to the Council in 1984. It argued for a policy that would require national government to exert controls over individual firms according to enterprise plans, negotiated with the unions. This would be backed up with legislation, co-ordinated at a European level: 'This would give trade unions much greater control in their companies, cut down on tax havens, require firms to pay compensation to communities they abandon and extend tax and customs controls and the policing service necessary to enforce the controls. Above all there needs to be a European wide agreement to stop the incentive competition which has so helped the transnationals at the expense of public funds.'

Even without such legislation, however, the report claimed

that there was still an important role for local authorities in attempting to make transnationals more accountable in the UK. The key to the control of transnationals — ultimately supported by legislation — was to be found through building the trade unions' bargaining strength. This was to be through the development of international trade union links in the factories and regions as well as at national level within the companies, capable of matching the international managements controlling them.

As the GLC found through direct contact with trade unionists involved, such links were fraught with problems, and required considerable resources: the expense of travel and accomodation, the problems of language and communication, the political divisions within the formal international trade union movement, and the sheer difficulty of piecing together the information about company plans and strategies. 'The first task of any national or local authority is to make these international links easier, by making resources available to facilitate the setting up of multi-lingual conferences, and to help with intensive research to find out the information about transnational companies which managements are refusing to disclose to their workers.'

The GLC emphasis on trade unions as a powerful force in shaping industrial policies — both nationally and locally — exposed certain conflicts of interest between the GLC and the unions, and between sections of the unions themselves, as substantial GLC resources were allocated to the London trade union movement. Throughout much of the work there were tensions between the GLC's policy of working primarily with rank and file stewards and the concerns of union full-time or senior lay officers, although these tensions rarely fitted conventional assumptions of shop-steward/full-time officer conflicts.

Steve Hart, a full-time TGWU District Officer covering the Ford Dagenham plant, commented: 'As unions, we're very slow and grinding when coming to decisions and policies, and we don't even consider a wide range of issues, but nevertheless our democratic procedures and structures in the TGWU are there. The GLC hasn't really taken account of those democratic structures.

'In Fords, I'm involved as an official, but by and large the GLC has been involved at the shop-floor convenor level. It is true that if I, as an official, or other officials had said "this is not on", then the GLC would probably have stopped, or gone through the formal structures, but the fact is that it hasn't been involved with the formal structures and there have been one or two problems in that respect.

'We have allowed money and the GLC to fill in gaps in our organisation in areas that we should have looked at. Paradoxically, while the GLC is assisting us in our democratic involvement with the company, in other ways it is quite undemocratic. As it happens, the GLC position tends to coincide with our views, but if it didn't coincide, the GLC would be capable of having a greater impact than us.

'It's got the money, expertise, information and so on just to sort of dominate us, to browbeat us. We would end up having a different position from where we started. Now what that position would be is irrelevant, it would have an impact over and above our democratic policies and organisation, which worries me really.'

Michael Ward agreed: 'It's a terrible danger for us in a lot of our work. Actually the resources that have gone into this are trivial compared with the resources we've put into servicing the trade union movement at a local level which have raised many of the same issues. If I was pushed, I would say that the transnationals work has been more cost-effective than the local resource centres — not all, some have been extraordinarily good — but in general I think that the transnationals work has been very cost-effective and very pioneering, very innovative and very important. Had we ever tried in policy terms to lead the trade unions, to lay down directions in policy, exercise a veto over material produced, or to produce negotiating demands as opposed to research-support papers, we would have been slaughtered, and rightly so.'

For most of the stewards on the shop floor, however, the potentially harmful influence of GLC cash was simply not an issue. Danny Pyman, a senior steward at the Unilever Purfleet plant, described the predominant problem being the endless task of trying to generate interest on the factory floor: 'I dread to think of the amount of GLC money that went into the Unilever seminars, but without those meetings, the stewards from the different plants sort of drift apart and lose interest. The level of moral support — knowing that there are people out there who do see it as an important question — is very important. It bucks you up.'

The Unilever seminars are nevertheless likely to have substantial implications for the national unions in the future. Branches and shop steward committees in Unilever are beginning to demand that the meetings are continued under the responsibility of their respective national bodies. The unions will not be able to match the level of funding provided by the GLC, which will make it much harder to organise extensive meetings of shop stewards given the costs of their travel and day's pay.

The were also more fundamental conflicts of interest. Although the GLC staff and councillors were sensitive to the need to avoid imposing GLC policies on the trade union movement, the Council had responsibilities and political priorities beyond trade unionism. There was, for example, considerable confusion on the purpose of the Ford Inquiry. It caused a lot of frustration amongst the Ford shop stewards. One steward, Joe Gordon, commented: 'Personally, I was fairly clear what I thought the purpose was, which was to bring out the maximum amount of information and then come forward with a result, which would hopefully justify the trade union position and enable us to campaign much more effectively — to be a major factor in changing Ford's policy; but one sensed other views around. One was that it was an academic exercise — a jolly nice exercise to find out how the transnationals work. Two, it was a publicity stunt to show that Fords were horrible. One of these two was dominant, rather than our own.

'Fords took the inquiry very seriously, they decided not to participate in it, but they sent a pretty senior figure to sort of sit in on it, and they've made enquiries as to when the results are to come out. Had it produced a clear and fast result, it would have had an impact on them, even if it had only shifted them one millimeter, and it would have enabled us to put democratic pressure on them and show that plant closures and such like are against the democratic wishes of the GLC and people of London — that sort of position — but that wasn't to be.'

The work-programme of TICL on the banking sector, run in close co-operation with the bank staff unions, unearthed similar, yet more serious problems. The policies published in the GLC's London Financial Strategy emphasised nationalisation as a route to effective reform of UK's financial institutions. But the staff of the financial institutions, looking at the experience of their counterparts in the public sector, believed there would be no guarantee that their hard won pay and conditions would be maintained. Nationalisation would be bitterly opposed by banking unions and staff associations.

The banking and finance unions are in many ways far stronger than is normally assumed, with about fifty per cent of staff in unions. Bank staff are well aware of the complex issues concerning massive funds in the hands of banks, pension funds, and other financial institutions, which should be channelled into UK investment to aid employment. This formed a further major theme of discussions organised in TICL, yet as Anne Simpson, a TICL staff member, explained: 'It has to be recognised that conflicts of interest can emerge between unions and local authorities: for example over nationalisation. The banking staff are essentially opposed to this cornerstone of GLC political strategy for the finance sector, yet the GLC's industrial strategy is firmly based on providing support for the development of policies by the unions themselves. Where does that leave all the platitudes about popular planning?'

Similarly, the Ford work involved the GLC considering ideas on import controls and protectionism which were greeted by the trade unions with considerable apprehension. Steve Hart commented: 'Import controls is the policy of literally all the trade unions, and is the position at the shop floor as well. It is quite clear though that the GLC position on this (if there is a position as such) is to, shall we say, not to stress it so much, and to have doubts about it. That came across at the GLC Inquiry where we made it clear where our position was with import controls. Although the GLC Inquiry result hasn't come out yet, I have no doubt that import controls would have been a contested area — whether or not that was a part of the required solution. It is a bit unsatisfactory really. On one hand, you can't expect a local authority to just jump when a trade union says jump, but there needs to be a more formal democratic relationship I think.'

Steve Riley, a rank and file steward, now branch secretary at Dagenham, disagreed that import controls form the only position at the shop floor. He explained the basis of a possible alternative policy to import controls — a policy which some of the officers at the GLC and some panel members were eager to develop: 'Workers in Britain and in other countries, through international ties and links, would co-operate together in terms of planning "unit build" (the number of cars built per worker) and have an agreed position on it, and also the level of cars they are producing and where they are going — taking into account that exports from one country to another can put that country under threat.

'The idea is to develop control over a transnational by those workers' agreements, and that over a long period of time, to establish those agreements amongst yourselves before you actually go anywhere near the company. Then you can go to the company and say "look, this is a joint international decision, and you either take it or leave it. If you leave it, then you are not going to be able to use that country or this country against (say) Britain, you're going to have to take us all on". That way you would actually control what the transnational is up to.

'It would also have to spread. It would be irrelevant if you were just trying to establish that in Ford without extending it to the other transnational component users, because then Ford would become more inefficient and less flexible than transnationals like General Motors, which would thrive above Ford. It would therefore have to be extended right the way through, through the whole industry.'

Steve Riley's proposals for controls to be agreed and bargained for by the unions are in many ways the logical extension of national combine organisation to the issue of the company's international production and trading policies, and have been echoed in the international trade union conferences supported by the GLC. The proposals seek to achieve on an international scale through workers' action what the conventional import control policy seeks to achieve on a national scale through government action. The approach has the advantage of facing up to the dilemmas of international economic democracy and justice posed by the global character of the transnationals.

Its disadvantage though, if seen in strictly trade union terms, is that the unity required across workforces in factories with hugely varying degrees of organisation, different kinds of problems, and conflicting ideological assumptions, is unlikely to reach the strength required without some form of political — government and party — support.

Conclusion

The GLC experience provides some lessons here, although clearly it cannot be simply extrapolated to a national level; the GLC lacked most of the crucial powers with which a government could back up trade union bargaining. But the GLC experience is important for this national and international policy debate in two ways.

At a general level it experimented with the scope for combining trade union with political action in a strategy for control over the transnationals. More specifically, it suggested two forms that the political contribution could take. Firstly, state authority can provide funds and facilities to enable trade union representatives to meet regularly, thereby building up trust, exchanging information, creating organisation, formulating and co-ordinating bargaining positions that would all be the necessary foundations for any agreed controls.

The second way it can help is to initiate and achieve the co-ordination of political controls in line with trade union controls. The GLC's scope was necessarily limited to co-ordination with a handful of European local authorities, but a national government could play a central role with other progressive governments, parties and local authorities, all of which would both encourage and sustain the trade unions in their efforts, and exert direct pressure on the company concerned. The evidence to the GLC's Ford Inquiry in particular indicated the kind of initiatives to be taken.

This of course does not overcome the problems of political differences between the trade unions and the political authority, as faced for example in the work on the banking sector. This is not simply a question of policy, but a complex relationship between different traditions of democratic organisation.

The GLC — like any other local authority — developed policies through the party political process independently of the views and concerns of any one particular community or group of workers. The organisations and groups it sought to involve through its policy of popular planning reflected these overall policies. The election mandate did not give the GLC the right to impose policies on trade unions, thus overriding their internal democracy, yet it was able to be selective in which unions or sections of unions it chose to work with and support — though this selection was relatively pragmatic and subtle.

In the vast majority of countries overseas, however, the traditions of 'political unionism', where the policy-making processes of unions and parties are far more inter-dependent, would present concepts of popular planning with stark problems. The selection of union organisations with which a political authority would choose to work would often simply be an internal party decision. If a local authority in the UK builds a partnership with a local authority overseas in order to foster an international local trade union organisation, the trade union involved overseas would almost certainly be the affiliate to the political party in local power.

If the UK authority chose not to work with local authorities overseas controlled by political organisations at odds with its own policies, it would be forced to seek partners in parties (and thus unions) in opposition. If such relations became stable and long-term, the political authorities would certainly be able to strengthen international trade union organisation; but it would also in the long run highlight the very real political divisions in the international trade union movement.

The GLC experience, in taking serious initiatives to support workers in transnationals, has demonstrated the need and potential for aligning electoral democracy with trade union democratic traditions, but has also highlighted political constraints and obstacles inherent in international trade unionism, for which there is no substitute when confronting transnational power. So far, British trade unionists have been able to ignore these political divisions — they are not reflected in Britain's trade union structure. But that may not always be the case. There could be, for instance, an 'alternative TUC' formed by the EEPTU and others. It would then be difficult for the 'official' TUC unions to co-operate with them in common action over (for example) Nissan.

That's one imaginable future. One steward from Kodak found it hard to imagine any serious future for the international links:

> Originally I supported the concept, then I got to the point where I couldn't see where it was going and decided it was probably a waste of time, but now I've actually been to County Hall and seen a little more of its workings, I decided that there is some practical application, and therefore I think it is again well worth supporting. So I've gone up and down, but I think it is very necessary with an international corporation like Kodak that you have an international representation for the workers.
>
> My fear is the difficulty of actually achieving it. If the company refuses any recognition on an international basis, how can you get them to do it? There is doubt as to the possibilities of achieving that, but I think I feel more confident now — it may take more time, but I think that there is now at least a chance.

Dan Gallin, General Secretary of the International Union of Foodworkers, has mixed feelings about such unofficial organisations: 'We have the problem of groups that have decided to enter the labour field to co-ordinate workers at an international level — which are basically self-appointed. They are not responsible to anybody, they have not been elected by anybody, they are not accountable to anybody. They have taken it upon themselves to co-ordinate workers internationally with the best of intentions, but the problem of accountability is one we have to face daily. We are confronted with some groups we think are doing more harm than good, and are divisive, and others on the contrary which have a positive attitude towards unions and understand that workers create unions because they need them.

'The quality that many unofficial groups outside the labour movement have is mobility and imagination, and in that respect, the trade union movement has a lot to learn. The disadvantages are very often a lack of a clear political perspective, a lot of confusion on the ultimate political objectives, and an undirected radicalism which doesn't lead anywhere, but I think we have to learn from each other.'

11
Municipal Landlords: The GLC's Property Strategy

From the time the new Labour administration took office until abolition in March 1986, the GLC tried to develop a property strategy which would support its aims of increasing employment and improving working conditions in London. There were two overlapping elements in this strategy. The first was the development of 'key sites' as they came to be known, and the second was related to building and letting industrial estates.

Since the property boom of the sixties and early seventies, community organisations in London had been campaigning against the development of office blocks and luxury hotels at the expense of local, affordable housing. A number of the GLC Labour councillors who took office in 1981 came in, as Mike Ward, GLC Chair of Industry and Employment said, 'on the backs of years of campaigning around land issues. We came in on an agenda of doing what we could on these issues, and our agenda was set by our knowledge of, and involvement in those battles over the years.'

The GLC ultimately bought a number of sites where pressure for speculative and office development was greatest. These included Coin Street in the Waterloo area, Battlebridge Basin near King's Cross and the Courage's site in North Southwark. The aim, as the study of the Courage's development later in this chapter shows, was to develop a mix of housing and industrial uses with and for the local residents. These projects would not have existed but for a history of organised struggle on the part of local groups.

The origin of the programme for building industrial estates

was quite different. When Labour came in there was no systematic factory building programme in hand, though in the past the GLC, and the London County Council before it, had built industrial estates to let. The Industry and Employment Committee was keen to get an industrial building programme underway. As Mike Ward said:

> On any reading you'd probably build industrial estates in London given the role of the land market in London's economy and the way in which land prices have gone up. Most industrial building, unless edging towards the studio type development, probably runs counter to the strategy the market would turn up — which would be luxury housing and office development. The returns for industrial estates take longer and are lower.

The justification for a local authority building factories was that the market was not doing it. More persuasive still, the programme could be launched quickly. The land and resources were available with few other projects competing, and the GLC already had a large Valuation Department able to manage the work.

Early on in the new administration's history the Industry and Employment Committee reviewed all its land holdings and industrial property. The review showed that the GLC had accumulated large land holdings through the years. For many sites no plans had been drawn up, though they might, like Battersea Rise (a terrace of disused shops), have been in Council ownership since the early years of the century! The Committee decided to sell some of these sites, in order to raise finance (and capital allocations from central government) for its capital programmes including factory building, housing and London Transport. Michael Ward says: 'We raised millions by selling freeholds, like the freeholds of office blocks on Kingsway'. Some of this capital went to finance the GLC plans for 700,000 square feet of new industrial floorspace in London.

Industrial Letting and the 'Good Employer' Programme

Many later problems had their roots in the fact that the Industry and Employment Committee started a programme to build factories before they had worked out how this was related to their employment policies. At first the factory building programme was viewed as a technical matter; whilst members of the Committee had certain ideas about the uses to which such a programme could be put, to the officers in departments like Valuation it was not much different from what they had always done, that is, building and managing property. In Mike Ward's words the programme was not given 'top priority'. The main emphasis was on starting to build industrial units given that there was a considerable time lag between drawing up the plans and completing the build.

The development programme for the estates was running effectively by the end of the financial year 1982/3. Running effectively that is, says Mike Ward, 'according to its own lights; and other things weren't. So even though there were contradictions between that and some other areas of policy, it was not a priority for getting the Industry and Employment Branch to work on — it was an area where *something* was happening, you at least had the physical minimum.'

Although shaping the factory building programme to wider employment objectives was not seen as a priority by the Industry and Employment Committee, certain concessions to those objectives were made. The most prominent of these was the 'Good Employer' programme. From December 1981 onwards the majority of firms moving into GLC industrial units, whether refurbished or newly built, signed 'good employer' clauses in their leases. These were to try and ensure that firms occupying GLC premises at least complied with existing employment laws (many small firms do not) and in addition provided a 'fair deal' for homeworkers and a 'fair wage' for their employees.

However, from December 1981 to April 1985, when two GLC posts were created to develop the Good Employer programme, no monitoring of any kind was done to determine whether firms were keeping to these clauses in their agreements, far less to do anything about firms who were not complying. Effectively during this time, the signed agreements were not worth the paper they were written on. The Industry and Employment Committee established them but then did not consider the issue of monitoring or implementation: the administrative and management structures of the GLC were not geared up to deal with these issues, and politicians had other competing priorities.

The Valuation Department of the Council handled all property matters including property lettings and so it fell to them to implement the 'good employer' programme. This meant attaching details of the clauses to letters offering firms the lease or tenancy of an industrial unit. The offer was dependent on the acceptance of the terms and conditions of the lease or tendancy, including the 'good employer' clauses. However, it became obvious once staff were employed to monitor the programme that signing 'good employer' clauses and keeping to them were entirely different matters.

A report to the Industry and Employment Committee in 1984 successfully recommended that 'good employer' clauses should continue to be included in new industrial leases and tenancies. There were a number of dissenting voices — in particular the Valuation Department who considered that such clauses put potential tenants off GLC premises and therefore put at risk rental income from the estates. However, it was ultimately agreed that two posts should be created to monitor the programme and that some £15,000 should be committed to publicity.

The two monitoring posts were not filled until after April 1985 — less than a year to go to abolition. The priority was to find out what was happening on GLC estates, and to make sure that the managers of firms on the estates were aware of their responsibilities and that workers knew their employment rights.

The first task of the two new officers was to write a booklet for workers in firms on GLC estates. The equal opportunities officer at GLEB, the Low Pay Unit and a couple of trade union officers gave a great deal of help. The 'good employer' booklet, as it was called, was written to accompany a big poster in four languages drawing employees' attention to what their employers had agreed in their leases to provide. It took three months to get the booklet printed in which time the two officers organised a pilot study of one of the industrial estates in Hackney (Long Street), and started to visit other GLC industrial estates. What they found was just what you would expect amongst small employers concentrated for the most part in fragmented, ill-organised and low paid industries like clothing and furniture. As far as they could see from this initial survey, there was little difference between the terms and conditions of employment for workers in GLC industrial estates and those you would expect to find on many private estates.

Where there was a difference was in safety standards. GLC premises were inspected for fire and safety hazards and were generally built or constructed with fire safety in mind. They were therefore not the hazardous places that you regularly read about going up in smoke and killing several of the workers.

However, what the 'lease compliance' officers did find was disturbing enough. As one of them described it:

Virtually, none of the firms visited in this initial period had written contracts of employment, several clothing firms gave below the minimum holiday entitlement guaranteed by the Clothing Wages Council and paid less than Wage Council rates. The majority of firms had first aid boxes, but few had anyone trained in first aid; none had a company safety policy or even knew that they were required to provide one and the vast majority of firms required to have fire certificates (those who employed more than 10 people above the ground floor, or more than 20 people on the ground floor) did not! None of the firms displayed the statutory notices informing employees of their employment rights as required in the good employer agreement, and again most did not know that they were required to do this. There were no Trade Union members in any of the firms we visited.

It became clear in this initial monitoring period that employers divided into two categories — those who knew very little about their legal responsibilities and those who thought nothing of flouting their 'good employer' contracts.

The attitude of employers to the monitoring varied considerably. No firm refused to answer the questions, but several were reluctant. A common response was: 'We haven't heard anything about all this before, so why is the GLC visiting us now?' Another comment was: 'Why do you need to know all this information — you should do something about the rates, not waste my time.' Yet another retort was: 'We're doing everything right, you don't need to talk to us.' Other employers seemed genuinely ignorant of what was required of them and wanted to know where they could obtain help or information.

In the following six months the GLC workers concentrated their energies on distributing posters and booklets to as many firms and workers as possible, monitoring further industrial estates all over London and developing a monitoring procedure for firms who wanted to move into GLC premises in the Hackney Road Area and on the Courage's site.

In all some 300 firms in GLC premises were visited during the programme and employers interviewed about their employment practices in well over half of these firms. The rest of the firms were either one or two person businesses, or else were firms where the employer could not be contacted. The results of this work supported the earlier findings. In every case employers were in breach of their 'good employer' contract. In some cases the infringement was minor, where for example an employer had not displayed the terms and conditions of the 'good employer' agreement for employees to see. In other cases the breach was much more serious, for instance where employees did not have written contracts of employment, or where they got no guaranteed payment when laid off. Pay, working conditions and terms of employment tended to be worst in clothing firms, and a great deal better in computer firms.

The Problems

There were many problems associated with establishing the 'good employer' programme. A key concern was lack of information and co-operation from the GLC's Valuation Department. The crux of the matter was that the Valuation Department regarded the 'good employer' programme at best as a waste of time and at worst as an additional impediment to getting property let. That was their first and foremost (and, some have said, only) objective. The information which valuers required from would-be tenants was largely limited to the firms' likely ability to stay in business and keep on paying rent. The Department kept a database called 'Land Terrier', the source of all wisdom on industrial property and tenants. The only information which was routinely stored on it was the name of the firm, the size of the unit and what it was being used for. No information was available on the numbers of people employed in the firms, what the part-time/full-time and male/female breakdown was, whether the firm was new or had moved from another area.

As a result, the compliance officers could often only find out this information indirectly — guessing the numbers employed from the square footage of the unit — or by a visit. Many of the firms that were visited turned out to be partnerships or else employ only one or two people: as the aim of the programme was to improve working conditions in GLC premises, visiting these firms was not a particularly productive use of valuable time. Another problem was the difficulty of contacting firms: the limited information that the valuers kept on computer about firms was outdated almost as soon as it was collected — firms went into liquidation, changed their names, took over other units or moved on. The only person with accurate information about the firms on an industrial estate at any time tended to be the caretaker — if indeed an estate had one. Some of these problems could have been remedied if the Valuation Department had developed an efficient system for collecting basic information from firms, about employment rather than only about financial security.

The second major problem was how to handle firms who were breaking their 'good employer' clauses. The aim of the 'good employer' programme was to encourage and persuade small and medium sized firms to comply with their agreements. Obviously in the last resort the GLC could have used its power as landlord to remove firms who continued flagrantly to ignore important areas of their agreements. However, the GLC was abolished at the point where this second phase of the 'good employer' programme, compliance, was just beginning. At abolition a number of firms had been sent letters about absence of fire certificates, fire exit signs and written contracts of employment for their staff. We will never know if they put these things right, or what further steps we could have taken where firms refused.

Nonetheless, it was apparent from the outset that if finding out whether a firm's employment practices were in order was difficult, getting firms to comply with the employment conditions of their leases would be even harder. As we have already said the attitude of the Valuation Department was not at all co-operative. In addition the firms in GLC estates tended to employ fewer than twenty people; many of the employees were ethnic minority workers — many of whom in the clothing firms were part-time women workers; often the firms were family-owned and in very few instances did workers belong to a union. For these reasons it would have been very hard for workers in these firms to pursue their employment rights without fear of victimisation.

Reflections on the Factory Building Programme

The policy on who to build factories for, and who to let existing industrial property to, was never successfully integrated into the GLC industrial policy. For instance, what size and type of firm did the GLC want to encourage? In 1983 the GLC published a document which said that small firms did not provide, on the whole, good working conditions, nor did they create jobs on any worthwhile scale: therefore the GLC should not provide assistance for them. In practice there were some exceptions, including ethnic minority businesses, co-operatives and firms in sectors dominated by small firms. However the industrial building programme as it developed, controlled by the Valuation Department, catered for *any* small firms. Mike Ward's view in retrospect was that the industrial building programme should have been specifically linked from the start to providing premises for ethnic minority businesses, co-operatives and the like: the type of firms which the GLC considered it politically valuable to support. This was never done and, said Ward, 'the interests that dominated the factory building programme had a degree of institutional independence' — in effect they did pretty much what they liked!

What the management of the estates lacked was a common employment policy, and what the Industry and Employment Branch lacked was people who could draw together officers in different departments and knock a common policy together. The run-up to abolition exacerbated internal conflicts. By August 1985 the GLC's fate was firmly sealed and by this stage the Valuation Department was already tugging loose from the main GLC organisation. Once it was known that GLC property would pass to the London Residuary Body the way was open for the valuation staff to secure their future (at least in the short term) with the new body. It was known that under the LRB the only consideration would be the 'efficient' letting, managing and sale of property: 'good employer' clauses and other minor distractions would be a thing of the past!

Finally, the scattered nature of the sites, and the very mixed nature of the lets, meant that the GLC had no organised outside constituency to work with to monitor and pressure employers to comply with lease conditions and it was virtually impossible to develop such a constituency. This distinguished the industrial estates lettings from the 'key sites' development, where the GLC hoped that by working with organised community groups, they could implement a more effective property-based employment strategy.

The Plan for the Courage's Site

The list of 'key sites' in GLC property plans had emerged from community pressure on Labour politicans before the election. As Ted Bowman of the North Southwark Community Development

Group described the sites, they were 'particular areas of London which because of their proximity to commercial interests — that's the West End, the City, Waterloo, Covent Garden, Spital-fields, North Southwark — were vulnerable to finance capital trying to grab the land, against the best interest of local needs'.

The old Courage's bottling plant on the south side of Southwark Bridge closed down in 1981 — and with it went some 2000 jobs. This was a major blow to an area which already had high rates of unemployment even by inner London standards. The site, near the City, was ripe for office development, and this is what probably would have happened if it hadn't been for the determination of local community organisations.

There were already some 11 million square feet of office space in North Southwark and planning permission had been granted for a further five million square feet. With over 4,000 families on the housing waiting list community organisations wanted hous-ing and jobs that local people had a chance of getting — not another office block! Ted Bowman, chair of the North Southwark Community Development Group representing many of the local community organisations, put it like this: 'In 1972 the local com-munity along the riverside became aware that Southwark Coun-cil had plans to develop the riverside and North Southwark ... the planning at the time by the local authority was with a view of having offices, tourist activities, hotels, things like that — cer-tainly no emphasis whatever on public housing, or the things that go with it, like open space. And certainly they weren't to any extent at that time trying to maintain or encourage industrial jobs.'

And so the North Southwark Community Development Group was formed to fight the redevelopment plans; plans which had taken no account of, nor even consulted the com-munity on, what they felt were the needs of their area.

Ted describes the Council's policies at the time as 'bizarre — they wanted offices, but they needed homes for people to live in. If you give the land up for other uses then you don't have the land for housing.' Land in North Southwark was going for 'studio type residential purposes, offices and "up-market" work-shops. Studio residential accommodation now fetches £150,000, you know — so anybody on the dole can quite easily get hold of one of these £150,000 houses!'

A year after the new Labour administration was returned to County Hall with positive planning policies for North Southwark, a new breed of Labour councillors got control of

Southwark Council. They then jettisoned the old North
Southwark plan for a new plan, explains Ted Bowman. The new
plan had a different emphasis — away from offices into housing
and from tourist attractions into industrial jobs. The North
Southwark Development Group were consulted on the plan —
and 'there was overwhelming support by local organisations and
people for the plan'.

The new plan gave support to the emerging Community
Areas Policy (CAP) coming from the GLC. As Ted saw it the
CAP was an attempt to 'initiate local action into positive reality'.
The Community Areas Working Party was one of the first
structures to be set up in the new GLC policy and 'into that went
money, quite a lot of money, GLC money. And it's fair to say
that unless politicians sometimes put their money where their
mouth is, nothing will happen.'

In this instance something did happen, and quickly. In 1983
the GLC bought the derelict Courage's site for some £2.5 million,
as a result of organised pressure from the local community. As Ted
Bowman explained:

> We'd been and marked it as a site, and George [Nicholson] who was
> the Chair of Planning was a worker for our group and so it wasn't
> without notice by him and myself and others in this group, and so
> we applied for it to be bought under Community Areas funding, and
> that was duly done. There was a need to get the site, and then look at
> how one designed (and used) it. The place had been more or less a
> derelict site for two years. The GLC bought the site quietly and then
> things began to move very, very quickly — and it just spotlights that
> it can be done.

One part of the site was designated for residential use and the
other for industrial use. Thirty industrial units — including
twenty four workshops for small businesses and six larger units
with showroom space — were planned for the industrial area.
The residential site was to be developed by Southwark Council
and included plans for sheltered housing for elderly tenants,
family housing and flats for single people. Plans for the whole
site were drawn up by members' and officers' working parties
from the GLC and Southwark Council. Representatives from the
North Southwark Community Development Group were
involved in the working parties, but as we shall see later did not
have enough imput over issues like disabled access: as Ted put it
'no doubt there's things we've missed.'

How the Plan Developed

The GLC did not appoint anybody within Industry and Employment to work specifically on the proposals for the Courage site until the summer of 1984. Looking back this was a mistake as it meant valuable time was wasted. It also meant that the only GLC officers involved in the project up to that point were concerned solely with technical issues like designing the units and not with the wider social concerns — who were the units for and how were they to be used. As we shall see this caused problems later.

When the GLC did appoint a new worker, Liz Williamson, her brief was to work with community groups and trade unions to develop employment plans for key GLC sites — one of which was Courage's. One of the first things she did was contact the main community and trade union groups in the Courage's area. She explained that the GLC wanted to set up some sort of forum which would involve the community groups more in planning the employment side of the Courage's site. Although the community groups already had a long history of involvement in the site, it had primarily been on the housing side, she said.

So the aim of the new forum was to focus on employment. The North Southwark Community Development Group and the Southwark Trade Union Support Unit were very positive about the idea. They wanted to have a say and had drawn up some ideas about the structure this should take, said Liz. The forum set up a Consultative Policy Panel which included GLC and Southwark councillors and officers and representatives of various local community and trade union groups. This group later became a more formal body — the Courage's Advisory Group (CAG).

The issue of race was not one which had been of particular concern at the start of the Courage's campaign. The North Southwark Development Group was from the start largely white, and the needs of black and ethnic minority workers were given little thought. It was only when the consultative panel was forming that the issue of black and ethnic minority workers, and indeed other groups of people discriminated against in housing and job markets, became a key focus for the work.

It was recognised from the start that the industrial development proposed for the Courage site could not replace all the jobs lost from the original bottling plant. 'The aim of the Consultative Policy Panel was to provide jobs specifically for working-class people in the community who had experienced particularly high unemployment levels — especially women, black and ethnic minority workers and those with disabilities. The aim was not simply a quantitative one however — the panel was also concerned to provide skilled jobs, so the objective was also a qualitative one,' reports Liz Williamson.

The members emphasised that local people's skills should be improved through training schemes; that good working practices and conditions should be provided by employers; that childcare facilities should be provided to enable more women to participate in the labour market and that the general well-being of employees on the site should be considered in any lettings policy. To try and ensure good quality jobs the panel intended to vet applicants for the units and require them to sign 'good employer' leases. They also considered the kind of employers and businesses that they wanted to see in the new industrial units. They particularly wanted to encourage both old and new manufacturing industry. The sectors to work on were quite easily identifiable, says Liz Williamson, because the local community was able to say, 'Oh we've always had print here for years and we've always had food and drink.' They were also well aware of the new industries that they wanted to see in Southwark which could offer better paid, better skilled work. But, adds Liz, they recognised 'that the people we were trying to cater for *weren't* better skilled, so then the issue of training came in.'

The consultative panel also wanted to give priority in lettings to businesses who provided good training and career prospects for women and ethnic minority workers, to co-operatives and to firms employing people with disabilities. The whole thrust of the Courage's plan was to provide job opportunities in the new units to the more disadvantaged sections of the workforce and to try and ensure that the jobs on offer provided good pay and conditions.

This employment plan did not happen overnight — it took the better part of a year to put together and an enormous amount of effort from people in the local community and GLC officers in the Industry and Employment Branch. However, it was one thing developing policies for the Courage's site, it was quite another making them happen.

Obstructions, Delays and Abolition

By the time the GLC was abolished in March 1986 the first

phases of the housing refurbishment and development on the Courage's site were complete and the industrial units were virtually ready to let. But the employment strategy that had been the result of so many hours of meetings and work had been lost.

On 1 April 1986 all the units on the Courage's site became the property of the London Residuary Body. Subsequently, the smaller units were leased by the LRB to Southwark (who had already taken over responsibility for the housing on the site). The LRB, not a notably radical organisation, certainly has no intention of implementing the lettings policy developed by the Courage's Advisory Group and consultative panel and the most likely outcome in the longer term is that the units will be sold off to private enterprise. The Courage's Advisory Group decided to disband in August 1986 as they saw no point in attempting to play some much reduced role in monitoring only the small units leased by Southwark. The employment strategy for the site had been developed for a mix of large and small units; without the larger units the ideas that had been worked out around childcare and training, to give only two examples, were unworkable. Although abolition of the GLC was the most obvious reason why the employment plan for Courage's did not happen, there have been a number of other problems which hampered progress on getting the units let according to the consultative panel's (and later CAG's) agreed policy.

The Bureaucracy Divided

Community groups and people who did not work for the GLC saw it as one organisation with common aims. Yet different departments held very different views and ways of working. Although the GLC's manifesto committed it to working closely with local groups to decide what should happen in particular areas, the message was not successfully acted on in every department. The divisions were clearest yet again between old established, technical departments such as Valuation and new units like the Industry and Employment Branch set up by the incoming Labour politicans. Stephanie Blackwell, a worker with one of the groups affiliated to the CAG as it now was, recalls: 'I had this idea that everybody in the GLC was working along the same lines, and then when we started working on the Courage's site it just seemed like time after time we were held back by valuers.' The Industry and Employment Branch backed the community organisations and the councillors supported the aims of the Courage's project, but did not have sufficient time to push officers from the Valuation Department into line over agreed Council policy on every occasion. These problems were exacerbated by inadequate management and administrative practices.

The fiasco over advertising the Courage's units illustrates the experience of the community groups. The GLC Valuation Department had responsibility for letting and advertising industrial units. However, in line with agreed Council rental and lettings policy, Courage's Advisory Group wanted to ensure that the units were not only advertised in the usual property journals but were also advertised in the black and ethnic press and made known to co-operatives and women's businesses. As Steph pointed out, 'if you want to reach the black community you don't advertise in the *Financial Times*.' Therefore in January 1986, with barely three months to go before abolition, CAG provided the valuers responsible for advertising the Courage's units with a comprehensive list of journals and magazines to be used. However, when the valuers finally informed CAG of where they intended to advertise, many of the black, ethnic and women's press journals were not included. When CAG tried to find out why, they were told by the valuers that there was no budget. This was clearly a stalling tactic as a specific marketing programme had already been agreed by Council members. The saga did not end there — the next problem was about when certain of the advertising material could be sent out. Steph Blackwell continues the story:

> Apparently anything to do with advertising he [the Courage's valuer] was not allowed to handle and it had to go back to this other guy in valuers who was always off sick. There was no one to cover for him and apparently nobody else on God's earth who could decide when our advertising went out. He was off sick for over six weeks. Our frustration was boiling over because we wanted to go on this. Eventually this guy did come back and it became a standing joke. One day somebody saw him in the corridor and rushed up to try and get a decision, but he disappeared again ... I could almost believe he was a plant.

The advertising fiasco was not an isolated incident: it illustrates how difficult it was for an alliance of community organisations and GLC officers working on employment plans to get imaginative new projects to actually happen — even when they

had been fully sanctioned as official Council policy. Bureaucracies like the GLC do not change overnight and it was clear
from the start that some of the technical departments had no
idea about working with the community and what is more saw
no value in it. To the valuers, Courage's was just another site —
they saw no reason why they should treat it any differently from
any other industrial development.

When the valuers briefed the architects' department, for
example, no allowance was made for disabled access to the
industrial units. In drawing up the site plans architects did not
question this omission even though the GLC's stated aim was to
improved job opportunities for people with disabilities. CAG
subsequently successfully fought for facilities for people with
disabilities for at least part of the site. All that seemed to matter
for the professional departments was that a site should be
bought, built on and let as quickly and with as little interference
as possible. That is not to say that individual valuers were not
sometimes sympathetic to the wider objectives of schemes but
on the whole they tried to go their own way.

Ted Bowman sums up some of the problems that GLC
schemes like Courage's, which originated from the local people,
and which involved the community in sharing decision-making,
encountered in dealing with the bureaucracy:

> If I were to advise anybody that's getting involved with council
> officers now, I say don't do anything you don't want to do, be
> suspicious of them, read every report — 'cos what they say and
> what's in a report sometimes are not the same. Well I don't have any
> regard for them see — they have thwarted us many times, officers, in
> the past. But I've got to like them (Industry and Employment
> officers) in the Courage's site, whereas once I didn't — because I
> didn't have the respect for them, and in a way, perhaps I was wrong,
> you should treat everybody with respect until you know they're not
> — but my experience in this world, is give everybody a hard time,
> you'll find what they're like.

Mike Ward reaches similar conclusions and stresses the fact
that the GLC departments were not all part of one happy family
working towards common goals: 'Some colleagues believed what
valuers were saying to them. They thought they were engaging
in a rational debate not a power struggle. They were not equal to
the war they were fighting.'

Issues and Lessons

Private developers and investors in the property market are not generally interested in building industrial units for small and medium sized firms in inner London. That is not where the money is to be made. Large profits for developers come from building office blocks, luxury housing and expensive hotels: the only types of industrial building which might be taken on by the private market are specialist users — such as computer software units — where high rents can be realised. This implies that the property market will seek to develop sites like Courage's in ways which will not meet the needs of local people. For these reasons the public sector has a continuing role in industrial property development, developing sites where it is financially possible for housing and industrial uses. But the GLC experience suggests this can only be done effectively in alliance with local tenants, residents and community groups. It also shows there is a great deal of potential for local authorities to use their powers and expertise to be more than traditional private sector estate agents or property speculators, but that it is by no means easy to harness that potential.

One of the main lessons from the GLC's attempts to use property in different ways — either by working with community organisations or attempting to improve employment conditions in smaller firms — was the need to tackle the entrenched power of established council departments. These departments had essential technical expertise but they worked to criteria which were inappropriate to the aim of the Labour administration, and fiercely resisted the reorientation of their work to serve the ends of employment policy. Not nearly enough thought, effort or staff time was put by the Industry and Employment Branch into this battle to get control of property policy and target it towards particular groups of workers or firms, and it was very difficult to find staff who had the relevant technical skills who were willing to use them for innovative economic and social purposes.

Interestingly, although opponents of this new property strategy argued that they were defending efficient property development against expensive 'social' aims, the GLC's estates management had been efficient by its own standards. Industry and Employment quite quickly discovered that the estates programme was costing £6 million per year to manage and was bringing in £5 million in rent.

What was needed was a major reorganisation of finance and

information systems in order to assess and make decisions on property management, since many of the existing budgeted figures were meaningless: for example the figure for rents gave the total which *should* have been collected, not actual rental income. As Chair of Industry and Employment, Mike Ward set up an industrial trading account, an innovation the valuers strongly resisted and to which the Finance Department gave a low priority. The aim was to gain tighter control of the property budgets and spending since, as he put it, 'there was no particular reason for running an indiscriminate industrial property programme at a loss'.

So what should the GLC have been aiming for? Mike Ward summed up his view of the lessons learned:

> What we needed was a property management division reporting directly to Industry and Employment with all the social values we were trying to develop. We would have needed a good manager at the head of this division — not necessarily a technical person. We could and should have generated a large rental income. The development of industrial property in the London land market is almost a social objective as it accepts lower than market return on capital investment. But we need to make it more discriminating.

From another angle, GLC experience also suggests that local authorities should be more flexible, looking at a wider range of industrial development beyond small and medium sized manufacturing units. Recording studios or food processing units provide two possible examples. Perhaps also in the future the public sector should be taking some part in the development and management of office space, but again more clearly targeted to particular types of use and particular areas — Stratford in East London could have been one possibility.

To develop and to defend the property projects which help provide appropriate employment with decent working conditions for the Londoners most in need of them, required however more than an internal reorganisation within the Council. It required new methods of working with outside groups. The 'key sites' experiences were important for all their problems, because they showed what was possible.

Working with community groups changes the property development process in crucial ways. First it provides consistent pressure on a council to develop appropriate policies for local needs. This pressure keeps sympathetic councillors interested, and ensures that the projects take on a political priority within the authority. It also keeps sympathetic officers working to overcome resistance to innovate projects.

Second, working with pressure groups provides information on local needs, which is not rapidly available otherwise. It helps ensure the project is targeted to people who most need to benefit — although that of course may involve choices between the interests of different groups and work to ensure all relevant groups have a voice. And it also provides crucial information on the additional services which are required to give target groups of people access to the employment possibilities generated. The most important related services tend to be training and childcare, and projects in these areas need developing early on in association with the building and estate management processes.

Third, work with outside groups provides a means to monitor and defend property projects from the pressures towards low wage sweatshops on the one hand, or prestige projects out of reach of local people on the other. The employers monitored in the 'good employer' programme could be subjected to no such consistent pressure; a large local site, however, where the development has involved organised community groups, can be subjected to much more effective monitoring and control.

Local authority property projects which run deliberately against the logic of the property market are most effective — perhaps only effective — where the authority puts its resources and organising power into an alliance with organised groups in the communities they are trying to help.

12
Docklands for the People

Introduction

At the time that the new Labour GLC came to power morale in Docklands was low. The property boom of the 1970s had been a boom not for Docklanders, but for private luxury developers who planned offices, hotels and private leisure facilities for those with high incomes, excluding the majority of people in Docklands itself.

These trends were reinforced by the London Docklands Development Corporation, the LDDC: set up by the Thatcher government in 1980. It took over many of the powers of the elected local authorities; three boroughs and the GLC. Battles to keep the docks open had failed; all but the Royal Docks were shut down by the Port of London Authority (PLA) and it was just a matter of time before they too would go. Riverside wharves were hit by recession and lack of investment, industry was in rapid decline. Redundancies were running at over 2,000 per year. The ambitious and vital 'new build' housing programme of the Docklands boroughs and the GLC, which had dominated the plans for Docklands in the 1970s, was in tatters. Government cuts and the LDDC take-over of vast tracts of local authority housing land meant that the development of amenities and opportunities for the local community would be retarded.

No-one held out much hope of gaining control of or influencing the LDDC: the boroughs were on the whole politically dormant and the Department of the Environment under Michael Heseltine was quite clearly going to take a hard line in support of

Credit: Martin Mayer/Network

A Wapping resident watches as new building work starts on luxury flats, while the chances for jobs and homes for rent for local people disappear.

commercial development and against public involvement. In this atmosphere local groups looked to the new GLC for help.

Though critics would say concrete gains were few, for many community groups the material and political impact of the GLC was considerable. Some of this was due to the astonishing popularity of the GLC throughout London from 1984 onwards, but a large part of the GLC's success in Docklands was because of its achievements. By supporting local groups the GLC was, for a short time, able to lift the low morale in Docklands and help to generate and build on existing political confidence and self organisation, most of which has outlasted the GLC itself.

What Could the GLC Do?

The GLC did not start out with many advantages on its side. Its reputation in Docklands had been at an almost permanently low level for twenty odd years. As the principal housing redevelopment agency for the East End since the war, the GLC was responsible for some of the worst housing schemes in London, including the notorious Canning Town tower blocks, one of which was Ronan Point, the tower block wrecked by a gas explosion. The housing shortage in Docklands was, and still is, extreme. In 1981 3,650 people were homeless in Newham, with 17,000 on the waiting lists in the three Docklands boroughs of Newham, Tower Hamlets and Southwark.

As a housing landlord the GLC was not exactly the people's friend. Connie Hunt, a tenants' association member on the Pier Estate, remembers when local tenants' associations and local mums went on a demonstration to County Hall in 1978. 'We were called the Housewives' Army by the media and I'm quite proud of that', she remembers, but when the Housewives' Army reached County Hall they were told by the Tory leader of the time to 'go back to North Woolwich where they belonged'.

Nor had previous GLC administrations done anything to help Docklanders struggle against the commercial developments that threatened their prospects of a house and a job. The GLC owned the freehold of St Katherine's Docks near Tower Bridge. They sold it to the developers Taylor Woodrow, enabling them to build the first luxury development in Docklands, making an estimated profit of over £200 million. St Katherine's became for the community a hated symbol of how they lose out to developers. At the same time, for the developers and financiers, St

Katherine's was a symbol of them of the new Docklands, where the 'West End would be brought to the East End'. It was this that local people were prepared to fight against, and it was partly because of these new pressures that community groups grew up in Docklands for ten years before the 1981 GLC came along. There were a variety of campaigns involving tenants and trade unions over private housing and factory closures, and against office and luxury development on both sides of the river.

In 1980 some of the action groups and trade unions began lobbying the Labour opposition at the GLC. They pressed for funding for Docklands resource centres, and for policies which reflected the needs of their Docklands community. In the absence of any lead from the boroughs, they looked to the GLC to take a positive political lead in the bitter battle against the LDDC. Expectations, however, were not high. There were LDDC plans afoot for an Enterprise Zone that would reduce the powers of local politicians even further. And the Government forced through a Special Development Order on Hays Wharf to circumvent any potential delaying move by a new GLC administration.

Labour's manifesto reflected many of the communities' concerns. It committed the new GLC to a campaign against the LDDC, 'because fundamentally what local people want and what the LDDC want are entirely different'; to supporting plans for public housing and jobs; to attempting to prevent any further run down of the docks and local industry. On all these issues the GLC promised to work in close collaboration with Docklands people themselves.

By the time Labour took power, its manifesto committments were already seriously undermined: the Government was cutting back on the GLC's strategic powers. Its power to decide on planning applications in Docklands was almost entirely removed in 1981, and the Department of the Environment was downgrading the status of the GLC's Greater London Development Plan (in the past a statutory plan) as fast as it could. Most of the GLC's housing land in Docklands was transferred to the LDDC, its residual planning powers were taken over by the LDDC (except some influence over major road building) and its house building programme was all but terminated by the Government. All that was left was transport planning functions, the control of some river piers and the Thames Barrier (though these were not unimportant powers). Its role then was confined to the use of its considerable discretionary spending powers to support campaigns and local organisations (for example through grants, spending on employment initiatives, childcare projects, training schemes) and whatever political authority it could muster.

What Could the Boroughs Do?

Even before the abolition of the GLC, any predictions about the future of Docklands usually depended on the boroughs, rather than the GLC. There were five Boroughs involved in Docklands in the 1970s — Southwark, Lewisham, Greenwich, Newham and Tower Hamlets. Until the mid-1980s Southwark, Tower Hamlets and Newham were somewhat notorious for their right-wing, secretive Labour policies and practices. They believed in public housing but also did deals with the big developers on Hays Wharf, Surrey Docks and the London Docks. They wanted the local authorities to control Docklands development, but did not want the community organisations to have much of a say.

Their policies did not in any way reflect the new thinking among some local councils and activists about equal opportunities, employment, community action, campaigning and cultural politics. Ted Bowman from North Southwark Community Development Group describes Southwark Council during the 1970s as 'a council that turned its back on the local community, that didn't need to look at the problems that exist far from the Town Hall. But more than that it was exploitative in the interest of millionaire developers, against the needs of the people of Southwark, which were for housing, jobs and open space.' The Labour parties within the boroughs slowly moved to respond to local groups pressing these needs, and the old guard struggled to keep control.

The first breakthrough for the new politics came in 1982 when an entirely new-style Labour administration took over in Southwark from what has often been called the 'Bermondsey Mafia' under John O'Grady, long time council leader. Southwark provided the GLC with its first major political ally in Docklands, an ally for a new form of political intervention. Significant shifts in the same direction took place in both Newham and Tower Hamlets, but not large enough to dislodge the ruling groups of concillors who had controlled the Boroughs through the 1960s and 1970s.

Greenwich and Lewisham were more sympathetic to community groups in Docklands in the 1970s, but when the government decided not to include Greenwich and Lewisham within the LDDC designated area their political significance in the main issue in Docklands — the conflict with the LDDC — was at first largely irrelevant. Then came the giant schemes such as Canary Wharf, the East London River Crossing and the STOLport, all affecting these two boroughs and drawing them into the battles with the LDDC.

So, although there were many issues on which the GLC and the boroughs were strongly opposed to the LDDC, the local authorities could only register that opposition in a formal and powerless way. The GLC's good intentions were in danger of being rendered politically sterile if there was no action in support of alternative plans in Docklands itself. Not only that but the comparative budgets were grossly unequal. The LDDC spent £205 million of public money between 1981 and 1984 in Docklands. The budget for 1985/6 was £73 million. The GLC and the Greater London Enterprise Board (GLEB) together on the other hand had an annual budget for Docklands of less than £2 million. The government increased the cash limit for the LDDC, while lowering the cash limits of the boroughs and the GLC. While the GLC could argue these points within its Council chamber, power to do anything about them could only be sought in an alliance with local people; an alliance which strengthened those organisations and did not undermine them or make them dependent on it.

The next sections are case studies of the ways in which the alliance between the GLC, borough councils and local organisations was forged, problematically and otherwise. The case of the People's Plan for the Royal Docks — where local groups drew up their economic plan for the area — shows how the GLC used its limited power in Docklands for the benefit of local people. It is also an example of how a local campaign, the Campaign Against the Airport, made use of a 'political lead' in the battle against the LDDC. The process of drawing up the plan is discussed in some detail to show how a local authority can work supportively — though not without problems — with local people on a day-to-day basis. The project illustrates the different ways of going beyond traditional lines of 'consultation', to reach wider sections of the community.

In contrast with the GLC's direct involvement in the People's Plan, the case of the Rotherhithe Community Planning Centre illustrates how the GLC could use its limited powers for maximum effect in an alliance with local people indirectly through grant aid. It is also a case of the 'new economics' of funding independent resource centres that are deeply rooted in and influenced by their surrounding communities. Finally there is a short summary of the GLC's work with trade unions drawing up plans for the future of the river, the backbone of London's Docklands.

All these cases show how the GLC combined with community groups, trade unions and local boroughs to use their 'clout' in an area where all popular organisations were, and are, severely weakened by the government and the LDDC.

From the Campaign Against the Airport to the People's Plan for the Royal Docks

> I walk through the docks sometimes and I always think to myself what a waste, what a terrible waste.
>
> The People's Plan for the Royal Docks

In November 1981 the LDDC announced its support for proposals by Mowlem, the construction company, to build a Short Take Off and Landing Airport (a STOLport), using the space between the King George V and the Albert Docks as a runway. This would obviously dramatically affect any future use of these docks themselves, as well as affecting the entire area. From the beginning the scheme was largely 'supply led', meaning that the initiative came from the supplier, rather than from any demand from potential users. The only airline company that came forward to support it openly was the small regional airline Brymon Airways, owned by ex-racing driver Bill Bryce. The STOLport appears to have been the idea of Bryce and John Mowlem. Bryce saw it as an opportunity to fly De Havilland Twin Otters and Dash 7s into a site close to central London, while Mowlem were clearly interested in an important and possibly prestigious contract. Mowlem also saw it as a way into other major infrastructure contracts, for example the Docklands Light Railway which would serve the STOLport (a contract they have since won).

Before the STOLport was given planning permission, the LDDC issued STOLport publicity leaflets, announcing that the scheme would create up to 5,000 new jobs in Docklands. A Gallup Poll of local opinion was commissioned, and on the morning of the poll Capital Radio, LBC and Thames television news repeated the LDDC's claims that the STOLport would

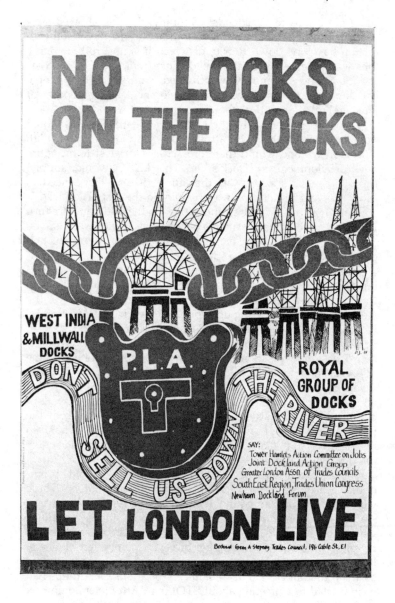

Local Docklands residents had been fighting closures for years before the involvement of the Popular Planning Unit.

bring 5,000 jobs to Docklands. Naturally, the Poll showed support for the airport. Since this first announcement, the job prediction has gone down to 500, of which it is unsure how many jobs would be newly created (as distinct from transfers of existing jobs). The community was divided, with some local people clutching at any promised new development and prospects of jobs, and others sceptical about the benefits it would bring.

The 'idea' promoted by the LDDC was that STOLport would put Newham on the map, attract office development and high tech industry and would therefore act as a catalyst to an entire new development in Docklands. The LDDC would supply, through public monies, all the infrastructure work needed; Mowlems and Brymon Airways would do the rest. The LDDC's support for this project is indicative of their 'dream' to turn Docklands into a businessman's (sic) paradise, with water sports on the weekends, expensive and luxury flats on the river, and office buildings close to the 'city'.

At this stage, the only local consultation that had been carried out was the Gallup Poll. Many local people, who couldn't afford the West End of London, let alone short air trips to Paris for the weekend, were expressing opposition to the LDDC's 'dream'. Lil Hopes, Chair of the Newham Tenants' Federation and soon to become the Chair of the Campaign Against the Airport, describes a conversation she had with a representative of the LDDC at the time. 'When I asked what the benefits of STOLport would be to the people of Newham, his answer was that when you want to go abroad you won't have to go to the trouble of getting a taxi to Gatwick, you can get an aeroplane from the heart of Docklands. I said I would show him around Newham, so he could see how many people could afford to go abroad, never mind a taxi to Gatwick.'

The next stage in the LDDC's strategy was to hold 'promotional' meetings for the STOLport in the community. These were held in May and June 1982 and on a very ad hoc basis. Accidentally, Connie Hunt found out about these 'meetings' when booking a local church hall. Having been involved in tenants' campaigns for a number of years she phoned Mowlem, listed in the church book as organising the meeting, and was told by them that all Docklands tenants' associations and groups had been invited to a meeting about STOLport. After telephoning six other local tenants' associations who knew nothing of these meetings she immediately became suspicious of the LDDC's strategy for STOLport. Lil Hopes and the Newham Tenants

Federation had not been informed either, although these promotional meetings were now being billed as 'consultation'. Pat
Vicks, a local tower blocks resident, said at the time, 'They said
they would send out petitions, but there's been nothing at all.
The only thing we read is what is in the local newspaper. Other
than that no one has knocked on our doors, or been in our
shopping centres asking us what we think about it.'

Lil, Connie and others decided to find out more about the
STOLport — what kind of aircraft it would use, what a Dash 7
was, and other plans the LDDC had. They rang aircraft
magazines and found that the Dash 7 was quoted as the 'quiet
aircraft'. Realising that no aircraft could ever be 'quiet', they
suspected the entire motivation behind the project. The claims of
'thousands of jobs to be created in Docklands' had a distinctly
suspicious ring to it.

In fact, the trend in the airline business had been cutbacks.
British Airways had sacked over 20,000 staff, some airlines were
defaulting on loans or going bust. The growth of the 1950s and
1960s, on which the wealth of the larger airlines and airline
manufacturers was based, had disappeared.

More local residents became concerned. The more they talked
together the more they realised that the LDDC could bring in
any type of jets or even helicopters if they got the go ahead on
STOL. It wasn't just the noise that the STOL would create either.
Tower block residents in the STOL's flight path were concerned
for their safety. Local trade unions were concerned about the
jobs claims, and the chance local people would have of getting
some of the promised jobs.

The Campaign Against the Airport held its first meeting in
May 1982. They resolved to start leafletting, and began holding
public meetings where all residents were invited. Lil continued
her research into the proposals, and local resource centres such
as JDAG — the Joint Docklands Action Group — and the Docklands Forum became further involved.

It soon was apparent that the enormity of the change the
STOLport would bring to Docklands demanded a response that
was much bigger than the campaigns over tower blocks which
local people had previously organised. They needed more allies,
with backing, and not least they needed the confidence to take it
on. 'We were used to fighting small things like housing issues.
We really thought that ordinary people like us couldn't argue
with the LDDC,' says Connie Hunt.

At the same time, the GLC's Popular Planning Unit, the PPU,

was anxious to help local people in local campaigns to build up alternative plans for their areas. They began by talking to local groups, particularly the Joint Docklands Action Group (JDAG). JDAG suggested the PPU come down to Docklands and go to a Campaign Against the Airport meeting. The Campaign had decided that 'it was really important to get the statutory bodies, Newham Council and the GLC, backing our demand for a public inquiry into the airport, and coming out against it, remembers Connie. Ed Googe, Chair of Planning at the GLC, went down to Docklands and talked about how the GLC could help.

It was important for the PPU to get the politicians involved from the start; and to show that this time the GLC could do something concrete. Wtihout the politicians the GLC planning officers may well have supported the airport; and if the GLC's proposals for help were not concrete, local suspicion would have ruled out any relationship at all. As the Campaign gained momentum it became the priority of the growing Popular Planning Unit in its first year, the first step being to put the local people's case to the GLC Planning Committee and win their support. After pressure from the campaign the GLC decided to stand with the local people against the airport. The battle had begun.

The GLC and the Airport

In its manifesto of 1981 the GLC had made Docklands a high political priority. Its policies for jobs for local people, public housing and improving local transport were in complete conflict with the LDDC's 'dream' for Docklands. The GLC also saw the airport as unnecessary in the development of London's airport and transport systems.

There were doubts about the airport's viability if it was limited to the Dash 7, but if it did expand to include noisier planes and helicopters it would be dangerous and intrusive for local people. The GLC also contested the LDDC claims to create 'thousands of jobs' from STOLport. In the *Newham Recorder* of August 1984 the LDDC declared that 'STOLport should directly provide between 350-450 jobs within six years, but the dramatic catalytic effect must produce a dramatic increase in commercial interest in Docklands. A major increase in associated and secondary employment will follow.' Mr Pope, a local resident, expressed the state of employment in Docklands and the demoralisation of its workforce at an early meeting of the Campaign Against the Airport: 'If it's a success there'll be planes like shuttlecocks, and there won't be any jobs except lavatory cleaners'. To increase employment in the area, and raise the skills of the local people, the GLC and the other Docklands boroughs, notably Newham, preferred an alternative use for the docks, including a ship repair facility, modern cargo handling, equipment for Euro shipping, industrial development and housing development for rent. The STOLport, straight up the middle of the Royal Docks, would devastate the possibility of this ever happening.

Many local people expected that Newham Council would support the development of the STOLport. Its leader, Jack Hart, was on the board of the LDDC, and there was a feeling of 'if you can't beat them, join them' amongst some of Newham's councillors. But if the links between local people and local authorities that were beginning with the PPU were to be strengthened, Newham needed to be with the GLC and the Campaign and against the LDDC. Strong lobbying by local people and the Campaign ensured that Newham came out against the airport. The final vote, 18 for the airport and 37 against, was significant because it implied not only a vote against the airport but an alliance with local people against the LDDC. Greenwich Council also became an objector to the airport.

Amongst other things, the GLC could uniquely offer the alliance technical evidence from its Scientific Services Branch on matters of noise regulations, runway lengths, and flight take off paths. On the other hand, the local campaign could inform and feed back local opinion in a way which the GLC, sited in County Hall, could not.

The People's Plan for Docklands

Interestingly, it was Mowlem and not the LDDC who applied for planning permission to build the STOLport, and a public inquiry into their application was announced by the Secretary of State to begin in June 1983. For local people the announcement was a type of victory; at least they would be able to present their opposition to the scheme in an official way. As well, local people felt it was important to put to the inquiry their own strongly felt ideas about the development of Docklands as a whole.

The Campaign needed to answer Mowlem's and the LDDC's

claims that the STOLport would act as a catalyst to the development of the area, and address the fact that the LDDC had not considered the STOLport in the context of any other options for the Royal Docks. How the Campaign should do that, and how the PPU could help, became the main question.

There were already alternatives to STOLport in people's minds. At the Campaign's meetings, local people felt there was still life left in the Docks, and that tourist facilities and leisure industries were possibilities for development. So that the alternatives could be made more explicit (and there was a lot of work to be done) the Campaign in conjunction with the Newham Docklands Forum decided that a 'people's plan' should be drawn up with the assistance of the Popular Planning Unit.

The Newham Docklands Forum — comprising tenants groups, tower block campaigns, the National Union of Teachers, allotments groups and local trades councils — had been active in the area around docks closures, leading the 'No Lock on the Docks' campaign in the 1970s. Large areas of Docklands have less black and other ethnic minority groups than London as a whole, reflecting a history of racial discrimination in public housing as well as the existence of a stable white population. While many local black people were involved in local campaigns in Newham and Tower Hamlets, few organised in Docklands around specifically race orientated issues. The West Docklands Action Group have a large Asian membership, but they campaign around wider issues affecting the entire area of west Docklands itself. The Newham Docklands Forum included black members as individuals.

The Forum agreed to take responsibility for drawing up the plan, while the Campaign would stick to the immediate issues around the STOLport. The Campaign could then use the plan to strengthen its opposition. As the PPU had access to money, the first thing the Newham Docklands Forum decided they needed was funds for a base from which to organise the plan, specifically a shopfront in a central local shopping area to legitimise the plan in local people's eyes, and to provide a stable working environment to get it all together. With the assistance of Newham Council and the PPU, it was set up in Pier Parade, North Woolwich. They called it the People's Plan Centre. Time was short. The inquiry was to start in June 1983, the GLC lawyers estimating that the People's Plan could be presented in September. The Forum decided they needed to employ a team of people to collect information and contact local people to collect their ideas. Funds were also needed for publicity and public meetings. In accordance with their policy of employing local people in local resource centres, the GLC approved £14,000 for five staff over five months to prepare the plan.

All people who applied for the jobs were invited to a large public meeting to discuss the project. The workers appointed were local people with detailed knowledge of the area and of the needs of particular groups, but with no experience of a project like this. Tracey Hastings was leaving school in May, but had strong views on the need for water sports facilities on the docks and river. Daphne Clarke and Annette Fry were local mothers both involved in local childcare groups and a Toy Library. Bill Hart, an ex-tugman, had a deep commitment to seeing the docks used for shipping and boat building, and Gary Cooke, a young ex-TGWU shop steward, was interested in projects that could use new technology in a socially useful way.

A GLC representative was voted on to a steering committee set up to organise the plan, though in retrospect it might have been better if the GLC representative had been there only in an advisory capacity. Despite a formal equality, the GLC had all the power of funding the organisation, and could have easily dominated the Plan's development.

The centre's first task was to contact local people. They learnt quickly that there were more efficient ways of doing this when the first letters posted out received a poor response. So they began more informally, speaking at mothers' and toddlers' groups, keep fit classes, even at the interval of bingo sessions in a local community centre. They sought out and went wherever people were getting together, from the pub to the seventy five companies still in the docks. They talked to workers in the local bus garage and visited shop stewards in the few remaining factories in Silvertown. Sometimes they simply carried out door interviews, sometimes they visited specific local people at centres such as the Kennard Street Health Centre. One idea which worked particularly well was 'surgeries', where all houses in a locality were leafletted that a 'surgery on the people's plan' would take place nearby to hear people's ideas. In particular they felt women's needs were neglected in the area and distributed a questionnaire for women only.

All these discussions about the plan had three main purposes, summed up when the plan was written: 'to get as detailed a picture as possible of the needs and problems facing local people, to weigh up the advantages and resources of the area, both human and physical, and to encourage people to put forward and develop together their ideas for solving these problems and making the best use of the area's assets'.

With PPU help, a paper on the plan was distributed to every house in Docklands. 'So what is a People's Plan?' asked the paper. 'The Plan will start from *our* needs, rather than developers' profits ... the need for secure jobs, for prompt and sensitive health care, and a good education for our kids.'

Meanwhile, the GLC's Scientific Branch was building a relationship with the Campaign Against the Airport, breaking down complicated information, answering their questions. Once this was established it provided a key with which the Campaign could 'unlock' other GLC departments. GLC involvement in the plan gave it more credibility with local people, who were suspicious of its worth. 'People are inclined to think that we, the workers and campaigners, are just somebody's mum or dad or some school leaver, and they think that we don't know,' said Connie Hunt. 'If you say we have the backing of the GLC, they will come along to a meeting.' As this happened, more local people brought their skills and ideas to the plan. Keith Luck, a postman from Silvertown, painted a series of artist's impressions of the new houses the plan advocated.

Pressure of time meant that many issues concerning the management of the Centre's workers were not adequately thought through, on both the PPU and the Centre's side. There were several moments of crisis and serious divisions that were a long time in being resolved.

However, as the centre progressed issues such as employment, transport, housing, the elderly, childcare, education, and recreation emerged, with ideas for improvement and alternatives to current provision building the basis of the plan.

Above all the Plan was first and foremost about jobs. 'It is also about sports and recreation but you can't live on sports. It is also about housing but it is not enough to build houses, there has to be work for the people you want to live in them. The Plan suggests better shopping facilities and provision for entertainment but these are not much use if you don't have a wage. With one in four on the dole in Newham's Docklands, many people are desperate for work.' Jobs were always number one on the agenda at 'surgeries'. The need for jobs caring for people and children was expressed by home helps, unemployed centres and mother and toddlers groups. The demand for jobs on the river was expressed at a surgery in Custom House, a meeting in Barnwood Court, a ship repair workers meeting, and meetings with TGWU representatives. From women in the keep fit classes to women shop stewards in Tate and Lyle at Silvertown the demand was for well-paid part-time jobs. Trade unionists working for the large corporations like Tate and Lyle, STC and Unilever found common demands with unemployed people discussing cooperatives; that is jobs under local control. Training facilities were also in demand, especially for women to find new skills. Obviously pay and job security were high on the agenda for all people attending, and given the high incidence of unemployment and relatively low paid, unskilled jobs available, this was also an area where racial discrimination was operating, and therefore of concern to black residents.

In November 1982 the GLC commissioned a study of the potential for cargo handling in the docks. Consultants were instructed to work with the local groups and trade unions. Bob Colenutt from JDAG remembers that 'a lot of emphasis was on ship repair and how to keep it in the area, and on how wonderful these dry docks were. We had a lot of instinct about repair of ships and the market that could be there in the future. So we needed the study to be done.' A summary of the first study was published in the GLC Industry and Employment Branch paper, *Jobs for a Change*, and showed what the GLC and local people had suspected: 'There is evidence that shipping lines with small and medium sized ships would use an upstream dock like the Royals. The PLA has misused opportunities in maintaining cargo handling. With limited investment there are definite prospects for the docks.' The report backed the idea in the People's Plan, and both the Boiler Makers Union and the TGWU, whose members in the docks as well as at Heathrow Airport were affected by the LDDC's developments, became involved although the Forum was criticised for not involving them more.

Ideas for jobs went beyond reviving the traditional Docklands skills, however. Gary Cooke remembers: 'There were also plans for a co-op to make lampshades which if you go to Harrods you pay £60 for but they can be made cheaply and can be sold cheaply for the local people. There were other ideas for co-ops producing heat pumps which are now imported from America. There is a company in Docklands that said if we can produce a heat pump they'd help design it and they'd have no problem selling it. There's all the people who maybe live in houses and their roofs leak, and there's toolmakers, engineers standing outside the pubs because they can't afford to go in. There is no end of things that can be done.'

Annette Fry found similarities with the local women: 'The clothing industry is another area where women can come in ... you know there are terrific dressmakers, sewers, lacemakers, batik makers — all these skills that have just been forgotten and disregarded.' The Plan suggested that all these skills could profitably be turned into providing local people with local jobs. By the beginning of September 1983 the plan had been drafted and the Newham Docklands Forum were preparing the final draft for submission to the public inquiry.

The Public Inquiry

Unless a campaign wins a public inquiry they are, in themselves, of limited use. They tend to deflect resources and energy away from other issues the campaign is working on, and provide an arena for demoralisation and despair. They can be, however, an important focus for a campaign's work, and though the terms of reference of the STOLport Inquiry were very narrow (limited to runway length, noise considerations etc.), it is unlikely that the local people would have drawn up the People's Plan without the threat STOLport posed to the area and the deadline of the inquiry.

As the Inquiry commenced the finished Plan was distributed in published form to every household in Docklands as part of the Newham Docklands Forum campaign for alternatives in the area. The LDDC and Mowlem were very hostile to the very idea of a People's Plan, and objected to its presentation at the inquiry. 'It is unheard of to have a People's Plan in a planning inquiry,' they said. 'While we will listen to the GLC and Newham Council's views, we cannot accept the suggestions of some local people as relevant evidence.' This is not surprising, given their past record in the consideration of social guidelines for town planning. The 1983 Royal Town Planning Institute and the Commission for Racial Equality report 'Planning for a Multi-racial Britain' has not been considered by the LDDC, nor does it appear to have implemented any of its recommendations for equal access. The GLC insisted that the People's Plan be heard, and although they and the Forum gave separate evidence, their drive to broaden the inquiry into the future of the area as a whole backed up the Forum's stand on their Plan.

Through two days the People's Plan for the Royal Docks was presented to the inquiry by fourteen different witnesses. Joe Jacubait began, telling how his boat building and ship repair business had been forced out of the docks by re-organisation, and compulsory purchases, and yet could have expanded. Pat Olley talked about the North Woolwich Resource Centre, a local idea to provide training for local women, and illustrated that this was the type of development local people wanted, not a STOLport. Sue McDowell from the Tower Blocks Campaign brought the issue of housing into the inquiry, showing how the land in the docks could provide houses for local people to get them out of their 'high rise hells'. STOLport would dramatically affect the possibility of increased local housing in the docks, she explained.

Morris Foley from the TGWU described how the docks could be used for a transport interchange, linking water, rail and road in a way that would revitalise the area and take heavy lorries off the road. STOLport was not part of any transport system, he argued, and would not assist in greater access being obtained by local people to recreation facilities and jobs.

Although the LDDC and Mowlem frequently raised objections to the Plan being presented on points of order, it was allowed to run its course, and by the end of it local people felt that at the very least their views had been presented in a positive way, and at the very most their Campaign would be strengthened. The GLC had assisted in legal costs for the Campaign to employ its own lawyer. This meant it was not alienated in any of the processes, and was well equipped to follow future legal and technical steps in the process from the inquiry to the possible granting of planning permission.

On 13 August 1984 the Inquiry Inspector recommended to the Secretary of State that 'outline planning permission' be granted to Mowlem, subject to a number of conditions limiting the length of the runway, requiring noise barriers to be set, limiting hours of operation, restricting ground running of engines, restricting night maintenance, banning helicopters and banning club and recreation flying. By a legal agreement, however, the enforcement of these conditions was placed in the hands of the LDDC, who had by this time had lost all credibility with the local community. As Joe Smythe from Newham Trades Council said at a meeting of local authorities opposed to the airport: 'Who are you going to ring up at 7 o'clock in the evening when you hear engines running too loud, or count too many planes coming in?

By the time the LDDC get here, it will have stopped. And then it will be their word against ours.'

The Quiet Aircraft?

The level of noise permitted at STOLport (surrounded by residential sites) and the methods of assessing that noise level were among the crucial questions in the STOLport debate. The Campaign Against the Airport, the GLC, Newham Docklands Forum, Newham Council, Greenwich Council, Lewisham Council, JDAG, and other local groups argued throughout the inquiry and through the People's Plan that this issue be resolved right there and then, and that the noise levels decided upon must be consistent with the LDDC's claims that the STOLport would only run Dash 7s and similar small aircraft. This crucial question, however, was only decided *after* the inquiry had finished. The Inquiry Inspector said that it must be sorted out, but as the Department of Transport and Mowlem, the LDDC and Brymon decided on this question separate from the Inquiry, the GLC, the Campaign Against the Airport and others demanded that the Inquiry be re-opened for noise levels and their monitoring to be discussed. Obviously the noise levels chosen would affect the type of aircraft allowed into STOLport. In the end the noise levels chosen were such that they excluded British Aerospace BA 146 jets but it is significant that in the recent route licencing procedures taking place in March 1987, an airline 'X' is already proposing that the runway be lengthened to allow BA 146s to fly.

The demand to re-open the Inquiry failed, and the GLC's legal and other resources disappeared when it was abolished in March 1986. But the essential conflict in Docklands which puts the LDDC, the government and corporate capital on one side advocating a Docklands for the well-heeled and image conscious city worker; and the Newham Docklands Forum, the major local unions, the GLC and rather uncertainly Newham Council on the other; will continue.

The community have by no means stopped opposing the airport and other LDDC developments which do not consider their needs. There have been sit-ins over compulsory purchase orders on the docks, demonstrations against private housing, public meetings over the use of the river, festivals to celebrate the potential for accessible and local recreation, and plays in empty warehouses to illustrate what local people have to contibute to their area.

The People's Plan Centre, refunded by Newham Council after the abolition of the GLC, still remains, though without any full-time workers.

After the Campaign Against the Airport had seen the details of the planning application, local people were even more concerned about the effects of the 'Airport' (as they now call it). A meeting in March 1986, over four years after the LDDC had announced its intention to build a STOLport in the docks, was one of the largest Campaign meetings held. 'People are more together, more organised, more confident,' says Connie, who goes down to the Centre almost every day. 'They know they have a right now to public resources, the GLC showed us that.'

Community Links — Rotherhithe Community Planning Centre

While the People's Plan Centre was building alternatives to current developments in Docklands, on the other side of the river community groups, with the help of Southwark Council and the GLC, set up the Rotherhithe Community Planning Centre. The Centre has different origins and objectives from the People's Plan Centre, and has had a different relationship with the GLC as a consequence. It is an example of 'arms length' funding, with the GLC playing a 'supporting' role, and of the 'new left' economic policies of funding largely autonomous local organisations. This section is about the processes and development of this new approach, to illustrate how an alliance with local groups and trade unions can work.

Southwark childcare, playground and health groups were involved in issues of land planning. Tenants' associations were only too aware that land had to be found if new housing for local people was to be built. The LDDC had initially control over 657 acres of public land, with a further 1500 acres acquired by compulsory purchase between 1981 and 1987. Only two per cent of the population in Docklands could afford the houses promoted by the LDDC. There was an urgent need to campaign for public accountability over the uses of publicly owned land.

In 1980 Southwark groups formed a local steering group to look at these issues. They decided they needed a central place to meet, and if possible people to work full time to gather know-ledge and ideas about planning and the alternatives to existing developments. In this way, the Centre grew out of broader aims than the People's Plan Centre, growing as it did out of the Campaign Against the Airport.

The steering group were wary of going to the GLC for support. Relations with the GLC and Southwark Council over the redevelopment of Surrey Docks and over poor GLC housing in the downtown areas were fractured. Southwark Council had antagonised local groups by adopting an initial policy of refusing to recognise or co-operate with the LDDC. This had backfired, and instead of rallying local people in a campaign against the LDDC as originally intended, it led to a bitter split with local tenants who argued that the Council was not helping them to negotiate with the LDDC over much needed grants and premises. In the end the steering group decided to apply for a grant to the GLC, and both Councils gave the Centre enthusiastic backing. It was seen as an opportunity to achieve better feedback on issues affecting Docklands, from the grass roots level to the Council level. Besides supporting local autonomous organ-isations, real 'consultation' was not possible within the confines of both Town Halls.

The LDDC's impact on the local area, especially as far as housing and jobs was concerned, was the first issue addressed. 90 per cent of housing on LDDC owned land is private, and there are direct links between this fact and the quality and type of jobs consequently available. Obviously the perception of local people and the two Councils on this differed, but the GLC's Planning Committee was determined to preserve the autonomy of the Centre in exploring this issue. Julie Donovan, a worker at the Centre, explains; 'How can they [the GLC] in their big organ-isation know what is right for people in Rotherhithe and Bermondsey?

'But they can get people who can represent them a bit more than they could, to get on with it and do it. That is the way they touch people's lives. No matter how good something up there is in the bureaucracy, it doesn't reach ordinary people. It is getting out locally and giving small amounts of money to lots of different local groups that is important.'

In some ways there was a 'double autonomy' operating within the Centre itself. They worked cautiously so as not to interfere in or take over from local campaigns and tenants' groups. The GLC's role was to provide the funding and political back-up where necessary. The delineation of these roles, however, was vulnerable as the experience was a new one.

An example of the levels of interaction that ensued is provided in the case of the Centre's work with a campaign against the closure of a local hospital, St Olaves. The Rotherhithe Centre helped the campaign to draft a report on health needs in the area, and proposals for the expansion of a wing. The campaign group itself applied to the GLC Popular Planning Unit for £750 to draw up an alternative plan for health provision at St Olaves, and a leaflet based on interviews with local people. The grant was agreed in line with the GLC's policies of creating jobs from health services. The campaign, with the help of the Centre, are now talking to the local health authority, which responded to their suggestions of expansion.

In a chain of autonomous organisations, it is difficult to see where any consistency in policies would arise. Through different channels, however, the GLC's policies were brought down to a local community level. For example, the GLC's anti-racist campaign had heightened the awareness of professional workers at the Centre to the racism that can divide communities. So they kept a distance from divisive campaigns, 'telling the group that we think it is racist, if it is,' explains Alan Turkie, a Centre worker, 'and that we are not prepared to collude with it'. The Centre could then feed back to the GLC experiences of local communities and the ways they dealt with racism.

This was also the case with the GLC's work on developing disability policies and projects. A representative from the GLC Disability Resource Unit came to the Centre to talk about the needs of the disabled, encouraging the professional workers there to be aware of the issues.

At the same time, the Centre felt that one of its flaws was that it employed three professional workers who did not live in its direct area. During 1985/6 it therefore pursued a policy of employing local people, which affected other resource centres the GLC funded. This turned out to have tremendous practical and policy advantages, as local people brought local knowledge and commitment to resource centres. 'When it's something like Docklands,' says Julie Donovan, a local resident and worker at the Centre, 'it is quite hard to draw the line between what is work and what is personal.' This policy also helped to cut down any antagonism local groups may have felt towards the Centre, and thus by implication the GLC, 'muscling in' on their campaigns.

As some projects were completed, people became more confident that the Centre and the GLC could actually provide practical support to local needs. As part of its work with Anscott Road Tenants' Association, for example, the Centre worked on the Anscott Road Nature Garden, providing physical help, contacting environment groups and the London Wildlife Trust, getting grants for new trees to be planted and arranging skips. This practical support was vital in projects like the Docklands Armada to Parliament. The Armada, a flotilla of boats representing local groups travelling up the Thames to Westminster, celebrates the alternatives to current development in Docklands, and the alliance that has built up around related issues.

In April 1984, 3,000 people and many local groups, including the People's Plan Centre and the Campaign Against the Airport, took part in the first Armada, taking with them the People's Charter for Docklands, organised by the Democracy for Docklands Campaign. The GLC paid for the hire of the boats, and provided tents, marquees and entertainment at the Jubilee Gardens, focus for many previous marches and demonstrations from the People's March for Jobs to the Hiroshima Day march. Ken Livingstone met the boats on their arrival at Festival Pier, and congratulated local groups and the Rotherhithe Centre on the organisation of the Armada. It has now become a major project for the Rotherhithe Centre annually.

Although the projects outlined above seem marginal and small, they boosted the low morale of local groups. A major issue in Docklands was housing, as previously explained. This next section holds a magnifying glass to a local campaign on housing, that maintained its autonomy from the Rotherhithe Centre, Southwark Council and the GLC, but achieved their concrete support and backing without losing its original aims and direction.

'Just to the east of the old Chambers Wharf and cold storage buildings at Bermondsey is a piece of land which the property developers and the LDDC would describe as one of the most attractive investment propositions in Docklands,' runs a Rotherhithe Planning Centre report. 'This area is known as Cherry Garden Pier, and includes a stretch of river frontage with superb views of the Thames, Tower Bridge and the City. The area has been derelict for ten years.'

When the LDDC bought the land, local residents were initially relieved. They assumed that a plan previously drawn up by Southwark Council for council housing would now go ahead.

They soon discovered that the LDDC's plan was for luxury housing consisting of high river frontage blocks. If allowed to succeed, it would effectively block the access and view of the river enjoyed by existing council residents, and the prices of the houses and flats would exclude them from remaining there.

At a Cherry Garden and Millpond Tenants' Association meeting, Alan Turkie from the Rotherhithe Centre suggested they get together with other local groups. They did that and formed the Cherry Garden Action Group. With the GLC funded Poster Project they launched a campaign: 'Think Again LDDC'. The Action Committee was firm. 'These blocks along the front of us, no way are we going to stand for them,' they said to the LDDC. The issue of public housing was one that all local residents felt, and the campaign mobilised local people relatively easily in comparison to the wider issue of Docklands development explored by the People's Plan Centre.

In March 1985 the LDDC offered one third of the site to local housing associations for rented homes, intending to buy off the Cherry Gardens campaign with a compromise after they had ensured the scheme received bad publicity. The Action Group decided to continue pressing for *all* of the site to be developed for local people, at rents or prices they could afford, with gardens and open access to the river views. 'They really don't like bad publicity,' says Beryl Donovan, local resident. 'If you make enough fuss, the LDDC will hold back, for a time anyway.' In January 1986, after considerable pressure from the Cherry Garden Action Group, the Rotherhithe Planning Centre, Southwark Council and the GLC, and LDDC gave way.

They released over half the land to Southwark Council, who, as originally intended, plan to build between fifty and seventy homes for rent. Without the LDDC's budget and with cut backs enforced by central government, they will have to borrow £4.8 million to make this a reality.

Although the GLC influence was small in this case, funding the Rotherhithe Centre to assist in the practicalities of the campaign, its resources and political backing were vital to the victory. Beryl Donovan feels that this can't be underestimated: 'If you are just one or two local groups the LDDC are just going to say that you are rabble rousers. But if you form your committee and alliances, we can all stand together as ordinary people. Then you get so much more done.' Echoes of the experience of women in the coalfields during the 1984 Miners Strike are heard in her description of the effect the 'politicisation' of the campaign had on her life.

So far, we have discussed the GLC's support, direct and indirect, for community action. But there were also the distinct interests and views of workers in Docklands to take into account.

When the GLC held its first workshop with TGWU dockers to discuss the future of the dock industry in London, one docker said that the GLC had come along 'ten years too late'. To a large extent this was true. While the docks had been steadily closing over a twenty year period, local authorities like the GLC had done little to stem the decline or ally themselves with dock workers or the unions in their struggle against the dock employers.

In 1985, with all the upstream docks closed, what could the GLC do? The docks appeared to be in the grip of an inevitable decline, caused by containerisation, changing patterns of world trade and missed opportunities by the Port of London Authority.

Although the wider community had been involved in protests against the closure of Hays Wharf, the West India Dock and the Royal Docks, the gradual desertion of the Thames by shipping companies and wharfingers — the wharf owners — seemed to have gone too far for any positive action. The dockers themselves were feeling demoralised. Continued cut backs by the PLA combined with a climate of anti-trade unionism had cut their numbers from 10,000 in 1970 to less than 2,000 by the mid-1980s. Dockers had bent over backwards to accommodate new working practices and make Tilbury Docks more attractive to shipping lines. Yet still the work did not come.

The GLC manifesto of 1981 had committed the new administration to keeping the docks open, although at the time all the upstream docks were on the point of closure. Tilbury Docks (outside the GLC area) were open but struggling due to the slump in world trade. Yet little practical contact between the GLC and unions took place for some time.

In December 1984 a new Docklands Team was created in the GLC, with one of its main tasks being to develop the GLC's work on the use of the river. This team soon discovered that the GLC was already involved in many aspects of the use of the river. It was responsible for river piers, the Thames barrier, and licensing passenger boats, and was the strategic planning authority. It coordinated a riverside development watchdog committee called the Thames-side Consultative Committee and its Freight Unit had undertaken detailed research into freight uses of the river and the viability of individual wharves.

But there was no overall economic, transport or planning strategy for the river. The GLC had close relationships with the community groups of Docklands, as outlined previously, but there was no working relationship with dock workers (predominantly white men) or with river users.

The Docklands Team worked closely with the TGWU to establish a Use of the River Working Party to bring together river interests including trade unions, boroughs and community groups. One of its first projects was to produce a manifesto for the use of the river.

The main aims of the Use of the River Manifesto were the promotion of the river for the transport of goods, the protection of existing jobs on the river, the resistance to luxury development on the riverbank, planning the riverside to benefit local people, investigation of new ideas for transport on the river, and pressure for recreational use of the river and the docks by residents of the docklands boroughs. This Manifesto and the Working Party provided the background to the first major GLC contacts with the grass roots of the dock workers unions. Workshops were organised by the Popular Planning Unit and the TGWU at which stewards and branch officials in the riverside wharves, watermen and lightermen, and Tilbury Dock workers discussed their views on the future of the dock industry on the Thames.

Though the initial reaction was sceptical, 'another talk shop' which was happening too late, the mood of the workshop changed when discussion began on what changes in the use and control of the river the workforce would demand from a future government. The threat of GLC abolition and the impending takeover of GLC river functions by the Thames Water Authority also prompted a strong response. At the same time, a slight upturn in river trade and some success by Tilbury in winning new shipping lines created the feeling that there was some real point in the discussions. Out of the workshops and discussions on the use of the river evolved the idea of setting up an entirely new democratically based London River Authority. Its functions would combine many of those of the GLC, Thames Water and the PLA — a government quango. Two large conferences were called to discuss the future of freight transport on the Thames and the problems of the administration of the Thames.

The TGWU at local and regional level gave its full backing to this proposal and is now involved in the process of pressing for the new authority to be established. The TGWU along with other river interests and the riverside local authorities will have seats on the governing committee.

The Use of the River work is now being taken forward by the Docklands Consultative Committee, run by the docklands boroughs following the abolition of the GLC. This work is only a small part of what needs to be done on the river. Reports commissioned by the GLC have shown that extensive public intervention, exercised through a new river authority for London, is essential if the potential of the Thames for freight transport or public recreation is to be realised. An investment plan backed by new scales of charges and incentives for river use is a vital ingredient of any new strategy.

Some Conclusions and Reflections

The Popular Planning Unit, combined with other initiatives by trade unions, community groups and local authorities, started the ball rolling for a new strategy for Docklands based on local needs. But there were problems within the GLC itself. In some ways it sounds as though the GLC was united as an organisation, in providing local people in Docklands with the resources to fight the changes in their area and put forward positive alternatives. But a lot of local people active in Docklands politics have had experience of previous 'well meaning' local authorities and dismiss this as 'hype'. The GLC in reality didn't run as a united machine, it became responsive when new policies, people and resources were channelled in different ways. 'It's just that there were new parts being grafted on which were more responsive,' says Andy Copeland, a worker at JDAG during the GLC developments. 'Sometimes they happened to get the right bits working.'

However true this may be, the politicians that came to the new GLC were seen as different from previous Labour politicians. As Ted Bowman, from North Southwark Community Development Group, says, 'there is no doubt in my mind that if there hadn't been some drive, political drive, political will to look at the needs deeply and not peripherally, then it wouldn't have been a success. There is no doubt that the GLC said "we are going to put our money where our mouth is". And initiatives in Docklands would never have come about unless there was that real political will.'

GLC support has definitely strengthened some local organisations, and shown that a determined local authority working closely with local groups can give a major boost to a demoralised area. Using its resources skillfully, in for instance buying land and funding organisations, it can also help people to win. The GLC and Southwark Council enabled local groups to win major property battles at Coin Street, Courages Brewery and Cherry Garden. These were won against the force of the property market and the government operating against them. They are exceptions, but they give a glimpse of what popular planning can achieve in helping to redistribute public resources fairly, and build an alliance between the public and its accountable local authority, in a way that achieves a working democracy.

Clearly in the Royal Docks, the People's Plan and the activities surrounding it helped to stimulate and develop a 'constituency' of people who had the knowledge and confidence to pressure not only other governmental organisations, but the GLC itself. Although the People's Plan was not a blueprint for planning in the area, it encouraged people to make their needs and desires more explicit.

If the GLC had more power to intervene in a positive way to build houses and infrastructure and to invest, problems no doubt would have developed over exactly what should and could be done, and under whose control it would be. Popular planning is in many ways a lot easier when the local authority and the local community are united in opposition to those with real power and much greater resources. In the case of Docklands, common opposition to the LDDC became the basis of a strong bond between the GLC and local people. This unity would have been more difficult to achieve in a situation where the GLC had all the power on its own.

Despite the many problems the GLC did, for a while, help the vision of a future Docklands to be on the agenda for debate, an agenda summed up with the words the Docklands Armada carried to Parliament: Docklands for the People, Give Us Back Our Land.

13
Our Health in Whose Hands? Health Emergencies and the Struggle for Better Health Care in London

Introduction

Health care is an obvious area of concern for a local authority like the GLC committed to the welfare of Londoners. It is both urgently and desperately needed as a service. It is also a big employer: over 200,000 people work in London's hospitals, surgeries and clinics.

There is an LCC tradition of local authority involvement in the organisation of hospital supplies and the design and manufacture of ambulances through direct labour. So the GLC's activities in the 1980s are not entirely without precedent even though the approach has differed. The approach of the recent Labour administration has been to recognise that health is a wider issue in fact than the Health Service. It has been seen to be linked to social, psychological and economic circumstances. Thus the work of the GLC in the period 1982-1986 on, for example, food, energy and the environment can be seen to relate to health. So also can the investigations of health at work, the chronicling of the effects of One Person Operation on the buses and on the underground, the dangers of homeworkers materials, the impact of asbestos and support for the campaign against it, the setting up of the Hazards Centre and the City Centre (which have publicised work hazards including tenosynovitis), and the Fords public hearing where the sewing machinists' loss of use of their hands through tenosynovitis and the effects of the stress of assembly line work were described. The London Industrial Strategy on Health Care summed this up by saying that

When the GLC was able to fund the Health Emergency campaigns, it provided a valuable means of bringing together local people trying to keep their hospitals open, and workers fighting for decent pay.

medicine was of limited significance:

> Our conditions of life are a far more important influence on how long we live and how well we are. Governments and local authorities wishing to improve health must pay attention to the quality of our work and home lives. Responsibilities for health cannot be hived off to a particular authority or government department ... the social changes needed to improve our health are as much to do with issues of power and relationships between people, as our physical conditions of life.

The following account is about only one aspect of the GLC's support for work around health — the funding of three London Health Emergency Workers who collect and disseminate information on the Health Service and produce a newspaper 'Health Emergency', and the backing for local groups in the boroughs, either by financing full-time workers or by small grants for publicity and research.

However even this relatively narrow study has tremendous ramifications because many people and organisations have come into contact with Health Emergency in London in the three years or so of its existence. This is not then an exhaustive history. I have drawn out instead themes from interviews with people involved in four areas of London (Hackney, Hillingdon, Tower Hamlets and Harrow), and with two of the co-ordinators. These were done between September and December 1985. The hope is that this partial chronicling will be a contribution to understanding the part a local authority can play in raising awareness of the problems in our health service and the needs for better health care.

Background

Since 1976 resources for health care in London have been cut; this policy is known as RAWP, after the Resources Allocation Working Party. It was argued that London had a disproportionate amount of resources because of the financing of the large teaching hospitals.

The smaller hospitals and the mental hospitals had however been under-capitalised. The attempt at re-allocation took no account of the social pattern of illness in working class inner city areas. It also presumed a model of high technology health practice.

But unfortunately for Londoners' health care in the last ten years, the flaws in the original policy have been compounded. Its reallocation came to justify cuts. It thus laid the basis for the Conservative government's offensive to reduce the cost of the health service in the 1980s. This has been waged on several fronts — cuts, the intensification of work, 'through-put', the increased speed in which patients pass through hospital and back into 'the community', or the imposition of 'competitive' tendering for cleaning, laundry and catering which forced down the wages of directly employed workers or gave the contracts to private contractors. This has been accompanied by anti-trade union legislation and an attempt to reduce the power of public service trades unionism. The government has encouraged the growth of private medicine, which has made use of public facilities and the skills of health workers. There is a real danger that the Health Service, which despite all its inadequacies has been still an impressive demonstration that public responsibility for care is more effective and more humane than the profit motive, will decline into a secondary service for the poor, employing a demoralised and badly paid workforce.

The 1970s saw a series of strikes by low paid hospital workers. These had several notable features. There was a strong sense of rank and file democracy. Women and ethnic minority workers played an important part. A stress on the value and responsibility of the work accompanied explanations of the reasons for wage militancy. In several cases resistance from the workers in the Health Service combined with community support. Health workers went outwards to gain support.

Trade unionists, community and women's groups combined to defend the Elizabeth Garrett Anderson Hospital in Euston. In March 1977 staff at Hounslow occupied, arguing for a community hospital. In July a work-in started to save Plaistow Maternity Hospital. In June 1978 there was a work-in in defence of Bethnal Green Hospital. Out of these experiences and others like them in the 1970s there emerged a consciousness of the need not only to link workers and the community in the effort to defend the health service but also to campaign for a more appropriate health care. The arguments were being made for more democratic and egalitarian relations between health workers, more say for the local community and greater involvement of patients. The demand for user control was greatly influenced by the emphasis of the women's movement on 'our bodies, ourselves'. There was considerable discussion in women's groups of the hierarchical relations in the health service and the need for more information about women's health. The stress on individual choice extended to an understanding of the social and economic factors which blocked this. For example it was argued that while reproductive technology technically made control possible, in its present social form it increased the control of professionals over child birth. By the late 1970s a 'politics of health' had emerged which argued not only for more resources but for an approach to health care which recognised the need for long-term care and the links to work, housing, food, and the environment, and was open to alternative medicine.

Various attempts were made in the 1970s to overcome the fragmentation of the groups concerned with health. There was the London Alliance of Stewards for Health Workers (LASH) in 1972 and its magazine 'Baclash'. In 1973 the rank and file paper 'Hospital Worker' was started and the All London Health Workers Alliance appeared with organisational energy coming from the International Socialists (later Socialist Workers Party). In the mid-1970s Fightback campaigns against the cuts developed. Politics of Health groups formed in the late 1970s, and women's groups got together at a conference on Women and Health in February 1979.

In 1979 a group of socialists working in the state spelled out the contradictions in resisting the oppressive aspects of the capitalist state while attempting to secure the improvement of conditions through state provision. *In and Against the State*, first as a pamphlet, then as a book, expressed the unease about welfare which had been growing throughout the 1970s among some radicals. It included discussion of the health service.

In the 1980s the Conservatives' attack on public services forced a change of emphasis. The strength of the mobilisation to defend the health service was not sufficient to prevent cuts in 1982. However it did force the government to make a public commitment to maintain the NHS in the 1983 election.

The London Industrial Strategy comments grimly:

> Had there been no resistance to hospital closures the picture might well have been bleaker.

It is discouraging to think that over a decade of intense struggle has apparently simply prevented worse from happening. In the present era far from creating a better health service it has not been possible to even defend the inadequate one in existence.

Origins

The historical origins of new social combinations of people acting for change has a dimension of time which for convenience can be called a beginning. But every individual brings into any social organisation a series of origins.

Even among the small group of people I interviewed about their involvement in Health Emergency, there is a wealth of experience of working for health, of being patients, of health service trades unionism, of fights against the cuts, of occupations, of campaigns, of women's group discussions, of struggles in the black community for greater power to determine health provision, and of the creation of alternative health practices. In commenting on the last three years people consequently draw on memories of their commitment in the last decade. In one case memory of health service struggles went back as far as 1949.

The original group was Hackney Health Emergency. Lucy de Groot, one of the founding members, worked at the time for Hackney Trade Union Support Unit:

> In Hackney what had happened was that we realised, with I suppose a shock, in December 1982, that there were serious proposals to finally close St Leonards.

St Leonard's hospital had been threatened with closure before and there had been a strong campaign to save it in the 1970s. This time it was in danger because of the 'Fowler cuts'.

> All over London in that period of '82 after the Fowler cuts, the health authorities were kind of slashing around to find money wherever they could.

A meeting was held in December 1982 in St Leonards, between the Community Health Council, Hackney Borough Council and the embryonic campaign which was emerging out of the Trades Council Health Sub-Committee. While each of these were approaching the health service from differing angles they were united in the need to safeguard existing services and St Leonards in particular.

In January 1983 Hackney Health Emergency was formally launched. Lucy de Groot stresses the importance of the basic combination of interest from the community, the council and the unions. She also points out this combination was a result of a much longer historical process.

The 1982 Health Service dispute immediately pre-dated the development of these health campaigns and a lot of the contacts that we had in Hackney ... had come out of the work that the Trades Council and other trade unionists had done in support of the Health Service workers in the '82 dispute. And whilst it was immediately about pay, I think people were very awae that it was about more than that. It was about the kind of evaluation of the Health Service as a whole and there was a lot of local support for the health workers in that very long dispute in 1982 ... the health campaigns very much came out of an existing tradition of campaigning and fighting for better services and against cuts and closures and so on, which had existed certainly in areas like Hackney, for many, many years.

Morris Kolander, a porter at Barts and active in NUPE, has worked in the NHS since 1949. He was involved in the strike of '82, 'against the cuts which were inflicted upon us, unsocial hours, less wages and all the rest of it.' He became involved in the Hackney Health Emergency group because the closures 'highlighted' the longer term policy of cuts:

I think we felt that the time had — I suppose it was time we made a stand ... It was nothing really new in a sense, I mean we had many marches and campaigns over closures over a number of years.

Having fought for St Leonards 'the first time round ... when it came up again, I suppose they thought, let's have another go'.

Lucy de Groot observes that it was apparent that the cuts were not peculiar to Hackney.

We thought this is silly, there's no point in us just going in alone ... we should get together with other people facing similar problems in London.

Battersea and Wandsworth trades council were trying to defend the South London Women's Hospital. They joined with Hackney to organise a meeting at County Hall in the Spring of 1983 of people from community health campaigns, health trades unions, and Labour Party groups. The meeting was attended by seventeen community based health campaigns, twenty two NHS Union branches, six trades councils and the Greater London Association of Trades Councils (GLATCs), and full-time officers from the South East Region of the TUC (SERTUC) NHS Co-ordinating Committee.

Dick Muskett, a member of NUPE, was the trade union

nominee on the Wandsworth Health Authority at the time. He supported the idea of an all London organisation because 'there was no one taking an overview ... it wasn't just a cut here and a cut there, it was a consistency of cuts'. It was impossible to quantify and assess the impact of the proposed cuts for London as a whole without such an overview. 'The GLC was the appropriate place that information should be logged and aggregated and then put out.'

There were three research workers who were on the health panel in the GLC, which had been set up as a sub-committee of the Finance and General Purposes Committee. They were not able to take on the work of finding out the scale of the cuts. However the Industry and Employment Committee, concerned particularly with the jobs angle, did employ two consultants to gather this information. It was also possible to give small grants of up to £750 for publicity and information about the effect of the cuts to the local campaigns through the Popular Planning Unit of the Industry and Employment Branch. £475 was given towards a pamphlet 'London's Health Service on the Danger List' and a day school organised with the Popular Planning Unit for health workers and members of local health campaigns.

It was evident though that there was the need for some kind of permanent funding for research and information and a means of helping local campaigns in a more systematic way. People started ringing County Hall with information and queries about the health cuts and some of them got involved in local health groups.

The aim of London Health Emergency was

> to provide research, information and other forms of assistance to NHS trade unionists and community-based health campaigns in London, to assist in their efforts to preserve jobs and services within the NHS.

It was considered 'to be of vital importance to establish and develop working links between trade unions and the community'. It was intended, as the GLC committee report said, that the project 'would encourage the development of local plans drawn up by both workers and users of the NHS for a more effective and locally responsible service'. The project was to 'alert the general public of the effect in health service facilities, if the proposed cuts in jobs take place'.

The fact that both John MacDonnell, then chair of the Finance and General Purposes Committee, and Michael Ward, chair of the Industry and Employment Committee, had a special interest in the health service was politically important within the GLC. Also important in the establishing of Health Emergency were the close trade union links which existed in Hackney and Wandsworth with NUPE and COHSE.

From the start there was a conscious attempt to establish alliances between the Community Health Councils, the boroughs, the community groups, and the unions. In Hackney the first workers, Julie Bromwich and Jenny Webber, job shared. Both were active in the local trade union movement. Julie Bromwich had written a history of NUPE's involvement in the health service while on a trade union course at the London School of Economics. Mike Walker, a health worker from Guildford, who had been on the same course and written the complementary history of COHSE, was also involved in the formation of London Health Emergency. He was though really carried along by events and other people's enthusiasm, feeling dubious about the project. He was 'hesitant' about working on a London-wide basis. He thought it would 'stretch' their ogranisational capacity. He had seen a series of attempts to set up trades union and shop stewards' campaigns nationally which had collapsed.

After the strike of 1982 there was in his view a 'deterioration in the militancy of London NHS ancillary staff, especially London East'.

He was consequently wary of a London-wide venture and had to be persuaded they could organise on this basis. He was also not sure about the links between the unions and the community, concerned that the community side would become paramount and the workers' interests be neglected.

In retrospect, he reflects,

> I must admit I took very much a sectarian — almost a sectarian view.
> Now if you are in Hackney, there are plenty of pressure groups ... and they are very easy to link in with the hospital workers, the problem in Hackney I always felt was that the workers themselves had ... they feel they'd their heyday. I meant it was a mental thing. I think a lot of them thought, you know, oh, this can never be as good as it was in '76 ... It's very hard to do anything in Hackney because it's all been done before about ten times as big.

Not all the money came from the GLC. Some came from local boroughs and the health workers who had received money from other trade unionists in '82 gave what they had saved from this dispute to the Health Emergency Groups.

At the same time by Autumn 1983 public concern about health cuts was mounting:

> It was a real crunch point in which people's fears overspilled, it was the first time that people really started attending DHA's en masse.

There was a large and angry meeting in Hackney that September where about two thousand people pressurised the DHA not to close St Leonards. Tony Benn and Rodney Bickerstaffe spoke. Lucy de Groot remembers:

> The town hall chamber was absolutely packed, and in fact the meeting had to be closed because of the activities of the Health Authority members, who refused to accept the strength of local feeling against the closure.

In this intense atmosphere the DHA postponed the decision, and though they did in fact close St Leonards as a hospital with beds a few months later, the fight to save St Leonards through an occupation continued until Summer 1984. It collapsed after the DHA took an unprecedented step of taking out injunctions against the whole of NUPE. As a compromise, though, useful community health services were kept going in the building, which in Morris Kolander's words

> were still standing ... as a monument to our struggle I think.

So St Leonard's has not become a completely wasted resource, a useless shell like Poplar on the Isle of Dogs and many other hospitals.

Mike Walker was 'taping' the events of Hackney the day after the Town Hall demonstration, and the news flashes were coming in from Hillingdon, where also there was resistance to cuts at Hayes Cottage Hospital and Northwood and Pinner Hospital. At this point Mike Walker was the COHSE Hillingdon branch secretary. Hayes Cottage Hospital was occupied one week before it was due to be closed on October 31, 1983. Only Margery Bane, a hospital domestic, and a couple of other ancillary workers, were unionised in the cottage hospital. People joined the union after they occupied. Despite this lack of formal organisational experience the occupation, led by ancillary workers, proceeded with considerable speed and efficiency. Margery Bane commented:

> the nurses didn't want responsibility of initiating anything but everyone worked alongside us.

The patients signed declarations saying they refused to be moved.

> It helped that the local T&G branch secretary just happened to be in the hospital for a hernia operation, so he got the patients' side sewn up.

Hayes got support from NUPE, from local trade unions, pensioners' tenants and many other people, for Hayes was popular in the community. Margery Bane said:

> This is a real working community hospital. As well as the beds there are other facilities; a mother and baby clinic, a community psychiatric clinic, family planning and there is an emergency unit.

Northwood and Pinner's occupation was led by a Labour Party matron in a middle class Tory area. But it was a First World War Memorial Hospital and local people were stirred. Mike Walker describes pickets being dropped off in Rolls Royce's and Daimlers, and prayer meetings being held outside the hospital.

Presumably somewhat taken aback, the DHA reversed its original decision on temporary closure and decided on public consultation with a view to permanent closure. The occupation had won a reprieve.

From these two occupations Hillingdon Health Emergency was formed. Pete Marshall, the COHSE regional official, explains:

> There wasn't actually a formal Health Emergency there until activity started around those hospitals, but there were two separate groups of people originally. There was a group of users, patients, patients' relations, a local group from the community who wanted to keep the hospital open and there were workers who were afraid for their jobs and were basically seeing the unions' role being to negotiate the best deal for them.

When the GLC was able to fund a Health Emergency group it provided a valuable means of bringing these two together.

In the Hayes occupation the involvement of the local trade council had meant links with the Trades Union Support Unit group, a GLC funded group which assists local trade unionists with information and research. Steve Clair, a worker for the Support Unit, was seconded for two months to help. Margery Bane paid him an impressive tribute:

We would have been lost without Steve. He was like an anchorman.

Hillingdon had been one of the early groups which in the summer of 1983 had applied to the Industry and Employment Branch's Popular Planning Unit for money for publicity. Margery Bane, Steve Clair and Mike Walker commented that this had made a difference in getting the campaign launched. When I interviewed Mike Walker in 1985 he stressed how the discussion of the most efffective way to use the £750 had involved people. The small grant was not only useful in itself but organisationally strenthening.

When Hillingdon Health Emergency was formed, Mike Walker became the local worker. It was among the eight groups funded by the GLC. He continued to be COHSE branch secretary.

Early in 1984 there was another rebellion in the area. On May 23, hospital workers in Hillingdon took strike action against privatisation partly inspired by the Barking cleaners' stand against Crothalls. There were large numbers of women involved. Asian women played an important part.

Hillingdon Health Emergency had already put proposals for a 'unified trade union response to privatisation' to Health Emergency Groups. The strike confirmed the resolve — resistance to privatisation has been an important aspect of Health Emergency work.

These sudden eruptions of militancy from workers who had not had the experience of resistance or even a great deal of trade union involvement were in response to specific threats. Hospital workers in Hillingdon had not even been affected much by the 1982 strike. While they lacked experience in organisation, they had not known the disheartening defeats of the East Londoners. The coincidence of the GLC funding London Health Emergency strengthened these new rebellions and helped to gain some support: for example leaflets were translated into Punjabi as some of the Asian strikers were Sikh women, and also into Hindi and Spanish. But funding alone was not enough. Mike Walker stresses the determination of the Asian women, mainly domestics, and the existence of strong community networks which provided organisational back-up for the strike. These networks served as a complementary form of organising to the formal organisation of trade unionism.

The Structure of London Health Emergency

When London Health Emergency's information centre was funded by the GLC through the Finance and General Purposes and Industry and Employment Committees, Dick Muskett says the emphasis was on saving jobs in the health service, and on the overall role of the NHS in the London economy as a large employer, supplier and purchaser. This was consistent with the aims of the Industry and Employment Committee and with a much older tradition, established in the days of the LCC, of concern about the welfare of London's workforce and the responsibility of public bodies to be good employers and use their purchasing power responsibly. This principle is the opposite to the free-for-all negligence of privatisation.

There was another element in the work of the Industry and Employment Branch which was important. It tried to develop alternatives to job loss through supporting people's plans to improve working conditions and relationships and extend workers' control over the social uses of their products or the social forms through which their service was expressed. The links between workplace and community which were made in Hackney and Hillingdon were clearly crucial steps towards this process. Another element was the provision of clear information about the implications of policy and health needs so these could be widely understood and discussed and resolutions reached. But the making of alternatives from below is not an easy process.

Dick Muskett said that in the original conception they pushed people's plans 'very strongly'. They envisaged

> health service workers and consumers working out a better way to plan the health service. That never really happened but that was really built in quite strongly in the early stages. That was what we wanted to see happen. I don't think anybody's really taken it on.

In fact the main bulk of the work of the information office of three workers has been the struggle to defend the health service, through making information available. This does contain of course an implicit alternative, for the democratisation of the NHS would require major changes in its structure.

Since April 1984 the office has produced a newspaper 'Health Emergency' which has been an important means of conveying information about the local groups, about cuts, closures, strikes, privatisation, private medicine, the false rhetoric of community care without resources, racism in the NHS, women's health needs and many other health issues. It is distributed in bundles to Health Emergency groups and trade union branches.

They also cover big demonstrations, conferences and events like the GLC Jobs Festivals. About 1,000 copies go to individuals by post. 'We don't have a machinery to sell so its basically a free distribution,' John Lister, one of the workers at the Information Office, told me.

Apart from the newspaper, the office itself serves as an information exchange. John Lister said that they try

> to provide information bringing together all the sources we have got available London wide, so that the local districts can draw in this information. We try to obviously publicise events in particular districts where we want support and we try also to mediate between London struggles and struggles in the health service elsewhere.

The information is thus partly about activities. But it is also about the health service more generally.

Kevin Flack pointed out that there was no other organisation 'putting together facts and figures on a London wide basis'. So even local councils will not 'necessarily know what the health plans are for the health district they cover'.

Another area they had investigated was privatisation. 'We think we've got the most comprehensive files on things like private companies that are tendering for the contracts.'

They worked with other labour and trade union research groups, including local trade union support units like Merton and Hillingdon. They also linked in with the research done by the GLC's Health Panel, and had had contact with another group funded by the GLC which is concerned with health and safety in employment, the Hazards Centre. While part of a network of research and information groups, they were clear that their focus had to be on the health service. They did not just sit and wait for people to tell them what was going on but sent an outreach worker 'into the field' to find out. In getting the information they collected out to people, they wanted it to be of use to people in the unions but also to 'people who just take an interest in the cuts'. They had thus gone to the TUC and Labour Party Conferences and done fringe meetings but they had also gone on the radio and sent out press releases and were used by journalists writing on the health service. Both of them stressed that information was a basis for democratic control of health care. Both were convinced that it would have been impossible to build up the range of support and contacts without GLC financing.

GLC Funding and Democratic Involvement

The resources which have gone to Health Emergency to provide information have been part of a wider GLC strategy to democratise the access to information about policy and to enable people to develop their own alternatives. In getting out information about a public service, Health Emergency is one aspect of a struggle to open up the stage and get the resources back to the people from whom they came. In the last four years a curious battle has been going on of little state (GLC) versus big state (central government).

Though at the moment David has fallen to Goliath, nonetheless in the course of the combat resources have been distributed and a new more active relation has been made between local government and the public. This relation has revealed political dimensions to the endeavour to extend the democratic process beyond a franchise or the right of combination to wider aspects of everyday life. If this is to be built upon in the future it is important to examine the details of the structures which have come into existence.

Public resources of time and money clearly require forms of accountability. One solution is to employ people to check and monitor, thus swelling the numbers of state officials. While this has been done by the GLC the attempt has also been made to create less bureaucratic alternatives. One way of doing this is to have voluntary groupings as democratic 'watch-dogs'.

London Health Emergency has a steering committee which includes trade unionists. Pete Marshall is a regional officer for the health service union, COHSE. He looks after branches in

West London and is on the Health Emergency steering committee. He points out that health service trade unionism is full of
inter-union conflict. Unity is a considerable achievement.
London Health Emergency has got representatives from all the
major unions and the two major unions, COHSE and NUPE, are
both nationally affiliated to London Health Emergency.

Another time-honoured manner of exerting a degree of control in the labour movement has been through affiliation. In
Autumn 1985 Health Emergency had 175 affiliated groups. 150
were in London and 25 outside London. Besides the local campaigns, unions and union branches, they include pensioners'
groups, community groups and a few trades councils. This too is
quite an achievement.

However if state monitoring can lead to unwieldy bureaucracies, voluntary efforts at accountability are not without their
difficulties. The London Health Emergency at the centre has the
problem common to information networks of ensuring that
people do stay involved. It is hard though sometimes to keep all
local health campaigns in touch with the centre.

It is not surprising that for people whose living connection
was to the local group, the central office had a rather shadowy
existence. It goes without saying that the mysterious workings of
the Industry and Employment Committee or Finance and
General Purposes within County Hall were well nigh incompre-
hensible. There was an administrative reality — time spent in
applications for grants, or the cautious custom of paying grants
in stages which ignored the problems of how the bills and the
rates were to be paid. But political contact with the GLC seemed
to be rather an affair of chance — an indication perhaps that
there is still a long way to go in this opening up of the state, even
at a local level.

The local groups themselves who were autonomously funded
by the GLC are not without certain structural problems. Again of
course these organisational dilemmas are not peculiar to the
health emergency groups. Nor are they simply the result of being
tangled up with a local authority. Eight groups received funding
from the GLC for a full-time worker in Autumn 1985. But groups
existed in most of the London boroughs. Harrow Health Emergency does not have a paid full-timer. But they did have a small
publicity grant through the Popular Planning Delegated
Authority in the Spring of 1984. In Autumn 1984 they received
£500 for organising a conference on alternatives in the NHS
through 'Jobs Year'. They have also been able to rely on back-up

from the Harrow Resources Centre which has been invaluable, for it is hard to sustain a group in Harrow, which has real health problems but not the dramatic deprivation of an area like Tower Hamlets. Also as Haf Evans explained both she and Tom O'Malley 'have other jobs which are very demanding and also neither of us are based on Harrow'. If the Resource Centre goes 'it would be a big loss for us'. The GLC projects are thus part of an interconnecting web. Their collapse will have a spin off effect. So even a group like Harrow which will not experience the loss of a full-time worker will be affected by abolition.

Local organising in Harrow can be dispiriting in a period like the present. Rosie Newbiggen, the Resource Centre Worker, who has helped the Health Emergency group with information and research, said:

> When there's only a small number of you, its quite easy to get quite disillusioned ... also just because of the political climate, you just sort of feel very isolated and very frustrated.

She thought it important that they met regularly and sat down and went carefully over what they were doing — despite the lack of dramatic triumphs.

A paid worker did mean an assured security and continuity for a local group. It meant also the resources to 'produce information'. It enabled time to be spent on working with community groups to convince them of the need to take up the work.

Tim Thompson has been working on a study of housing and health in Tower Hamlets. He was given some hours of paid employment through the GLC's Popular Planning Unit, as an outreach worker in liaison with the Trades Council's Alternative Economic Strategy group, to study areas of need which might create employment. His work has made him aware of the considerable body of research which was done on conditions in Tower Hamlets which was never used. The idea of holding a Health Inquiry came out of this realisation of the need to publicise the knowledge of both local people and professional experts about the health service and the impact of environmental factors on health in the Borough. He explained that people in the Health Emergency group became very discouraged when they realised that just showing opposition would not change the DHA's policies. In this downturn it was especially important that there was GLC backing to see them through. This had given them the leeway to change tack and 'be a bit more subtle in the approach'.

This had led into the Health Inquiry. He argued:

> You're a paid worker so you don't get so fed up as you would just doing it in your spare time. And the fact that the GLC is there providing that support and saying it's worthwhile is important.

The advantages have however to be set against the disadvantages. Myra Garrett, the Health Emergency worker in Tower Hamlets, is GLC funded and knew this enabled her to work in a wider sphere. Still, there were snags:

> People say, oh well, they're getting on with it. They don't really need — I can skip this meeting because it's being seen to. So, in a sense we have less input from our members in setting priorities and staff than we did when we didn't have a paid worker.

It is one of the grisly facts of organising, of course, that after the initial honeymoon period there is a tendency for input to be negative. Apart from the dedicated few, people turn up when they are fed up about something. Not surprisingly the Health Emergency Worker's job can be demanding and somewhat nerve wracking. Being responsible to the committee is grand as a political theory. In human terms though it means there is a numerical reversal of the normal employer-employee relation. There is in this case one employee and a group of symbolic 'employers'. A committee can demand long and self-sacrificing hours or disagree uncomfortably with the worker's priorities. As Mike Walker puts it,

> they're saying 'Do more research, do more research', and you're already working 66-70 hours a week ... and there's no support structure, you just feel isolated a lot of the time and trade unions are the worst employers.

He saw the linking of health workers in the borough as the most vital aspect of his work but the results were necessarily long-term.

The funding of health emergency workers has revealed a whole range of activities which are needed locally around health needs. Consequently the job can be several rolled into one. These might include documenting a borough's health in relation to environmental and industrial factors, briefing people on Community Health Councils, putting pressure on the DHAs, developing a local policy on health, going around keeping trade unionists informed and in contact with one another and with community groups, producing clear and popular material on health, organising meetings, inquiries, or other action, working with alternative health groups who want to be within the NHS and finding new forms through which people whose voices have been ignored can express their health needs. Added to all these the ideal Health Emergency worker could be expected to possess a good background knowledge of health issues, of the administrative structure of the health service, of the health service trade unions, and of the local boroughs. They would also need to know of current struggles, and of the companies which are privatising services. Perhaps statistical skills and historical knowledge might be an advantage — and indeed the ability to work with people.

As Lucy de Groot observes,

> there's a whole range of jobs which imply a whole range of skills ...
> No one person can combine them all.

Yet she could see a two-way tension. One one side 'a campaign can basically get lazy'. People start to expect miracles of a worker, who cannot be a substitute for a group of people active in their workplace or in the community — the group perhaps also fears the power which the information held by a paid worker can give. The Health Emergency Worker can be torn between trying to serve the campaign and work to their own view of priorities, doing the immediate tasks and yet working out a long-term strategy. All this is made worse at a time of crisis in the NHS.

Particular organisational forms have political implications. The opportunity to improve the effectiveness of organisation came with GLC funding. This gives the opportunity to consider what Lucy de Groot calls 'a difficult dynamic' — how to balance the need for a continuing established structure with the continuing involvement of people in creative politics. Certainly a financed worker can be a great strength, at best in combination with a buoyant organising group, or at worst as a buffer in the bad times. But the worker, as Lucy de Groot stresses, cannot be a replacement for grass-roots organisation. 'Workers don't solve problems and shouldn't be expected to.'

One of the undoubted strengths of Health Emergency has been the diversity of experience which its supporters brought to it. But the strains and stresses emerge more clearly when it becomes evident that any victories are going to be hard won. Sometimes tensions about everyday organisational matters can be more submerged disagreements about political aims or even about what constitutes politics. Reflecting on these different traditions, Lucy de Groot observes:

> I think it is probably fair to say that in many ways most active trade unionists, certainly at the kind of level of local area health service workers, have not really been much affected by developments in organisation or style of operating, and they come to the campaign with very specific kinds of needs. And many of the community activists, and particularly some of the women who've been involved in community campaigns or have come from a more explicitly feminist kind of tradition, are very keen that the *process* is as important as the product.

Women played a crucial role in starting Health Emergency. Mike Walker, for instance, referred to Lucy de Groot and Andrea Campbel (a Hackney COHSE activist at that time) as 'the two founding sisters of the campaign'. They brought understandings about organisation from movements which had broken with labour movement formalities — they wanted to organise with people where they were rather than expecting Mohammed to come to the mountain.

> We spent a long time at the beginning saying that people could contribute in whatever way was most suitable to them, that coming to meetings was only one way of contributing,

Lucy de Groot remembered. They also tried to develop more imaginative forms of activity: for example, in the Summer of 1984, together with CND Hackney Health Emergency delivered enormous cheques, demonstrating the cost of Trident compared to the cost of hospitals that were being cut. But in the practical day to day organising it was hard to keep this up and remain concerned about how meetings were held and how people communicated with one another, and to keep on encouraging women and ethnic minority members to take on more in the unions. It also proved an effort to hold people who wanted to see results immediately, or new people who wanted to make changes in the group.

The different aspects of Health Emergency — quite apart from the problems of involvement — require a combination of organisational forms. The campaigning work is different from working out policy, the effort to enable health needs to be expressed is different again.

From the point of view of a local Health Emergency it is hard to balance these contrary assumptions and organisational forms. However their combination in Health Emergency as a whole illustrates in microcosm a wider debate on how to create political structures which both foster the skills and creativity of everyone involved and achieve specific objectives.

Health Emergencies and Trade Unions

The idea that local authorities share responsibility with trade unions to safeguard working conditions and should work with trade unions to secure jobs, develop training, encourage equality and a greater degree of control by the workforce, assist in the application of skills and link these with the needs of the community is new in its present manifestation. It has precedents, it is true, in the early days of the Labour Party when some of these were aspects of Independent Labour Party involvement on local councils. It still existed in East London even after World War II. But such precedents had been so decisively buried and almost completely forgotten that it was as if the GLC had started something entirely new.

It is not surprising that the attempt has been fraught with difficulties. Trade unions have enough problems of their own and the health service trade unions in London are no exception. For a start there is no automatic support between them, as Pete Marshall pointed out. Moreover branches within the same union can be cut off from one another. There is not surprisingly a weariness among the more experienced rank and file militants after a decade of cuts. The mobilisation against privatisation has not been whole-hearted.

The Barking Hospital cleaners were left to struggle, for over a year, without much real support, against a contractor, Crothalls, who tried to reduce wages and increase the hours, without much real support. It is hardly surprising that workers have accepted wage cuts to keep their jobs. The pressure of work at all levels of the NHS is terrible and the stress of dealing with frustrated patients is considerable. Hospitals are increasingly dirty, often unsafe places to work. The workforce is divided by rank, and in different unions. Racism and sexism exist in the NHS and little is being done to combat either.

After the upsurge of 1982 there has been a disgruntled quiet among London hospital workers, interrupted by eruptions on a local basis to defend jobs, resist privatisation, and save particular hospitals. These have brought many people new to trade unionism into resistance, especially women and people from ethnic minorities. But heroic isolated struggles have often been defeated or fended off cuts which have been enforced later. There seemed to be general agreement among the people I interviewed that morale was low among rank and file health workers — especially in East London.

Dave Carr, who works as a porter at the London Hospital, became involved with Tower Hamlets Health Emergency through the enquiry. He argues that the initial problem was that the 'roots' of trade unionism in the NHS were in unionisation pushed by the management:

> It's not grass roots, it's not through struggle. In 1948 when it was all nationalised it was Join the union, Join the union. And the actual branch structure wasn't struggled and fought for — it was given on a plate.

Though his contact with Tower Hamlets Health Emergency was relatively recent, Dave Carr recognised that the health emergency group could be important in putting the health workers' case across, and contacting other unions and local people. He accepts that they have a useful role because they have the time to find out information which workers do not. In December 1986 he had just been delegated by the stewards' committee to liaise with the Health Campaign. This formal recognition was the result of a long effort to build up confidence and break down suspicion. This hidden labour of contact and liaison is put in jeopardy now, of course, by the consequences of abolition, just as much as the more visible work of the GLC.

Commenting on the suspicion from the union side, Dave Carr said:

> I think it was for reasons of mistrust — who the Health Emergency was operated by, the fact that the people in it weren't workers. What the aim of Health Emergency was was unclear.

Jayne Harrill, assistant admissions officer at the London Hospital and a NALGO member, is also convinced of the need for the Health Emergency group. She was involved in the struggles to save St Andrews Casualty at Bow and Mile End Hospital, which were supported by Health Emergency. She noted a better response in Tower Hamlets from 'users' than from 'workers'. She wants more trade unionists to come forward and explain the conditions in which they are working. Along with Dave Carr, she gave evidence to the Health Inquiry. She believes that health workers in Tower Hamlets are just beginning to connect to Health Emergency and that this is the result of a great deal of work and effort. She mentioned that the newspaper, 'Siren', produced by Tower Hamlets Health Emergency has had an important role. It has started to carry articles about very specific groups' of workers problems:

> There's been things about the rats in the catering stores and now I've got members down there and they're really impressed to sort of see their little workplace written about.

The emerging connection is now of course at risk:

> Well I think it's a shame if they lose their base, because I think it's really good having a base, you know and having a phone number to phone up and the Ansaphone if Myra's not there. So you know you can always phone up and find out what's going on. I think it's just beginning to sort of get more well known within the hospital as well. It takes ages.

Jayne Harrill believes that the Health Emergency group has a useful role and regrets the suspicion of local trade unions towards it. She says the reasons are partly to do with accountability. Myra Garrett is not elected, so the unions say, why should they accept her?

> They've thrown that in her face, well you're not elected who do you represent? You represent nobody. Which is a fair enough comment, but even so, I think she's there and she's there to do that particular job, and so, you know we get no money and no time to do things in the hospital, so while she's there, you know, we may as well use her.

The other grounds of suspicion are to do with the boundaries of authority:

> I think the Health Campaign's got a big problem if they want to try

and work with the big unions in the hospital, because they just see anyone interfering as an encroachment on their bit of power.

There is a narrow division between jealously safeguarding a power patch and the principle of trade union autonomy. Dependence on the 'little state' of the local authority might be all very well when there is support for trade union rights, but could undermine the responsibility to represent members' interests if things change and the 'little state' is guided by anti-trade union policies.

Pete Marshall mentioned another problem for trade unionists in relation to Health Emergency groups. Some of the local groups had been more geared to the inadequacies of the health service than the pay and conditions of the workers. Already under attack from the government, workers can 'see campaigns for the health service as being criticisms of themselves as workers, saying you are not providing a good enough health service'.

As Morris Kolander put it,

> the public are a very funny people ... they will moan ... but they don't seem to see where the problems start from.

It is noteworthy, though, that despite the short time in which links have developed between the GLC (through the Health Emergency groups), and the Community groups and the workers, there does exist a core of trade unionists who are firmly committed to strengthening the combination.

There is also a realisation that a change has been initiated in trying to restore resources to working class people and other unprivileged groups. While these resources have been partly contributed by them, they have not been returned to people who have little in social benefits. Yet it has been complacently assumed that employers should receive grants or loans or help through the provision of an infrastructure, with only a hopeful trust that this will benefit employees. Pete Marshall believes that as more and more groups of people came to feel the practical effect of support from a local authority, the right-wing propaganda that the GLC was giving 'money to all these daft groups' began to have less impact. When you are desperately struggling to save a local hospital and someone comes from a local authority to bring support and explain you could get help as long as you are a representative body to do a leaflet it all seems a lot less daft. For after all you gave them the money in the first place. It is coming back to where it is needed. Pete Marshall is convinced that Health Emergency has brought many people who would not see themselves as politically in support of Labour to agree with the GLC's practical backing for a better health service — a deeply emotional issue.

This has not been simply because of the resources made available: The people directly concerned have been the judges of how they should be brought to fruition:

> Whatever the problems are, instead of trying to do it for the people they [the GLC] allowed people to do it for themselves.

And they explained what they were doing. They did not take it for granted that people 'ought' to be grateful or loyal.

There are strong bonds of personal respect in Hackney between trade unionists like Morris Kolander and the people in the local Health Emergency. He paid a tribute to those who had worked in the group:

> Their names should be up in, you know, in a roll of honour in a sense for what they did ... you give time, you give money you know, and your life in a sense to that campaign, because that's part of life. It's just one part of the struggle for better things for people.

To respect the labours and endeavour of your own is a recognition of the importance of sustaining movements of change by caring for one another.

Jane Foot, who was the Health Emergency worker in Hackney in Autumn 1985, made the same observation from the other vantage point:

> One of the real pleasures of the job has been the daily contact with trade unionists who have been so dedicated in campaigning for hospitals. I just don't know how they keep going under the pressure. People who work in hospitals and are active in the union. I'm just really impressed about how they do it and hold down a job like that.

In places where the links are less established it has been much less encouraging. Harrow Health Emergency described low morale among NHS staff in the face of private medicine, conflict between rank and file members and the official structures of the union, and lack of active resistance to privatisation.

By working with the trade union movement the GLC Industry

and Employment Branch has landed in the midst of the complex, shifting, often tense, relation between rank and file and the trade union official structure. Because it was committed to working with both wings of the trade union movement rather than being content with informal liaison at the top, it has not been easy to evade confusion and sometimes conflicts. Health Emergency has been no exception.

John Lister was aware that in a conflict between a union and the rank and file the way in which stories were reported in 'Health Emergency' could be a sensitive issue. The central office needed to work at both levels. He could see that faith in purely rank and file initiatives, without structural backing, ignored the historical weakness of rank and file movements which had persistently collapsed in the 1970s from lack of resources. If Health Emergency had started as simply a small group of leftists working with the rank and file they would not have been able to involve those people who are not 'simply the hyper-activists in the union'. The GLC resources had enabled the ideas of Health Emergency to reach out more widely. This base had resulted in the affiliations from trade union branches and had made the officials in the unions more prepared to work with the Health Emergency.

Although the scale of the work has been great it has still not been sufficient. Morris Kolander's regret is that it has still not been possible to 'bring resistance together under one umbrella with enough power to do something'.

Health Emergencies and Community Groups

The GLC did not invent the idea of linking workers and users — which is after all of long currency in the labour movement. In fact the efforts of the 1970s to work in political combination were an influence on the politics of the GLC Labour Group. Nonetheless in the few years of its embattled existence the resources which the GLC has been able to put into building these connections, both through funding labour time and coordination, have given these greater strength. Overall, as Pete Marshall maintains, Health Emergencies have been a good example of this. For people are profoundly roused over some health issues.

Nonetheless there has been an inevitable unevenness in community involvement. An obvious problem has been how 'the community' is to be represented.

One of the snags in what has been called the GLCs 'rainbow coalition' has been an oversimplification of constituencies, so that once categorised into a deserving group, you are presented as a homogenised package. It is assumed you share interests and opinions with the rest of your category. While this is sometimes valid, in other cases it is not true and blurs political differences.

The policy of enabling local groups to put public resources in operation to meet needs has meant that new, more direct democratic forms have been brought into local politics. There is the electoral democracy of the franchise which selected the councillors and there is the participatory democracy of the community. The aim has been to extend democratic control in a more active manner. This new approach to the local state has not been without problems. Reflecting on the rapid learning process which has been taking place Jane Foot concludes that we need to observe these conflicting democratic processes in practice much more closely. There is indeed a struggle to restate what democracy means abroad in our society but it is far from being 'perfected'.

Despite these critical reservations there is plenty of evidence in the Health Emergencies work that the policy of getting resources out to people to put their case themselves, and the attempt to make democratic involvement an active process rather than a passive matter of a vote and a hope, has begun to lay the basis for a fundamental reconception of the meaning of welfare. The pressure for the NHS to change in response to women's health needs has already been mentioned. It was a contributory factor in the initial politics of Health Emergency, and from this political experience has come a tradition of linking workers and users.

However, while the segmentation of black workers is institutionally visible in the Health Service, the need to extend opportunities for equality in the Health Service and the health problems of black people are only beginning to be expressed. The anti-racist commitment of the GLC can be said to have been of use here in making more visible inequalities which have been ignored by the white majority. The ramifications of this inequality are clearly extensive and the points made here are simply those revealed through the sources I consulted and not intended as a comprehensive statement about racial injustice in the NHS as a whole.

Clara Arokiasky, speaking at the London Black Women's Health Action Project Conference, backed by the GLC Women's

Committee and attended by Tower Hamlets Emergency among
other groups, stated on 25 October 1985:

> Although the women's health movement has made significant efforts
> towards changing hospital practice, for the black community there is
> little progress, and we have a long way to go still.

Myra Garrett said black people and other ethnic minorities were
under-represented on DHAs. Small and obvious modifications
like multi-lingual signs and information were often still ignored
in the NHS. Jane Foot observed that the Health Service keeps
refusing to acknowledge that there are any special health needs,
while not doing the investigative work required to determine
whether this is the case.

> You can identify illnesses that only black people get, in the same way
> that women's health campaigns are very much focussed on the ill-
> nesses that only women get, i.e. gynaecological and obstetric ... But
> what we don't have is the statistics about whether more women than
> men get heart attacks or more black people than white get some
> other illness.

Yet even an illness lke sickle cell disease, which affects people of
African, Afro-Caribbean, Asian, Mediterranean and Middle East
origin, is not greatly researched and information is not widely
available. The London Black Women's Health Action Project
Newsletter states that there is a need for screening, for early
diagnosis and for counselling — because of the distressing psychological effects. The Newsletter remarks:

> One has to question whether the lack of provision for sufferers has
> anything to do with the origin of the people.

Two groups which have worked with Tower Hamlets Health
Emergency have been especially concerned with the issues of
black and ethnic minority women's health. These are the Black
Women's Health Action Project and the Maternity Services
Liaison Scheme, both of which received some funding from the
GLC's Women's Committee. Both submitted evidence to the
Tower Hamlets Health Emergency.

The approach of the Black Women's Health Action Project is
to go into people's homes to learn about the health needs of the
women. Shamis Dirijaid explains: 'We are starting at the bottom,
on the grass roots level, going in every household, talking to

women, giving them opinions, writing down things, or recording'.

They are careful to give their findings back to the women so they can alter them if they are not an accurate representation.

> And I think one of the good things is that we can win the trust of the people — and I think if you have that, then nothing can stop you.

She is enthusiastic about the newsletter as a means of communicating the health needs of ethnic minority groups — for the same reason as Jayne Harrill, really. Stories were directly relevant to the people who read about themselves in the paper.

The Maternity Services Liaison Scheme works with women whose mother tongue is not English, in the Chinese/Vietnamese community and with Somali women, Bengali women and other ethnic minority women. They offer advice and support on all aspects of pregnancy, childbirth and post-natal care. They have been funded as a voluntary group — they are now thinking of the need to become more securely established. They have formed close working links with workers in the NHS and with the Health Authority. They stress that they are not simply interpreters but Community Health Workers. Amidst cuts and the deprivation in Tower Hamlets, women in the ethnic minority communities face added problems as a result of racism.

The work of these two groups indicates the need for funding to be much more substantial for research into the health of ethnic minorities, and for the training and employment of people with medical skills who are from the communities themselves, have an understanding of health needs and are prepared to work at the grass-roots starting from problems as they are experienced.

If someone were to do a kind of social audit on black people's use of the health service this might also reveal more immediate inequalities. In the 1960s the manner in which middle class people were able to get greater advantages from the welfare state was shown. Similar patterns could be observed among ethnic minorities in Britain now. Amidst the general crisis in welfare and the material factors of poverty and class there are also a series of cultural barriers which exclude ethnic minority users. What this really amounts to is a relative exclusion from the social wealth to which these groups have contributed. With small resources the GLC tried to push this inequality back somewhat. Health has been an important terrain for this struggle.

What Do Patients Want? Some Observation from Health Emergency

Lucy de Groot explained that in the original conception of Health Emergency they had tried 'not to just take the assumption of existing levels of provision and the existing type of provision but to actually say what do people actually need. Actually want.'

In an immediate sense the answer is obvious. People want not to have to wait for a year, or stand around in waiting rooms or be treated with contempt. They do not need there to be barriers of language. They do not want to deliver amidst cockroaches because cuts have been made on the cleaning, or die of salmonella poisoning because of unsanitary kitchens. There are many obvious needs. But Health Emergency groups have also enabled some wants and needs to be expressed which are less apparent, which surface less quickly and require more searching and more time. As Jane Foot observed:

> It's very clear there are people from different backgrounds and different cultures who are still not using the National Health Service because it doesn't provide the health service they want.

She pointed to one example of this: the use of herbal remedies and homeopathic medicine by people from Cyprus and the West Indies. This is yet another example of groups who are paying twice over — for the NHS in their taxes and, because it does not meet their health needs, for alternative remedies.

Alternative health is sometimes dismissed as private medicine. But some alternative health practitioners would like to be within the NHS. Also the demand for differing forms of health care is being expressed by community groups. Jane Foot cited the Hackney Pensioners' enthusiastic response to alternative health in their Pensioners' Health Festival. Many of the bodily needs of ageing are so obviously made worse by poverty, damp housing, fear and stress, that interconnecting approaches to health are clearly relevant. It is harder to recover from illness because of depression and if one is categorised as a useless and unwanted person. Lily Cook has been in a Pensioners' Health discussion group and went to the Hackney Health Festival which was backed by Health Emergency. She explained why the holistic approach of alternative health was important:

> We don't want to be packed off with pills ... Once you go into a home you're destroyed bodily and mentally. You're just treated like a

cabbage ... When you go to the doctor he doesn't want to be bothered. You're old. You're written off. It's not right. You've got a lot to offer.

Needs are sometimes hard to express because they are rooted in a particular social existence. Jane Foot gave the example of the professional concern in Hackney about the use of casualty rather than the GPs. This is an 'irrational' health 'need'. It clogs up the over worked casualty service. Doctors in Hackney believe if they can improve the GP service this will produce 'rational' patients who will not use casualty 'wrongly'. Jane Foot said this ignored the panic in the night in a tower block in Hackney on a dangerous estate with a sick child and no phone which made a mother take a child in a car or a taxi to casualty rather than trying to reach a GP or a locum substituting for the usual doctor. Health needs too are notoriously ambiguous. Jane Foot described how people will complain about their GPs but rarely be prepared to criticise openly. At our most vulnerable we are at once dissatisfied and dependent.

One of the slogans of the women's movement has been 'A Woman's Right to Choose'. But this presumes a middle class patient earnestly consulting *Our Bodies, Ourselves*. Myra Garrett pointed out that on issues like maternity, '... you can't have a campaign about choice ... The campaign is about having enough knowledge and information to be able to make a choice.' Because needs are rooted in our specific circumstances and because they are ambiguous, reaching often in apparently opposite directions, they do not always turn easily into demands around which campaigns can be made.

Both Myra Garrett and Jane Foot were active in the anti-cuts campaign of the mid 1970s. The lack of support for these was identified then as being because people felt ambivalent about defending services which they found 'inappropriate' and sometimes 'offensive'. Jane Foot felt this has not changed and 'is especially true for women, who are the main consumers of the welfare state and the biggest group of people whose lives are really materially affected by the welfare state'.

But at the same time the acute threat to the welfare state as it is can increase the division between the two approaches, the formal campaigners to defend and the community networks which sustain and seek expression for alternative approaches to health care. Both Myra Garrett and Jane Foot expressed a tension in combining the necessary defence of beds, hospitals, and working conditions with the very different work of encouraging groups to express needs and present alternatives. Myra Garrett referred to 'a pull and stress between the two things'. Jane Foot said they had different time scales and required different kinds of work.

Perhaps the difficulty goes deeper too and connects to 'the crisis of perception' which Lucy de Groot described. The problem of what kind of health service people want is made harder to answer because it is linked to questions about what kind of science and technology we want, what kind of conception we have of our bodies and indeed what we mean by 'welfare'. All these conceptions and creations are not fixed entities. They were all made by people, fashioned out of particular historical interpretations of need. So they will be refashioned. This is a daunting task in the abstract. Nonetheless in practice there is the insistence on the right to have more information about health and the use of resources for the Tower Hamlets Inquiry or the Harrow Conference on alternative health care. There is the Black Women's Health Action Project going into women's homes, building trust. There are Hackney Pensioners rejecting their dismissal as helpless victims and asserting a sense of power and demanding time for relaxation and pleasure. Hackney Health Emergency has worked too with another group, 'Health in Homerton', a community project funded by the GLC Women's Committee. One of the workers, Jo Robinson, who was trained as a midwife, found that women in an antenatal group needed to talk about relationships as well as the physical changes which pregnancy brought and needed more information about what choices were available around childbirth. The group came to act as a collective means for working out what they wanted. As Jo Robinson said,

> Women in a group can use each others personal experiences. It's a way of feeling more confident about getting what you want from the health service.

These barriers of lack of confidence and self-identity can be shifted. Even amidst the collapse of the NHS people are developing approaches in which there is the potential to move, through exchanging experience, to reshaping what is desired. But this can be a dispiriting process unless changes can be achieved. As the Black Women's Health Action Project puts it in their Newsletter,

It is about time that professionals in the Health Service try to be
aware of the facts that are raised by Black Community groups themselves. They are in a better position to reflect their communities'
problems. Only by feed-back system will we be able to understand
the problems and deal with them.

The difficulties which the last three years have revealed have
been the sheer extent of the cuts and the offensive against public
health care, combined with uncertainty about what 'people
actually need — actually want'. Perhaps it has not been so much
a straightforward retreat, as a kind of side stepping to reassess a
strategy. Needs and wants resist transplanting too glibly into
plans and programmes. More basic work comes first to make it
possible for people to discriminate between options and conceive
new possibilities. There is no doubt that GLC backing has contributed to this. The strengthening and realisation of this process
among users of the health service involves the democratising of
the NHS. For curing and caring means listening. It necessarily
involves the struggle for better working relations and conditions
— for without these it is unlikely that workers in the health service will respond to patients more humanely. Thus both
resources and a change in consciousness are equally needed.

What Do Workers Want? Some Observations from Health Emergency

It is true, as Dick Muskett said, that alternative plans have not
sprouted like mushrooms in the three years of GLC funding for
Health Emergency. But even my relatively superficial investigation revealed a great deal of what might be described as
'alternative' thinking. I mean by this simply the practical recognition of how many things are being badly done at present and a
range of conceptions of how relationships among workers and
patients could be better. Perhaps it is a longer term process —
the mulling over of approaches — especially in a period in which
there is a fundamental contesting of concepts about health care.
Perhaps too the formation of plans requires a political context in
which there is a realistic expectation that they might be implemented. Nonetheless the relatively small resources which have
been put at the disposal of users of London's health service and
of workers in the health service to draw on their experience and
to conceive of ways of improving the NHS have contributed to

debates and ideas which go much further than the more visible and obvious criticism of low pay, long hours, stressful working conditions, the harmful effect of privatisation and the lack of resources. What follows is a sketch of what a small group of trade unionists said to me. It is intended to be read as an indicator of the possibilities of an approach to developing policy which draws on the observations of people concerned. While the abolition of the GLC will cut this process short it could be developed by the Labour Party on a national basis and by Labour Councils in their areas. Thus instead of a political party making its programme and policy from within, this approach assumes that the political party releases resources to enable and assist people to express and exchange and co-ordinate the wealth of understanding already in their possession.

Both internal debates in the Labour Party and the threat of abolition of the GLC in the last few years have raised again the very basic radical issue of democracy. Health Emergency has helped to foster a climate of discussion around democracy which has been wary of quick answers but insistent in the application of the principle in far-reaching ways. The implications of the democratisation of health care would require extensive changes in our society. So while central government has been increasing its direct control over public services, a countervailing tendency has emerged for groups of users and health workers to enquire how the District Health Authority might be changed or Community Health Councils improved. It would be an exaggerated claim to suggest this was a mass preoccupation. Nonetheless the habit of enquiry has taken hold now and is manifesting itself in small ways. For instance in June 1985 the London Health Democratisation launched its charter demanding election, accountability, trade union representation and greater involvement of users in health care. Several London boroughs have started to do work on health in relation to social and environmental issues in their areas. This has now been taken up by councils outside London.

On the form of democratisation there is considerable uncertainty. For instance there have been proposals for restoring local authorities' powers over health. The assumption that decentralisation automatically guarantees democratic services is questionable — Peter Marshall was wary of the equation of local with 'democratic', arguing that you could get Tory controlled health authorities on a local basis who would not see the need for the democratic provision of health. He believed the Health

Service could be made better but the first step was to be clear about the different approaches towards democratisation which jostled each other on the left:

> The problem is that the Health Service has been under such a threat over the last few years that people have been putting more of their energy into just defending what there is at the moment and possibly that's a failure, that we haven't looked at how to improve the service, because the Health Service could be improved greatly without even talking about further funding. But that needs really radical changes. The sort of changes that are needed are only going to come with a change of Government. I think that we should be clear because there needs to be far more democratic control of the Health Service ... There are various points of view about how you achieve democratic control.

He thinks it important that people on the left get their ideas together about what kind of Health Service is needed, as this is the only chance of influencing a Labour Government in the future to overhaul the NHS.

He thinks the '45 Labour Government's combination of conceding power to the consultants and the medical model were flaws in the creation of the NHS from the start:

> When the Health Service was set up the problem was there from day one. Bevan said it at the time — that he would have to stuff their mouths with gold to get this very basic service. I mean we have a National Sickness Service not a Health Service. We have a repair service where you take your body in every now and again to have repairs, rather than a service providing genuine health care that actually looks after people at all stages of their lives.

Nye Bevan himself did in fact believe that workers should have 'a far greater share in the management of their work and the policies that govern it'. The snag seems to have been that he conceived health workers as simply doctors. Without denying doctors an important contribution, other heath workers clearly have a range of skills and knowledge to contribute. Doctors' control could mean control of an elite within the workforce. As David Widgery points out it was 'professional self-rule' rather than 'workers' control'.

'Workers' control' as an abstract slogan does not *solve* the problem of the right alternative to the existing structure, any more than local authority control. The phrase itself is not a magical guarantee of democracy for it blandly ignores the present inequalities of rank in the NHS, the inequalities between men and women, and the racism which can be reproduced in the trade unions. Obviously it also misses out patients.

However while not a sufficient guarantee of democracy in itself, it is clearly part of a process of democratisation of the NHS. Jayne Harrill made the point that the lack of democracy contributes to the bureaucratic impersonality of the service. She gave an example of this. Registrars tend to call in more people than there are beds to take — presumably hoping for vacancies. The admissions officer consequently has to turn the extra people away. Not surprisingly patients are likely to be upset, especially as the same person can be turned away several times. They get cross with the clerk. But the registrar gives no thought to the effect on the clerk and the clerk has no means of communicating the problem. The bureaucratic hierarchy means managers are too frightened to confront doctors. In the lower ranks passive resistance appears as a result. Pete Marshall said that ironically lack of control contributes to ill-health among health workers. Illness becomes a negative rebellion against the scarce resources and run-down of the service by the government. The carers themselves simply collapse physically — a bitter inversion of the proverbial 'Physician heal thyself'.

Lack of workers' control in the health service means that a great wealth of practical understanding of administration and health care is wasted. There is a lack of co-operative communication. Instead, the hierarchy reproduces itself in sectionalism as a defensive response:

> You only have to walk into a hospital and you will see fifteen different uniforms. I mean everybody's got a uniform to mark exactly who they are and if you negotiate with the Health Service, there are so many different grades and disciplines and groups of workers. It's used very much to divide the workers as well against one another. A lot of the disputes arise in overlaps about who does what job, who should be doing this and who shouldn't.

If there were not a hierarchy what would there be? There seems to be a curious lacuna here. How are large scale administrative systems to be made more accountable, more responsive, more prepared to change methods of working, more effective and more democratic? This is a vast subject and a local authority-backed information service in one town can hardly be expected to pull out an alternative administrative system like a rabbit from a hat. Yet it is a pressing problem, for the health service can hardly become more caring if the people who work in it themselves do not experience working in relationships of freedom, care, consideration and equality. You cannot plan how people relate but you can ensure circumstances which influence their inter-connecting.

It is worth remembering that the hospital, as well as being a repair shop, is also the repository of many human fears and fantasies about the unknown, about the body and its decay, about the mysteries of birth and death. It is a place where intimacy, absurdity and tragedy combine with authority and bureaucracy. It is a place where people therefore can feel very nervous indeed. Even the visit to a GP is hardly straightforward. We seek out GPs for a multiplicity of reasons, psychological as well as physical. Also physical illness generates emotional complaint and distress. Jeannette Mitchell, speaking at the GLC Conference on the NHS, pointed out the limits of an approach to the politics of health which could not express 'compassion' but simply reverted to a reflex exhortation 'to struggle more'. The will to transform the structure of the health service is not only then a matter of democratic control but of changing the relationships between carer and patient. It has to have the strength, in Jeanette Mitchell's words, to 'acknowledge all the pain and suffering that comes through the door of the general practice'.

Within the NHS and despite the crisis in health care, amazingly, health workers, at every level, endeavour to do this still. But the structure of the service makes it harder than need be. Their frequent discouragement is the tragic social cost. It should be within our human capacity as a society to improve rather than undermine our health service, instead of allowing the pecuniary interest of a few people of privilege to be masked pathetically as the workings of fate and the market. But even if we are able to reverse the present cruel and dishonourable folly it is well to be aware of the complexity of hope and anxiety which is in operation, rather than repeating slogans which are as the sounding of brass. Perhaps the notion of control itself, which is so deeply ingrained in the secular radical psyche, comes up against limits. For perhaps there are indeed circumstances when we want to be able to hand over control in trust without being subordinated or denied our humanity in the giving.

It is of course the case that health workers — of all kinds — encounter people in acute states of pain and anxiety. As an everyday affair they see panic and resilience, hysteria and humour, rage and gratitude, ecstatic joy and small sensual pleasures. But it is after all a job, and they do want more pay and they want to go out or get home themselves.

Despite low morale in the face of the onslaught on public health care, the realisation of the dignity, value and responsibility of the work persistently surfaces. This is recognised more as a feature of nursing or being a doctor. Yet in a more fragmented way it presents itself among domestic and ancillary workers too. Here too there is an alternative potential — even though the Health Service is often negligent of its own human resources.

The striking Barking cleaners, who received help from Health Emergency and from GLC's Industry and Employment Committee, argued that their experience in cleaning Barking Hospital would not be replaced by the Crothall's contract. The skills they had developed had been completely dismissed and disregarded. As one striker argued, in an interview for 'Jobs for a Change',

> We've been here years, we know the job, the patients and the wards and the staff. We know what the problems are, we check who can and can't have sugar in their drinks, who's on special diets when we hand meals out. It's frightening to see all that ignored.
>
> Domestics are part of a team. We care for patients too, the nurses rely on us.

Morris Kolander, speaking from his experience as a porter for many years, made a similar observation:

> Ancillary workers I think are treated too casually ... I think it's not appreciated enough what they do ... I mean they often get abused by the press when they take action because they appear to be the unskilled telling the doctors what to do, those sort of nasty remarks. And afterwards I feel like saying to those people, you know, you should come and see for yourself what we do and what skill we have, which is an unrecognised skill. We are actually responsible for a part of a hospital. Because without that sort of back-up you'd have doctors cooking their own meals, nurses having to push their own patients around.

He argues ancillary workers could as a group come up with the answers to administrative problems instead of having to put up with the mistakes of others.

So while aspects of medical work require a marking out of

responsibility, other aspects require more collective forms in which responsibility, thought and care are distributed more equally. It goes without saying that people whose working lives are constantly revealing these two facets of medicine are the best equipped to begin to devise alternatives, and that in reconstructing a more democratic health service the skills and responsibility could be extended and recompensed with greater generosity from society.

Within the existing health service, there have been small-scale attempts to work more democratically. An attempt to pool these experiences and learn from them could be a valuable resource for restructuring.

The London Industrial Strategy on Health Care suggests in accord with this approach that ancillary or nursing work should precede medical training and that staff could 'develop their knowledge and skills', moving more freely between jobs. As words on paper this idea can glance off the consciousness. But when it has been even partially experienced and seen to make sense it opens up tremendous possibilities for improving health care.

There is another body of experience which could contribute a great deal of knowledge to the development of alternative ways of administering the health service. In 1981, Margery Bane talked about what had been learned through organising and maintaining the occupation at Hayes Cottage Hospital:

> You have to have a good understanding of the health service and how it works ... a hospital occupation is completely different from a factory occupation; we tried to keep patients' relatives involved all the time ... a lot still are ... the occupation committee was totally open, anyone could come along to meetings ... pickets had their own committees too ... towards the end of the occupation pickets were coming forward and saying they wanted more and more responsibility.

To the question, 'How was work organised?' she replied:

> Ancillaries could do their own rotas. The nursing staff just got on with their work — we didn't interfere, we kept out of the patient area, we didn't want to be disruptive.

And when she was asked what it was like inside the hospital, she responded:

It was lovely running it ourselves. I think it was run much better ...
Management came and said it was their hospital and we told them to
go away ...

We were like one big happy family. It was a joy to come to work.
It was *your* hospital.

Mike Walker maintains the first hospital occupation was in 1922
in Nottingham. Occupations obviously have a special atmosphere; nonetheless, many have continued over considerable
periods and must have developed forms and processes. You
would think that after sixty years of this kind of thing some
alternative administrative systems might have been conceived to
be practicable in the Health Service. It might have occurred to
some policy maker that here was a living body of evidence that
all health workers could play a much more responsible and valuable part in health care than had been recognised. And if indeed
such skills are nearer at hand and proven in action, why go to all
the toil, trouble and expense of importing elderly and high rank-
ing military gentlemen to supervise the administration of health
in East London?

Conclusion

As I did the interviews for this account of London Health Emergency in the autumn of 1985, everyone knew that the abolition of
the GLC was imminent. Everyone I talked with felt apprehensive
about the implications for the work they were doing, and for
those who were paid, there was anxiety about their own futures.
Shamis Dirir expressed this graphically:

I think the GLC although they have done mistakes themselves, I
mean where they put their money and all that — I think they've done
very, very well for community organisation, because there's a lot of
community organisation would never function if they didn't have
this GLC money ...

I think the GLC was great, but now it's to be abolished we don't
know what we are going to do. I think a lot of people are worried,
and I don't know what is going to happen, we have to wait and see
...

I don't know what is going to happen really and who are they
going to fund and who they are not going to. So you never know
anything. We are in the dark. I really don't know.

Amidst this uncertainty she was resolved somehow to continue the work with Somali women.

John Lister and Kevin Flack hoped to be able to keep the central information service going by building up affiliations and extending its sphere to the Health Service nationally. John Lister said he hoped other local authorities would take up work on health, as Southwark, Hackney, Greenwich, and Lambeth were already. There was evidently a need for the information they provided on health. The period of funding by the GLC had had the positive effect of demonstrating this, even though it was not to be continued.

Some of the local groups will carry on, on a voluntary basis. Harrow were least affected because they had no full-time worker, but Tom O'Malley and Haf Evans agreed they were dependent on the background work of Rosie Newbiggen at the Resource Centre — also threatened with abolition. Morris Kolander said wearily he was worried how the work of convening meetings and providing information would get done in Hackney. Shamis Dirir and Jayne Harrill believed the Tower Hamlets Health Emergency worker Myra Garrett would somehow still go on — like John Brown's body — beyond abolition, money or no money, unstoppable by government.

As Jayne Harrill put it, 'I think Myra probably will carry on doing some of the work. She is quite well known. A lot of people know her, they know Myra Garrett, Health Enquiry, you know, so it's recognised that she's the person to contact.'

It is true that even if the Health Emergencies collapse locally, the network of people they have brought together will still be there in a fragmented state and could be reactivated when the need arises. But this will be for defensive resistance. It will be a return to the patterns of the 1970s in much harsher circumstances. Jane Foot said she thought the campaigning side would continue. What will be in danger from the withdrawal of resources is the more long-term discussion of what kind of health service we need — not by policy makers at the top whom it is customary to pay large sums to think on behalf of others, but by people at the grass-roots, who know from their experience the consequences of decisions. The beginnings had been made of getting some resources out to encourage this process. A concept was taking shape that there could be another means of creating a system of health care which drew on what Jean Spray, a health visitor and a member of Brent Community Health Council, described at the GLC-funded conference on the NHS as 'the hidden experience of health workers'.

Two concepts of politics have co-existed and presumably interacted in Health Emergency. One stresses the clear cut pro-gramme of demands, necessary for campaigning but merely the tip of the iceberg. Another expresses more submerged feelings and doubts. It is inchoate, harder to express, but it goes deeper into 'the hidden experience'. Many people feel tugged in both directions and struggle to find a balance.

Jean Spray said at the conference on alternatives in the NHS that she had often felt herself perplexed at meetings, sitting thinking

> you've got to make a decision, Oh, my god shall I go for local government control, or perhaps it's the trade unionists or ... and for a long time I used to sit thinking I've got to choose one of these models and I don't know which one to choose and I'll fail if I don't choose one, because it means I haven't got the answer. And I've been a health activist too for many years. And then finally you begin to realise there isn't an answer because we haven't had the debate.

Democracy is not just a choice between routes, in this concept of politics, but a process of articulating understandings gained through your own practice and observation. It is about clearing and creating ways. But if these are to be anything more than by-ways there has to be the means of effecting change. Briefly the municipal majesty of County Hall was turned back to the reforming usage of its LCC origins. For a few years the bulky citadel threw its weight on the side of people who expected little from government. This was not only through its provision of funding and the resources of space, time and labour. The GLC has also had, as Pete Marshall reflected, a legitimising role. From a purely grass-roots perspective it is easy to dismiss this as intangible and unimportant. But this is to miss crucial factors about rule and power — which is always visible, on stage, in control of the loud speakers. The GLC challenged Westminster. The bad tempered response of the Government in simply abolishing its opponent is perceived by many Londoners as an act of political pique.

Nobody was sure, though, whether the way thus far cleared was to be kept open. There was some feeling that the Labour Party should learn from the work of Health Emergency, that there should be some way in which a socialist party took notice of the experience of workers, community activists and the people who had become involved in local health struggles — though nobody seemed particularly sure how this could be done. It certainly would enlarge the active support for Labour politics if such an association were to be developed. Pete Marshall pointed out how strongly people felt on the subject and how they would respond to the commitment to health care and practical political support. It was also recognised that there were many unresolved questions among socialists active around health.

It was not, then, an alternative programme which was being presented by Health Emergencies, but a readiness to engage and listen to a variety of viewpoints from people directly involved. There was general agreement that the Labour Party's policy should not ignore the weight of evidence gathered in the process of campaigning and simply revert to an approach which saw a health service as needing only more of the same to be improved. Better health care is partly a question of resources, partly a matter of a radical rethink of what is needed.

Several people also noted spin off effects in the GLC's impact on trade unions. Mike Walker said COHSE, had begun to discuss child care and women's role in the home as unpaid carers. Indeed Hillingdon and District COHSE, with Hillingdon Health Emergency, produced a broadsheet with clear arguments on workplace nurseries in hospitals. It is replete with historical allusions indicating Mike Walker's hand at work. Pete Marshall said it was hard to establish influences precisely but he was sure the GLC had contributed to a greater awareness of equal opportunities for women and black people in COHSE and to discussion of gay and lesbian rights in the union. There were creches at meetings, for instance, now. There had been resolutions about gays and lesbians in the union, without the outrage the leadership had assumed. Jayne Harrill had got hold of the GLC's equal opportunities policy through NALGO and it had helped her as a trade unionist to show the inadequacies in some of the proposals from management.

Nonetheless, everyone agreed abolition was a major set-back. Morris Kolander drew on his forty years of experience to find the necessary fortitude to face this and keep going:

> There are peaks and troughs. We're either up or we're down. But I think we're never really down. I think there's a need to — I suppose re-organise in a sense ... rethink how to approach the problem. So you don't just have a failure and say that's it. You've got to build on what's left. You cover what you can before you've lost. You don't

just walk away. You don't walk away. You say, Well what can we do next?

Those of us with less experience can learn from this resolution. Many people have fought to make the Health Service and despite its inadequacies it is inconceivable that people will not continue to fight by some means or other to safeguard this battered Bevanite legacy — GLC or no GLC. It is impossible to believe, even in this time of discouragement, that the greater hope it embodies will be forgotten. For memory is most resilient. And surely, in Jane Foot's words, people will again

> come up with their dreams about a health service — the kind of health service that could meet their needs, that would be there when they wanted it, and provide the service that they wanted, that would comfort, that would care for them.

As the saying goes, from small acorns, mighty oak trees grow — and survive bad weather.

14
Reggae on the Rates: The 'Jobs for a Change' Festivals

Introduction

Twenty thousand people are packed into the County Hall car-park. Despite repeated requests to get down, many of them have climbed up the buildings, and are hanging precariously from the noble municipal balconies and columns. The light is beginning to fade from the sky. The faces in the crowd seem to merge together. They surge and sway like a single living organism.

The Smiths are due to play at 8 p.m., and the people are baying for them: *'Smiths! Smiths! Smiths!'* The people have been packed along South Bank for over eight hours now. Many are drunk, quite a few are drugged, and all are euphoric. Extra stewards have been sent down to add their weight to the crush barriers in front of the stage, but even so the barriers are beginning to buckle inwards, and it seems impossible that they will hold. The girls at the front of the crowd are so crushed their faces are straining with fear.

'This is a bit worrying,' I tell the Stage Manager, a hippy-looking character with his hair in a pony-tail. 'People are going to get hurt.' He surveys the situation with experienced eyes. 'It's alright,' he says briefly. 'When they faint, the stewards will just yank them out and carry them round the side.' His sang-froid is reassuring, but the tension is still unbearable, and I'm desperate for the show to get on. But it can only get on when everything is ready — when all the gear is in position on stage and thoroughly tested and sound-checked. Stevie, the Stage Manager, knows

Credit: GLC

With numbers over half a million (according to the London Standard), *the Jobs for A Change Festivals were bigger than Woodstock.*

that the most dangerous crowd of all is a disappointed one, so everything has to be right.

Stevie has a last word over his control mike with the man at the mixing desk in the middle of the crowd, and glances at me significantly. 'Ready?' I ask. 'Yes.' he says. '*Go!*' I dash up to the mike centre stage. An immense roar greets me — not for myself, but because the crowd knows that we are about to begin. Even more, they are cheering because Ken Livingstone has come up to the mike beside me. Amazingly, this roar of greeting for Ken is bigger than the roar which will greet the Smiths in a few minutes time, and it completely drowns out my words: 'Ladies and Gentlemen. In a minute we'll be having a band that you all want to hear. But first we have a speaker you'll also want to hear: Ken Livingstone, the leader of the GLC!'

For a minute or two Ken is unable to start his speech because of the noise, but eventually he gets underway. He is talking to the biggest and the youngest audience of his political career . . .

The two big 'Jobs for a Change' Festivals mounted by the

Industry and Employment Branch attracted enormous crowds. The first festival was held on South Bank, spreading over Jubilee Gardens, the riverside, the Queen Elizabeth Hall, the National Film Theatre, and County Hall itself, with up to 100,000 people attending. The second one, held in Battersea Park in July 1985 — involving five music stages spread around the park, a large number of exhibition and performance tents and some 250 stalls — was the largest event put on by the GLC throughout the Labour Administration. The Police estimate for the numbers attending it was 250,000, whereas the *London Evening Standard* gave a figure of half a million. Yet the festival attracted virtually no media coverage at all, despite the fact that something approaching one Londoner in every ten attended it. The mention in the *Standard* only came a couple of days later in a shock-horror piece about the litter the festival had left behind.

If the numbers who attended the three smaller 'Jobs Year' festivals are added in, along with those who attended the 'Giro Shows' in the boroughs and the programme of Concerts for the Unemployed in major London venues, the total 'gate' for events promoted by the GLC's Industry and Employment Committee in 1984 and 1985 must be very close to a million. This is undoubtedly an extraordinary achievement. But what does this achievement mean?

There is no doubt that most of these people thoroughly enjoyed themselves at the festivals and other events. If nothing else, these events must have left people with the feeling that since the GLC gave them all such a good time, the GLC was a 'nice' organisation and was worth supporting. Some might say that this is enough, and already justifies the expense involved. But the festivals aimed to do more than this. They aimed to promote certain ideas about the London economy and the GLC's policies towards it. To what extent were they successful in this aim?

A festival may attract a huge number of people, and in doing so it would seem to fulfill most politicians' dreams. But in actual fact the mood at a festival is not one that is conducive to an interchange of ideas. It is extremely difficult to go beyond a situation where people at the festival merely enjoy themselves. Only an exceptional orator can harness a crowd's mass energy and turn it back on the crowd, and in doing so get across ideas about politics and policies. Most speakers are simply marginalised by the crowd's energy and will. The only thing that gets through is music — and music appeals to the heart rather than the head.

The festivals were intended to go beyond 'mere' enjoyment. Local authorities, after all, have a tradition of organising festive occasions. Royal weddings get celebrated, municipal fireworks are let off on 5 November, grants are given to street parties and Arts Festivals. In what ways were the GLC festivals a departure from local authority traditions? And, above all, what *effect* did they have?

Jobs Year 1985

The first Jobs for a Change festival, held in July 1984, came about because Mike Ward, chair of Industry and Employment, and people concerned with publicity in the Branch realized that the initiatives being taken by the GLC in the area of employment weren't 'getting through' to people. It was thought that a Jobs festival might bring the issue more to the public eye. Initially (such was people's innocence at the time) it was thought that this festival could be organised by officers within the branch as a kind of second job on top of their other duties. But eventually, very late in the day, good sense prevailed, and four people were taken on as consultants to organise the festival. The four were Tony Hollingsworth, Ken Hulme, Sue Beardon and David Bradford. As well as organising the 1984 festival itself, the brief of these four was also to mount a major exhibition about the work of the I and E Committee. In the event, getting together this exhibition took at least half their working hours, largely owing to the low level of co-operation they received from members of the Branch. Despite their work, it's doubtful whether the exhibition made much of an impact during the day. But the festival itself — including all the exhibitions and stalls mounted by outside organisations, as well as the music, theatre, cabaret and other cultural events — was a triumphant success, and there was general agreement that another one should be held the following year.

Meanwhile, the GLC's Anti-Racist year was drawaing to a close, and — once again, rather late in the day — it was agreed that 1985 should be Jobs Year. It was decided that in addition to the second festival, there should be a programme of events throughout the year based on the theme of unemployment and the GLC's attempts to create jobs and deal with other problems connected with the economy. Dick Muskett, who had previously worked in the Industry and Employment Branch's Project

Development Unit, was appointed full-time co-ordinator of Jobs Year. He recruited around him a team that included Ken Hulme and Tony Hollingsworth, and set about organising the year.

He describes his aims as follows:

> We wanted to get across by a whole variety of different events and happenings the idea that unemployment was a disaster that was round Londoners' necks, and that even the employment we did have was increasingly low-paid, that people worked under bad conditions, that there were severe inequalities in people's work. We wanted to keep the idea permanently there, so that it was a constant nagging thing in the public's head that there must be an alternative to what's happening to the London economy.
>
> Obviously the remedies, or the ideas for remedies, are what you have to get across in the end. But you have to get the idea firmly established that the problem is very real and facing us now and is going to get worse, before you can get people to say, well okay, what is the alternative?

Peace Year (1983) and Anti-Racist Year (1984) had both been very successful. Largely because of a series of brilliant and expensive poster-campaigns, both these 'theme years' had been very visible to the public, and had undoubtedly created a considerable awareness of the issues involved. By the time Jobs Year was thought up, however, circumstances had changed. The Council was now in a constant state of conflict with the Government and the courts, and one result of this was the introduction, early on in Jobs Year, of severe restrictions on Council spending and, in particular, on advertising. As Dick Muskett puts it, 'We spent the whole of the spring and summer of '85 veering from one court case and one injunction to another, trying to find gaps in between them where we could do things, and very often being nipped in the bud at the last minute.'

But as happened so often in the GLC's work, these restrictions on GLC powers turned out in many ways to be an advantage. They forced the Council to find original solutions; and often these solutions meant a greater co-operation with outside groups than might otherwise have been the case, and a greater attention to small, localised details rather than an exclusive emphasis on the grander scale of things. As Dick Muskett explains, this was certainly the case with Jobs Year:

> Once the year was underway, we could see that having lots of expensive poster campaigns wasn't going to be possible. So we decided

instead to put a lot of stress on sponsoring and working with local organisations doing local things. I think that has been a success. To give you examples: during the course of the late summer we sponsored dozens and dozens of events at a very local level where perhaps a tenants' organisation on an estate, or a youth club in an area, wanted to put on something that highlighted the pressing problem which they saw for their community, which was unemployment and low pay. Because of the flexibility which we had been able to achieve, we were able to put quite small sums of money at the disposal of these communities to put on events on the estates or in the streets that were very much about entertainment and enjoyment, but also were clearly about unemployment as a problem for us around here.

As well as working with communities in this way, we've done an increasing amount of work with trade union groups. What we've done is to work on the principle that the problem wasn't just unemployment but the spread of low pay and deteriorating conditions. We decided to work with groups of low-paid workers through the unions that attempt to organise those sectors, and put on events specifically for groups of workers in a particular industry. So we've done a very successful event with people who work in shops in the West End. Not necessarily the group that you'd immediately think of as being the most oppressed and the most deprived, but nonetheless people who work quite long hours on low pay and often in very poor conditions. ... Certainly, the USDAW (shopworkers) stewards in the West End who were involved in organising the 'Shop-Workers' Ball', as we called it, were enthusiastic beyond my belief. They were just very impressed that a local authority could actually work with them in that way on the issues that were confronting them — you know, seven day trading, the abolition of the Wages Councils, and so on.

In addition to these 'small events' there was an extraordinary range of other activities during Jobs Year, including the local 'Giro Shows' (one of these was held in almost every London borough) and the larger 'Concerts for the Unemployed' (which brought some of the best acts in the world to London for a mere £2 entry fee for people with a UB40). These numerous events had an important spin-off. They ensured that the Jobs Year logo appeared in the music papers and the London listings magazines almost every single week throughout 1985. This kind of continual publicity — which was often related to specific industry and employment issues, according to the event being organised — must have had an important cumulative effect during the year. However, important and original though all these smaller events were, the festivals were clearly the centrepieces of both 1984 and Jobs Year 1985.

Before going on to look at these in detail, one final point worth making about all the Jobs Year Events, both large and small, is that they all involved the use of considerable resources and a very high degree of organisation. (Dick Muskett estimates that the total budget for Jobs Year was £650,000, of which the Battersea Park festival consumed £200,000.) Peter Jenner is the manager of Billy Bragg and Hank Wangford, two performers who played not only at many of the Jobs Year events (including both the large festivals) but also for many other GLC events in the previous theme years. Besides a general interest in the more radical end of the music industry, he has a particular interest in music festivals, since he helped organise the big free concerts in Hyde Park in the late sixties and early seventies. He has watched the GLC's growing involvement in music events with close attention:

> They were awfully cocked up, a lot of the earlier events, because they'd never done anything like that before. It took them a long time to come to terms with commercialism — you know, to hire PAs because they were good rather than because they were run by nice chaps; to hire security people, because you need security in case fascists appear. ... But the great thing about the GLC which surprised us all was the spirit with which they wanted to do things, the scale of what they did, and also the speed with which they learnt ... One of the reasons they were doing them, of course, was for PR — to demonstrate that the Council was involved in your environment, and part of your environment was the cultural environment. They weren't just being cultural to fulfill their cultural quota. They were out there to do things to make themselves popular. So they had to do good events.

The kind of hard-headed professionalism Peter Jenner describes may be necessary for everyone's enjoyment and for the event to go off well, but it does not necessarily accord easily with a political message concerned with collectivity, power-sharing and popular involvement in decision-taking. Overruling this contradiction was one of the hassles GLC festivals had to take on.

Furthermore, while the 1984 festival had a more dramatically *political* feel to it, the Battersea Park festival, according to many who attended both events, succeeded more in strictly cultural terms. While there's no doubt that the political climate of the times was in part responsible, this may well be another example of a tension between professional criteria and political criteria. Looked at in this light, the very professionalism of the Battersea Park festival might be judged to have muted the festival's political impact so that it only succeeded as a 'cultural event'. However, one of the basic arguments underlying this chapter is that the cultural (in its broadest sense) *is* political. From this point of view, the Battersea Park festival may well have been just as important in the long term as the earlier festival on South Bank.

Putting the Message Across From the Stage

What are the ingredients of a good festival? And if the aim is to put across certain political ideas in a festival, how do you go about that? Dick Muskett summarises the thinking behind the GLC jobs festivals as follows:

> If you're doing something large-scale and open-air, I think that you start from the idea that you're going to lay on different sorts of entertainment, diversion, amusement, whatever, to suit different age-groups, different racial groups, different interests — so you have a mix of things. You recognise that the classic scenario of a festival is popular music, and that is always the central, focal theme to it. You then have to work out how you can try to ensure that the popular music doesn't dominate everything else: that there is scope for people with children, scope for older people, scope for people who have completely different cultural interests from the mainstream young pop audience. And then if you have a theme that you want to get across, you have to try and work out how you can make that theme run through all those different bits of entertainment.

Amongst all the various ingredients that Dick is talking about here, the dominant one will always be the main stage and it is here that you would expect the political message to be most clearly put across. No matter how much diversity is aimed at in the festival's organisation, the main stage — the people on it, and the music that is played from it — will always tend to be the unifying focus of the occasion. As Tony Hollingsworth puts it: 'The main stage gives a sense of direction to everything. It gives the heartbeat of the festival. It gets everyone on that line of enjoying themselves.'

It follows from this that the choice of music to be played from the main stage will have a crucial bearing on the overall political message conveyed during the day. Dick Muskett explains that there was a conscious effort with the Jobs festivals to hire bands who were willing to identify themselves with the cause the festivals were trying to put across:

> All the bands we've had are people who've been prepared to make a comment about unemployment, whether through their songs, or, if they just play music which is music for itself, in comments to the press. That's a sort of base-line for putting on music, that they're prepared to put themselves on the line in that way.

This kind of policy towards music is one of the ingredients that can help a festival take on a certain political flavour. But the number of singers like Billy Bragg whose words are directly political is limited, and in any case the words of songs tend to get lost when they're amplified in the open air. So, Muskett adds, if the idea is to get across clear political ideas, you can also

> put up a speaker to say a few words in the middle of the music. The fatal mistake would be to put up a speaker who's going to go on at great length to an audience of basically young people and make them feel alienated and bored. It has to be somebody who has a certain ability to communicate.

Ken Livingstone is undoubtedly a speaker with a certain ability to communicate, and his speeches at the festivals were effective as far as speeches went. But as Ken himself makes clear, the kind of communication that is achieved in such a situation can be limited and unsatisfactory:

> Usually when I speak, I get up in a room or a hall, and I can see everyone. You can see each individual face and you can see movement, and it's a conversational tone — I don't know exactly where it's going to take me. But you can't do that with this sort of huge rally of 50,000 people or more. You can't see individual faces. It's a sea of little pale dots of faces, and you can't see people's individual movement. You can only get in terms of feedback what comes out of the roar and the noise that you get, whether it's applause or shouting or whatever. And therefore it's a very unsatisfactory way of communicating a political message — particularly when they're all standing there dying to see Morrisey and the Smiths!

Ken adds that during the 1984 festival he made several speeches as the day went on, and his speeches changed during the day as he got higher and higher on what was happening:

The last one, just before the Smiths, was like a fascist rally! You know, you walk out to see all those people under the arc-lights and so on. In a way, it's totally opposed to everything else we've been talking about and doing at the GLC. And I found that the speech was much more sort of rabble-rousing and 'bash the government'.

In the end, then, it seems that though the main stage of a festival may be the focus of the occasion, the amount of political information put over on the stage, whether by speeches or by other means, is always going to be rather limited. In fact it makes a lot of sense to see the speakers as *performers* rather than communicators, in a similar way to the musicians. They contribute to the general atmosphere of the occasion, rather than being (as they are likely to see themselves) the point during the occasion when the *real* message is conveyed. Certainly, that is how Ken Livingstone saw himself:

> Speaking is part of helping to make the day. Like having a particular band on, or having sort of rubber balloons for the kids to bounce up and down on. Equally, seeing Ken Livingstone — not having to listen to him for more than three or four minutes — you can say, 'Oh we saw Ken Livingtone as well. He was on before Morrisey and the Smiths.' In that sense, it's part of the day. It makes me part of the carnival generally.

Round the Edges

Most people I talked to who attended the festivals agreed that whatever political information they gathered from them came not so much from the central stage, but from the stalls, exhibitions and other activities round the edges of the festival. Gordon Donald, who attended both festivals, said that what he thought was being explored at the events was 'whether you could do something like that and bring out the politics'. He didn't think that much politics did come through in the end, but 'at least it was an attempt, and some lessons have been learnt from it'. When I asked him whether the organisers could have tried to push the politics any harder, he said:

> It depends on whether you think an orthodox way of pushing the politics is how you achieve things. I would have hoped that we were finding other ways of doing it rather than the traditional ones of Ken Livingstone having to get up and make a speech.

A festival is about communication of values and ideals, rather than slogans and messages. If people just wander around and try and soak in everything, they'll be taking away with them not just different images, but also all the stickers and the pamphlets and the books and the leaflets that are available there. And maybe a lot will get lost on the way home, but some of them will be read — a lot more than they'd ever come across ordinarily.

Helen Archer is 26. Like Gordon, she was unemployed at the time she came to the festivals, which she had read about in the London listings magazines. Like most people, she came to the festivals with a groups of friends:

> I came mainly for the music — but we didn't actually stay and listen to the music all day, because there were so many things going on round the outside. We went round the stalls and had a look at those sort of things. The people I went with had actually come from different places in England, so they were very interested, because they didn't know what was happening in London sort of on a ground level.
>
> I thought the festivals were good not only as entertainment, but as a ground for giving people information — for something that people would go to that wouldn't normally get that sort of information. And it was done in a very easy manner. It was laid back, rather than being thrown at you.

The festivals were planned in such a way that political information would come through *all* the events at different levels of detail. The stage was only one component of this, and it was never really expected that the information conveyed from the stage would be very full. In Tony Hollingsworth's words, the stage 'gives a general feeling of a political happening. But in the sense of there being detailed politics and messages going over, that comes over in the constituents of all the bits of it, the exhibitions and the stalls.'

In addition to the exhibitions, the GLC mounted a series of debates and workshops about economic issues at both festivals. In the 1984 South Bank festival these took place in County Hall, and included a five-hour rolling debate in the Council Chamber about abolition. At Battersea, a special tent was given over to question-and-answer sessions about the London Industrial Strategy, with leading GLC officers and politicians taking part. However, the GLC's own work was only a small part of the information available. Dick Muskett explains:

In the Battersea Park festival we spent a fair bit of money assisting community groups to put on exhibitions that they couldn't afford to put on themselves. They had the good ideas, we provided the money so they had the chance to come there. So it wasn't just glossy exhibitions put on by GLEB and the GLC. It was the downtown community groups saying: here's an exhibition about our ideas for our area, which is in a real mess.

Some 50 local groups took advantage of this offer to mount exhibitions, with, in some cases, groups like Co-operative Development Agencies across London combining to put on a single exhibition about their work. But a lot more groups had decided after the experience of the previous year's festival (where they had been given exhibition space in County Hall) that they preferred to do stalls out in the main throng of the crowd rather than being confined inside a tent. Over 200 local organisations eventually contributed to the festival in this way. Because of their contribution, the amount of political information on offer at the festival was very considerable. The reports of the groups who put on exhibitions and stalls show that in most cases there was an extremely good take-up of their wares, with people saying they'd come along to the next meeting of the groups concerned, and expressing their interest in a variety of other ways.

Bringing together all these different groups was not only an important way of providing political information for the people who visited the festival. It was also important for the groups themselves. In Tony Hollingsworth's words, it gave them

that sense of being involved in something much bigger than just themselves. A group putting on a stall was no longer just a co-operative in the middle of Haringey or Brent. They were all brought together and there were ten of them in a row, all being co-operatives, and all being proud to say 'we are co-operatives', and not being knocked for it. That meant a lot for them. It gave them a lot of support and confidence, as well as making new contacts with each other.

Cultural and Political Diversity

There is no doubt that a certain amount of overt politics was on offer at the festivals. However, everyone I talked to agreed that the 'politics' of the festivals were contained as much in the general *image* that the festivals created as in any overt statements made from the stage or elsewhere.

This is most obviously the case in the actual physical lay-out of a festival. For example, there is a danger in such events that a large, dominating stage with a powerful PA system can easily have an authoritarian feeling to it — Ken Livingstone even used the word 'fascist'. The organisers of the festivals were aware of this problem, and tried hard to counteract it, as Tony Hollingsworth explains:

> The stage is the heartbeat of the occasion, but it shouldn't be dictatorial, it shouldn't impose too much. The festival as a whole should be fluid, non-fixed. You have to set up a structure that people can *play* in. It has to be left to them to use the occasion how they want. You have to design it to give choices.

Tony's use of words like 'choice', 'fluid' and 'play' begins to describe aspects of the *image* that the festivals provided. They suggest, to put it very simply, that the image was quite a democratic one, as well as being one that was about enjoyment. A festival, by its nature, offers people the opportunity to decide for themselves what they want to do, within parameters that the organisers try to make as wide as they possibly can.

But besides a vague general feeling of democracy and enjoyment, the image of the festivals also contained some more specific characteristics that made important implicit statements about the kind of politics the GLC was trying to evolve. One of the most significant of these was an image of cultural and political diversity. The attempt to achieve this diversity was at the heart of the planning of the festivals. For almost everyone who attended them, it was the most striking and stimulating feature of the occasions. It is likely that it had far more effect on changing people's political awareness than any of the information put over about the issue of jobs. Dick Muskett describes the kinds of concerns in the organisation of the festivals that were necessary to achieve this diversity:

> You have to make sure that there isn't an oppressive feeling anywhere. You have to make sure — you damn well better make sure — that women don't feel offended by what is going on, that they don't feel oppressed by the performance of particular musicians. You make sure that there are facilities for people who aren't particularly mobile, people with disabilities. You make absolutely sure that there is plenty of space — and safe space — for children. You try and make sure that there's a diversity of music that will appeal to the different cultures that exist in London, that are part of London — so that it

isn't just young white bands, but there's music for different age groups and different cultures. You try and get a global feel to it, so that there's something for everybody there, and it meshes together at the edges.

A run-down of the programme at Battersea gives a clear idea of the diversity of what was on offer there. This leaves aside all the exhibitions, stalls and workshops, which have already been mentioned, and also the very large number of food and drink tents which, like everything else, aimed to appeal to a wide cultural and ethnic cross-section of London's population (so that the variety of different types of national food was in itself greater than most people at the festival would have ever come across before). Music at Battersea was provided from five stages, each with a different musical policy. One, the 'Cowboys for Jobs' stage, was simply there for people from the music world to fool around on. A second stage was devoted exclusively to African and Latin music, while a third was given over to DJs and rapping. Between them, these two stages catered for well over 10,000 people, many of whom never left them all day. A fourth stage was given over to the 'up-and-coming, raunchy end of the pop market', with bands like the Pogues attracting a largely young, pop-conscious audience. Finally, there was the main stage, which, Tony says, 'had to be in itself made representative of a total, multi-ethnic policy — so it started with Ravi Shankar from India, and went through Thomas Mapfumo from Africa, to Aswad from Britain, via Orchestral Manoeuvers in the Dark, very poppy, and Billy Bragg and Working Week and the Communards.'

In addition to the music, there was a wide variety of other events and entertainment that people could choose from. A children's area included inflatables, pony-rides, face-painting, badge-making, clowns, story-telling, children's theatre, and 'teas for mums and dads'. This area was sufficiently well-staffed to cater for several thousand children during the day, in addition to which there was also a fairground as a more traditional form of entertainment. A theatre tent well away from the noisy areas put on six theatre groups during the day, while several other theatre groups roamed freely round the site performing in the open air. There was also a poetry and cabaret tent in which some sixteen acts appeared. One of the high-points in this tent was a reading of their own poetry by a group of miners' wives. There was also an art exhibition, featuring again work from the mining communities, and there was a sports area, with football and cricket and other games, and a martial arts display.

There really was 'something for everybody' at Battersea Park, and all the advertising for the festival made it quite clear that this kind of diversity was going to be on offer. The same variety and diversity was also found at the earlier festival on South Bank in 1984. One person who came to that festival was Anne Scargill, who had come down to London for the weekend with a group of miners' wives. Coming from Yorkshire, and being something of a star in her own right, she is perhaps an atypical visitor to the festival, but on the other hand, as someone from outside London, she responded with particular surprise and pleasure to things that Londoners might be more likely to take for granted, as her account illustrates:

Twelve of us came down in a bus, and for a lot of these miners' wives they'd never been to London before. It was a terrific day, that. The hospitality here was tremendous, and it were another world to us in Yorkshire, you know, to see the things that were happening, the way of life. I mean to say, we'd never been to a festival like that. It were beyond our comprehension to get all these people together, it were a new world opened up to us. There was an atmosphere I can hardly describe. Maureen Eckersly was with me, and she's older than me, she's fifty. She said, 'Oh, I feel like a little kiddy again, isn't it strange, it's like going to a fair!'

We met a lot of people that day — I mean various types of people. People with punk hairdos and people who were very young came up and talked to us about the strike. And I've not got anything against people who are way-out or anything, it's up to them how they want to live, but it surprised me that so many people wanted to talk to us and ask us how we were going on. We didn't have any disparaging remarks thrown at us at all.

And the steel bands, they fascinated us, because as I say we've not been in this Caribbean type atmosphere. You brought all the cultures together, really, didn't you. You brought the steel bands, you brought the rock'n'roll, and you collated it altogether for us to see, all the different cultures.

It were an education to us in a way to see all this. The GLC broadened our outlook a lot. They say travel broadens the mind, and it does. You meet different people, you learn things. We met the dockers, and Connie from the docks who had done so much work for the docks, and we realised that there were a role for women to play in life. In our esteem she seemed great. Here were Connie battling in what were a man's environment. And we thought we'd been held back, we're miners' wives, but here's Connie coming to the forefront

and doing things, and we can do 'em too. It gave us a lot of inspiration meeting Connie.

You'd be surprised who came up to us and said hello, you're
miners' wives, good luck with your struggle. They did seem
genuinely concerned for us, and we found that a lot of the coloured
people were more concerned that the whites. Because I think that
they can identify with us — and we can identify with their struggle
as well better now. We know what harassment they're getting
because we're getting it now. We're witnessing it because we're in a
struggle, so we could identify with their struggle.

If one of the GLC's political achievements was to reach
beyond the white, male, working-class base of traditional labour
movement politics and create the beginnings of a new coalition
of interests that also included women and black people and a
wide variety of ethnic, cultural and other groupings, then this
potential coalition was made visible and actual at the festivals.
This was a crucial part of the image that the festivals communicated. As Ken Livingstone said, summing up this aspect of
the occasions, 'So many people would have come away seeing all
the alternative forces brought to bear there.'

Openness

There was another important aspect of the GLC's image which
was forcefully conveyed during the festivals. This was a feeling
of 'openness' that reflected the GLC's attempt to open up part of
the state and its resources to ordinary Londoners and to share
some of the power with them. I've already mentioned that one of
the aims of both festivals was to give local groups and organisations round London the opportunity to make use of the
festival by putting on stalls and exhibitions to tell people about
their work. For Dick Muskett, the symbolic importance of this
was every bit as important as the actual political information the
groups conveyed to the public:

> The politics in inviting these groups to participate is the attempt to
> make people feel that the ideas we're working out at the GLC are not
> done in some detached way, but that we're working out ideas with
> groups of local people across London, with people who work in dif-
> ferent industries, with people in different communities.
>
> I think the aim has got to be to get across to people that we are
> not an authority or body that somehow stands above you and hands

you down nice things and tells you what to think. What we are trying to say is that we're an authority that is of you: you elected us, we're part of you, we're just the same as you, we're Londoners like you. We have to make them feel that this particular council is accessible and answerable to them and that what we do is not just for them but is of them.

It might sound silly to say it's about sincerity and trust, but that's what it comes down to. Either you believe and trust that people have the ability and the power and the right to do things themselves, or else you're just another bit of the state handing down the goodies.

What we're trying to do is part of a fairly significant move that's taken place in the last few years which recognises that you have to get to people where they are, you can't preach to them. You can't say: this is what you should think. You have to meet them on their own ground, where they live, and work with them in that way. The British labour movement has been too patronising. I think we've tried to turn that round and say that we're working with you, we're organising something with you. We're not doing it to you, we're doing it with you. I think there's been a success in that.

For those of us who had been working at County Hall since the early days of the Labour administration, one of the striking changes that had taken place was in the kind of people who came to County Hall and were encountered strolling around the corridors. Gradually, the visiting dignitaries and officials of former times were replaced by a cross-section of Londoners, ranging from punks and rastas at one end to parties of Bangladeshi old-age pensioners at the other — all of them uncowed by their august surroundings and treating the place as if it was their own. At the July 1984 festival, this aspect of the change at County Hall reached an exuberant high-point. Throughout the day, County Hall swarmed with young punks, skinheads, rastafarians and a host of other Londoners. They camped on the grand staircase (in the past reserved for VIPs only) and in the wood-panelled corridors of the Principal Floor. Throughout the day the Council Chamber was used for a rolling debate on the abolition of the GLC, which at one point was also given over to speeches by Anne Scargill and the miners' wives.

The atmosphere was quite extraordinary — no one at County Hall had ever seen anything like it before. Ken Livingstone describes the feeling:

People were sort of wandering in and just getting really happy and excited and talking. And there was an incredibly mutually supportive atmosphere in the whole building. I've just never felt anything like it before or afterwards in a political gathering. And yet most people would say they hadn't come to a political gathering at all. It was just a little bit of politics dropped into a series of bands. And yet it was absolutely electrifying. The buzz people got back and forward from each other was incredible. You just saw the enthusiasm that could be unleashed by a genuine socialist movement — I mean, how many people it would sweep along and capture, and how rapidly they'd develop and grow. And how exhilarating that would be, that sort of mood.

Gordon Donald, summing up the image the festivals conveyed to him about the GLC, said:

At one level, the festivals were just another social provision by a local authority. But I think at another level they were beginning to raise people's expectations of what they can expect from an authority — an authority that isn't so distant or 'other'. It's much closer to what we want and like.

Pop and Politics

Of the different aspects of the festivals that have been discussed here, there is one aspect which, as Dick Muskett, Tony Hollingsworth and others have pointed out, is at the very centre of things, providing the focus that holds everything else together: the music. When Ken Livingstone talked earlier about a festival gathering together 'all the alternative forces', he included in this the musicians:

An awful lot of the rock industry has not been terribly political, but it broadly has been a progressive voice over the last twenty years. On balance, most of the individuals in it are either apolitical or to the left. So if you're talking about building an alternative Britain — I mean building a left Britain — those sorts of elements are going to play a major role in the groundwork of opinion.

What did the musicians themselves feel about these festivals — and did the festivals have any political impact on *them*?

The bands chosen to play were generally ones who were in sympathy with the GLC and its policies, and special efforts were made to get a good representation of women's bands and black bands, and a variety of different types of music. They were not necessarily picked for their success in the charts and the straight commercial world. Dick Muskett recalls that at one point in 1985 there was a possibility of getting Bruce Springsteen to do the summer festival, Springsteen's politics apparently not being too far away from some of the GLC's:

> If we'd had Springsteen or somebody of that stature, we'd have lost everything. You wouldn't have had a quarter of a million or half a million, you'd have had two million there, and it really would have been unworkable. In fact, a lot of the bands we put on are bands that are almost pub bands, and have got their own local following. There's a certain familiarity about them. If they can come, then hopefully it's going to be a relaxed day. It's not going to be enormous surging crowds that are unpleasant to be in. It's going to be a day when you can sit down on the grass and have a picnic, or you can go and get a beer or whatever when you want a drink. That's probably much better than doing it with mega-stars. Let the mega-stars go to Wembley.

Peter Jenner believes the GLC festivals did have a profound effect on the musicians themselves. The great surprise, in fact, was that the GLC was willing to put on popular music at all:

> It was the first time in my experience that a local Council put money into pop music in a major way and saw that its job was to provide popular culture and fun culture, as well as heavy and high art culture. And suddenly I found my artists being employed by the GLC — and equally that other artists, and sorts of people I was interested in, doing the sorts of things I was interested in, were being financed by the GLC in terms of employment. Even above market rates! That was nice about the GLC. They tried to close down a little bit on the top earnings and push up the bottom earnings . . .

On reflection, Peter thinks that the reason the GLC did this was that the GLC leadership was part of a generation that had grown up with popular music, and for whom rock music and electric guitars 'were not the music of the devil or some ghastly aberration of capitalism'.

Peter adds that, at least for Billy Bragg, working with the GLC and doing miners' benefits was a radicalising experience. 'It made him, for instance, really realise the importance of the women's movement, because he came across some of these women's groups, and that gave him a perception of how women are treated and so on which probably wouldn't have happened otherwise.' Conversations I had with musicians during and after the festivals seemed to bear out what Peter is claiming here. In particular, I remember at the 1985 Christmas Concert for the Unemployed in Finsbury Park finding that all the bands who were lined up to play during the evening had disappeared into the Madness caravan parked at the back of the site. When I went in there to tell them who was on next, I half expected to find an exotic drug party going on. There were a dozen or so musicians crowded together in the confined space, several of them forced to sit on the floor. But there wasn't a drug in sight. Instead of getting stoned, they were all vociferously arguing about politics.

Mike Campbell, the manager of Aswad, probably summed up the feelings of many musicians when he said, 'As far as we're concerned, the GLC has been very worthwhile. I don't know what they're going to replace it with. There's going to be quite a few wasted years while they try and sort everything out.' The fact that so many musicians were prepared to play for the GLC, and that in doing so their interest in politics was heightened, is of considerable significance for the music industry and for popular culture generally. A lot of people say that an involvement in politics somehow kills creativity, and that in any alliance between music and politics, music must suffer. Yet it now seems that many musicians are entering into just such an alliance. This was seen clearly at the GLC festivals, and, partly as a result of these festivals (along with the benefits for the miners strike), it has led to the formation of Red Wedge, the cultural organisation that has devoted itself to drumming up support for the Labour Party.

In fact, of course, there is nothing so very new in this. There has always been a critical, rebellious strand of opinion in the arts, and this has expressed itself in more or less overtly political commitment according to the situation of the artist and the general ethos of the time. Amongst embattled communities and cultures, music is naturally used for the expression of political ideas. Black music, in particular, frequently has a political content, and for many women the fact of playing music at all has been regarded as a political statement. As for mainstream British pop itself, the history of political attitudes within the industry has been closely bound up with wider generational changes on the one hand, and with the political complexion of the government (whether it was Conservative or Labour) on the other. In general, a Labour government has tended to blunt pop's political edge, turning pop rebellion into more individualistic directions — though an exception to this rule is the Rock Against Racism movement of the 1976-79 Callaghan period (a time, admittedly, in which the distinction between Labour and Tory became rather blurred).

It's no great surprise, then, that the excesses of Tory monetarism, coupled with the political disaffection of pop's main constituency (urban youth), have led a large number of musicians to take up explicitly anti-Thatcher (and, quite often, pro-Labour) positions. In particular, Peter Jenner singles out two issues that have had a profoundly radicalising effect on musicians. One of these was the miners' strike, which was supported by a large number of musicians, doubtless because so many of them come from working-class backgrounds. The other was the *abolition* of the GLC. If many musicians had already enjoyed working with the GLC and sympathised with its politics, then abolition was seen as an unwarranted attack that affected musicians directly. Peter Jenner explains:

> The GLC had done a lot for musicians, and that turned me on for a start. Then I realised they were doing the same for the gay and lesbian and black groups, and all the other things which were put up as 'look at this absurd waste of tax-payers' money'. I could see that *I* was under the category of absurd waste of tax-payers' money! And that in their own way a lot of these other things were doing a lot of good, in the same way as with the pop things. That came through, I suspect, for quite a lot of the musicians, who I think probably wouldn't have agreed with all that before, or hadn't thought about it. One felt that maybe some of what the GLC did was a bit absurd, but that on the whole they were trying to do things which needed to be done. And then you saw that it was being attacked. It was being attacked in a malicious way, for no very good reason other than the fact that the government didn't like it.

At the same time, changes in the music industry itself have propelled many musicians to take stock of themselves and their relation to their work and their audience. With the great boom period of the record industry now over, record companies are increasingly relying on the star system to make their profits. They are less willing to sign on new artists in any numbers, preferring instead to spend large amounts of money on promoting and marketing a few chosen stars to ensure that they sell records by the million. This is stultifying for many musicians. They resent the lack of opportunities for new bands, they resent the predictability and unadventurousness of the music that gets promoted, and they resent the way stars are packaged and treated like just another product. As Peter Jenner says:

A lot of the artists involved in Red Wedge, for example, are aware that something has to be done about the music industry, because the way it's going is obscene. I mean, nobody listens to Radio One or Capital Radio. No one's got any time for it. Even go and speak to the people who are running it, they have no time for it. They all know it's junk!

Most of the interesting new music is in fact now being provided by the 'indies', the small independent record companies; and it hasn't gone unnoticed among musicians that the GLC, as part of its cultural industries policy, gave financial support to the indies through GLEB as a way of countering the dead hand of the major companies and their domination of the industry.

These various changes in society at large and in the music industry itself have led to a considerable re-evaluation amongst musicians about their role, and about the uses to which their music is put. One of the most important achievements of the GLC festivals was that they succeeded in providing a political focus both for musicians who were beginning to take up more critical positions towards society and for the tens of thousands of disaffected young people who formed their audiences in London. In this way, the GLC began to reach out to a youth constituency as no political party has succeeded in doing for several decades. The degree to which the festivals helped sharpen the political awareness of this constituency must be one of the key yardsticks by which the success of the festivals should be judged — for, as Ken Livingstone points out, 'if you want to transform society in Britain, you've got to have massive support amongst youth. That's where you start from.' From this point of view, the roar of acclaim with which the Smiths fans greeted Ken when he appeared to talk to them in the County Hall car-park was encouraging. But, as Ken himself is at pains to point out, such moments are fragile. If young people are to be won over to politics in a more permanent way, politics itself has got to change:

You can only reach that constituency by sharing your power with it. No amount of packaging or gimmickry will actually do it. Yes, Red Wedge has had an effect and an impact in creating support for the Labour Party. But to really make an impact, Neil Kinnock and the rest of the leadership have got to open up the channels of influence to young people. If that starts to happen the thing will really take off. And also, Neil Kinnock and the others will be changed by the process. But clearly there's going to be a lot of people round Neil saying: 'Just use it for the votes, and keep them in a box and don't let them out, because it might frighten the older voters!' And if that is the case, well, we'll get a few more votes out of it, but the potential of it won't be realised. I mean, young people are not fools. They want to know what's in it for them. What influence are they going to have on the way policy develops? Will they actually be consulted after there's a Labour Government?

Ken's conclusion, however, is that young people will indeed become increasingly involved; and because of the nature of today's youth, he is optimistic about the possibilities for the future:

Over the last month they've been having all these seminal early sixties films on TV, like Saturday Night and Sunday Morning, and A Kind of Loving, and A Taste of Honey. And I've been watching those with Kate, who's ten years younger than me, and she keeps complaining I keep turning into a sociology lecturer, because *it is such a different Britain*! Incredible! When you look at how un-street-wise those people are in those films, how lacking in style or confidence. For all the unemployment and for all the fears that people have, there's still so much more knowledge and confidence that young people have today in that age group. Now, if Thatcherism and Reaganism carried on for a decade longer, would we all be pushed back into how things were before? Would everyone's horizons be narrowed sufficiently that they could get dragooned back into that sort of world? I don't think so. I don't think you can roll it back. For all the economic pressures, still people are hanging onto bits of personal liberation that were grabbed hold of in the sixties and seventies. Women are particularly — in fact they're still continuing to encroach. So in my view, when you hit another period of economic upturn, in global terms, and confidence starts to return, you start from a much higher level of personal politics and confidence than we did when we ran into the sixties.

Conclusion

Over and above their value in affecting the political awareness of the people who attended them, the GLC Jobs Festivals were well worth doing *anyway*, simply because they gave people a good time. This might seem an obvious point, but it's one that's worth makig to counter an accusation that has been levelled against the festivals along with many other of the GLC's activities (like, for example, its grants to minority groups): the accusation that these activities were ways of 'buying support' for the Council and its activities. Behind this accusation is the view that it is somehow illegitimate for a local council to provide popular entertainment for the people in its area, and to subsidise this entertainment out of the rates. Yet why on earth shouldn't a local authority do this? Cultural activities like ballet and opera have been subsidised out of the rates for decades. All that was different about the GLC's pop festivals was that they were on a much larger scale, and the entertainment provided included popular culture.

It was also, as Tony Hollingsworth point out, very cost effective entertainment. Whereas seats at Covent Garden are subsidised by rates and taxpayers to the tune of £20 per person, the total of cost of a full day's entertainment at Battersea Park for over 250,000 people was in the region of £200,000 — less than £1 per head. This was more than it would normally have cost an individual to see just one of the bands on stage, let alone the twenty or so who were playing. So, as Tony says, 'it is just as exceptionally cheap way of putting on a show for people'. As for 'buying support', Dick Muskett is scornfully dismissive of this:

> People in the 1980s in this country are quite acutely aware of the way they are being manipulated. Everybody knows the story about Saatchi and Saatchi and Sir Gordon Reece changing Margaret Thatcher's image. If people got the impression that all we were doing was buying their votes or buying their loyalty by giving them a rock concert, we would have failed. Not just that we would have failed; I personally feel I would have failed, because that's not what I want to do. You may as well stand on Westminister Bridge and give five pound notes away if that's all you're going to do.

But, to return to the central argument, the Jobs Festivals in particular aimed to do more than simply entertain. They also aimed to put over certain political ideas. On the surface these political ideas were about the problem of unemployment. The festivals aimed to draw people's attention to this problem, and to suggest that the GLC was trying to do something about it. The aim was probably achieved to a degree. Because of the 'title' on the stage, because of the speeches, because of the information being disseminated round the fringes, most people at the festivals must have been aware that the occasions were in some way and at some level about the problem of unemployment. But how deeply people were aware of this, and even more how much they became aware of the GLC's policies in relation to employment, must have depended on the degree to which they listened closely to the speeches, and the degree to which they visited the exhibitions and picked up literature from the stalls. Probably, only a small minority (still measured in thousands) became more closely acquainted with the issue in these ways. However, almost everyone who went to the festivals must have been aware that whatever the GLC's policies on employment were, they were policies that had some kind of relation with the myriad of local organisations who put on stalls and exhibitions during the festivals. This particular political point — that the GLC was trying to develop its ideas in association with local workplace and community groups — must have come over fairly forcibly to quite a high proportion of the people at the festival, whatever else they made of the occasion.

In addition — and in the end, this must surely have been the more powerful impression — the festivals conveyed aspects of the GLC's policies through certain images that were part and parcel of the texture of the festivals as events. One of these images was the affirmation that London is composed of many different cultures, age-groupings, ethnic minorities and so on, and that all of these — black, white, women, men, old, young, with or without disabilities — have legitimate political interests and have the right to be heard and to celebrate their own particular identity along with everyone else. In this respect the festivals were a concrete embodiment of an ideal of a particular kind of equality that was one of the GLC's most important contributions to contemporary political life in Britain. At the same time, the festivals, in their generally loose and easy-going character, their spirit of fun, their informality, also provided an image of a local authority as open and approachable.

Finally, the festivals marked an important political and social moment in London in the degree to which they brought together very large numbers of young people and invited them to develop a political awareness of their situation in today's society. The festivals were able to do this because they involved the enthusiastic co-operation of progressive popular musicians. Earlier movements involving music and politics such as Rock Against Racism had a much sharper political focus, but nevertheless the festivals played a part in developing a political constituency amongst youth, the effects of which are likely to have an increasing impact both on the Labour Party and on British politics generally.

No great claims are being made here. The politics of the festivals was low-key and muted, and intentionally so. Above all, the festivals were a nice day out for Londoners, and that's how they were mainly appreciated. But in their way, they did communicate a kind of politics, and that politics was important. When people think back to the days of the GLC, one of the things they will particularly remember about the GLC will be those days out in July 1984 and July 1985 — and this memory will be, in part, a political one. Whether this political impact of the festivals was great or small, there is no doubt that the festivals represented an interesting break both with traditional *left* attitudes and traditional *local authority* attitudes towards popular (and commercial) culture. Writing in *New Socialist* in February 1986, Tony Banks MP (formerly chair of the GLC Arts and Recreation Committee) and Alan Tonkins, a senior officer with the Arts and Recreation Committee, characterised these attitudes as follows:

> The left has never taken cultural politics seriously, let alone recognised that access to certain forms of culture delivers a tremendous source of social power. Labour Party intellectuals have been complicit with dominant definitions of culture: the arts and sports as morally improving, culture as conservative national heritage or as elite excellence which working-class people are deprived of and need to be educated to enjoy.
>
> Moreover, socialists have always been embarrassed about dealing with the other major area of provision: the mass leisure industries.

The GLC's willingness to engage with popular and commercial culture, which was a feature of many GLC initiatives in the cultural field, reflected the discussions about cultural policy that were taking place in both the Arts and Recreation Committee and the Industry and Employment branch. These discussions were particularly concerned with the question: who should decide what culture is of value, and how should they decide it? It was recognized that attempts to answer this question in the past had confronted two problems. On the one hand, cultural provision by the state had historically favoured 'elite' minority arts that in general were consumed only by the middle classes. On the other hand, while the market has been sometimes a more democratic method than the state of determining what culture people want (and are therefore willing to pay for), the market has been greatly distorted by the control exercised over it by large multinational companies. The GLC responded to these problems in two ways. Firstly, it shifted its own subsidy policies so that they included popular cultural forms as well as the traditional minority ones. Secondly, it instituted a policy of direct investment into the smaller independent cultural production and distribution companies so as to expand the choice available on the market.

These policies marked an important movement away from attitudes on the left which have contributed to the left's marginalisation in Britain over recent decades. Closely bound up with this shift in emphasis lies another important change which has been particularly noticeable in the GLC festivals. This is to do with an attitude of the left towards *pleasure* itself. At one point Dick Muskett said, 'I think there's a strand of puritanism on the left which really has to be got rid of if socialism is ever going to be a truly popular thing.' This comment of Dick's reminded me of Billy Bragg's evaluation of the Battersea Park festival when he was interviewed for Jobs for a Change: 'I think the festival was a great day, and what it did was show people that socialism is something that can be enjoyable.' When I quoted this to Dick, he said:

> I think we should have that engraved on our hearts. ... How many times do you hear politicians hark back to the days of 1945, as if that was some sort of heyday in the development of British socialism? Yet if I ask my mother about that period — and she was a Labour voter — she will say it was a time when there was rationing and austerity and power cuts, and it didn't seem like a honey moon period for the British working class at all. It seemed pretty fucking miserable, even if things were maybe going to improve as a result of it.
>
> I think we have to ditch that puritan aspect. Bragg's right. Socialism has to be seen to be an enjoyable, living thing that people involve themselves in.

Ken Livingstone's response to this seems to me a fitting way of ending this chapter:

> It's not just a strand of puritanism on the left. It's a strand of puritanism in all Christian societies. You can also pinpoint the origin of it, which is St. Paul and his self-hatred and his self-loathing and the move away from a basic underlying humanity of Christianity into bureaucracy and rigidity and anti-semitism and so on. And that has been reinforced century after century in the Christian world. It as an echo in every part of our culture, even in people whose parents and grandparents have been committed atheists for years. The underlying cultural ethos determined by that early reactionary Christianity — which, by the way, is totally out of keeping with what Christ was

saying — lives with us in every aspect, and it infects our left-wing politics as much as right-wing politics. It's an inability to come to terms with yourself physically and emotionally, to relate easily to others. It's all driving everybody in. And it's obviously a very important part of the engine of capital, in the sense that it drives people — you have to strive to achieve, to control, to dominate. I see all that flowing together. And therefore an alternative world, a co-operative one, is going to mean quite major, fundamental changes in things like that, so that things *will* be enjoyable, people *will* relate easier to each other, they *will* be able to come to terms with themselves, their own bodies, their own sexuality and so on.

So much of the leadership of the British left is so intricately bound up with the old ways and attitudes of looking at things — sort of containing it all, and seeing it as strong leaders, and so on. Yet what's interesting is that the British left hasn't produced a more 'strong leader' type than Arthur Scargill in a generation; and yet he immediately slotted into all that at the festival and loved it, and you saw him actually blossom and come out of that. He found that an absolutely elating day.

And that's why reactionary politicians concentrate so much of their fire on popular music, on liberalising sexuality, and so on. Because they're aware that if you start to loosen those bonds, you actually call into question a whole lot of property relations as well — the whole balance of power between capital and labour. That is an absolutely frightening thing for the British establishment, to see those sorts of things being brought into the open and talked about.

15
Conclusion

I think the GLC is guilty of claiming that it was doing things it wasn't. Because it was doing things in a *better* way, and was in Thatcher Britain such a bloody breath of fresh air, I think it got away with murder. But in terms of exciting and challenging people to come forward with ideas, if it had gone into a second term, I suspect that the GLC would have had quite a hard time, because a lot of its existing practices would have been challenged by groups of people who would have had the confidence and would have had sufficient time to look at things clearly. I think that's particularly true of black groups. I think the second stage would have been a lot more challenging to the local state than the first stage.

GLC Industry and Employment officer

The GLC set itself up to be criticised and criticised it was — and not just by the government. The GLC politicians, in rhetoric and sometimes in practice, set out to open up the local government process to ordinary Londoners. How limited and partial was their success, the chapters of this book demonstrate. But the opening up was real: as one person interviewed for this book said, you did not realise how open County Hall was until you saw it after March 1986, its echoing corridors empty now of the people who still pay for it through their rates and taxes. And the rising expectations were real, too, if painful and frustrating. Many of the GLC politicians and staff had worked hard to create the expectations and the links between the GLC and different London communities; to create, in other words, a constituency which in turn would pressure *them* to produce more effective policy. If that pressure had increased, if in a sense that constituency had turned on them and forced them to be much more responsive, then many of them would have felt they had succeeded.

This argument picks up where the book's introduction left off. All the chapters in this book are about the growing (and creative) tension between expectations and pressures and what was actually done. The GLC must in part be judged by what it left behind, what it helped to create 'out there' amongst the people who outlasted it. And raising expectations, encouraging people to make demands, to organise and to have confidence in their dealings with the government they pay rates and taxes for, was an end in itself, as well as a way of working on economic policy.

The GLC's experiments in shifting power, where they happened, were one more round in an old debate: how to extend effective democracy beyond the political franchise to increase democratic control over the economy and over state economic policy. In the process people rediscovered another old truth: where popular initiative and control grew, there was far more change than elsewhere. It will help to draw conclusions about these experiments if we start by summarising where they fitted into the council's employment policies.

There were five main ways in which the GLC used its spending powers for employment purposes. It invested in the development or maintenance of employment in the private and co-operative sectors. It used its purchasing activities through contract compliance to try to improve working conditions in the private sector. It spent money on the development of public service employment under its own control. It resourced the provision of services which were essentially plugging gaps in welfare state provision: notably training and child care. And it provided resources for the development of organisation of the labour movement, and other popular movements, organisations and campaigns. Of these, the last constitutes most of what was initially seen as 'popular planning'*: supporting people seeking to develop 'alternative plans', to take more control of their economic lives, to pressure the state including the GLC itself.

By the end, as the chapters make clear, people had become

---

* As should be clear from all the chapters of this book while there was a unit in the GLC Industry and Employment Branch called Popular Planning, the practices which we are including under that heading went much wider, involving many of the people working in the research, contracts compliance, grant giving, industrial and area development units in the Branch.

much clearer that the active development of outside alliances and pressure groups was an essential part of *all* the different areas of spending. Summarising the lessons about why this is so, how it has to be done, and the contradictions involved in a notion of alliances between the state and popularly based organisations, is the subject of this conclusion.

Creative Contradictions

Let us start with the central lesson: democratising state policy-making processes is a creative but inherently contradictory process: messy, unsatisfactory, necessarily incomplete. And that is if you do it properly!

The reasons for this stem from several central contradictions which emerged every time the GLC tried seriously to transfer control and resources from itself to others.

In the first place, the GLC, as a part of the state, was an employer and provider of services. As such it was an institution with interests of its own, as well as a political body with a set of wider political commitments. A commitment to popular planning amongst its own employees and users of its own services created much more internal conflict than resourcing such popular planning elsewhere. As a result — and the chapters of this book show this up sharply — the GLC was most effective in democratising economic activity in areas away from its own in-house staff and transport employees. The industrial democracy efforts were weak within its walls (including within GLEB), and there was little popular planning of transport services. The closer any state body gets to democratising its own activities, the more serious the conflicts will be.

Second, efforts by the GLC to democratise economic policy were bedevilled at the start by the assumption of consensus between the GLC and what at first was seen as a relatively homogeneous constituency. The more naive discussions of popular planning tended to assume that somehow the GLC would agree with the proposals in alternative plans, and, more strongly, would invest in the plans, in other words that the GLC and 'the people' could be partners without major difficulties. This assumption of consensus tended to run through enterprise planning, industrial democracy, and local plans for area development. But in fact, from the start, the GLC was subject to conflicting demands.

Issues concerned with anti-racism and women's employment led to the most drastic breaches in this assumption of consensus. The reason of course is that they illustrate most strongly a central problem for popular planning: that there are conflicts of interest among working people. And some groups have historically benefitted from an organised relation to Labour authorities. The initial illusion of homogeneity, the evidence in this book suggests, was in part because the 'constituency' for employment work was at first seen in terms of the organised labour movement, especially skilled workers. As pressure developed to devote more resources to people outside that network, especially women and black people, conflicts developed. To reach the least privileged Londoners, the GLC needed to shift its assumptions about the organisations it worked with, and the whole pattern of its funding. When the GLC did not do this it was rightly criticised; when it did make an effort, it was attacked from another angle for interfering with unions and community groups, often predominantly white and male, properly constituted and going their own way, thank you very much.

Which brings us to the third contradiction. The GLC talked of decentralising and sharing power. But in general, of course, the GLC had final power — within the constraints set by government — over the use of resources. It had its own criteria for using these resources, whether for service provision or investment, and only to a very limited extent indeed did it give that power up. At the very least, it had the power to turn down groups applying for grants; and increasingly it pushed its priorities, for example on anti-racism, on groups it did fund and work with, and it monitored their output. All the development of participation, then, even where it was successful, was within the constraints of the GLC holding onto much of the final power of decision.

In other words there are conflicts of interest between people and the state, centred on the loss of autonomy for groups who accept resources. All that people working for the state can do, when they are trying to transfer power and resources to outside groups, is to be clear about the precise extent and limits of what is on offer. The state cannot be a popular resource centre itself, it is too powerful an institution in its own right. It can only offer resources with strings attached, but be sure that the strings are visible so that people can make their own decisions and have a realistic basis for exerting pressure. The inherent and finally unresolvable tension comes from the fact that the elected politicians have to have policies and priorities, but progressive and innovative policies can only be developed if people *outside* the state can be given the facilities to develop them. A central argument of this book is that this tension between representative democracy on the one hand — choosing political priorities, winning democratic support for them, and sticking to them — and decentralising resources on the other hand — passing them over to people in the community to control and use — is a messy, but politically important tension, essential to increasing economic democracy.

Politicians, especially Labour ones, have a strong bias towards staying in control of what is going on. Many of the Labour Party's current proposals and policies contain neat models of how everything should have a bit of 'participation', though controlled from the top. But the great virtue of the GLC was that it let this cat out of the bag. Though it didn't democratise nearly as much as it said it did, it did demonstrate the possibilities, the creativity which can be released and the pressures for innovation which can be generated when a lot of people are given a look in, and not immediately boxed into predetermined structures. Without that creativity and pressure — that noise and mess — not much new will be achieved. That is the argument of the rest of this conclusion.

Where Do Ideas Come From?

The first set of arguments for democracy is about the need to go looking for information and ideas. There was an interesting tension within the last GLC administration about where ideas came from. On the one hand, the GLC itself had a strong sense of strategy, of how policies should relate to each other, which was one of its strengths. While the vision was often hopelessly over-ambitious, at least it was there, and gave people wanting the organisation to do something different something to latch on to. But on the other hand, this book demonstrates that in practice many of the most creative and innovative policies came from information and ideas provided by workers, consumers or communities affected by the economic polices the GLC was trying to challenge or by the economic situations it was trying to change. Where the GLC politicians and staff sat in County Hall or the offices of GLEB, or shielded themselves from outside pressure, they tended to become captive to establishment ideas.

The chapters of this book show the extent to which there is a wealth of knowledge and ideas, especially about better uses of public funds, going to waste in the decaying London economy. They also show the limited extent to which the GLC managed to draw on and build on those ideas. The GLC officers who went to talk to those working in firms and services, and living in run-down areas of the inner city, were looking for an alternative view of economic need and economic policy; an alternative to the view of managers and planners both in the private sector and in the public sector (where many are increasingly adopting the market-led assumptions of Thatcher's economics).

The extent to which they found those alternative views runs through the whole book. In some cases, including the in-house GLC workers, the ideas were listened to too late: the Woolwich ferry workers, for example, who could see the potential of their ship repair facility but who could not get their management to listen, and whose sense of waste was heightened by the fact that it was a public facility built up over the years on their skills and used by the local community. In other cases, the views of those who worked for a public service became crucial to the GLC's alternative plans for that service: the engineers at the Aldenham bus works, for example, who contrasted long-term viability and a socially responsible use of their skills, expertise and productive capacity with the narrow and short-term commercial calculations of London Transport management, or the community organis-ations who had ideas for the better use of central London land than speculative office building.

In other areas of work, the chapters show the extent to which GLC funding allowed people to develop and sometimes imple-ment their own ideas of what should be done. The Health Emergency campaigners, for example, who, between fighting job cuts, developed their own ideas of what a better health service could be like. Or the Women's Employment Project workers, who developed innovative training schemes and saw the possi-bilites of improving and developing the school meals service, by involving workers and parents. Or the childcare workers and campaigners who developed provision for the huge variety of needs of children and parents in different circumstances. Or the furniture workers who presented a different view of their indus-try and of the possibilities of public funding.

The list of ideas was endless. Behind all people's judgements is a sense of the social value of their own skills and contribution; and a strong sense that public money should be spent in a socially responsible and accountable manner. For all of these people, their wasted knowledge and skills are a social waste and also an individual indignity. And for many of them, the best thing the GLC did was give them the resources and encouragement to think for themselves. However critical people were of the GLC generally, they tended to come back to that: 'it's the fact that initiative is welcomed'; 'it's a different relationship, a discussion ... a different concept of consultation'.

The GLC's attempts to draw on these ideas and this experience provide some strong lessons about the politics of this process. The most important lesson is that the learning process, if it is to be effective, has to be a genuine exchange, offering as well as listening, and returning to people the results of discussions. It sounds obvious but in practice it is not, nor is it easy. People have low expectations of local or national government. Many people, such as the bus workers, community campaigners, black groups, were rightly suspicious when the GLC arrived looking for information: would the GLC just appropriate their ideas for its own benefit, and in the end, use the ideas against them? Those actually employed by the GLC — twice bitten — were the most suspicious of all.

Their suspicions had good grounds. In the private sector, many workers have been confronted by management who realise that workers have untapped knowledge which could be of financial value: 'the gold in workers' minds', as they have enviously described it. The implication is clear: 'and we'll dig it out'! This recognition has led to the introduction of 'quality circles' in factories: occasional, brief periods when small groups of workers are brought together entirely separately from the union, to discuss how production can be improved. The aim is to increase productivity and thereby increase company profits. Their calculations do not take into account the social costs of redundancies, factory closures and personal stress which might well result from the way these increases in productivity are extracted. In effect 'the gold' is stolen. Public sector management has a poor record in consulting its workforce at all, let alone using its workers' ideas to improve services; it rarely works with rather than in opposition to its workforce; and with the growing commercial pressures on the public sector, the pressures on public sector workers are becoming much more severe. None of this leads to trust in suggestions of collaboration. And community groups too have good grounds for suspicion of all local councils, whom they have often spent their time lobbying and opposing.

The GLC tried, some of the time, to do it differently: to learn but not steal, to give as well as to take. This was most complex where the GLC was itself the employer, in GLEB, or in in-house services, facing constraints of legality, finance and the market. Its ambitions looked like trying to sit on both sides of the fence at once, and some groups of workers feel that they gained nothing from the deal, especially those who participated in GLEB enterprises which have now gone under, or those who felt ignored within the GLC itself.

Too often the GLC used people's ideas without acknowledgement or return, and thereby lost support and allies. But sometimes it put its principles into practice. Again, it should have been obvious, but the genuine astonishment of trade union activists who, after the GLC had interviewed them on their ideas, got back a transcript of the discussion, plus comments and offers of collaboration, speaks for itself. At times the GLC also provided information to people which they could use in return — access to technical information, for example, from its own resources — demonstrating that the process could be a genuine exchange. There were a number of attempts to put the GLC's research skills at the service of people who wanted to research their own situation: the bus and tube workers involved in investigating the effects of one person operation felt the experience had been productive, though they had criticisms, and they certainly changed the council's view of the issues, as well as strengthening their own self-organisation.

At its best in the GLC, this process of learning and providing information both strengthened people's capacity to control their own situation, and shifted the council's conception of how it could spend its money effectively. The Aldenham workers used their knowledge of the factory, of their own skills, of the engineering needs of the transport service, *and* the information supplied by the GLC, to build up a powerful case for keeping the works open, aimed at convincing management and the Council. The energy policy workers worked with tenants' groups to learn about needs and possibilities, then provided information which the tenants could use for organisation and campaigning. *Only* if people get back knowledge and resources that they can use there and then, can a local authority go on learning and asking people to give up their free time to, in effect, help it do its job properly. And this will only happen if there is a conscious 'politics of knowledge' in the authority: principles to be worked from about looking for knowledge and ideas, bringing people together to develop ideas and work out what they want, providing the resources for this to be possible, encouraging criticism, and always giving back relevant information (including about the authority itself) in exchange.

Economic Policy as Process

The second major argument for democracy is that, not only is work with outside organisations essential for people in the state to work out what they want to do, it is also generally essential for getting it done. On the whole, alternative policies were not successfully implemented solely from inside County Hall; they also needed an outside base of pressure and support. The outside pressure involved people in: supporting the council against opposition; keeping the GLC to its principles and promises; and doing a lot of the actual work themselves. The chapters of this book have examples of all of this.

In other words, strengthening the capacity for self-organisation of workers, of tenants, of women's groups and black groups was not only a basis for learning, it was also an essential basis for effective intervention in London's economy. Our experience leads us to argue that unless socialists use the state resources over which they win political control to make working-class organisations — in the community as well as in production — one of the driving forces of their economic strategy, then that strategy will largely fail. And furthermore, the results will not last.

One reason for this is that the kind of economic policies discussed in this book, running against the logic of the capitalist market and against conventional wisdom, all involve taking sides, and imply conflict against entrenched interests. This is clear in the public sector examples in this book, where many policies were blocked by entrenched interests within the council, and only partly unblocked by pressure from below. Where that pressure failed, policies fell: in-house policy on low wages is a good example.

In the private sector, policies which favoured devising new products for need, and took the interests of workers into account implied supporting and spreading a challenge to management's unaccountable powers to manage. For while management would value a worker's suggestion, elicited through a quality circle, for reorganising the lay-out of the factory to increase the flow of production for instance, it would see proposals put through the trade union about new products or a new investment strategy as subversive, a challenge to management's prerogative. Supporting and developing these challenges to management prerogatives is an essential basis of alternative economic strategy.

The experiences of the previous chapters provide vivid evidence, positive and negative, for these conclusions. Where there were no organised groups, outside the GLC, pressing for action and working with the Council, often little got done. An example would be the attempt to use the conditions on the lease of the GLC's industrial properties as a lever to improve workers' wages and conditions. it failed because the GLC had not found a way to work with unions and local organisations to build up a base of workers who could make use of that lever. Other property initiatives, for instance new sites developed with the involvement of organised groups, where the GLC could work with local organisations, were much more successful. Or take the example of alternative production to armaments: the achievements of the Greater London Conversion Council fell far short of its ambitions largely because of the difficulties in achieving any close working relationship with workers in any part of the arms industry.

Where the GLC supported and worked with organised groups, much more was achieved. For example, on alternative energy strategies, where the GLC and the London Energy and Employment Network established a base amongst tenants, local borough councillors and the 'alternative energy movement', the GLC's policies had a lasting impact. Where the GLC joined up with and supported groups already working on childcare and training projects for women, innovative projects mushroomed, and many are still in existence. And working to create links between trade unionists within the same transnational and thereby to increase their power was really the only way the GLC could have the slightest influence on the operation of the big transnational firms.

Successes and failures in GLEB, though, are more complex, because market pressures on weak firms are no respecters of the efforts of workers. In principle, GLEB treated the promotion of workers' organisation and involvement in its firms as an end in itself, as well as a way to improve and turn round the operation of the company. Involvement of the workforce, with the costs to them involved, undoubtedly helped turn round some firms, and in the discussion of the furniture industry, the CD investment is an example of where involving the workforce might have made a major difference. In some cases collective bargaining and trade union organisation was strengthened through GLEB's initiatives. But where many workers worked very hard, and made sacrifices — and put themselves in some difficult positions — to try to turn round companies which have since gone to the wall, the result has sometimes been disillusion. One of the complications of 'popular planning' through intervention in the private market is that the state can draw people into collaboration in a situation where it lacks all control over the fate of the firm, and hence undermine their confidence.

If outside pressure forces change within the authority, in the two areas of black employment and women's employment the failure of the GLC to work with organisations that existed, or to help build up organisations and infrastructure where they were missing, were central reasons for the GLC's very limited success in these areas. The Industry and Employment Branch, despite a verbal commitment to these two issues, failed at least in the early years to build up the kind of base necessary to generate projects, support and pressure on those inside. And in other areas, property work for instance, overcoming blocks on progress within the council from technical departments who disagreed with council policy was substantially the result of harassment from outside groups.

Finally, the support of outside organisation is crucial to the lasting nature of anything achieved. Most Labour authorities will not be functioning, as the GLC was, with an axe over their heads, but they will still want their changes to last and the more their actions both bring direct benefits worth defending, *and* help create organisations capable of defending and building on them, the more likely those changes are to last. Funding the voluntary sector turned out to be an enormously effective way of getting policies implemented and work done. And where the GLC funding helped to create organisations clearly fulfilling a need, and with a strong constituency of support, renewed funding by other authorities and organisations has been common.

It follows from the importance to our economic strategy of people's own economic knowledge and power, that GLC support for trade union and community organisations was not just a Good Thing in itself; it was central to its achievements. The next sections consider the process of developing this support, and the issues involved.

Local Authorities and Trade Unions: Working Relations

At first, the Labour GLC saw its natural allies in employment policy to be the organised labour movement in London. Its initial partner was the constituency of regional and local trade union officials, who were consulted on the manifesto, and invited on to the Board of GLEB and later on to the London Transport Board. Conflicting with this conception from early on was the set of experiences outlined in the introduction, which led people in the GLC to emphasise working with shop floor workers, and to see the GLC in effect as a potential resource centre for the wider London labour movement.

The chapters in this book leave no doubt about the importance for economic and employment policy of effective working relations with trade unions. But they also show that this must mean close and direct relationships between the public authority and trade union representatives at the workplace. It is not enough to liaise with trade union officials. Where there is still some trade union strength in London, in the public sector, and in some of the older skilled trades, it is only at the workplace level that the unions have the detailed knowledge and power necessary to a strategy for intervening in production in the interests of working people. Even where, as in much of the London economy, trade union organisation is very weak, a local authority seeking to intervene in production still needs to draw directly on the workforce, while helping to strengthen unionisation in these areas.

To argue this is not to denigrate or to suggest by-passing trade union officials. Far from it; effective working relations with trade union officials were a crucial part of much of the work described here, from campaigning against health cuts, through strengthening trade unions in GLEB companies, to investigating one person operation on London's buses and trying to save London Transport's engineering works. Many trade union officials worked with the GLC, increasingly used it as a resource, saw its input as useful. But all of the activities just cited also crucially involved work directly with shop floor trade unionists. Without these working relations, a local authority, however well-intentioned, will end up relying on management, accepting management arguments and propping up the status quo. Moreover, it is at the workplace that much of the power lies to implement changes resisted by the employers, whether in the public or private sector.

These working relations between local authority staff and active lay trade unionists need to be thought out and argued for by politicians. The local authority has a legitimate interest in working conditions and employment in its area; work with local trade unionists is essential to developing policy, and can be done in a way that strengthens the local labour movement rather than creating client networks or undermining trade union autonomy. But to achieve this involves experience, having something to offer as well as to learn, honesty about what is on offer, explicit choices about who to work with so that relations with the state are not the property of any small faction, and deliberate attempts to strengthen organisation, not be divisive. In the weak state of the London labour movement in the 1970s, it became clear that a local authority could provide an important contribution to labour organisation, which both officials and activists could draw on, whether or not they agreed with all the GLC's policies.

This relationship between the public authority and workplace representatives is very important where the local authority is itself the employer. In many towns and cities the local authority is either directly or indirectly the largest employer. The new GLC was, as we have seen, committed to introducing some form of industrial democracy for its own workers and for London Transport, but did not have a clear idea of what structures they wanted, nor of how to convert doubting trade unionists to their view. In LT, working relations developed ad hoc with officials, convenors and stewards, and became very productive of policy; in the GLC itself this rarely happened. In fact the GLC's record on public sector industrial democracy was poor, and GLEB itself had no internal industrial democracy, only the standard bargaining relations.

This history suggests some lessons. First, lower paid staff have to see some tangible benefits, before demands can be made on them for wider participation. Second, there has to be a change in the managerial relationship between councillors and public authority workers. So long as relations between lower grade staff and councillors pass solely through senior staff or through union structures dominated by the more privileged sections of the staff, it is impossible to develop even the beginnings of a political alliance to transform the local authority's own administration. Third, the councillors have to develop active working relations with, in particular, unions representing lower grade manual and non-manual staff, and support organising by these unions, as well as taking seriously their views and ideas on their jobs and on the services they provide. Furthermore, they will have to ally themselves with these unions, in opposition to higher paid staff defending privileges such as the GLC closed grading system.

On formal structures for industrial democracy in the public sector, the relevant chapters raise more questions than they answer. Some of the trade unionists involved argue that public sector services, such as London Transport, need Board members from the workforce. Others disagree, and argue only for more sympathetic Board members and an extension of collective bargaining to incorporate wider issues. The same debates re-appear in the discussion of the experience of enterprise planning in GLEB: do worker directors undermine effective collective bargaining? The chapter shows the variety of experiment, and argues for the importance of social or public ownership as a precondition for lasting progress in economic democracy.

Any idea of an alliance between the political management of the public authority and the workers' representatives involves potential conflicts of interest for the unions. An alliance is only appropriate on certain issues — e.g. the quality of service, forms of management, possibilities for extending municipal activity — while on others trade unon autonomy must be maintained — e.g. wage negotiations.

In many ways existing trade union structures are not adequate for the task either of developing and implementing industrial policies or for effective industrial democracy in the public sector. For instance few unions have mechanisms for bringing together workplace representatives on a sector basis for analysing developments in an industry or service. In the private sector the sectoral base of many unions is limited to one aspect of the sector, e.g. either the production side or the retail side in food or furniture, while the problems facing the industry now concern the relationship between the two. Also trade unions in the public sector have little experience of seeking links to users of the services they provide, or the community in which they are based. Their structures are almost exclusively geared to collective bargaining over immediate, defensive needs surrounding the employment contract.

An economic policy based on workers' knowledge, initiative and power requires trade unionists to play a more active role. This in turn implies a need for structures where they can meet as producers, across the sectional divisions of the workforce and with the information and time to consider the wider context of their work and to plan ahead. And it implies new patterns of work, and new areas for bargaining. These pressures from local authorities for change in the unions' role have coincided with other parallel pressures. The recession and government policies towards the public sector have blurred the line between defensive and offensive trade union action. Trade unionists at all levels have found it necessary to make leaps of imagination and organisation simply in order to survive. For instance, in London, these included proposals for a better service from NUPE refuse collectors fighting privatisation in Wandsworth; unity between competing unions, COHSE and NUPE, through the Health Emergency campaigns; links with the community by the local TGWU co-ordinating committees; international co-ordination by workers in transnationals such as Ford and Kodak.

Exactly how trade unions adapt to increase their economic influence in alliance with local and national authorities is a matter finally for them and their own democratic procedures. But public authorities committed to democratising economic policy have a legitimate interest in working with the trade unions on this. In our experience over the four years 1981-85, the public authority can provide a variety of forms of support for changes which gather an internal momentum of their own. For instance the GLC's funding of sector-wide trade union workshops in furniture led the shop stewards and officials concerned to press the union to organise regular London-wide meetings of workplace representatives. The possibility of GLC funding was one factor which led local health campaigns to set up a London-wide Health Emergency Campaign. Meetings supported by the GLC between telecom workers and community organisations concerned with communications, led them to a lasting joint campaign. The initiative taken by the GLC and the local council in Val De Marne, to establish contact between unions and local councils on a European basis, led as we saw to a joint 'Standing Conference of Kodak Unions', to a European trade union newspaper and to more informal — and perhaps more important — relationships of trust, and channels for the regular exchange of information.

In developing this working relationship, one of the most important things local authorities have to offer, as opposed to take, is resources for education and information work. Trade unions are always hard pressed for research resources and information, and any new working relation makes new demands. The information and skills of planning, of gaining an overview, identifying the trends, calculating the costs and benefit have always been the monopoly of managements, whether industrial management or government. Much of the Industry and Employment Branch's 'educational' work, reported in passing in several of the previous chapters — on the GLC as an employer, on work with the furniture union, on the transnationals etc. — consisted of helping to break that monopoly by enabling workers from scattered workplaces to exchange information and piece together the full picture, by sharing relevant research done at the GLC or by academics, by funding workers to have time off where it could not be negotiated, and by employing trade union tutors where this proved useful. This work grew in importance as the implications of rooting economic strategy in popular organisations became clearer and the potential gains from working with the GLC became clearer to trade unionists.

From the start, there had been a commitment in GLC policy to build on innovation and new ideas — 'alternative plans' — by trade unionists. It quickly became clear that hopes based on the Lucas Plan model were unrealistic in the context of 1980s London; but in the wake of this, the importance of work on new uses of technology, and on developing trade unionists' ability to deal with technological change and its implications, became clearer.

For example, the introduction of computer controlled manufacturing and design into the furniture and clothing industries internationally has contributed to a major restructuring in which London companies have been at a disadvantage due to their slowness to invest in the new technologies. The backwardness of the employers poses a problem for those trade unionists who remain in employment and who want to be in a position to exert some control over the timing, design and application of the new technology. The popular planning workshops with trade unionists in the furniture industry provided those who attended with the opportunity to educate themselves about the most advanced technologies in their industry, to explore its implications and dangers, and to develop their own ideas about its application. GLEB's technology networks provided material, ideas, and practical experience of the new technologies. Local authorities can in this way help trade unionists gain expertise from outside their immediate employment; expertise to devise strategies and bargaining demands necessary to work with public authorities on responses to the crisis in the industry.

Political Choices: Women, Race and Popular Planning

People don't think there's a racial division of labour in England ...
GLC Industry and Employment officer

There were a number of inherent contradictions in the priorities of the Labour GLC; the one that came to loom largest was between on the one hand the expressed intention to develop employment policy benefiting women and black people, and on the other, the commitment to work with the organised trade union movement and with other established groups (such as community groups) as the political base of employment policy.

The contradiction lay partly in the low level of unionisation of parts of the London economy where women and black people were predominantly employed, in the low level of involvement of those groups in many unions to which they did belong, in the historic hostility or at best indifference of much of the trade union movement to the particular needs of women and black workers, in the high levels of unemployment which fell disproportionately on black people. It also lay, however, in the racism and sexism historically built into the organisation of the local state itself, in the failure of the labour movement to value and support black workplace and community struggle, and in the resultant alienation and low expectations of both groups in relation to both the local state and the trade unions.

The GLC experience demonstrates that making a priority of women's work and black employment involves major changes in the conception of economic strategy, including popular planning. This is one of the most important conclusions from this book, emphasised by the quote at the beginning of the conclusion.

If working with outside organisations becomes a tenet of economic policy, and if time, as always in the GLC, presses, then unless explicit choices are made about which organisations to involve, there will be a tendency for Labour authorities to work with the trade union movement and other organisations which they know or recognise. In the GLC in the early days this bias was in fact defended by some as the most efficient way of working, as the chapter on women's work documents. While we have just argued that this is an important part of policy making, it precisely excludes the groups most in need, both within unions and outside them. Without an explicit effort to rectify this, popular planning will simply reinforce relative privilege, and further exclude other groups from influence.

Several chapters in this book show how limited were the GLC's efforts to shift this bias in employment policy, and suggest some strong lessons from this history.

First, popular planning needs an explicit rethinking and redirection of its starting points. One of the GLC officers most involved in struggling to develop work on black employment argues that the GLC failed to recognise and start from the strong and effective organisations which do exist in the black community, for example in the struggles around education. These groups organising against racism in education, creating links between teachers, students and parents, setting up supplementary education, were not properly valued by the GLC as one of the communities' own starting points for work around training and employment. Instead of imposing its own view of appropriate forms of organisation, popular planning has to recognise and build on the existing forms of organisation, and the immediate needs of the communities it wants to reach: whether women's centres, childcare, or black community organisations.

The women's chapter argues that this implies putting resources into supporting and helping to develop a stronger 'infrastructure' of independent organisations serving the needs of women which can in turn effectively pressure the local authorities for changes in policies and use of resources. It was this, the GLC officer argued at the beginning of this chapter, which had been largely neglected by Industry and Employment, despite the rhetoric.

The women's chapter discusses some of the new ways of working which this involves in terms of publicity, organising help, educational work, encouragement, good 'outreach' and development work, hiring practices, pressure and sheer nerve. Many of these points also apply to working with all the less skilled, less organised groups in the community or at work, more generally. As someone put it, the point being made is *not*, 'Everything was perfect, we just didn't do it on women'. The point was that popular planning tends to reinforce divisions between groups unless conscious efforts are made to push the other way, hard.

However, those involved in black employment also identified a problem with this strategy of developing groups through funding. State funding and state interference can *weaken* effective and independent organisations, exacerbating political divisions and dragging the aims of the organisation towards those more acceptable to the local state. This effect can be worst where the groups being funded have interests which are in sharpest opposition to the local state as presently organised, which includes many black groups. Disillusion with what the state actually delivers in these circumstances can lead to demoralisation. As a result, many black groups thought long and hard before applying for state resources. And the GLC officer quoted above argued that small sums of funding, which could be used flexibly, and more resources in the form of staff time for educational work, were more appropriate than large grants to the needs of the community.

The discussion of employment work with both women and black people constantly returned to the distribution of resources within the GLC, resources that is in terms of staff time as well as money to spend. Shifting funds and support towards women and black people not only implies innovative working methods; it also implies removing staff time and money from areas where people are pushing hard for them, and results might be rapid, and applying them to areas where the gains are slow, less tangible, and less immediate in terms of 'jobs created'. It means concentrating on areas of the economy other than the manufacturing sectors with more skilled and organised workers, spending on training and childcare, resourcing organisations outside the traditional labour movement. It also means breaking down traditional categories of work within the Council: as one GLC officer put it, 'racism' is the experience linking the workplace and community for black people; there can therefore be be no neat divisions between 'employment' work and other issues, to fit into council departments.

This did not mean that women and black people had no organisations: both had many with a far larger and more active popular base than many labour movement institutions in London, and many of them worked with the Women's Committee and the Ethnic Minorities Committee. In particular many black organisations have demonstrated the ability to link workplace and community, workers and users, in struggles against racism in employment and service provision. Health, education, and a number of black workers' strikes in London are all examples of this. But despite many individual efforts, Industry and Employment as a branch never learned from these initiatives or built on the strength of these forms of organisation in developing and proposing employment strategies.

Such a shift in perspective requires Labour politicians to take a strong political stand, since it comes up against opposition from both unions and established community organisations. It was the issue of race which provoked the sharpest contradictions of this kind in the GLC. These contradictions came through very clearly when the GLC did try to pressure groups they were funding to implement the equal opportunities policies, especially on the question of anti-racist practice. The GLC's conditions for giving grants included specific clauses on equal opportunities. A number of the groups, especially those already established, objected on principle to this as outside interference. On several occasions the GLC rejected, threatened or refused to renew grants on these grounds, for example to some unemployed centres and in the case of some campaigning groups which were all white and refused to take seriously the need to develop an anti-racist practice in their work and hiring.

The same issue arose in relation to the unions. The women's chapter discusses some of the difficulties of raising the issues of racism and sexism in work with the unions. A number of the other chapters, including those on campaigning over health cuts, on OPO on the buses and tubes, and on the transnationals, touch on this. The work with unions often focussed on white, skilled male workers in areas like engineering: often easier to get off the ground than work in less organised, largely female sectors like retailing or office work; and easier too than focussing on the needs of the often well unionised but neglected groups of black workers, for example catering workers within the public sector.

The GLC was seriously criticised for this bias in a number of forums, including in a conference and public inquiry into the economy of West London. Where the GLC did take on the issue, the level of hostility it could provoke demonstrated the scale of the problem it should have been facing. For example, the GLC sponsored an investigation into racism in the trade unions: several trade unions objected, considering it to be an unjustified interference in their internal affairs. The GLC in this case did persist, arguing that its policy commitment to fighting racism in employment gave it the right to pressure the unions on this issue. The Popular Planning Unit followed this up with workshops on racism with the TUC, but few other resources were put into support work with black trade unionists.

Within the Industry and Employment Branch, the women's chapter argues, a major reason for the small proportion of resources which went to women outside was the failure of women inside to organise successfully to extract them. Or, to put it another way, the group of women working on women's employment never had enough time and control over the work, or a budget. On the question of race, the position of employment officers within the council was even more difficult. The officers who worked seriously on the issue, mainly towards the end, never felt in control of their work, and became frustrated by lack of progress.

This is partly because the research and policy work earlier on, largely done by white officers, had not focussed on the issue of race. While the sexual division of labour and the need to challenge it was at least in principle an accepted starting point for debates on women's employment work, no serious work was developed in the early years of the Industry and Employment Branch on the racial division of labour in London, its evolution, and the institutionalisation of racism embedded in it. This issue was not a major theme in any of the private and public sector research work. As a result, although GLEB was challenged early on by the Ethnic Minorities Unit about the failure to fund more black businesses, and although the Equal Opportunities Unit for the council as a whole did succeed in increasing sharply the numbers of black people employed by the council, the Industry and Employment Branch spent few of its resources promoting black employment and the organisation of black workers.

Rather late on, a debate developed concerning the funding of black business. The GLC had decided not to concentrate private sector investment on small firms, on the grounds of their poor employment practices and small capacity to generate employment. However, GLEB did in fact fund small businesses and co-ops, and in the face of high unemployment and the experience of racism within employment, many black people saw more funding for black businesses as essential: a means to employment, and to some degree of self-determination. More research and popular planning work might have provided the basis for a more radical approach, linking producers, including co-ops, users and consumers in sectors which employed many black workers (such as food). A focus on the racial division of labour might have guided the choice of sectors to concentrate on, and would certainly have focussed attention earlier on the employment practices of the major public sector employers.

As it was, the funds for black employment projects, as for women's employment projects, were generally underspent. An in-house equal opportunities policy was successfully established, but there was little attempt to break down the major divisions of labour or radically to improve the pay and conditions for the lower paid — often black and female — staff. In London Transport, which the GLC controlled until 1984, no effort was made to change the internal racial division of labour, which kept black people, especially black women, in the lower paying jobs, or indeed to prevent some reorganisation and job redesign which was making their situation worse. Some early GLC decisions, such as buying more OPO buses, made their job situation even more precarious. The efforts of some of the new London Transport Board members established, though too late, an equal opportunities adviser in LT. But there was little sustained attempt to support pressure groups of black and women transport workers, such as an Equal Opportuntiies Pressure Group organised by some LT workers, so that they could have exerted effective pressure on management (a tactic which might also have been resisted by the unions on the grounds of divisive interference).

In GLEB, the conflict with which this section began reappeared. GLEB's stated internal commitment to equal opportunities was not effective, as the composition of its own staff indicated. There was a contradiction in their policy process in that, while equal opportunities was to be promoted through the process of enterprise planning, enterprise planning was too often interpreted as a consensual process where a tacit agreement to procrastinate on equal opportunities could emerge between GLEB, unions and management. The exceptions, such as *Universal Books*, in the enterprise planning chapter, demonstrate what could be done. Elsewhere, as the chapter on enterprise planning comments, GLEB's work with management, and GLC work with trade unionists, could leave no effective lobby for those excluded, that is those not yet employed or organised: those the equal opportunities policies were meant to prioritise.

Here then is a case where the manifesto, agreed through the electoral process and elaborated through the council committees, came into conflict with the interests of some organised groups, including some within the labour movement. It also came into conflict with an easier life for people working in the council: it is always easier to work with existing constituencies than to go out and find or help create new ones, and then to fight for them.

In effect, only two things would have created a different pattern of employment work, more oriented towards those who needed it most. First, more staff with more power, from early on, whose job was to work specifically on the issues of women's employment and black employment, as well as to push others to incorporate that perspective into their work. And second, more resources for these people to develop work and outside pressure on the GLC on these issues. The Women's Committee and the Ethnic Minorities Committee developed these links much more effectively, but this was not a substitute for also bringing these priorities into the centre of the employment work.

Finally, however, such a shift in funding would not have solved the contradictions: on the contrary it would have probably sharpened them, as the quote at the beginning of the conclusion suggests. There is an inherent problem for people in relatively weak social and political positions becoming involved in a relatively unreconstructed local state, however many well-meaning individuals are trying to change it from within. Many community based groups, especially among women and in the black community, have a well-founded alienation from the local and national state, and from the labour movement, and put a strong emphasis on autonomy. How far can a part of the state go in supporting truly independent organisations in order that they might put more pressure on the state and thus increase conflict? Many black groups were very suspicious, and unwilling to risk the inevitable loss of autonomy involved in state finance. There are conflicting views of the GLC, both there in the quote at the beginning of the conclusion: on the one hand it did little, on the other, it did enough to open itself to serious pressure particularly from black groups.

Perhaps, then, not only should popular planning be part of all policy making, but more strongly, one major determinant of employment policy should be its potential impact on organisation inside and outside work: especially where people's organisational capacity, or capacity to pressure the state is weak. An example given by one interviewee was training, where a training project might be used to help and reinforce an existing community based scheme. The same argument has been made about GLEB: its most useful effects may be in strengthening the union side of collective bargaining, and increasing unionisation, and the most durable effects of the GLC may be in the area of strengthening people's confidence and capacity to make demands on the state.

State Support: Democracy and Accountability

'You never felt you could influence GLC policy?'
'Oh God no, it was like dealing with mud most of the time.'
Trade union resource centre worker, funded by the GLC

It follows from the argument of the last two sections that one of the most useful tools of GLC employment policy consisted in giving people resources so that they could do things for themselves: run projects, provide services, campaign, and pressure the government, managements, or the GLC itself. The expanding grants programme was a recognition of how effective this kind of resourcing was; at the same time, it raised a series of issues about democracy and accountability which are worth exploring in a bit more detail.

We began by saying that the GLC was experimenting with what it might mean to extend democracy beyond the ballot. This was generally construed by the politicians and the new GLC officers as responding to outside pressure, and opening up the resources, information and, to some extent, the power of the council, to ordinary Londoners.

There were a number of experiments with institutions for doing this. One, used for example by the Women's Committee (and by many other Women's Committees around the country), was to co-opt members from outside the council. Another was to hold open meetings, and advertise widely for applicants for funding. The Industry and Employment Committee used neither of these, and was slower than the Women's Committee or the Ethnic Minorities Unit to reach people with no initial connections with the GLC.

Industry and Employment was however under enormous pressure from the start to assist firms in trouble, and to fund support networks: trade union resource centres and cooperative development agencies. There were also demands for support from a wide range of community and campaigning groups.

One of the strengths of the GLC, and one of the positive lessons, was its flexibility in response to these pressures: work with campaigns was clearly seen as useful to employment policy, and there was no assumption that all the initiatives had to be local authority-led.

Some of the most effective resourcing was in response to popular resistance to imposed job loss or privatisation: the campaign against the LDDC's decision to promote an airport in

Docklands; the campaign of the National Communication Union against the privatisation of British Telecom; the threat of Ford workers to strike against the closure of the Dagenham foundry. Or it might be a more diffuse discontent: the discontent of transport workers over the introduction of OPO; the anxieties of construction workers faced with the run down of Direct Labour Organisations. Or sometimes the GLC was asked for support or involvement in a joint initiative by a well established workers' or community organisation struggling for greater control over their situation: for instance the Ford Workers Combine, or the Coin Street Action Group, in Waterloo. This necessary diversity of starting points requires a flexibility on the part of the local authority, a concern to listen and investigate before deciding on priorities, and a willingness to share power and decentralise resources without being able to predict the outcome.

In the process of responding to these kinds of pressures, many of the staff working for the Industry and Employment Committee developed a strong sense of their *own* accountability to the people they worked with, as well as upwards to the politicians. It is worth spelling this out, because the implication of taking democracy wider than the ballot box is that the process goes wider than the politicians. The skills and commitment required of local government officers change substantially, since they come to include working with outside groups and taking responsibility for those relationships. As one of the new staff put it: 'It gives you a political validity if you can show that the people you are supposed to be representing are actually putting demands on you.' Extending democracy, creating more open government, involves hiring people who can implement that.

It also involves, as was discovered, developing clear criteria about who should be worked with and supported, what support is necessary, what rules and demands should be put on those funded and why, and what sort of relationship could and should be developed with groups once funded.

These are questions about political choices and autonomy. A political authority will make choices about who it will support and work with, on the basis of its manifesto commitments and general principles, *and* its own interests as part of the state. This power of the state to accept, reject and control will conflict with autonomy for groups considering applying for funding, and therefore will affect who applies. Being funded by the state is always a constraint of some sort. Having said this, some of the choices for the state are more straightforward than others, and some groups get more space than others.

For example, in Docklands a local group *supporting* the STOL-port approached the GLC for funds, arguing: 'the GLC claims to support local people, we are local people so it should support our group.' The GLC turned down the application, mainly because the group's aims were quite contrary to council policy for the Docklands area. Less straightforwardly, the GLC had a poor record in funding pressure groups seeking to make council services better and more accountable, and only partly because its direct services to the public were so limited. It funded the London Transport Passenger Committee (abolished when LRT was established), but otherwise had established few groups directly to pressure the Council. The work of the London Energy and Employment Network (described in chapter 7) was an example of work with tenants' groups aimed in part at pressing local authorities for better heating and insulation in Council housing, but this pressure of course fell mainly on local borough councils.

Surveying the Industry and Employment Branch's funding, some would say that the further away an issue was from the council's immediate interests, the more effective was the funding of pressure groups; some would also say cynically that this is inevitable. But it is not entirely true, especially of the GLC as a whole: politicians can set out to increase the democratic pressure on themselves. In the Women's Committee and Ethnic Minority Committees they did it to a rather substantial extent; there should have been more of it, sooner, in Industry and Employment too.

Can this kind of resourcing, then — 'popular planning' if a label is useful — be Labour's way of developing and deepening representative democracy? Is it an effective counter to the Tories' informal ways of *subverting* representative democracy, built into the long-established relationships between private business and local and national government? This depends on the relationship built up with the groups funded by the authority. On this, the experiences recounted in the chapters contain what might be summarised as a tentative list of principles.

First, the funding must *not* simply respond to pressure; the pattern of groups funded has to correspond to general political aims. This means that the pattern of funding and support (including staff time) has to be monitored, or it cannot be accountable. Where funding is not going to priority groups (women, for example) then something has to be done about it: and that means time and resources for staff to go out and help to develop the organisations which can make use of the available funding. That also means making hard choices about not funding other groups. All this constitutes a more council-led process in the early stages, with the authority actively developing a constituency.

Second, to achieve that, staff doing the funding and 'popular planning' have to be integrated into the policy-making process as a whole, rather than hived off into a corner. Recommending grants and working directly with the grant-aided groups is an immensely political job. The grants staff are those who are subject to the most direct pressure from outside, and also those whose work is most directly monitored. They need to be involved in a two-way relationship with other staff working on policy, which rarely happened in the GLC. The same applies to others involved mainly in 'popular planning' work who often did not work with other staff developing industrial policy or policy for directly-run services.

Third, to return to the issue of autonomy: while the authority may at times fund groups with whom it does not wholly agree, it will always be working within its own interests and policies. It therefore needs to be very clear about what are the demands being made on funded groups — the GLC was often muddled — and it needs to provide a lot more support to allow groups funded to use funds, and fulfill conditions effectively. The women's chapter contains some particularly eloquent material on this issue. Having done that, it needs to keep its hands off the rest of the group's activities, and leave it to develop, so long as it uses the resources as it stated that it would. There is always a risk that local authority resources or involvement undermine the independence and strength of community and trade union organisations, making them dependent on council resources, and undermining their accountability to their real constituents who are also the source of their power.

If the group and its constituents become divided, the point of resourcing it — to create organisations with the strength to criticise and resist the Council, to put demands on it and work with it — is undermined. This brings us to the fourth lesson: procedures have to be devised whereby the groups funded *can* influence the council. As the quotation at the head of this section, from someone who knew the council quite well, suggests, the GLC was not very good at this. Furthermore, as things got bigger, busier, more fraught, it got worse, not better.

The result was that many groups who wanted to contribute

more gave up in frustration because the GLC was so amorphous, hectic, impenetrable and unresponsive. Looking back, people feel that it should have been a specific responsibility of some staff to develop this kind of feedback, and use it. However, the implication of that in turn is probably that the GLC spread itself too wide: it could only have used feedback from groups funded if it had concentrated resources on fewer areas of work, and developed a much more conscious internal process of relating funding, policy, and other sorts of spending in the areas chosen.

This brings us back to the central issue. There can be no straightforward alliances between 'the people' and a part of the local state. The local state itself is a far from homogeneous entity, as the groups discovered who got caught in internal conflict within the authority. Politicians and officers to some extent pursue self-interested ends. But there can also be a lot of genuine goodwill about extending democracy and making policy and spending effective. As a result, more democratic economic policy is a complicated and fraught, negotiated process. Politicians have to accept that organisations they have supported turn on them: for example in the chapter on transnationals trade unionists working in the City institutions disagreed with GLC policies towards these institutions, and there were arguments with the unions in the motor industry about import controls. Criticisms of their record on racism and black employment were often the hardest for some politicians to swallow.

In addition, 'popular planning' has to be flexible: the GLC moved rather rapidly away from the idea that 'an alternative plan' — on paper — was necessarily the desired product. The chapter on enterprise planning argues this particularly clearly. Whether in enterprises, in sectors or areas, the work has turned out to be a continuing process with a variety of objectives, depending on the state of the organisation concerned and the circumstances it faces. These might include an extension of collective bargaining; new links with people in related parts of the economy for public service workers organising with service users as in Health Emergency; trade unionists on the production side making contact with workers in retailing; women and black people successfully challenging divisions arising from gender or race; an organisation developing more effective means of spreading information or learning how to monitor and investigate management more effectively; and so on. Plans or written reports have proved important only under particular conditions: mainly when the campaign needs a public focus or has the opportunity of a public platform. For instance at least two 'people's plans' (for the Royal Docks and for Coin Street) were produced for public inquiries.

Finally, the resourcing must include education and self-education projects. The Industry and Employment Branch spent over £100,000 a year on explicitly educational resources. Some of this went to 'Popular Planning Projects' which were created by the Industry and Employment Branch and ILEA in several Adult Education Institutes and other centres, to provide know-how, research and support for groups not organised through the trade unions or any established campaigning or community groups; for instance young people on an estate with ideas for a service needed on the estate, homeless people wanting to put pressure on the local council, homeworkers wanting to meet together and do something about their conditions. This educational work offers to a popularly based economic strategy an additional method for involving the less organised in collective initiatives about their local economy: learning democratic economic planning by trying to do it.

The aim, at least, of resourcing is now much clearer. It is to contribute to a process whereby workers and communities can gain more collective control, first over council policy, and secondly, over their own economic circumstances. In Britain at present, where people have such low expectations — this was another major lesson — of achieving either of these, that constitutes a major and important aim of economic policy.

There is a major snag which has to be weighed against the benefits: one of the effects of this kind of economic policy is that it attracts to the state people who have been previously working in community organising, and what is loosely called the voluntary sector. And within the state, it can draw into bureaucratic roles people who were union organisers. In both cases, it can weaken outside organisation, in addition to any effect of the funding in creating dependence on the state. And that in turn can create, not an effective and continuing political process, but rather a breed of slightly more benevolent bureaucrats: how to prevent this (without abolishing any more councils!) would be a useful subject of discussion.

Messy, Very!: Issues for National Economic Policy

If you look at the Labour Party's economic policies, they actually seem to be almost the same as they were twenty years ago, whereas a lot of things that the GLC raised, are really fundamental things about the Labour Party's economic strategy, and I think more effort should have been put into disseminating that, so it's not lost.

Women's Employment Project Worker

Moves towards economic democracy are neither tidy nor peaceful. Such moves as occurred through the GLC created enormous and uncomfortable pressures, external and internal: many of the pressures, from the point of view of the local government staff who suffered them, self inflicted. Myths were created, accusations abounded, people got burned out; all these are problems. But those pressures were highly creative from the point of view of new directions in local economic policy making. However, it all does sound just that: very local. What does it have to do with the national level of economic policy making? In our view, a great deal.

A good place to start to draw implications from the GLC for national policy would be the GLC's popularity. It was that rare beast in British politics, a popular Left Labour authority, and popular well beyond any natural Labour constituency, insofar as such a thing remains. There were a lot of reasons for this. Ted Heath blamed it on the government's ineptitude, especially the then Environment Secretary Patrick Jenkin. It may have had to do with Ken Livingstone's talents on TV chat shows. Some of it resulted from plainly sensible and successful transport policies. Partly it was because the GLC did *not* run a number of the public services people most complain about, like housing and social services. But quite a bit was to do with the unprecedented openness with which the administration operated: from turning County Hall (of all places) into an accessible town hall, through the pop festivals, to the endless stream of campaigns, information and demands for participation. For all the problems, more open, and popular, it undoubtedly was, and this in itself has lessons for a national Labour government.

Labour governments may not face abolition, but they always face economic crisis, and very serious opposition, if they try to do anything radical. The relative weakness of the British economy, the position of the City as a financial centre potentially subject to very volatile flows of funds, the resultant vulnerability to balance of payments crises and the need for loans: all this has been an axe for the economic establishment to wield against successive Labour governments. Few manifesto commitments survive this process, and nor, most importantly, does the margin of support which puts Labour in power in the first place.

The Labour GLC did not succeed in holding off the hostility of national government, but it did manage to carry out considerably more of its manifesto than recent Labour Governments have done. It did not lose support under attack, at least until it started to tear itself apart internally over rate capping. And it left at least some changes behind it in terms of what people know and expect of government.

We think that, despite the difference in scale and the difference in *function* of national and local government, this history — the successes and the failures — holds some lessons for national politics.

There are lessons about public openness, information and accountability. We have a pathologically secretive national government, far worse than many other industrialised capitalist countries, and the Labour Party historically has done nothing to change this. The Labour GLC kept its electoral mandate alive by using council resources to explain and campaign for its policies. It also made the information available in the GLC accessible to a very wide range of people in the community and the London workforce. It raised people's expectations, often unreasonably high, and it opened itself more than is usual to effective criticism. And as a result it made unusually available the public sector resources people had paid for through their rates and taxes.

A Labour government — and the Labour Party now — would gain a great deal from a much greater commitment to this kind of openness. While many of the specifics of the GLC's activity were those of local government, the benefits of more open government are more general. Labour governments, too, could raise people's expectations of the state, make its resources more available, be more open about internal conflict and conflict with the civil service and the City, open itself more to criticism by providing more material for criticism to latch on to. In the long run, despite the embarrassment at times involved, such accessibility is highly constructive: so long as the policies being proposed do genuinely bring benefits.

This is all the more true the more interventionist the policies. Many of the lessons of the GLC stem from its highly interventionist line, in both the public and private sector. Consider first the lessons in the public sector. One of the lessons for many people who went to work in the GLC was to discover just how badly much of the public sector was managed, with inappropriate criteria leading to ever more short-sighted and wasteful decisions about the management of public sector assets. Against this, the GLC drew on, and encouraged, active support for its transport policies on fares and services; it developed alternative criteria for managing public transport services; it worked with unions on the future of the engineering works and conductors on buses, and put people on the LT Board who also talked directly to the unions; it funded a stroppier passenger committee than had previously been seen; it tried — and failed against government opposition to the spending — to get better criteria established of need for public transport; it investigated women's transport needs; it provided detailed information about services. The point of this catalogue is the contrast with the hands-off, and increasingly narrow commercial approach to the declining public sector under national control.

The lesson is that national policy towards the management of the public sector too wold be transformed if it was rethought as an active alliance between government, unions in the workplace and organised consumers of the service. The alternative to inappropriate commercial criteria is more of this kind of democracy.

This conception would undermine the time-honoured concept of 'tripartism', the idea of a three-way union-management-government partnership which still reappears in trade union and Labour proposals for managing the public sector, as for example in transport. There is no reason why a Labour government should regard itself as an equal partner in such discussions with the public sector management which it employs. On the contrary, it should come off the fence, and actively promote change, and a more socially responsible use of public sector assets, by working with unions and consumers, and helping both to develop their role in transforming public services, such as the Health Service, which are under national control.

Some of this implies decentralising: participation only works rather locally. But 'going local' in itself will not achieve much: it has to be decentralisation in order to democratise. To put the point at its simplest, if more resources for public services can be allied to more active popular control over how those resources are spent, then when the spending comes under attack, it will be defended. *And in the mean time it will be spent more effectively.*

There are some parallel though more complex lessons in the area of private sector industrial intervention. National thinking on industrial policy is still wedded to tripartism, still alive, though shaken by monetarism, in the corridors of NEDO. This concept of a partnership between labour and private capital, with government holding the ring, has delivered little, in industrial development or in promoting the real involvement of labour in industrial restructuring.

The GLEB history shows how difficult it is to establish a partnership between a public authority and workers in factories where the state invests. GLEB was frequently not open with unions and workers, and frequently failed to draw on the information they could have provided. It was caught up in worries about commercial confidentiality, and was trapped by the weakness of the firms where it invested, and its own difficulties in delivering a return for the commitment of the workers who come to it for assistance. Despite all this, the evidence shows how often GLEB fell captive to bad managements, and also shows the extent to which working more closely with labour could have extracted them from this, and offered new perspectives.

Labour governments have similarly been captive, and uncritical of private sector management. The GLC experience reinforces the view that Labour governments should seek to undertake industrial policy in an active alliance with labour, as a basis for a bargaining relation with private capital. The lessons from GLC policy do not add up to an alternative model to tripartitism, but they suggest a starting point: a break with the defensive psychology of the labour movement whereby workers' demands are always 'sectional', and with the civil service view that only a three way dialogue can produce policies in the interests of the majority. And they suggest a principle: that the people Labour represent are a fertile source of policies in their own interests, and of support for those policies.

There is, though, another set of lessons. Labour does not only represent those in unions; over 60 per cent of the labour force is now outside unions, through unemployment, privatisation, and the increase in non-union firms, from high tech firms to sweat shops. This concluding chapter has analysed some of the lessons from the GLC experience about the need to create new constituencies for employment policy, to find ways of working with the non-unionised, those whose subordination is reinforced by the organised labour movement, diverse community-based groups and consumers of public services. All these experiences contain lessons for national policy. Intervention in public or private sectors needs to draw on, and encourage initiative by, a much wider range of organisations than the Labour Part has typically identified as its base.

Developing pressure and raising expectations will, the GLC experience suggests, mean new demands on the public sector, pressures for better management and better spending criteria. One of the interesting aspects of GLC policy was the attempt — not very successful — to use the different powers of the public sector together to influence the economy of London. Purchasing, direct employment, contracting and compliance, transport spending, industrial investment were all to be related in the interests of more employment, better quality employment, and improved opportunities for women, black people and other disadvantaged groups. The intention is interesting and contains lessons. Overall, our national public sector is never seen in that light, and is completely uncoordinated. This could be changed. The public sector is so large, it determines the conditions for the private market; thinking in terms of co-ordination suggests new criteria for various branches of public spending. Thus, the GLC argued that much apparently 'social' spending could also be seen as a tool of economic policy, such as the 'social objectives' of GLEB's enterprise planning. The GLC argued that transport spending should be thought of, not simply as a way to provide transport, but also as a tool of direct and indirect employment policy. Trade unionists were quick to develop these ideas, and argue for wider and longer-term criteria for investment, and proper accounting of the costs of unemployment in the calculation of spending priorities.

New spending criteria of this kind *will not* be developed by current management, given a few new rules, or civil servants or even well-meaning advisers sitting in offices. It is no good simply calling for 'socialist managers' to be trained. Better public sector management can *only* be developed in association with trade unionists in the industries and services concerned.

One important casualty of monetarism has been the idea that the public sector has a duty to be a model employer. And one important reaction has been the growth of campaigning organisations with developing views on changes that are needed in the content and the control of the public services. The local state, not only the GLC, has supported the latter, and tried to reintroduce the former ideal; national policy ought to be able to build on these organisations, and this experience, if it is prepared to listen. Especially in the public sector, where in principle there is political and financial control, new models for the effective use of public ownership need developing, based on what has been done already. It needs more innovative research, more support for popular organisation, more encouragment and financing of local initiative. The process, we know, is messy and ridden with conflict. But it is the only way to look for new, more interventionist economic policies at national as well as local level.

All this goes against the grain of conventional labour movement as well as establishment economic thinking. There has always been a current of thought in the labour movement which based socialist economic policy in the organisation and ideas of working-class people in the workplace and community, from trade unionists influenced by Marx to socialist intellectuals such as William Morris and G.D.H. Cole. But this has been dominated and pushed to the margins by the more powerful rationalist tradition which considered planning to be the responsibility of specially bred professionals. As Beatrice Webb, a leading advocate and practitioner of this latter position, put it: 'It is our opinion that the average sensual man [sic] can only describe his needs. He cannot prescribe the remedies.'

It is this latter view which has generally dominated Labour when in power. Rarely if ever has the — describing it broadly — 'popular control' perspective had a taste of power. The Labour leadership has seen the purpose of state intervention and economic policy as being to guide the economy more efficiently than the market could do, not to lay down the conditions for increasing popular control; indeed, for them, a Labour government is itself democratic control.

It is this perspective which is challenged by the experience of the GLC. The GLC did not institute 'popular control' or anything like it. And there was always, as many chapters of this book have shown, a conflict within the GLC between its sweeping, strategic aims for sectors of the economy, and its principles of working with outside groups. But the fact that more than one person, reflecting on the institution from the outside, could describe the GLC's interest in, and openness to, the ideas and needs of ordinary people as a 'revolution' in the attitudes of the state to its citizens suggests a path for change.

The Livingstone GLC came at a time when the failure of the alliance between national Labour politicians and union leaders to deliver change — even improved public services — in the face of opposition had undermined popular confidence in the power of the state in progressive hands to plan for social need. Indeed it was in substantial part a product of this crisis. Some of the councillors in the last GLC administration and many of the officers who worked for them were influenced by this experience, and were looking for the chance to experiment with a different approach, based in part on supporting and encouraging initiatives from trade unionists and community organisations, as well as a more active interventionist use of public sector powers. We hope we have shown the experience was rich in lessons and insights, at least as much from the failures as the successes.

In summary, to learn from the GLC would be to make democracy a central aim of Labour economic policy; a policy which would not only deliver improvements in services and material life, but also develop a process of democratising the economy — starting with the public sector.

Now what? At present some Labour leaders, notably current employment spokesperson John Prescott, have recognised the potential of local initiatives for creating jobs. But these local efforts, like the shop stewards' plans of the mid-1970s, will face strong opposition from the City and the Treasury. They will only avoid the same fate as those plans if they are built on the kind of popular base which this book has been arguing Labour authorities must help to develop. These lessons still seem too risky and too democratic for most of the Labour leadership. The GLC was only one experience among many. In the end, it will have achieved something lasting only if its work contributed to strengthening the pressures from popular organisations on this leadership. Its experience shows that Labour's plans for jobs can only be effective if Labour, nationally and locally, makes it own electorate the driving force of its economic policy.

Acknowledgements

The GLC as Employer

Especial thanks to Pat Masters for her comments on all drafts and her contribution to the ideas in the chapter. Thanks to all those who agreed to be interviewed, in particular John Carr, Jimmy Fitzpatrick, Degraft Nunoo, Judith Hunt and those GLC workers who attended trade union workshops. Many of the points made in this chapter are theirs.

Women's Work

Many thanks to all the people quoted in the chapter, who gave their time to be interviewed, and to Sue Sharpe for much of the interviewing. Particular thanks to those who read and commented on the different drafts: The Haringey Women's Employment Project, Mandy Cook, Irene Breughel and Mandy Snell. None of those who contributed are responsible for the final version of this chapter.

Transport Engineering

Particular thanks to Julia Tinsley, Tom Holland and Dan Skinner who gave time to be interviewed, and read the final version of this chapter. Thank you, too, to all the London Transport engineering workers who worked with me, patiently explained their understanding and ideas to me, and helped me do my job at the GLC. Thanks too to Dave Wetzel for being interviewed and providing material, Irene Breughel for comments on the draft and to Chris Lakin for allowing his report to be quoted.

None of these people are responsible for how their help has been used here.

OPO

· This chapter owes its content to Jeannette Mitchell, Brian Collins, George Collins, Tina Mackay, Mike Joffe; and also to Ollie Jackson, Terry Allen, Regional Officer of the TGWU London Bus Section (who gave the project official backing as well as his enthusiasm and support) and all the other trade unionists and other people who worked on the OPO and health project on the London Buses, and on the videos on the buses and the tubes. Thanks to Brian Collins, Steve Johnson, Ron Young, and Ollie Jackson for giving time to be interviewed. The final version of the chapter is Maureen's responsibility alone.

Furniture

Thanks to FTAT shop stewards for the fascinating, and enjoyable discussions at their trade union workshops. I hope that I have accurately recorded their views. Thanks also to Mike Best, Mike Cooley, Mayerline Frow, Jamie Gough, Robin Murray, John Palmer, Ernie Scarbrow, Nick Sharman and Mike Ward for useful discussion about industrial strategy, and to Doreen Massey for helpful comments on an earlier draft. I am also grateful to the Open University for providing me with the funds to finish this work after the abolition of the GLC.

Enterprise Planning

Thanks to Hilary Wainwright for much editing and some interviewing; and to Doreen Massey for her comments. As well as the author's interviews, the chapter was also based on interviews carried out by Julie Hayes, research officer for the South East Region TUC, who is writing a report on enterprise planning for SERTUC members. Material for one of the Co-op case studies was supplied by Liz Heron, and other material on GLEB and co-ops by Lliane Phillips. Finally, most thanks to all those people, workers and management, in GLEB firms, in GLEB, and in unions, who gave time and help; none of them are responsible for the way their interviews have been used.

Construction

This chapter owes a lot to Frank Campbell, who did the interviewing on which it is based. Frank died before the chapter was written: it would have been better and richer if he had been there to work on it. Particular thanks for help to Pete Turner but he is not responsible for the outcome.

Technology

Very many thanks to the interviewees for this chapter: John Butler, Angie Barst, Julie Betteridge, Mike Cooley, Peta Sissons, Shaun Murphy, Bill Niven, Mike Ward, Ron Edwards, John Chowcat and also to Mary Moore at LIN who wrote a wonderful account of her work and ideas from which the chapter quotes. Thanks also to Sue Sharpe who did much of the interviewing.

Jobs Festivals

Thanks a lot to all those interviewed: musicians, organisers, punters and politicians.

Transnationals

Thanks to the Transnational Information Exchange, to shop stewards from Unilever, Kodak, Philips and Fords who attended trade union workshops. Thanks also to Steve Riley and to Alan Hayling for discussions on the ideas in the chapter. And thanks to Sheila Rowbotham for doing some of the interviewing.

Docklands

Very many thanks to Bob Colenutt and Betty Presho for all their help and criticism, and many thanks to all the following people for interviews: Jim Kennedy, Docklands Forum; Ted Bowman, North Southwark Community Development Group; Andy Copeland, Joint Docklands Action Group; Beryl and Con Donovan, Cherry Garden Action Group; Julie Donovan and Joanne Donovan, Rotherhithe Community Planning Centre; Alan Turkie, Rotherhithe Community Planning Centre; Connie Hunt, People's Plan Centre; Eddie Corbett, People's Plan Centre. Interviews were also used from BBC Transcripts of Docklands 1983, from Morris Foley, Annette Fry, Joe and Wally James, Lynne Warne and Pat Vicks, Ann Nicholson, Frank and Myrtle Lester.

Health Emergencies

Thank you to all the following people for interviews and advice: Lucy de Groot, one of the initiators of Hackney Health Emergency; Dick Muskett, involved in the setting up of London Health Emergency; Jane Foot, Hackney Health Emergency worker in 1985; Morris Kolander, NUPE steward at Barts involved in Hackney Health Emergency; Michael Walker, Hillingdon Health Emergency worker; Haf Evans, Rosie Newbiggen, Tom O'Malley, involved in Harrow Health Emergency; Myra Garrett, Tower Hamlets Health Emergency worker; Tim Thompson, outreach worker funded by Popular Planning Unit working on health and the environment; John Lister and Kevin Flack, two of the co-ordinators of London Health Emergency; Peter Marshall, West London regional official, involved in the Health Emergency Steering Committee; Shamis Dirir, worker in Black Women's Health Action Project, funded by GLC Women's Committee and other organisations, with links to Tower Hamlets Health Emergency; Dave Carr, NUPE member at the ondon Hospital; Jayne Harrill, NUPE member at the London Hospital; and people at the Maternity Services Liaison Scheme, funded by GLC Women's Committee. The chapter also draws on a typescript by Liz Heron on the occupations at Hillingdon, Autumn 1983, and on the typescript of a conference on the NHS funded by the Popular Planning Unit 1984. I am grateful for all the people involved for their help and time. The conclusions are of course my own, and none of the people interviewed bear responsibility for my interpretation.

Property

Thanks to Steph Blackwell of the Waterloo Employment Project, Ted Bowman from the North Southwark Community Development Group, and Liz Williamson and all in the GLC 'Areas' Unit, for help and enthusiasm for writing this up.

Conclusions

Thanks to Gail Lewis, Mandy Cook, Lucy de Groot, Sheila Rowbotham, Pat Masters and Slim Hallett for discussions which enormously improved the content. Only the editors are responsible for the outcome, however.

Sources of Further Information

Further information about many of the policies and issues discussed in this book can be found in the following GLC publications. They are all available from:

London Strategic Policy Unit (LSPU)
Middlesex House
20 Vauxhall Bridge Road,
London SW1V 2SB

The London Labour Plan

The London Industrial Strategy

The London Training Legacy: the Work of the Greater London Training Board

Racism Within Trade Unions

Other sources of further information for the individual chapters are as follows.

The Chapters on Public Transport

The two videos mentioned are both available through the LSPU (Transport Unit). The report on the bus study, *Bus Work and Health Report*, is published by the Birmingham Trade Union Resource Centre, and is available through the LSPU Transport Unit, as are a number of pamphlets on London's buses and underground, including *London's Buses — Back on the Road; Notes from the Underground; The Bus Worker's Little Red Book*.

Women's Work

The LSPU has several reports relevant to women's private sector work: *Where There's Muck There's Money* (on the cleaning industry); *Sunset Industries* (on textiles and clothing); and *Faulty Towers* (on the hotel industry).

Further information on women's work in London can be obtained from the Women's Unit of LSPU.

Industrial Democracy, Socially Useful Production, and the Furniture Industry

The GLEB strategy for the furniture industry is further discussed in: *Turning the Tables*, published by the Greater London Enterprise Board (63-67 Newington Causeway, London SE1); and in: *Veneer*, the workers' report on the furniture industry, published by The Furniture, Timber and Allied Trade Unions, and available from LSPU. Background to the industrial and technology strategies generally can be found in: *State Intervention in Industry, A Workers' Inquiry*, by Coventry, Newcastle and North Tyneside Trades Councils, published by Spokesman Press, Nottingham, 1981; and also in: *The Lucas Plan: A New Trade Unionism in the Making?*, by Hilary Wainwright and Dave Elliott, published by Allison and Busby. The GLEB publication *Saving Jobs. Shaping the Future* discusses enterprise planning. The South East Region TUC's report on enterprise planning will shortly be available from SERTUC (Congress House, Great Russell St., London WC1.)

Labour's Plans for Construction

Two videos about contract compliance and equalities in the construction industry are available from LSPU. Further information can be obtained from *Checking Private Building Contractors*, a publication of the Sheffield Joint Works Group, Sheffield City Council.

Transnationals

The Ford Inquiry Report is available from LSPU.

Property Strategy

More information on the Courages Site can be obtained from The Waterloo Employment Project (Colombo St., SE1). Information on the progress of another big 'key site', Coin Street, can be obtained from Coin Street Community Builders (99 Upper Ground, London SE1 9PP).

Docklands

For more information on Docklands, contact the Docklands Consultative Committee Support Unit (c/o Newham Council, East Ham Town Hall, London E15.) The DCCSU can supply the following publications: *The East London File, Four Year Review of the LDDC* 1985. Other organisations able to supply information include the Joint Docklands Action Group (2 Cable St. London E1): People's Plan Centre (10 Pier Parade, London E16.); Rother-hithe Community Planning Centre (190 Southwark Park Road, London SE16); Cherry Garden Action Group (c/o Rotherhithe Community Planning Centre); Newham Docklands Forum (6 Addington Road, London E16).

London Health Emergencies

The interview material used for this chapter is deposited in the GLC archives at Clerkenwell, and with the History Workshop Centre. Documents used in preparing this chapter include *In the Service of London, Origins and Development of Council Employment* by Ellen Leopold (GLC 1985); *Taking Stock :A Documentary History of the GLC's Supplies Department* by Rodney Mace (GLC 1984); *Health in Danger* by David Widgery (Macmillan 1979); *Cuts and the NHS*, the Politics of Health Group Pamphlet No. 2 (BSSRS, 9 Poland St., W1); *The Political Economy of Health*, Lesley Doyal with Imogen Pennel (Pluto Press 1979); *In and Against the State*, London Edinburgh Weekend Return Group (Pluto Press 1980);

the GLC's committee report on London Health Emergency (code IEC 1153, 31.10.83); the London Black Women's Health Action Project Newsletter and London Wide Conference Report; the Maternity Services Liaison Scheme Annual Report; and many issues of *Health Emergency,* and *Jobs for a Change.*